Farm Policies and World Markets

Monitoring and Disciplining the International Trade Impacts of Agricultural Policies

World Scientific Studies in International Economics

(ISSN: 1793-3641)

Vol. 35 The Floating World: Issues in International Trade Theory
by Wilfred J. Ethier (University of Pennsylvania, USA)

Vol. 36 Trade Policy in Asia: Higher Education and Media Services
edited by Christopher Findlay (University of Adelaide, Australia), Hildegunn Kyvik Nordas (Organisation for Economic Co-operation and Development, France) & Gloria Pasadilla (APEC Secretariat, Singapore)

Vol. 37 The Path of World Trade Law in the 21st Century
by Steve Charnovitz (The George Washington University, USA)

Vol. 38 International Trade, Distribution and Development: Empirical Studies of Trade Policies
by Paul Brenton (The World Bank, USA)

Vol. 39 Evolving Patterns in Global Trade and Finance
by Sven W. Arndt (Claremont McKenna College, USA)

Vol. 40 Shadow Banking Within and Across National Borders
edited by Stijn Claessens (International Monetary Fund, USA), Douglas Evanoff (Federal Reserve Bank of Chicago, USA), George Kaufman (Loyola University Chicago, USA) & Luc Laeven (International Monetary Fund, USA)

Vol. 41 Modeling Developing Countries' Policies in General Equilibrium
by Jaime de Melo (FERDI, France & University of Geneva, Switzerland)

Vol. 42 Developing Countries in the World Economy
by Jaime de Melo (FERDI, France & University of Geneva, Switzerland)

Vol. 43 Farm Policies and World Markets: Monitoring and Disciplining the International Trade Impacts of Agricultural Policies
by Tim Josling (Stanford University, USA)

The complete list of the published volumes in the series can be found at
http://www.worldscientific.com/series/wssie

43 World Scientific Studies in International Economics

Farm Policies and World Markets

Monitoring and Disciplining the International Trade Impacts of Agricultural Policies

Tim Josling
Stanford University

World Scientific
NEW JERSEY • LONDON • SINGAPORE • BEIJING • SHANGHAI • HONG KONG • TAIPEI • CHENNAI

Published by

World Scientific Publishing Co. Pte. Ltd.
5 Toh Tuck Link, Singapore 596224
USA office: 27 Warren Street, Suite 401-402, Hackensack, NJ 07601
UK office: 57 Shelton Street, Covent Garden, London WC2H 9HE

Library of Congress Cataloging-in-Publication Data
Josling, Tim, 1940–
Farm policies and world markets : monitoring and disciplining the international trade impacts of agricultural policies / Tim Josling.
pages cm. -- (World Scientific studies in international economics ; 43)
Includes bibliographical references.
ISBN 978-9814616447
1. Agriculture and state. 2. Agriculture--Economic aspects. 3. International trade. 4. Produce trade. I. Title.
HD1415.J667 2015
382'.41--dc23

2014046947

British Library Cataloguing-in-Publication Data
A catalogue record for this book is available from the British Library.

In-house Editor: Li Hongyan

Printed in Singapore

Contents

About the Author

Tim Josling is an Emeritus Professor at the (former) Food Research Institute at Stanford University; a Senior Fellow by courtesy at the Freeman Spogli Institute for International Studies (FSI); and a faculty member at FSI's Europe Center. His research focuses on agricultural policy and food policy in industrialized nations; international trade in agricultural and food products; and the development of the multilateral trade regime. His recent research topics include the reform of the agricultural trading system in the World Trade Organization; the treatment of agriculture in bilateral trade agreements; the use of geographical indications in food markets; the role of health and safety regulations in trade; the impact of climate change legislation on agricultural trade policies; and the treatment of biofuel subsidies in the WTO.

Before coming to Stanford in 1978 Josling taught at the London School of Economics and the University of Reading, England. During this time he served as a Personal Advisor to the Secretary of State for Prices and Consumer Protection in the UK government, and as Advisor to the House of Lords Committee on Europe. He was also a member of the Secretariat of the President of the World Food Conference in 1974. His academic background includes a BSc in Agriculture from the University of London (Wye College), a MSc in Agricultural Economics from the University of Guelph, Canada, and a PhD in Agricultural Economics from Michigan State University. At Stanford, Josling currently teaches a course in the Economics and Political Economy of the Multilateral Trade System, in the International Relations program.

Josling is a member of the International Policy Council on Food and Agricultural Trade and former Chair of the Executive Committee of the International Agricultural

Trade Research Consortium. He held a Visiting Professorship at University College, London, in the United Kingdom, and is a past President of the UK Agricultural Economics Association. He has also been a Visiting Scholar at the Institute for International Economics in Washington. In 2004 he was made a Fellow of the American Agricultural Economics Association.

He lives with his wife in Northern California, with a son and daughter close by.

Preface and Acknowledgements

It is rare to be presented with the opportunity to look back at one's own academic writings and try to see whether the whole adds up to more than the sum of the parts. The request from World Scientific to put together a volume that drew on one's own writings on a topic of current interest in international economics was an irresistible invitation to indulge in such a retrospective endeavor. I hope that my attempt at following the thread of my writings on the measurement and disciplining of farm policies in developed countries proves useful as a contribution to the current debates on the development of multilateral restraints on subsidies, within and outside agriculture.

But this also presents an opportunity to reflect on how one came to the subject and who along the way contributed to one's development. My involvement with the agricultural sector began with a visit to a farm in post-war Holland. Ten years later I was still keen on farming and attended Wye College, the agricultural school of the University of London (now closed). But during my studies at Wye I became intrigued by the economics of farming and of marketing farm products. This in turn led to study at Guelph, in Canada, and to Michigan State University (MSU), in the USA. Major influences on my interest in public policy aspects of agricultural economics were Gerald I. Trant (later Deputy Minister of Agriculture in Canada and Executive Secretary of the World Food Council) at Guelph and Dale E. Hathaway (later Undersecretary for International Affairs at the US Department of Agriculture) at Michigan State. My initiation into international trade and trade policy was in the hands of Max Kreinin at MSU and Harry Johnson at the University of Chicago. After graduation I had the great good fortune to be a colleague of Harry Johnson's at the London School of Economics. This was a time of great activity in trade policy and I became immersed in the debate about the entry of the UK into the European Economic Community (which would later become the EU) much of which revolved around the adoption by the UK of the Common Agricultural Policy.

My interest in policy measurement stemmed from my work with Jim O'Hagan at the Food and Agricultural Organization of the United Nations in Rome. At his request I worked on a way of monitoring the extent to which developed country farm policy intruded on world markets and hence on other countries. The development of this indicator is discussed below in the Introduction to this volume. Suffice it to say that the adoption, in a modified form, of this indicator in the WTO

Agreement on Agriculture has proved to be a breakthrough in the benchmarking of farm policies and the adoption of schedules for the reduction of the most trade distorting aspects of these policies.

The establishment of the International Agricultural Trade Research Consortium (IATRC) in the early 1980s provided a fertile environment to work with other economists interested in trade and policy, including those from government agencies. At the time of the Uruguay Round the IATRC became a type of think tank as the issue of crafting multilateral disciplines on domestic policy rose to the top of the agenda. To my colleagues in the IATRC and others at the Food Research Institute (FRI) at Stanford goes my appreciation for intellectual stimulation and friendship that remains strong to this day.

I would also like to acknowledge the contribution of coauthors on four of the papers, Stefan Tangermann (on two papers), David Orden and David Blandford (one paper) and Klaus Mittenzwei (one paper), and to thank them for their encouragement to include these papers in this volume.

I acknowledge with thanks the willingness of the original publishers and copyright holders to give their permission to reprint the articles in this book, as detailed below.

Permission was granted by Westview Press for reprinting:

Josling, T. (1979). Agricultural protection and stabilization policies: Analysis of current neomercantilist practices. In J. S. Hillman and A. Schmitz (eds.), *International trade in agriculture: Theory and policy* (pp. 149–162). Boulder, CO: Westview Press.

Josling, T. (1981). Price, stock, and trade policies and the functioning of international grain markets. In A. Valdes (ed.), *Food security for developing countries* (pp. 161–184). Boulder, CO: Westview Press.

Josling, T. (1990). The GATT: Its historical role and importance to agricultural policy and trade. In H. J. Michelmann, J. C. Stabler, and G. G. Storey (eds.), *The political economy of agricultural trade and policy: Toward a new order for Europe and North America* (pp. 155–171). Boulder, CO: Westview Press.

The International Association of Agricultural Economists gave permission to reprint:

Josling, T., and Tangermann, S. (1990). Measuring protection levels in agriculture: A survey of approaches and results. In A. Maunder and A. Valdes (eds.), *Agriculture and governments in an interdependent world: Proceedings of the Twentieth International Conference of Agricultural Economists, held at Buenos Aires, Argentina, 24–31, August, 1988* (pp. 343–352). Aldershot, UK: Dartmouth.

John Wiley & Sons gave permission for the use of:

Josling, T. (1977). Government price policies and the structure of international agricultural trade. *Journal of Agricultural Economics, 28*(3), 261–277.

Josling, T. (1993). Agricultural trade issues in transatlantic trade relations. *World Economy, 16*(5), 553–573.

Josling, T. (2002). Competing paradigms in the OECD and their impact on the WTO agricultural talks. In L. Tweeten and S. R. Thompson (eds.), *Agricultural policy for the 21st century* (pp. 245–264). Ames, IA: Iowa State University Press.

Cambridge University Press gave permission to reprint:

Orden, D., Josling, T., and Blandford, D. (2011). The difficult task of disciplining domestic support. In D. Orden, D. Blandford and T. Josling (eds.), *WTO disciplines on agricultural support: Seeking a fair basis for trade* (pp. 391–432). Cambridge, UK: Cambridge University Press.

Josling, T., and Mittenzwei. K. (2013). Transparency and timeliness: The monitoring of agricultural policies in the WTO using OECD data. *World Trade Review, 12*(3), 533–547.

Oxford University Press gave permission for the use of:

Josling, T., and Tangermann, S. (2003). Production and export subsidies in agriculture: Lessons from GATT and WTO disputes involving the US and the EC. In E.-U. Petersmann and M. A. Pollack (eds.), *Transatlantic economic disputes: The EU, the US, and the WTO* (pp. 207–232). Oxford, UK: Oxford University Press.

Emerald Publishing Group gave permission to reprint:

Josling, T. (2009). Agricultural trade disputes in the WTO. In J. C. Hartigan (ed.), *Trade disputes and the dispute settlement understanding of the WTO: An interdisciplinary assessment* (pp. 245–282). Bingly, UK: Emerald Press.

Springer Science + Business Media gave permission of the use of:

Josling, T. (2010). WTO compliance and domestic farm policy change. In V. E. Ball, R. Fanfani and L. Gutierrez (eds.), *The economic impact of public support in agriculture: An international perspective* (Volume 7 in Studies in Productivity and Efficiency, edited by Rolf Fare, Shawna Grosskopf, and R. Robert Russell) (pp. 213–241). New York, NY: Springer.

The German Journal of Agricultural Economics gave permission for the use of:

Josling, T. (2010). Reflections on the exceptional treatment of agriculture in the WTO. *German Journal of Agricultural Economics, 19*, 19–32.

Littlefield Adams and Company gave permission for the use of:

Josling, T. E. (1981). Domestic agricultural price policies and their interaction through trade. In A. F. McCalla and T. E. Josling (eds.), *Imperfect markets in agricultural trade* (pp. 49–68). Montclair, NJ: Allanheld, Osmun.

The remaining article was not under copyright and was in the public domain:

Josling, T. (1993). Of models and measures: Some thoughts on the use and abuse of policy indicators. In M. D. Shane and H. von Witzke (eds.), *The environment, government policies, and international trade: A proceedings* (pp. 99–109). Washington, DC: Economic Research Service, United States Department of Agriculture.

Finally, I would like to thank the editorial staff at World Scientific for their expert support and friendly guidance in the production of this book.

Introduction

The interesting task of putting together a collection of one's essays on a particular theme allows an author the luxury of creating a sense of continuity that may not have been obvious at the time. The theme of this book, the development of the art of monitoring and disciplining the trade impacts of farm policies, captures a number of issues about which I have written over the years. The sections of the book reflect a progression from the question of how to monitor the impacts of farm policies on international markets, a concern of the 1960s, to the issue of the impact that particular types of policies have on the structure and performance of world markets, a key question in the 1970s (and more recently). The progression continues with the attempts to impose disciplines on domestic policies in the 1980s, first through the GATT and subsequently in the WTO, and the trade disputes that arose as a part of that disciplinary process. The progression concludes with the current questions about the monitoring of obligations on farm policy undertaken in the context of the World Trade Organization (WTO). Though most of the articles included here deal with the policies of developed countries, the issues themselves are of renewed significance today as emerging and middle-income countries enter the tricky world of agricultural and food policies.

Part I. Monitoring the Trade Impacts of Developed Country Farm Policies

The agricultural policies that were adopted by the industrial countries in the mid-part of the twentieth century defined the conditions on world markets for temperate zone farm products. The major players, the US and Europe, were in large part responsible for the "disarray" in world markets for farm products that was a feature of the 1960s. The nature of this disarray was summarized by D. Gale Johnson in a seminal work in 1973 as follows:

> Products from the land are being produced at high cost in some parts of the world while elsewhere farm products that can be produced at low cost cannot be sold at all or only with great difficulty. The prices of farm products are manipulated by most governments and without any real knowledge of the consequences of such manipulation. (Johnson, 1973, p. 17)

Governments in food deficit countries, such as Japan, Switzerland, Norway and Sweden maintained high prices for their domestic farmers as a way of keeping small farmers on the land and avoiding where possible the importation of staple foods.[1] Governments with farm production surplus to their domestic needs, particularly Canada, Australia and New Zealand, sought to expand markets overseas, to keep up domestic farm revenues and to avoid rapid adjustment in the farming sector. Meanwhile the countries of the young European Economic Community (EEC, later the EC and now the EU) decided to set a high internal price for their own farm products, requiring levies on imports that insulated their markets from low world prices and giving subsidies for exports so as to be able to move any surpluses onto world markets. The EEC Common Agricultural Policy (CAP) became the poster child for expensive food, high budget costs and disruption of world markets.

The US found itself caught between limiting production so as to support markets for its major export products and disposing of surpluses in whatever market would take them. A succession of Farm Bills from the 1950s to 1996 vacillated between the two approaches. At times large parts of US agricultural acreage were removed from production in an attempt to keep up world prices. The strategy was vulnerable to the possibility that other exporters could take advantage of the supply control in the US. Storing surplus grain was only a temporary expedient, until the grain could be absorbed on the domestic market or disposed of abroad. But disposing of surpluses was costly and disruptive to world markets, driving prices lower. The solution came in the form of sharp reductions in support prices, but such a move was resisted for years by the power of the farming establishment.

Serious attempts to estimate the impact of these domestic farm policies of industrial countries on international trade began in the 1970s. The complexity of these policies had stood in the way of a clear indication of their impact on domestic supply and demand, and hence on trade. The need for some form of indicator that would capture the essence of these domestic farm policies had been recognized in the Haberler Report presented to the GATT in 1958 (GATT, 1958), but that report concluded that the gap between world and domestic prices was the only available measure. The implication was that negotiations would have to focus on the level of domestic prices, a position untenable in the countries concerned. The inability of GATT contracting parties to negotiate directly on domestic policies was in part responsible for the failure of the Kennedy Round (1963–68) to agree on any trade disciplines in this area, settling instead for an ineffectual international commodity agreement. It was becoming clear by the end of the 1960s that the impact of "dueling" agricultural policies among developed countries was having a detrimental impact on developing countries as they sought to benefit themselves by

[1] Many of those policies persist to the present day and are ostensibly aimed at similar objectives.

engaging in international trade. But which policies had the most impact on other countries? And how might one approach the issue of monitoring changes for the better (or for the worse)? It was clear that some new approach to this issue was needed.

One such attempt to monitor developed country domestic farm policies began in the context of the FAO program of International Agricultural Adjustment and was continued by the OECD as a part of the lead up to the GATT Uruguay Round of trade negotiations. The first two articles reproduced in Section I deal with the development of this family of indicators (Producer and Consumer Subsidy Equivalents) and their use in trade policy discussions. There was at the time a parallel development of economic models that sought to give quantitative answers to the questions about the external effects of domestic farm policies. Included in this section is a third article that relates the indicators to the models, illustrating their mutual dependence.

The FAO PSEs

The concept of "international agricultural adjustment" subsumed a number of elements that were considered relevant for developing and developed countries in pursuing their agricultural and food policies. The emphasis was on improving the international environment for development and focusing national policies on taking advantage of that improved environment. The Eighteenth Session of the FAO Conference (the biennial meeting of the member governments) in 1975 agreed on eleven "guidelines" as a framework for implementing a Strategy of International Agricultural Adjustment (FAO, 1975). Guideline 3 addressed the issue of agricultural policies:

> National policies of developing countries should provide appropriate incentives for farmers to expand production and to promote the adaptation of structures within farming both to permit optimum use of available and suitable technology, and to promote social equity and fuller integration of the rural population into the national economy; national policies of developed countries should aim at the most rational use of their resources, having regard to the special needs and interests of developing countries and taking into account the need to ensure world food security.

The first part of the guideline shows how little has changed in forty years. The wording may appear dated but the emphasis on providing "appropriate incentives" is still relevant. Against the backdrop of the 1970s this admonition was particularly aimed at those countries that kept down the prices to farmers in order to satisfy the urban consumers. This tendency for countries to tax their farmers indirectly through actions to keep farm prices low was reinforced by macroeconomic policies that encouraged imports of foodstuffs (Kreuger, Schiff, and Valdes, 1991). There has at least been significant progress on this score, as confirmed by an extensive study of over eighty countries undertaken by the World Bank (Anderson, 2009).

The second part of this guideline clearly calls for developed countries to moderate their own policies with the interests of developing countries in mind. But of course the guideline did not constitute an obligation, and would not have been agreed if it had: getting agreement on the wording of the guideline was a contentious process in itself. But the FAO Conference committed itself to monitoring the extent to which the guidelines were being followed. In this connection, the FAO Secretariat prepared a report every two years that was designed to address the extent to which the guidelines were being followed. The Producer Subsidy Equivalent had been proposed in a concept paper in 1973 (FAO, 1973) and was developed more fully in 1975 (FAO, 1975). In 1977 it was used to monitor the compliance with the second part of guideline 3 (FAO, 1977), and subsequently updated for the next four biennial Conferences. By the time of the 1987 FAO Conference the issue of developed country agricultural policies was under discussion in the Uruguay Round and FAO member states had come to realize that the IAA guidelines were not generating any significant policy responses.

The concept of a subsidy equivalent as introduced in the 1973 paper and developed more fully in the 1975 report was simply that any policy instrument could be deconstructed into its effect on producers and on consumers and that these policies could therefore be represented by the transfer of an equivalent monetary amount. The Producer Subsidy Equivalent (PSE) was thus the subsidy paid to farmers that would be equivalent to the effect on the farmer of the current policies. Similarly, the Consumer Subsidy Equivalent (CSE) was the subsidy that would have been equivalent in terms of the impact on consumers of the current farm policies.[2] Where the producer gained more (higher PSE) than the consumer contributed (a smaller negative CSE), the difference must come from the taxpayer.

The particular indicators were chosen with three benefits in mind. First, they represented a way of extracting comparable and additive information from each policy instrument under consideration. Farmers gain from border protection, input subsidies, support prices and direct payments. Consumers lose from the border protection but can gain from direct subsidies on consumption. Adding up the subsidy equivalent of each type of transfer gives a total that can act as an indicator or benchmark. It can be expressed as a monetary amount, a percentage

[2] In the 1973 paper the consumer impact is measured as a tax (the Consumer Tax Equivalent). This was changed in the 1975 paper to the CSE improving symmetry at the expense of having a measure that contained mostly negative figures.

of total revenue or as an amount per unit of output.[3] The second benefit is that the indicator can be used as an input into a quantitative model in place of a simple tariff or price gap. However, this gives rise to problems as to whether transfers made in different ways have the same impact on output, a matter considered below. The third motivation was to move away from the simple comparison of domestic prices with "world prices" as had been common in earlier studies. Not only were such world prices difficult to find but the meaning of such a comparison raised conceptual issues.[4] Most applications of the PSE methodology have however made extensive use of world prices as a reference for what would happen to farm prices in the absence of the policy instrument concerned, at least in the calculation of market price support.

An early use of the PSE in explaining the impact of policies on world markets is contained in Article 1 in this volume. Written in the late 1970s it was an attempt to link the chaotic situation on world markets experienced over the decade with the operation of domestic farm policies in the major industrial countries. The paper makes use of the FAO calculations of PSEs and CESs for a few major products and countries to address the issues of how much of the instability in world markets is generated by the farm and food policies of the countries themselves. At that time the Tokyo Round of GATT negotiations was addressing the question of quantitative restrictions and non-tariff trade barriers but not the underlying causes of the problems of market instability. It would be nearly a decade before international negotiations faced up to these issues in the Uruguay Round.

The OECD PSEs

The FAO was not the only organization to calculate and interpret PSEs. In 1982 the OECD ministers mandated a report from the Agriculture and Trade Committees on ways to analyze the "approaches and methods for a balanced and gradual reduction of protection for agriculture" and to examine "the national policies and measures which have a significant impact on agricultural trade". In response to this request the Secretariat adopted (and adapted) the PSE as a way of comparing the comparing the trade impact of the various farm policies in use in its member countries (OECD, 1987). The OECD Ministers also adopted some principles for guiding agricultural policies and the PSE measure proved useful in the "monitoring and evaluation" of these principles, required of the Secretariat on an annual basis.

[3] It can also be expressed as a transfer per unit of input, such as land area, if one is interested in the impact on income distribution among farms of different size.

[4] The FAO had for many years published a series labeled "prices of international significance" that were essentially spot prices for several commodities in particular markets. This was often used as a measure of world prices despite its significant limitations.

This process has continued until the present.[5] The report on "Agricultural Policies in OECD Countries: Monitoring and Evaluation" is published annually by the OECD.

The 1982 OECD Trade Mandate was one of the precursors to the negotiations in the Uruguay Round.[6] In 1987 the OECD Council took note of the possible use of the PSEs in the context of the GATT Round. Subsequently the PSE cropped up in several manifestations in the Round. First, it was suggested by the US in its initial proposals for the agricultural modalities as a way of liberalizing trade: PSE reductions would be made by countries over a period until by the year 2000 all trade-distorting support would have been phased out. The Cairns Group (of agricultural exporting countries) also suggested the use of the PSE as a way of phasing out subsidies and tariffs in agriculture. The Nordic countries gave their blessing to this approach to disciplining domestic support, as did the Japanese with somewhat less enthusiasm. Even the EU, with a much more defensive posture on this matter, agreed on the possible use of an Aggregate Measurement of Support (AMS), a relative of the PSE, and gave it the name of a Support Measurement Estimate (SME). All major countries had moved to endorse the notion of negotiating on the basis of a proxy indicator for domestic policies. The AMS that emerged from the final stage of the Uruguay Round of GATT trade negotiations was markedly different from the OECD PSE, but its ability to capture the aggregated effects of various policy instruments in one indicator preserved the family resemblance. The relationship among these support measures in the early stages of the Uruguay Round is discussed in Article 2 in this volume.

As an aid to negotiations on agricultural trade the PSE has also been used in another context. In 1986 the US and Canada entered into the Canada–US Trade Agreement (a precursor to NAFTA). One difficulty was to allow free trade in grains between the two countries that had different farm policies and price support levels. The solution was to trigger tariff reductions by the relative level of support as given by the PSE. If one partner had a higher PSE for a grain then it was obliged to reduce the tariff. As a result of some fluctuations in PSEs in the following years, both countries reduced to zero the tariffs that they charged on trade among themselves.

In parallel with the increase in information about farm policies was a similar sea change in the art of modeling of these policies. This took two forms: increasingly detailed models of agricultural markets that incorporated the impact of policies on supply response and included quantitative restrictions and policy instruments that were dependent on market conditions; and whole-economy models that traced the impacts of policies on factor markets and trade flows. The first group of models was of a partial-equilibrium nature though they could accommodate

[5] The development of the OECD PSE is discussed in more detail in Legg (2003).

[6] Another precursor was the report from the Committee on Trade in Agriculture set up by the GATT in 1982 (Josling, Tangermann, and Warley, 1996, p. 111).

many commodities and countries. Notable examples of this genre were the models of Tyers and Anderson (1992) and Roningen and Dixit (1987). The second group of models used a general-equilibrium framework, necessitating considerable information on household behavior (as providers of labor as well as consumers) and on inter-industry flows of intermediate inputs. This Computable General Equilbrium (CGE) approach was facilitated by the pioneering work of Robinson (Robinson, 1990) and of Hertel who developed a database as well as template models that could be adapted to answer a wide range of specific questions (Hertel, 1997). Institutions such as the USDA Economic Research Service (ERS) and the OECD were simultaneously devoting resources to monitoring and modeling. The community of scholars interested in trade in farm products (both in academic and government circles) set up the International Agricultural Trade Research Consortium (IATRC) in 1980 to follow these exciting developments.[7]

At times it seemed as if there was a choice between devoting resources to modeling and improving the quantitative monitoring of policy developments. In fact, the two were complementary. Article 3, reproduced in this book, was an attempt to reconcile the ambitions of the modelers with the enthusiasm of the monitors. The argument is made that the best indicators for monitoring are those with a fixed definition (e.g. the impact on trade in a product arising from a particular policy instrument). The way in which the indicator is measured would be a choice based on data availability and convenience. Such unambiguous indicators could be the result of models (a market, multi-market or a general equilibrium model) and the quality of the indicator would presumably improve over time. This would be an alternative to the more usual process of defining the indicator by its formula (e.g. the ratio of domestic price to world price) rather than using a fixed definition (the domestic price in the absence of a particular policy). Of course, in practice, the formula approach is more convenient and the relationship between indicators and models will remain contentious.

The work that developed from the early studies of the FAO on International Agricultural Adjustment and the adoption of the PSE by the OECD as a way of monitoring developments in developed country policy in the context of the Uruguay Round of trade talks has continued to the present. Indeed, the collection of data through the notification of policy data to the WTO to show compliance with obligations has generated a new and complementary set of indicators (discussed in Section E below). The OECD has been expanding its coverage of PSE studies to include important non-OECD members, such as Brazil, Russia, China and Indonesia), and the Inter-American Development Bank has recently announced its own PSE database (Agrimonitor). FAO has developed a significant database

[7] The developments of modeling and of measuring at this time were described in Josling and Anderson (1993).

for agricultural policies in Africa (MAFAP) and it using this data in discussions with countries in the region. Indeed the proliferation of PSE-type databases has encouraged the OECD and IFPRI to attempt to coordinate Agricultural Policy Indicator work.

Part II. Domestic Policies and the Structure of International Markets

The monitoring and measurement of the impact of domestic farm policies on trade was a precondition for the effective discussion of the world market for agricultural goods in the 1970s. But many of the policies themselves were a reaction to world market conditions. So the behavior of the world market was influenced not just by the level of taxes and subsidies on consumers and producers but also by the responsiveness of these policies. The articles reproduced in this section illustrate the fundamental dilemma faced at that time: governments sought to isolate their domestic markets from world price developments but in doing so prevented the world markets from performing their useful functions. Moreover, the policies themselves caused tensions that went far beyond the occasional skirmish found in many other areas of trade. In particular the tensions between the US and the European Community (now the EU) over agricultural trade became topics of conversation for political leaders. A framework for resolving these issues at a multilateral level was not in sight at that time.

The structure of world markets will always depend on the policies of major trading partners. In a world where import markets are protected by simple tariffs and export subsidies are absent the world market will rise and fall with production or consumption variability. But that was not the situation in agricultural markets in the 1960s and 1970s. Many importing countries keyed their farm polices in terms of the desirable domestic price, and employed variable import levies (tariffs that varied inversely with the world price) or quotas (varied to manage domestic markets) to maintain those prices. Some exporters pursued similar objectives and varied export subsidies to maintain domestic prices when world markets were weak and export restrictions when world markets were strong. But such markets will have an inevitable tendency to be unstable. To see the possibility of a world-market failure imagine that the amount that importers wish to import at prices that are acceptable domestically is less that the amount that exporters would like to export at prices that they find acceptable. The market will not clear: there is a "policy-induced surplus" that will have to be removed from the market. The instruments for the removal are limited to building up stocks, finding new markets that would otherwise not be able to afford imports, or restricting production. Each of these mechanisms was employed by countries at that time in an attempt to isolate their domestic markets from international prices. Stocks, in exporting countries, rose when surpluses occurred, and even importing countries took advantage of low world prices to increase public stocks.[8] Food aid syphoned off some of the surpluses and supply control was used particularly in the US.

An attempt to represent the structural problem in world markets in straightforward (primarily graphical) terms is reproduced later in the book as Article 4. Written in 1977, it elaborates on some of the conclusions cited above about the dilemma of defensive policies leading to unstable prices on world markets that then validates more defensive reactions. In periods of surplus there is a glut on world markets exacerbated by the efforts to keep up prices to domestic producers and to use the world market as a dumping ground. In periods of shortage the attempt to keep consumer prices stable leads to export restrictions and in some cases to import subsidies. The effect is to exacerbate both the price plunges and the spikes.

The analysis is extended in Article 5 in this book, bringing in a variety of domestic support instruments and stocks policies that was used at that time to manage prices. Almost all policies have an effect on the structure and hence stability of markets. Thus deficiency payments (paying the producer the difference between the market price and some form of target price) will shift the import demand curve. But this in itself changes the structure of the world market (if the country is a significant player). If the exporter employs similar policy instruments then the effect on the stability of the market is amplified. The article shows that the impact of domestic target prices on world markets is not just confined to the protected import markets of the CAP, a common target for such complaints. It claims that the problem extends to the US target price policy and other similar schemes. The structure of the market determines both the stability of prices and the distribution of benefits from payments. A subsidy given by an exporter to domestic producers can be "captured" by an importing government through a tariff. The nature of domestic farm policies redistributes funds around from country to country through trade, as well as between consumers and producers within a country.

The focus of much of the concern over the instability of international markets and the consequent impact on developing countries was on the grain crops. Wheat was the major traded grain, and the most important as a source of imported food supplies for developing countries. Even those countries that had a diet dominated by rice or corn used wheat as a convenient source of nutrition for the urban population. Article 6 was written for a conference on food security (Valdes, 1981) and addresses the matter through a simple conceptualization of grain markets. The article starts

[8] However, private stocks were low as a result of the fixed-price policies on domestic market. Such stocks as were held by the private sector were either "pipeline" stocks or were held for speculation against world price variability.

with a series of identities for the world, involving production and the initial (carry-in) level of stocks and consumption and the final (carry-out) level of stocks. Thus any production fluctuation will show up in some or all of the other variables, no matter what international actions are in place. For any sub-system the addition of imports from and exports to other sub-systems preserves the identity. So a fall in production shows up for any one country as either more imports, less consumption, or lower carry-out stocks. This suggests a simple approach to food security: to trace the changes in production fluctuations to the changes in these other variables. An illustration from the wheat market over the period 1970 to 1976 shows a marked difference in the distribution of the incidence of production fluctuations between the developed countries and the USSR (at that time a peripatetic importer from the rest of the world). The developed countries were "running domestic policies that appear to obscure price signals to the users and consumers of wheat in part through stock policies that reflect strongly the changes in production" (Josling, 1981, p. 167). By contrast, the Soviet Union, though holding some production-related stocks was using trade to make up for their production instability and imposing more variation in availability on consumers than did developed countries (in spite of more closely regulated consumer prices). These issues of the incidence of production fluctuations were also pertinent in the recent price spikes of 2007/8 and 2010 in world rice and wheat markets.

These issues of price instability on world markets led to discussions about the feasibility of collective action. The main instruments that were suggested to control the price volatility on the world market involved commodity agreements that obliged countries to restrict exports and/or build up stocks at times of low prices. These policies carried with them the seeds of their own destruction. Unless all exporters adhered to the rules on exports and stocks there was always the problem of the free rider. And the burdens of controlling exports or holding stocks fell on some countries disproportionately. The alternative to commodity agreements was to establish rules to constrain government policies in the major commodities so as to improve the structure and hence stability of the markets for basic food and feed grains. This issue is the topic for the next section.

Part III. Disciplining Domestic Policies through the GATT and WTO

Political will to reform domestic agricultural policies to allow for a better functioning trade system finally emerged in the mid-1980s. Eventually a structure of multilateral disciplines was agreed in the WTO that could provide a framework for the co-existence of domestic farm policies and a viable trade system. The articles in this section discuss the background to the Agreement on Agriculture (AoA) that emerged from the Uruguay Round of GATT negotiations in 1994 and the apparent shift in paradigms that characterized the farm policy changes in the US and the EU. These paradigm shifts included changes in the prevailing view on the relationship between domestic and foreign trade policy.

The General Agreement on Tariffs and Trade (GATT) was an outcome of the establishment of the post-war economic institutions. Two such institutions were created at the Bretton Woods Conference in 1944, namely the World Bank and the International Monetary Fund. The negotiations on an institution that would oversee the trade system were somewhat delayed by fundamental differences between the US and the UK. The UN called for a Conference to create such an institution, and this was held in Havana in 1948. Meanwhile, a group of countries had been meeting to prepare a draft text for the Havana Charter, to agree on some tariff cuts to start the process, and to negotiate a code of conduct to give countries some assurance that the tariff cuts would not be unraveled by means of other (non-tariff) instruments (in effect the Articles of the GATT). When the Havana Charter was sent to governments for ratification, its weaknesses were only too apparent. In the US the Charter found few supporters and a variety of critics. Finally, President Truman decided in 1950 not to put the ratification to a vote in Congress and the institution that the Charter had established (the International Trade Organization) was stillborn. The GATT survived, as it did not require Congressional approval: countries were not "members" of the GATT but "contracting parties" agreeing to implement the agreements reached in the preparatory conferences on a provisional basis. This somewhat informal institution had remarkable success in its nearly 50 years of operation, finally being replaced by the World Trade Organization in 1994.

It is sometimes said that the GATT excluded agriculture from the reach of its articles. The reverse is closer to the truth: agriculture (or primary products) is mentioned several times, in contrast to other major sectors that are rarely singled out in the GATT. The problem has been one of special treatment rather than exclusion. The sensitivity of agriculture in discussions about trade stems from the nature of domestic farm and food policies. As mentioned above, countries like to be able to control these markets and trade rules get in the way. At the insistence of the US, two exceptions were made to the general principles of the GATT. In the GATT Article XI (General Elimination of Quantitative Restrictions), which prohibits non-tariff border measures, an exception is made (*inter alia*) for agricultural products when domestic supply restrictions are in place. This seemingly innocuous provision turned out to be a convenient loophole for domestic farm policies: even a weak and ineffective form of domestic supply control gave the importing country a case for introducing quotas or licenses on imports to strengthen domestic price levels. The other exception was to the prohibition of export subsidies and other subsidies that might increase exports under Article XVI (Subsidies), as revised in 1955. The revised article made the distinction between primary products and all others. In the case of primary products the obligation was to avoid subsidies that might yield to the exporting country more than an "equitable share" of the world market for that product. Though understandable in terms of domestic politics, the exception was responsible for much of the tensions surrounding agricultural markets in the 1980s.

These issues are outlined in Article 7, which was written at the time when the Uruguay Round was under negotiation. Besides reviewing the agricultural exceptions discussed above, it gives a perspective of the issues being negotiated in the Uruguay Round at that time. The article concludes with two possible scenarios: a breakdown in the talks and a reversion to unconstrained national farm policies that characterized the 1980s or a successful outcome that would mark a turning point in the international rules for national policies. As we know, the Uruguay Round was indeed concluded by the end of 1993, and the Agreement on Agriculture (AoA) became the framework for agricultural policies.

The question of exceptionalism is still relevant today. This is the topic of Article 8, which broadens the argument to include the treatment of agriculture as an exception in the AoA. Having gone some way to removing the special treatment of agriculture embedded in the GATT (by directly banning non-tariff import barriers and by putting a tight lid on export subsidies) the Uruguay Round introduced a separate set of rules (in the AoA) that seemed to extend exceptionalism.[9] But the question remains as to whether treating agricultural trade in a different way to that in other areas of commerce makes sense. The article raises the question as to what would be lost if the AoA were to come to an end? Tariffs would be governed by normal market access rules (which would mean a phasing out of tariff-rate quotas); export subsidies would be eliminated if the rules of the Subsidies and Countervailing Measures (SCM) Agreement were to be applied fully to agricultural trade; and domestic support (subsides, direct payments and provision of environmental public goods) would also be subject to the full obligations of the SCM rather than being restrained in sector-specific (and idiosyncratic) ways by the AoA.

The rules that countries are prepared to accept in institutions such as the WTO are ultimately conditioned by the domestic policies of those countries. These policies change with the emergence of new ideas of the relationship between government and the agricultural sector. These ideas influence the set of policies from which governments make choices. Hall (1993) refers to these ideas and the set of policies that are consistent with those ideas as "paradigms". This notion

[9] An interesting comparison is with the treatment of textiles and clothing in the Uruguay Round. This sector was dominated by import quotas and licenses introduced since the 1960s. The solution was to eliminate quotas over a defined period and thereafter to make no distinction in GATT rules between textiles and other areas of manufacturing.

has been adapted to describe policy changes in the area of agricultural products. Domestic paradigm shifts help to explain the possible outcomes of trade talks (and indeed the agenda for such talks). Article 9 elaborates on this theme with respect to the dramatic changes in farm policy in the EU and the US in the 1990s. The paper identifies several competing paradigms and the trade implications of each. The Uruguay Round AoA was in part the result of the paradigmatic changes in domestic policy that accompanied the movement to limit government involvement in the management of markets. As countries reduced their interventions in domestic markets and weakened their attempts to fix domestic prices that they signaled a willingness to see the world price play a greater role in clearing markets (by removing the structural impediments discussed in the first two sections above).

Part IV. Trade Conflicts over Domestic Policies

The process of introducing disciplines on farm policies involves two steps: first to agree on rules governing national behavior and then to establish a mechanism for resolving disputes that arise from the infringement (or supposed infringement) of those rules. The next group of articles looks at some of the disputes that have occurred in agricultural trade, in particular between the US and the EU. Though not alone in making use of the dispute settlement process of the GATT and the WTO, the US and the EU have tended to dominate the arena. This tension between the US and the EU in agricultural trade has a history spanning five decades, starting with the adoption of the Common Agricultural Policy by the EEC in the early 1960s (Josling and Tangermann, 2015). The US and the EU had developed somewhat different approaches to similar problems, such as the tendency for surpluses to accumulate under politically inspired fixed prices. As illustrated in the earlier sections of this book, this is a recipe for dysfunctional markets and mutual recriminations.

Some of the many transatlantic trade disputes in agriculture that were brought before the GATT are described in Article 10. The article was written at a time when the dispute over oilseed subsidies in the EU was proving the most difficult to resolve and when the GATT negotiations in the Uruguay Round had reached one of their several roadblocks. The future of the trade system seemed to have become hostage to a dispute over a few thousand tons of soybeans. Much of the rhetoric surrounding the dispute came from convenient, if not always accurate, demonization of the other party. The EU was seen in the US as a protectionist bastion and an irresponsible trade partner. The US was seen in the EU as being arrogant in demanding changes in the internal policies of other countries to favor its own agribusiness interests. What truth there was in these accusations was outweighed by the exaggerations: in fact the trade conflicts were often over small market shares important to particular national (in the EU) or corporate (in the US) interests. Trade philosophy played a minor role in the dramatic confrontations of the time (Josling, 1993). The mid-1980s had seen these transatlantic tensions reach new heights, as the EU (briefly) surpassed the US in agricultural exports (in 1986) and the US spent more on agricultural support than did the EU in that year.[10] Clearly something had to be done to resolve these disputes. Concluding the Uruguay Round was a first step to putting agricultural trade back on an even keel, and the inclusion of the trade impacts of domestic support policies was a major part of that process.

The creation of the WTO as the successor to the GATT provided both a significant new set of rules (as mentioned above) and a better way of litigating any perceived infractions of those rules. The WTO Dispute Settlement Understanding (DSU) set up a more effective procedure for resolving conflicts. The conflicts between the EU and the US over agriculture that kept the GATT dispute settlement process occupied are discussed in Article 11 from this later perspective. The conflicts that are discussed in this paper include several that related to export subsidies (wheat flour, pasta, poultry and sugar) and others that involved challenges to domestic subsidies (canned fruit, wine and oilseeds). Each of these cases showed the inadequacy of the GATT articles to constrain developed country farm policies. The contrast with the first few years of the WTO dispute settlement process is striking. Of the 231 consultations recorded by the WTO Secretariat between 1995 and mid-2001, only seven involved agricultural disputes between the EU and the US (Josling and Tangermann, 2003, p. 220). Of these cases only one (related to alleged EU export subsidies for processed cheese) involved subsidies.

This did not mean that the DSU was not important in the resolution of agricultural disputes. It was inevitable that several of the early dispute panels that were set up under the WTO were given the task of resolving some of the ongoing US-EU disputes that had been raised in the GATT, though these did not involve subsidies. Among these were the disputes over the ban on the importation of hormone treated beef into the EU and the operation of EU banana import quotas on products from Latin America and the Caribbean. The beef hormone case stemmed from the decision in 1988 to ban both the use of several hormones in animal production and the imports of beef and beef products from countries that used such growth enhancers. The banana case arose initially in 1992 when several Latin American countries complained about the distribution of import quotas into the EU. Later two other prominent disputes arose between the EU and the US: the use of Geographical Indications for foods from particular regions, and the approval

[10] US agricultural exports had plummeted in the period after 1981, in large part because of a sharp appreciation of the dollar against other currencies. A drought in the Midwest in 1983 also had an impact on US exports.

of foods and feedstuffs made from transgenic crops sold in the EU market.

The disputes that are referred to a panel under WTO procedures generate a wealth of information not only about the legal interpretation of the rules governing trade but also about the activities of governments themselves. For a period of a few months the spotlight is focused on the activities in question. The cases discussed in Article 12 illustrate this point. The banana case revealed a web of trade restrictions stemming from both the post-colonial policies of the EU members (particularly the UK and France) and the internal market for bananas within the EU itself. The policies were dictating the market structure to such an extent that the firms operating in the market were competing for the "rents" generated by the preference schemes. The creation of the single market in the EU (in 1993) forced the integration of the markets for "dollar" bananas in Germany and the Netherlands and the Caribbean bananas sold in France and the UK. Those firms that had a foothold in the UK and French markets were keen to hold onto their privileged access: those that were selling onto the German market wanted to expand in the EU market and resented the high tariffs that they faced. It took several years of litigation to resolve these issues to the satisfaction of the US (who had taken the part of one of the suppliers of Latin American bananas) and the EU (that was ultimately obliged to abandon the quota system that had been the cause of the conflict).

The beef hormone case also took several years to reach a mutually satisfactory solution. The US (along with Canada) claimed that the 1988 ban on beef imports violated the Sanitary and Phytosanitary (SPS) Agreement negotiated in the Uruguay Round. Once again, the dispute settlement process shed light on the impact of government policies on the marketplace. The amount of trade involved was small (barely US$100 million of imports of processed meat products) and the nature of the market suggested that there was an opportunity for the US beef producer to recognize that market segmentation could act in their favor. However, the US was determined to use the WTO dispute settlement process to resolve the issue that had eluded the weaker GATT arrangements. The combination of the SPS Agreement, that made it mandatory to employ risk assessment in designing and implementing health and safety standards, and the DSU that removed the possibility of stalling a panel decision by an unsatisfied member offered the US an opportunity to force the EU into compliance. However, the WTO dispute settlement process proved itself to be no match for internal political pressures and the case ended not with the EU changing its policies but with an agreement that a limited amount of hormone-free beef should be allowed in each year.

The other cases discussed in the article showed different aspects of the influence of farm policy on markets and market structure. In cases where groups of producers are granted exclusive use of their geographical names (as is common in wines in Europe, along with certain cheeses and meats) a monopoly is created that is protected by regulations from others using that name. The protection of geographical indications (GIs) was made mandatory in the Uruguay Round, through the Agreement on Trade–Related Intellectual Property (TRIPS). However, the means of ensuring that protection was left to individual governments. Whatever the merits of including the encouragement of protection of intellectual property (in effect restricting trade) in a set of rules designed to liberalize trade, the fact is that the EU and other countries that had made full use of such rules (e.g. Switzerland) insisted in their incorporation. The US objected in the WTO to the self-serving way that the EU was administering the system of GIs that seemed to favor European firms and farm groups, and the US view prevailed in the dispute. But it underscored the way in which markets can be fragmented and competition reduced by actions that seem "fair" on the surface but are in fact ways of distributing rents from established names that command a premium.

The impact of domestic farm policies on market structure was also behind the case brought by New Zealand and the US against Canada for allegedly subsidizing exports of cheese and other dairy products by supplying cheese factories with low-priced milk. In this case the Canadian government had contrived to allow milk surplus to domestic requirements to be sold at a low price to dairies. The significance of this case was that it involved domestic marketing laws but had an impact on exports similar to a (restricted) export subsidy. In the end, the Canadian government had to remove the provisions that were at fault. Once again, the DSU had shed light on a domestic marketing policy that was responsible for causing unacceptable problems for world markets.

Perhaps the most significant case involving agricultural policy and trade involved upland cotton in the US. Once again it was domestic farm policy that was distorting world markets. In this case the US market share had been increasing even when its production declined. Brazil challenged the US support program for upland cotton on the grounds that subsidies given to cotton processors for the use of domestic cotton contravened the GATT prohibition on discriminating against imported inputs, and that payments to cotton farmers reduced the market share of Brazilian cotton producers. The case took a close look at domestic support programs, and came to the conclusion that such subsidies when related to production levels had an unfair impact on the legitimate interests of foreign producers. However, the panel also found that paying farmers in ways that did not encourage more production did not violate WTO rules. So the arguments of economists and other observers that had resonated from the 1970s were validated by a judicial process: domestic price support programs that had been the feature of farm policy over four decades could cause serious injury to producers in other parts of the world.

Part V. Monitoring the Compliance of Country Policies with WTO Disciplines

Agreeing to discipline domestic policies raises the question of monitoring the adherence to the disciplines. The establishment of a firm legal basis for the trade rules and a more comprehensive system of dispute resolution rested on greater transparency in trade policies. This transparency is generally manifest in notifications by WTO member states to a Committee in the WTO that can undertake the monitoring and facilitate an assessment of compliance. For agricultural trade the obligation to notify policy conformity was particularly broad. This annual notification required information on the quantitative aspects of policies, primarily on support prices and subsidy costs.

Notification by governments of their compliance with obligations is an important part of a credible trade system. Being able to examine and interpret such notifications is step that turns mechanical and perfunctory notifications into information that adds to our understanding of the trade system. Though notifications to the WTO to demonstrate compliance with the Uruguay Round obligations are common in other areas of trade, the notification of support levels permissible in the Agreement on Agriculture have particular significance.[11] The extent to which countries were in compliance was then subject to discussion (and counter-notification) within the WTO Committee on Agriculture. Though the Committee itself does not rule on such compliance the process opens up the door to the assessment of the impact of these rules in disciplining domestic policies.

The experience of the first decade of domestic policy obligations is discussed in Article 13. This article links the earlier discussions of policy change and trade disputes to the Doha Round of trade negotiations underway at the time that the article was written. It begins with a review of the policy implications of the AoA for the US and the EU, concluding that the changes were subtle but important. A direct clash between farm policies in the US and EU had been avoided by the formula agreed at Blair House that provided partial shelter for those payments that were tied to acreage (and headage) limits. But the AoA did have some impact on policy choices and on the room for significant changes. Quantitative trade restrictions were translated into Tariff Rate Quotas (TRQs) that carried lower tariffs for a fixed

[11] Notifications to the Committee on Regional Trade Agreements have been improved to the extent that useful information on these agreements is now collected and collated by the WTO Secretariat; however, some recent agreements have not yet been notified. Notifications under the Subsidies and Countervailing Measures (SCM) agreement have been descriptive but been inadequate for other WTO members to assess the impact on trade (a part of the notification requirement). Among those notifications that have been useful are those that are presented to the Committee on Sanitary and Phytosanitary Measures (SPS Committee) and those notified to the committee that performs a similar function for Technical Barriers to Trade (TBT Committee). See Collins-Williams and Wolfe (2010) for a review of the broader issues of notification and transparency in the WTO.

quantity of imports. In principle these TRQs were a step towards improved market access, though in practice some of the TRQs have gone unfilled and the expansion of these quotas has not been continued since the AoA.

However, a monitoring system requires members of the WTO to comply with the notification rules. Not all countries have been notifying domestic support obligations in a timely and complete way. This has meant that the monitoring system has been somewhat less effective than originally intended. Though some of the delays may have been due to lack of data it is more likely that the lack of any sanctions for missing deadlines is the cause. Moreover, the method of notification has not been without problems. For instance, the way in which notifications are presented by countries makes the comparison across countries difficult.

One major issue is the calculation of "Aggregate Measurement of Support" (AMS) that is subject to limit within the schedules of Member States. One component of the AMS is the Market Price Support (MPS). This is calculated by applying the difference between an "administered price" and a "reference price" (based on world market conditions in the 1980s) and applying this price gap to an "eligible" quantity of the product that can receive support under the program. The administered price can be reduced by governments without a comparable drop in producer price (if the market is protected by tariffs); the reference price can be very different from current world prices (and hence give a misleading impression of the impact of the policy); and the eligible quantity can be interpreted by the government with little guidance from WTO documents. So the AMS has lost much of its significance as a way to monitor policy developments. This issue is discussed in detail in Article 14, with careful examination of the notifications from a number of countries (US, EU, Japan, India, China, the Philippines, Norway and Brazil).

The final article in the book relates to both transparency and monitoring. Article 15 was written to illustrate the relationship between two of the efforts to collect and present data on the level of government intervention in agricultural markets. The OECD, as mentioned above, has been collecting data on farm policies for its members since the mid-1980s, more recently expanding its country coverage to include some important non-members. The WTO has amassed a significant database of its own in the process of collecting notifications from members of their compliance with obligations under the AoA. The differences between the two databases are not trivial: they are, after all, collected for different purposes. But the argument in the paper reproduced here is that the two different datasets each give a dimension of the story of the impact of farm policies on world markets. The WTO database focuses on categorizing policies under the major headings of the AoA — market access, export competition and domestic support. Domestic support is further categorized as "green box", "blue box", or AMS (often called "amber box"). So the fit of policy instruments into these categories is necessary for monitoring compliance. The OECD database follows a classification that has evolved over the years to calculate the Producer Support Estimates (PSE)[12]. The three categories of transfer that are at the heart of the PSE calculations are the support given through output market price measures (MPS), that given by direct payments (DP), and that coming through input and capital market subsidies (ICS).[13] In addition to these components the cost of providing general services and various other measures such as taxation relief and subsidies from sub-national bodies are also calculated. The Total Support Estimate (TSE) includes the PSE along with the general services estimate (GSSE) and other miscellaneous unattributed transfers.[14]

The linkage with the WTO categories requires some disentangling of the categories. The MPS, as explained above, is calculated differently, as the OECD uses current international prices rather than fixed reference prices, actual farm process rather than administered prices, and total crop output rather than eligible quantities. Thus the OECD MPS adds information to the WTO MPS. Similarly the WTO Green Box calculation can be refined by relating payments to the categories that separate out those that require production and those that do not. In short, if the two databases are taken together, a fuller picture of support in the context of trade rules can be gained.

So the process of monitoring farm policies has come full circle. In the mid-1970s the FAO was interested in developing a monitoring device that would inform governments of the implications of their decisions for world markets. The markets themselves were unstable and unsuitable as a guide for domestic policy. By the 1980s the need for some disciplines on farm programs was patently clear, and the OECD began to build up a database that would provide a basis for discussion and negotiation. The GATT Uruguay Round provided such trade rules in the form of the Agreement on Agriculture. Not only did the disciplines on domestic support use a variant of the PSE developed by the FAO and the OECD (the AMS) but it put in place a monitoring system through country notifications. These notifications have, together with the increased transparency provided by dispute settlement panels, illuminated the murky world of farm policies.

---

[12] The name of the measure was changed from Producer Subsidy Equivalent to Producer Support Estimate in 1999, though the definition (and the acronym) was unchanged.

[13] Additional indicators that are derived from the PSE include the Producer Nominal Protection Coefficient (NPC) and the Producer Nominal Assistance Coefficient (NAC). These measures use the same information but relate the level of subsidy to the unsubsidized value — a form that is sometimes more convenient than relating support to the support-inclusive value.

[14] The OECD (in 2007) introduced some more classification detail in the category of direct payments within the PSE. These payments are now distinguished by whether they are based on input use; on area, animal numbers, receipts or income; whether those bases are current or historical; whether production is required or not; or whether based on "non-commodity criteria". The calculations of market price support and of output-based subsidies have not been changed.

References

Anderson, K. (Ed.). (2009). *Distortions to agricultural incentives: A global perspective 1955–2007*. London, Washington DC: Palgrave Macmillan, World Bank.

Collins-Williams, T., and Wolfe, R. (2010). Transparency as a trade policy tool: The WTO's cloudy windows. *World Trade Review, 9*(4), 551–581.

FAO. (1973). *Agricultural protection: Domestic policy and international trade*, C73/LIM/9, (International Agricultural Adjustment: Supporting Study No. 9), FAO, Rome.

FAO. (1975). *Agricultural protection and stabilization policies: A framework of measurement in the context of agricultural adjustment*, C75/LIM/2, FAO, Rome.

GATT. (1958). *Trends in international trade*, (Haberler Report), GATT, Geneva, October.

Hall, P. A. (1993). Policy paradigms, social learning, and the state: The case of economic policymaking in Britain. *Comparative Politics, 25*(3), 275–296

Hathaway, D. E. (1988). *Agriculture and the GATT: Rewriting the rules*. Washington, DC: Institute for International Studies.

Hertel, T. W. (Ed.). (1997). *Global trade analysis: Modeling and applications*. New York, NY: Cambridge University Press.

Johnson, D. G. (1973). *World agriculture in disarray*. London, UK: Macmillan.

Josling, T., Tangermann, S., and Warley, T. K. (1996). *Agriculture and the GATT*. London, UK: Macmillan.

Josling, T., and Anderson, K. (1993). The challenge to economists of multilateral trade negotiations on agricultural protection. *Food Research Institute Studies, 22*(3), 275–304.

Josling, T., and Tangermann, S. (2015). *Transatlantic food and agricultural trade policy: Fifty years of conflict and convergence*. Northampton, MA: Edward Elgar Press (forthcoming).

Kreuger, A. O., Schiff, M., and Valdes, A. (1991). *The political economy of agricultural pricing policies*. Baltimore, MD, Washington, DC: Johns Hopkins University Press, World Bank.

Legg, W. (2003). Agricultural subsidies: Measurement and use in policy evaluation. *Journal of Agricultural Economics, 54*(2), 175–200.

OECD. (1987). *National policies and international trade*. Paris: OECD.

Robinson, S. (1990). Analyzing agricultural trade liberalization with single country computable general equilibrium models. In I. Goldin and R. Knudsen (eds.), *Agricultural trade liberalization: Implications for developing countries* (pp. 201–224). Paris: OECD.

Roningen, V., and Dixit, P. M. (1987). How level is the playing field?: An economic analysis of agricultural policy reforms in industrial market economies. Foreign Agricultural Economic Report No. 239, Economic Research Service, USDA.

Tyers, R., and Anderson, K. (1992). *Disarray in world food markets: A quantitative assessment*. Cambridge, UK and New York, NY: Cambridge University Press.

WTO. (1994). *The results of the Uruguay Round of multilateral trade negotiations: The legal texts*. Geneva: GATT.

Part I

Monitoring the Trade Impacts of Developed Country Farm Policies

7
Agricultural Protection and Stabilization Policies: Analysis of Current Neomercantilist Practices

Timothy Josling

The years 1972-1977 were traumatic for those who had responsibility for food and agricultural policies of industrial nations. Old notions of the problems to be faced had to be discarded; well-established political alliances were shaken by new interests; entrenched policy instruments had to be resharpened in a new cause. It was a period of heightened uncertainty, and the responsibility of decisionmakers was widened to include concern with economic stability on the domestic front and with the security of food supplies to low-income countries abroad. But the experiences of that period should not be seen as an aberration, to be forgotten in more normal times. Indeed those experiences have illuminated many of the problems of the agricultural trading system for the past twenty-five years and put into sharper focus the relationship between domestic farm and food policies and the international market for temperate-zone agricultural products.

This chapter discusses those aspects of domestic agricultural policies of particular importance to the operation of the trading system. It also considers some empirical evidence on the reaction of governments in the wheat market to the period of high agricultural prices and the consequent implications of these reactions for international trade in wheat. Finally, the discussion is placed in the context of the Tokyo Round of international negotiations and the policy choices facing major governments in the next few years.

Domestic Agricultural Policies

Two things are remarkable about domestic agricultural policies of industrial countries: their durability and their flexibility. These are of course related, since any viable policy has to be responsive to circumstance, but the continued existence of these characteristics demands an explanation. Some would subscribe to the view that forty years of farm policies are an example of the ability of one sector of the population, through active lobbying and political cohesion, to derive a continuous stream of benefits in the form of transfer payments from the economy at large. Others would suggest that these policies survive because of bureaucratic vested interest and the inability of a modern economy to reject an entrenched set of government programs. Any policy, of course, will attract and create interests which will in turn work for its perpetuation, but it seems more useful to view developed-country farm policies as the response of a mixed economy (carried forward by general political consensus and supported by prevailing orthodoxy) to a particularly complex set of problems in an important sector.[1] Thus understood, the continuity of such programs may be attributed to the fact that they have fulfilled a need. In the context of the general expansion of government responsibility for economic management, they have offered a range of instruments of control that few administrations have felt able to forswear.

The problems to which farm policies have been addressed have changed over time. During the depression the concern was largely with rural spending power; in wartime, with maintaining strategic food supplies; in the postwar period, with the development of the economic potential of advanced agriculture; and afterward with the human adjustment problems caused by the success of modern technology. In recent years the problem of inflation has come to dominate all other domestic issues.[2] The instrumentalities have been similarly modified, at least in emphasis. Prewar legislation on marketing structures and control over supplies gave way in the postwar era to production incentives, then to adjustment assistance programs, and finally to consumer price measures. The pattern differed from country to country, and the armory of policy measures was built up to suit local conditions, but the same theme has been apparent in North America, Western Europe, Australasia, and Japan. The orthodoxy knew no frontiers, just as the problems themselves appeared to be spread throughout the trading system.[3]

It is this similarity that is at the heart of the problem of trade relations in agricultural markets and the source of the basic incompatibility of many domestic farm policies with a properly functioning world food system. It is because the same set of issues are of domestic concern in a number of countries at the same time that the autarkic solutions to those questions are inadequate and often self-defeating. This is indeed part of a broader problem. The fact that the modern mixed economy reacts to situations in much the same way throughout the developed world in agricultural as well as other matters is itself a major cause of tension in international commercial relations.[4] One aspect of such an economy is the extensive use by governments of price as an instrument of control, in contrast to a command economy with its emphasis on quantitative planning and to a laissez-faire economy in which control is related to market power and prices are a consequence of individual decisions rather than an instrument of government policy. Farm policies represent an example par excellence of such management by price. For our present purposes it is not necessary to explore the merits and demerits of such economic management as a whole. It is enough to note that the engine of farm and food policy in the last four decades has been government manipulation of the price at which major farm goods are sold on the domestic market and, as a consequence, the price paid by food manufacturers for agricultural raw material. Protection has meant price support, and stabilization has implied the stability of price levels. And once such ideas are implanted, the original problems of rural incomes, consumer welfare, and adjustment of the labor force become subordinate to the objective of domestic price maintenance. The tyranny of the domestic price objective for agricultural goods has dismayed a generation of economists who have argued for a more direct attack on the problems themselves and a greater degree of freedom in price formation.

The well-worn ground of alternative domestic farm policy approaches is not treated here. The external influence of price policies is more significant. Decisions taken in the name of domestic objectives help to decide the structure of world markets. In the case of basic foodstuffs such an influence is of fundamental importance. The performance of the world food system—the ability of the world to feed itself securely and at the least cost—can be hampered as much by the operation of such domestic price policies as by the more obvious hazards of climatic instability and crop disease. This appears to be the major lesson of recent years.

Recent Experience of Price Policies

The above conclusion is supported by empirical evidence on how governments in developed countries reacted to the sudden change in the balance of agricultural commodity markets from surplus to shortage. It was suggested earlier that an important legacy of thirty-five years of intervention in price fixing in domestic agricultural markets was a convenient anti-inflation device when prices unexpectedly rose on world markets. This is not to say that price rises did not occur domestically. Both producer prices and consumer prices rose steeply between 1972 and 1974. Table 1 shows the movement of wheat prices, calculated to include the effect of various subsidies and taxes, implicit and explicit. The pace of price rise differed from country to country, but none escaped the impact altogether. Costs to farmers had doubled over this period, and no government could have held the line on administered prices in the face of such pressure on profitability.

A research report prepared for the U.N. Food and Agriculture Organization (FAO) in conjunction with their ongoing work on "international agricultural adjustment" has traced the changes in the level of protection of six of the developed countries from 1968 to 1974 for some important temperate-zone commodities.[5] The problem of measurement of agricultural protection was approached first by separating the impact on producers (producer subsidy equivalent, or PSE) from that on consumers (consumer subsidy equivalent, or CSE). Major product price policies and input subsidies for the countries and commodities studied were then evaluated with respect to these two effects.[6] The conclusions were, broadly, that the relatively high level of producer protection of the 1960s evaporated suddenly in 1973-74, to be replaced by policies that often taxed producers and subsidized consumption.

This change in support levels is clearly shown in the lower part of Table 1, which gives the calculated levels of producer and consumer subsidy equivalents for wheat.[7] The figures illustrate that with the exception of the small Japanese wheat sector (which in any case has declined in size) producer protection was negligible in North America and negative in Europe and Australia in the harvest year 1974-75. Farm price support had, temporarily at least, been wound down with the aid of firm world markets. What is perhaps more striking is the size of the (positive) consumer subsidy programs in Australia, Japan, and the European Community (EC).[8] North American consumers did not benefit to the same extent. The instruments of policy that were responsible for this remarkable turnabout did not always change, but they were put to use in a different cause. The world price rise eliminated at a stroke the need for export subsidies and heralded into existence export levies and taxes to keep domestic prices down. In some cases import subsidies came into being, but more often consumers were subsidized directly to protect them from the world price boom. Taxpayers found themselves financing consumption as well as production.

The FAO study also examined total producer and consumer subsidy values, calculated by applying the percentage change (PSE and CSE) to total producer receipts from wheat sales and total consumer expen-

Table 1. Wheat Prices and Subsidy Equivalents of National Policies, 1971-72 to 1974-75

Country	Producer prices dollars, million tons				Consumer prices dollars, million tons			
	1971-72	1972-73	1973-74	1974-75	1971-72	1972-73	1973-74	1974-75
Australia	57.81	70.95	150.37	137.04	71.48	92.02	102.46	109.23
Canada	58.20	82.00	171.00	168.00	61.48	97.60	201.89	197.69
European Community (EC-6)	99.10	101.89	131.58	141.85	106.54	133.03	146.40	158.80
Japan	182.64	212.93	273.17	324.99	100.58	111.52	140.43	156.31
United Kingdom	78.62	86.32	100.90	143.05	58.11	86.32	143.54	134.73
United States	48.98	64.67	145.14	148.45	60.99	81.94	167.92	165.35
	Producer subsidy equivalents percent				Consumer subsidy equivalents percent			
	1971-72	1972-73	1973-74	1974-75	1971-72	1972-73	1973-74	1974-75
Australia	19.3	13.7	-12.4	-10.0	-19.4	-10.8	76.0	47.4
Canada	20.2	11.5	1.2	0.7	-37.7	-24.1	19.4	18.9
European Community (EC-6)	64.8	46.5	-39.9	-4.4	-53.3	-32.5	40.6	8.3
Japan	57.8	60.7	41.8	51.3	-26.8	-26.7	13.4	60.8
United Kingdom	28.4	18.1	10.6	-40.8	-1.8	-6.0	-2.3	43.8
United States	35.9	40.6	7.4	0.0	-24.6	-30.8	1.1	0.7

Source: U.N. Food and Agriculture Organization, Agricultural Protection and Stabilization Policies, C/75/LIM/2 (Rome: 1975). Revised in the light of data available since 1975.

ditures, including use for animal feed. These total values can be thought of as the amount of exchequer payments that would be necessary to compensate for a removal of price and nonprice policies. They indicate a dramatic switch from an implicit payment of $3.4 billion to producers in crop year 1971-72 to an effective tax of $0.7 billion in 1974-75. On the consumer side, the burden of $2.2 billion in 1971-72 is replaced by a bonus of $1.8 billion in 1974-75 under the price stabilization policies.[9] Sum of the two totals indicates that the residual "taxpayer" obligation falls marginally from $1.2 billion in 1971-72 to $1.1 billion in 1974-75.[10] When observed from a national point of view, these figures suggest a flexibility of national wheat policies that contributed usefully to the control of inflation. As prices rose the need for farm protection was reduced and the obligation to keep supplies on the domestic market secure became predominant. The farm policies survived by adaptation: the mixed economy utilized the instruments at hand to fight price rises.

Implications for International Trade

The period of high grain prices was also a time of great concern about global food supplies, leading up to the 1974 World Food Conference.[11] The effect of national policies on food supplies needs further elaboration. How was the trading system affected by such policy adaptations? And what might have been their impact on other countries less able to absorb higher wheat costs? To arrive at an estimate of such implications for the trading system requires further assumptions. In the calculations discussed below it was assumed that producers react with a one-year lag to the change in the level of a subsidy, and that in all the countries concerned the supply elasticity is 0.25.[12] Consumers (or users of wheat) react immediately to the change in their price, with price elasticity of -0.3. Thus, for any given year, the volume implication of a set of subsidies is the production effect of the previous year's PSE and the current year's CSE.[13] Table 2 gives the results of these calculations. They show that "supported" output accounted altogether for perhaps 8.1 million metric tons in 1972-73, but in 1974-75 production was perhaps 2.6 million tons *less* as a result of the policies pursued in the six countries, in particular the EC.[14] The consumption volume effects indicate a reduction in demand (at constant world prices) of 5.7 million tons in 1972-73, changing to an additional demand of 3.6 million tons in 1974-75 as a result of national policies.

Though it is inappropriate to apportion "blame" among countries, all of which are pursuing legitimate internal ends, it is interesting to cast the figures in terms of additional exports and imports from these six

Table 2. Estimated Policy-induced Production, Consumption and Trade Volume Effects, Wheat 1971-72 to 1974-75

Country	Production volume effect[a] million metric tons				Consumption volume effect[b] million metric tons			
	1971-72	1972-73	1973-74	1974-75	1971-72	1972-73	1973-74	1974-75
Australia	0.360	0.410	0.410	0.219	0.157	0.104	-0.707	-0.427
Canada	0.457	0.727	0.417	0.049	0.537	0.308	-0.279	-0.268
European Community (EC-6)	3.392	4.941	3.743	-3.242	4.205	2.691	-3.264	-0.645
Japan	0.067	0.058	0.046	0.021	0.418	0.425	-0.221	-1.883
United Kingdom	0.193	0.341	0.217	0.132	0.046	0.166	0.055	-1.222
United States	1.634	1.580	1.705	0.858	1.727	1.968	-0.068	-0.848
	Export volume effect[c] million metric tons				Import volume effect[d] million metric tons			
	1971-72	1972-73	1973-74	1974-75	1971-72	1972-73	1973-74	1974-75
Australia	0.517	0.514	-0.488	-0.799	--	--	--	--
Canada	0.994	1.035	0.138	-0.212	--	--	--	--
European Community (EC-6)	7.597	7.632	0.479	-3.887	--	--	--	--
Japan	--	--	--	--	0.485	0.483	-0.175	-0.982
United Kingdom	--	--	--	--	0.239	0.507	0.272	-1.898
United States	3.361	3.548	1.637	0.818	--	--	--	--

a Positive figures show the <u>increased</u> production calculated to result from the producer subsidy equivalents (as given in tables) - the production that would have been lost by the removal of those subsidies.

b Positive figures show the <u>reduced</u> consumption calculated to result from the consumer subsidy equivalents - i.e. the extra consumption that would have occurred without these 'subsidies.' When the subsidy itself becomes positive, this 'extra' consumption is negative.

c Positive figures show the <u>additional</u> export volume generated by the national policies; negative figures are a reduction in exports.

d Positive figures show the <u>reduction</u> of import volume attributed to the policies; negative figures are an increase in imports.

Source: Calculated by method described in the text from the figures in Table 2.

countries. For each country, the trade balance change is the sum of increased (or reduced) production and reduced (or increased) consumption arising from the policies. The lower part of Table 2 shows that the four exporting countries changed from a policy-induced surplus of over 12 million tons in 1971-72 to a deficit of 4 million tons in 1974-75. The two importing nations also changed from a policy-induced import-substitution of 0.7 million tons in 1971-72 to an impact-stimulation of 2.1 million tons in 1974-75.

The total impact of the effects on production and consumption and trade are indicated in Table 3. To countries outside this particular group, nearly 14 million tons of wheat were being "exported" as a result of farm policies in 1972-73. By 1973-74 this figure had dropped to 2 million tons, and in 1974-75 the "rest of the world" were denied over 6 million tons as a result of these domestic policies. The significance of these results is not only in the absolute size, though this is not in itself uninteresting in the context of the location of global production, but in the change from 1973 to 1975. The impact of the domestic price stability schemes was to reduce the amount of wheat available by almost 20 million tons. The magnitude of this figure is striking. World wheat stocks (excluding Soviet Russia and China) decreased by 23 million tons between 1972 and 1973 and by a further 5 million tons the next year. Average imports of wheat by developing countries for 1971-73 were about 22 million tons. Soviet purchases of grain in 1972-73 amounted to 20 million tons, and the world harvest shortfall below trend in that year was 31 million tons. Although no simple link exists between these figures and the behavior of the world market, it is clear that the countries considered had potentially a significant influence on the price and availability of grains in the rest of the world.

The Problem of World Market Structure

The empirical evidence from the wheat market over this period indicates the possible extent to which governments, in pursuit of domestic price stability objectives, unwittingly might have had a destabilizing effect on the world market. Much attention has been given in recent years to the question of whether reserves of basic food commodities are adequate to deal with world production fluctuations. The inference of the previous discussion is that the question of reserve policy must itself be set in a broader context. Pressure on world market prices, both to lower and to raise them, comes not just from the vagaries of the world harvest alone but also from the reactions of government policies to the world price movements themselves. When prices weaken,

Table 3. Aggregated Production, Consumption and Trade Effects, Wheat, 1971-72 to 1974-75

	1971-72	1972-73	1973-74	1974-75
Total production volume effect	6.1	8.1	6.3	-2.6
Total consumption volume effect	7.1	5.7	-4.5	-3.6
Total export volume effect	12.5	12.7	1.8	-4.1
Total import volume effect	0.7	1.0	0.1	-2.1
Net trade volume effect[a]	13.2	13.7	1.9	-6.2

a Positive figures show additional net export volume from this group of countries (i.e. extra exports plus reduction in imports); negative figures show a reduction in net exports. These totals also correspond to the aggregation of the production and consumption effects.

governments maintain production and restrict consumption by a variety of measures. When prices firm, production incentives are stifled and consumption levels maintained, causing the situation on the world market to deteriorate still further. The quantity of stocks needed to give a particular level of price stability, and hence to maintain consumption levels in low-income countries, is therefore greater the more the developed country governments are successful in their own price-stability objectives.[15]

At the risk of some exaggeration, the links between domestic policies and the structure and performance of the world trading system can be illustrated in the following way.[16] Suppose that the quantity imported into or exported from a developed country is entirely dependent on domestic price objectives. The exporter facing such an import market cannot compete by price means; for it is as if a quota had been fixed, where the import quantity was determined by the amount that will sell internally at the predetermined domestic price. Any excess supplies will be an embarrassment. They will be moved into residual outlets, such as food aid, or stored, or sold to markets perhaps in central-plan economies which can absorb surpluses without depressing domestic prices. But if exporters also maintain domestic price targets and do not vary export volumes with the market position, a further strain is put on prices. Generous use of export subsidies will further depress world price levels and lead to competition among national treasuries for limited market outlets in times of surplus, and export controls will further increase world prices when supplies are tight. Recalcitrant importers face determined exporters, and market price stability is the casualty.

The implications of such a trading structure occasioned by domestic policy objectives are far-reaching. There is a serious analytical question as to what does in fact determine world price levels when the interplay of commercial import demand and export supply is thwarted. The answer probably lies in the willingness of legislatures in developed-country exporters to appropriate funds for food aid and reserve accumulation and in the ability of the central-plan countries to rescue the trading system from its own self-imposed rigidities.[17] But on the high side of the market, food aid will be curtailed as its cost rises, predatory purchasing will be discontinued, and stocks will quickly be used up. Importing countries will be concerned with supply security and will step up efforts to become self-sufficient. In particular, developing countries with food deficits will be forced to adopt agricultural policies of their own which may in time lead to high-cost food production which they can ill afford. These symptoms have all been evident in the market for grains, particularly for wheat.[18]

This raises a question as to what might be done to alleviate the problems. How can one return to a market structure for temperate-zone agricultural commodities that combines the advantages of specialization (in particular, to lower the cost of food products to developing countries) with the degree of price stability that has become a vital element in the satisfactory management of a mixed economy? One can at least outline the type of policy initiatives that would seem to meet these problems at least in part. Some such policy changes have indeed already been evident recently. At the level of the individual country, the question of reserve stocks of food grain has entered into the general discussion of food procurement policies. Many developing countries have added storage capacity and improved distribution systems to enable them to counter production and price variability. On the international front the major grain trading nations have been meeting to discuss a new International Wheat Agreement, linked with negotiations both in the General Agreement on Tariffs and Trade (GATT) and the U.N. Conference on Trade and Development (UNCTAD). The FAO-inspired "Undertaking on World Food Security" has continued to concentrate the attention of governments on the formulation of reserve policies and to provide a channel for information on stock levels. The World Food Council in turn has generated ideas on stock policies which both distinguish the various objectives of such stocks and attempt to coordinate the attitudes of governments and international agencies on such objectives. Meanwhile, the improvement in the world supply situation for the main food grains has provided an opportunity for such schemes to be contemplated without the emotional atmosphere that clouded the issues at the World Food Conference.

Despite these developments, which themselves have reduced the risk of another food crisis, the major issues have not yet been faced. Two elements would appear to be essential to an improvement in the structure of the grain market. First, the major developed countries must come to accept an obligation, in their self-interest, to absorb more of the fluctuation in grain production than they have in the past. This means primarily that domestic price targets must be made responsive to world conditions—in the short run to absorb surpluses and alleviate shortages and in the long run to allow domestic markets to reflect the international valuation of grains relative to other products.[19] Secondly, these countries must themselves develop a common approach to stocks which allows them to avoid recourse to trade disruptive measures at times of market disturbance. Trade measures that look attractive from a country viewpoint together give rise to market structure problems: stocks policies that seem expensive to the individual country become a viable alternative if the burdens are shared. The benefit to developing countries comes largely as a result of a more certain alternative to domestic output expansion while not in itself reducing the value of wise investment in indigenous agriculture. The developed countries benefit from a more predictable basis on which to reformulate their own domestic farm and food supply policies. The gains from such cooperation spread far beyond the grain trade, extending to better commercial relationships in other fields. The danger of letting slip the opportunity is that the world may slide into the next food crisis with a world trade structure for basic foods as shaky as that which served so poorly in 1973.

Notes

1. The consensus can of course be misplaced, the orthodoxy wrong, and the mixed economy fallible in its response to problems. But in democratic societies the concept of an "error" in policy is itself problematic.

2. For a fuller discussion of these changes in agricultural policy in developed countries, see T. E. Josling, "Agricultural Policies in Developed Countries: A Review," *Journal of Agricultural Economics* 25 (September 1974), pp. 229-64; and J. S. Hillman and W. Henrichsmeyer, "Negotiations on Trade-Disruptive Measures," in *Trade Negotiations and the World Food Problem,* ed. W. Henrichsmeyer et al. (London: Trade Policy Research Centre, Ditchling Press, 1974).

3. For a comprehensive critique of these policies and discussion of

their development in the postwar period, see: D. G. Johnson, *World Agriculture in Disarray* (London: Macmillan St. Martin's Press, 1973).

4. But one must beware of placing the "horse" of domestic imperatives behind the "cart" of world trade. Harmony in commercial relationships must itself be shown to be of benefit before a democratic society will dismantle its own domestic defenses.

5. The author was engaged as a consultant to the FAO during preparation of the report and was responsible for the estimation of the trade effects of national policies discussed below. The FAO should not be held responsible for the interpretation of the report given here. See U.N. Food and Agriculture Organization, *Agricultural Protection and Stabilization Policies,* C/75/LIM/2 (Rome, 1975).

6. Thus a tariff or levy, where it demonstrably increased the price level in an importing country, was deemed to be a combination of a positive producer subsidy and a negative consumer subsidy, i.e., a consumer tax. A direct producer payment, however, although in practice likely to have a small impact on consumers, was held to contribute to the PSE but not the CSE. Most of the information on the levels of protection came from financial data, such as receipts from levies and taxes and payments under subsidy schemes. The per-unit equivalent of these payments and receipts was then applied to production and consumption volumes to calculate their protective effect. When quantitative restrictions were involved, "world prices" were used as estimates of the price levels in the absence of the programs considered.

7. In this chapter, illustration of the link between national policies and world markets will be restricted to one commodity, wheat, over 1971-74. Concentration on this product perhaps exaggerates the general policy change over the period in question. But wheat is the most important of the major traded commodities in a global context, one of particular interest to developing country importers. Subsidy equivalents are the percentage of actual producer receipts or consumer costs attributable to effects of the policies considered. The numbers have been revised from the original report in the light of data not available at the time of its preparation.

8. EC here refers to its original six members. The United Kingdom (U.K.) was treated separately from the original EC in order to make use of statistical series that start before it became a member.

9. This is not the actual financial cost of the programs. It is the notional difference between transfers to and from consumers and producers, much of which is borne through the tax system.

10. The dominance of the EC is noticeable. Of the countries included,

the mechanism for domestic price stability in the EC during the world price boom was perhaps the most complete. Variable export taxes and subsidies allowed a greater freedom to keep domestic prices stable, and the high original level of protection gave room for substantial changes in the incidence of the Common Agricultural Policy (CAP). The U.K. position is somewhat anomalous, since that country was at the beginning of the transition period to higher price levels within the EC over this period.

11. This concern is documented in World Food Conference, *Assessment of the World Food Situation,* E/CONF/65.3 (Rome, 1974); and in a later study: International Food Policy Research Institute, *Meeting Food Needs in the Developing World,* Research Report No. 1 (Washington, D.C., 1976). A more optimistic view of world supplies is given in D. D. Johnson, *World Food Problems and Prospects* (Washington, D.C.: American Enterprise Institute, 1975).

12. The elasticity of supply for the United States was taken as 0.1 for the years up to 1973 to allow for the effect of the set-aside program.

13. This convention is maintained in the tables, so that the production volume given for 1971-72, for instance, refers to the implications of the 1970-71 producer subsidy (applied to 1970-71 production levels) on output in 1971-72 harvest year.

14. Although the EC cannot strictly be considered a "country," over this period the policies in the six original members were reasonably in harmony. The six-member EC is included as a net exporter, though without the support of the CAP it is possible that the trade balance would switch to a deficit in wheat in some years.

15. For a comprehensive discussion of the food stocks issue, see U.N. Food and Agriculture Organization, *Food Reserve for World Food Security: A Consultant Study,* ESC: CSP/75/2 (Rome, 1975); and for an elaboration of the link between stocks and policy changes see T. E. Josling, "Towards our International System of Grain Reserves," in Henrichsmeyer, *Trade Negotiations.*

16. McCalla and Learn trod this path about a decade ago; see A. McCalla and E. Learn, "Non-Equilibrium Fixed Price Schemes in Agricultural Trade," *Agricultural Economics Research* (Washington, D.C.: U.S.D.A., October, 1967).

17. For a more formal treatment of this problem, see T. E. Josling, "Government Price Policies and the Structure of International Agricultural Trade, *Journal of Agricultural Economics,* Vol. 28 (Sept. 1977), pp. 261-277.

18. This is also the interpretation of other writers, most notably Johnson; see D. G. Johnson, "World Agriculture, Commodity Policy,

and Price Variability," *American Journal of Agricultural Economics* 57 (December 1975), pp. 823-28.

19. See T. K. Warley, "Western Trade in Agricultural Products," in *International Economic Relations of the Western World, 1959-1971. Volume 1: Politics and Trade,* ed. A Shenfield (R.I.I.A. and O.U.P., 1976); and T. E. Josling, *Agriculture in the Tokyo Round Negotiations,* Thames Essay No. 10 (London: Trade Policy Research Centre, 1977).

TIM JOSLING* AND STEFAN TANGERMANN**

Measuring Levels of Protection in Agriculture: A Survey of Approaches and Results

PURPOSE OF MEASURING PROTECTION IN AGRICULTURE

One fundamental element of policy analysis is to gauge the extent to which governments actually influence market conditions. This is the essence of measuring levels of protection. The level of protection is not in itself a measure of policy impacts. The same level of protection can have different effects, depending on such parameters as supply and demand response. However, the implicit assumption is usually made that there is a fairly robust relationship between protection levels and the magnitude of both sectoral income transfers and sectoral distortions in resource allocation.

The economist evaluating policies, and pointing to the economic cost of transferring sectoral income through the price system, and the politician seeking to expand export markets both look to the degree of protection as a yardstick of progress. Economists have frequently calculated the extent of agricultural protection inherent in domestic policies. Recently there has been a growing interest in using estimates of protection levels in the context of international policy discussions. A number of countries have proposed use of an 'aggregate measure' of government policies in the agricultural talks of the ongoing Uruguay Round of GATT negotiations.

Use of such an aggregate protection measure in international trade negotiations would be a significant departure from past practice. Traditionally trade talks have related to border policies such as tariffs, quantitative restrictions and export subsidies. In agriculture past negotiations have not led very far. One of the reasons is the difficulty of dealing adequately with the wide variety of agricultural policy instruments working at the border and domestically (Hathaway, 1987). Hence there is a point in trying an approach based on a comprehensive indicator such as the level of protection in agriculture.

The introduction of an aggregate measure of support into international trade negotiations would constitute a challenge for the agricultural economics profession. It would indicate the potential usefulness of economic analysis, but also require additional efforts. One of the tasks is to share with negotiators the experiences made with different approaches to measuring the level of protection in agriculture.

*Food Research Institute, Stanford University.
** Institute of Agricultural Economics, University of Göttingen.

TYPOLOGY OF PROTECTION MEASURES

Economists have developed, and applied in empirical work, a number of different indicators for measuring the level of protection, with differing meanings, uses and degrees of complexity. The most simple measure is the nominal rate of protection (NRP) which measures the difference between world and domestic prices.[1] In a situation where only border policies are applied, the NRP correctly measures the policy effects at the output level. In particular, in a tariffs-only world the NRP is equivalent to the tariff applying to the product concerned.[2] The NRP is relatively easy to estimate if reliable statistics on domestic and border prices are available.[3]

The most appropriate use of the NRP is in relation to policy effects on consumption. As long as non-price policies are not in existence, different NRPs for different products indicate the direction in which consumption may be distorted. Distortions of production incentives would, though, be correctly indicated by the NRP only if all policies would affect output prices.

More recently, a measure similar to the NRP has been introduced into the agricultural economics literature, the Price Adjustment Gap (PAG) as christened by Miller (1986) and the corresponding Nominal Rate of Assistance (NRA) as defined by Haszler and Parsons (1987). This indicator includes direct per-unit subsidies such as deficiency payments but not decoupled income transfers. This clarification is useful; payments tied to product output but which are not reflected in the market price must clearly be included in the protection measure.

More often than not, policies do not only affect output prices, but input prices as well. In such a situation, a more complex measure, the Effective Rate of Protection (ERP), is a better indication of the direction in which policies distort incentives to produce different products, since it measures the joint effect of input and output policies on value added.[4] Clearly the superiority of the ERP over the NRP is the more pronounced the more important input policies are and the smaller the share of value added in producer return is. ERP analysis is particularly appropriate in the study of policy impacts on processing activities, in particular where the raw products are agricultural commodities subject to high protection (Tangermann, 1986). Within agriculture, the superiority of ERPs over the NRPs is probably most significant in sectors such as grain-fed livestock.

Estimating ERPs is significantly more demanding than calculating NRPs. In addition to NRPs for the output and all inputs, technical information on input-output coefficients is needed, which is notoriously difficult to obtain on a representative basis. Hence, different studies could easily come up with widely different ERP estimates for the same activity. Since the non-protected value added is usually chosen as the base, the ERP becomes rather volatile, jumping around from huge positive to huge negative numbers when the denominator is close to zero – as it very often is.[5]

However, even the ERP may not provide a complete picture of all policy induced output distortions. There may be policies which affect prices of labour, capital and land employed in a given sector (say, an investment subsidy for agriculture). Such policies do not affect value added and they are therefore not included in traditional ERP measurement. Hence, going beyond the value-added concept of the ERP, one can push the analysis to the level of profits. This is done in the analysis of Domestic Resource Costs (DRC), widely used in the context of development policy for comparing private and social profitability of farming systems (Pearson and Monke, 1987). Of course, DRC calculations are even more demanding since they require a significantly larger amount of empirical information (for example, information on factor market policies and on factor-output coefficients). On the other hand, there is no doubt that factor market interventions are a typical feature of agricultural policies in many countries, such that the measurement of agricultural protection is not complete without inclusion of these policies.[6]

One further step would be to include the effects of macroeconomic policies. A particularly relevant candidate for inclusion is exchange rate distortion. In calculations of NRPs, ERPs and DRCs for developing countries, the effects of overvalued exchange rates, as often found in these countries, have sometimes been included. While inclusion of exchange rate distortions does not add information concerning distortions among traded goods, it does throw light on distortions between traded and non-traded goods. A recent example of this attempt to capture both the direct price policy impacts and also the indirect effects, through exchange rate distortions and general commercial policy, is the set of studies on 18 developing countries sponsored by the World Bank (Krueger, Schiff, Valdes, 1988).

Inclusion of exchange rate distortions is necessary when the analysis aims at the totality of all policy effects on individual sectors. On the other hand, exchange rate distortions usually are not an element of protection in the sense defined above (that is, policies targeted at individual sectors). Hence, depending on the purpose of measurement, exchange rate distortions can either be included or excluded.

All measures mentioned so far are partial in two dimensions. First, they take no account of general equilbrium effects in the domestic economy. Second, they work on the small country assumptions. The analysis can be expanded in both dimensions, though of course only at the cost of increased complexity and additional research investments. In particular, to include these dimensions one has to go beyond a purely statistical analysis and include more or less complete models full of assumptions on reaction coefficients.

General equilibrium effects, working through links such as factor prices, income distribution, public budgets and exchange rates, are the more important the larger the sector concerned. In developing countries, agriculture usually has a large share in total employment and GDP, and general equilibrium effects may be significant. In most developed countries, on the other hand, agriculture is relatively small. There, it may be interesting to use general equilibrium models for analysing the effects of agricultural policies on other sectors of the economy (Stoeckel, 1985). However, the general-equilibrium-adjusted rate of protection[7] in agriculture is probably only marginally different from the rate of protection measured in the traditional partial approach.[8] Hence, the construction and use of general equilibrium models for the sole purpose of measuring levels of protection more accurately would probably not be justified in industrialized countries.

The situation is different when it comes to the small country assumption. In a number of highly protectionist countries, agriculture is large in relation to the world market. In such cases domestic protection can significantly affect world market prices, and therefore distort the basis of comparison for protection measurement. In such cases, there may be a point in measuring the level of protection against the world prices that would have obtained in the absence of policies of the country concerned. Moreover, one can go even further and measure protection against those world prices which would prevail if all countries together would completely liberalize trade.[9] Clearly such measurement can be done only in the framework of trade models.

While all these types of protection measures have been used more or less frequently in agricultural economics analysis, one measure has recently received particular attention in the political sphere. The US, EC and Cairns Group proposals for the agricultural talks in the Uruguay Round each mention the possibility of negotiating on the Producer Subsidy Equivalent (PSE) of national policies, and the Canadian and Nordic proposals refer to the analytically similar Trade Distortion Equivalent (TDE). The PSE measure (and the corresponding Consumer Subsidy Equivalent, CSE) has earlier formed the basis for the OECD report on national policies and agricultural trade (OECD, 1987). The PSE is defined as the level of (per-unit) producer subsidy that would be necessary to replace the array of actual farm policies employed in a particular country in order to leave farm income unchanged. It can be thought of as the 'cash' value of policy transfers occasioned by price and non-price policies. The CSE is defined correspondingly.[10]

How does the PSE relate to the other protection measures? In the way the PSE was originally used, it probably comes closest to the ERP concept, in the sense that it includes input policies, but not factor market policies. The original PSE calculations did not include the effects of non-agricultural policies, both at a sectoral level (such as tariffs on fuel) and of macroeconomic nature (such as exchange rate distortions). Indeed, not even the effects of agricultural policies on inputs (feed prices in livestock production) were included. However, subsidies and taxes not reflected in prices were taken into account.

The PSE was based on the small country assumption and on existing world prices. It was expressed in money units per ton of output, as an aggregate sum of money, or as a percentage of actual domestic producer returns. In this way the problems resulting from the small base of value added in ERP measurement were avoided.

For the purpose of agricultural policy analysis a measure like the PSE has been found to be a flexible instrument, since it can be geared to the effects of the wide range of policies employed in agriculture. Data needs are manageable, and the assumptions required (or implicit) are limited and transparent. As a basis for international policy commitments, as in trade negotiations, the definitions can be adjusted to accord with what is politically agreeable (Tangermann, Josling, Pearson, 1987).

None of the protection measures presented above is immune to criticism. Some of them are not sufficiently comprehensive, others are too complex to be used in regular empirical work. Moreover, protection measures can contain very different amounts and types of information. In the end, the measure used in any particular context has to be tailored to the needs and the possibilities of the exercise concerned.

EMPIRICAL APPROACHES AND RESULTS

The suggestion that the effect of the various types of agricultural support policy on trade should be collected in an aggregate measure dates back at least to the Haberler Report (GATT, 1958). The issue was taken up in a GATT Committee, but no agreed method emerged from this discussion (GATT, 1962). Policy comparisons tended to be made on the basis of domestic price levels, relative to world or references prices. The one serious suggestion for bringing domestic policies under international agreement, the EC's *montant de soutien* proposal during the Kennedy Round, was based on the notion of binding the relationship between domestic prices and a reference price. Research on world markets also tended to emphasize the price-level differences among countries, ignoring the complexities of the policies themselves.

The first calculations of PSEs and CSEs was undertaken as a part of the FAO work on 'International Agricultural Adjustment' (IAA). The method was described in a paper for the 1973 FAO Conference, where it was applied to five commodities and five countries for the period 1968–70 (FAO, 1973). A follow-up paper for the 1975 Conference expanded the coverage to include six countries and six commodities, and extended the period to 1968–74 (FAO, 1975). At that Conference the FAO was given the task of monitoring adherence to the eleven 'Guidelines for International Agricultural Adjustment.' One of these guidelines stressed the need for developing countries to adopt domestic policies which provided 'appropriate incentives for farmers' and for developed countries to aim at a 'rational use of resources' in formulating their farm policies. The PSE calculations were used by FAO to address the issue of the incentive effect of policies.

The first sign of significant governmental interest in the comprehensive measurement of the impacts of domestic policies on international agricultural markets came in 1982, when the OECD ministers gave a mandate to the Organization to analyse the 'approaches and methods for a balanced and gradual reduction of protection for agriculture' and to examine the 'national policies and measures which have a significant impact on agricultural trade'. The OECD Secretariat adopted and modified the PSE/CSE measure and applied it to seven countries and twelve commodities, for the period 1979–81. After considerable internal discussion the results were released in published form (OECD, 1987).

The potential value of the study for trade negotiations was recognized by the OECD Council in May 1987, but it was the specific mention of the PSE measure in the US GATT proposal of July 1987 that focused attention on the OECD work and its usefulness. By this time the USDA had produced its own PSE study based broadly on the OECD method but including some non-OECD countries (USDA, 1987). The USDA results covered the 1982–84 time period. The OECD has since updated their own calculations to include the 1982–6 period. An updated version of the USDA study, with data through 1986, is also under preparation, with an expanded commodity and policy coverage for some countries.

The basic method used to construct the PSE is similar in all of these studies. Policies are classified into those that raise (or lower) the price level in the market and those that involve budget expenditures but do not directly influence price.[11] The transfers to producers are taken to be the sum of the price and non-price

TABLE 1 *Comparison of policy coverages, PSE studies*

FAO	OECD	USDA
Policies Included		
Market price support	Market price support	Market price support
Deficiency payments	Direct income support	Direct income support
Input subsidies	Indirect income support	Input policies
Storage subsidies	Extension + Research	Extension + Research
Transport subsidies	Structural policies	Marketing subsidies
	Sub-national measures	Controlled exchange rates
Policies Excluded		
Administrative costs	Administrative costs	Administrative costs
Income subsidies	Social Security benefits	Social Security benefits
Acreage control		
Extension + Research		
Structural policies		
Social Security benefits		

transfers – 'subsidy equivalent' of the included policies. The same transfers arising from different policies are treated equally. In the OECD and USDA studies the expenditure on 'long term' programmes – research, extension, environmental and structural payments – are also added in and allocated to individual commodities according to their share in output value.

Table 1 indicates the main differences in policy coverage among the three studies. The FAO study divided policies up into those that (artificially) increased the demand for 'farm-owned resources' as opposed to those that operated on the supply side. It was argued that the main problems of international agricultural trade stemmed from the demand-side policies, including market price support, input subsidies and storage and transportation assistance. Acreage control programmes, along with structural and factor market policies, research and extension and direct income payments (unrelated to output), were deemed to be supply-side policies, and of less direct interference with world markets. The OECD study chose a broader range of farm policies to include in the subsidy-equivalent calculations. Besides market price support and output related payment (such as deficiency payments), direct income transfers were included, along with specific taxation benefits, research and extension, structural measures, capital grants and interest subsidies. Though clearly having an effect on output, the increased heterogeneity of the policy instruments included put more strain on the assumption of equal-output impact per dollar of transfer.[12]

The USDA study adopted a similar classification of policies to that of the OECD, but added a new element. In the case of developing countries, where government policies dictated the exchange rate, it was felt that the degree of transfer to agriculture should be modified by the indirect transfers through exchange rate distortions. Consumer price indices were compared with those in the US to establish approximate 'purchasing power parity' exchange rates, which were then used in the PSE calculations. As a consequence, the USDA results for developing countries should be treated with care: they include effects not

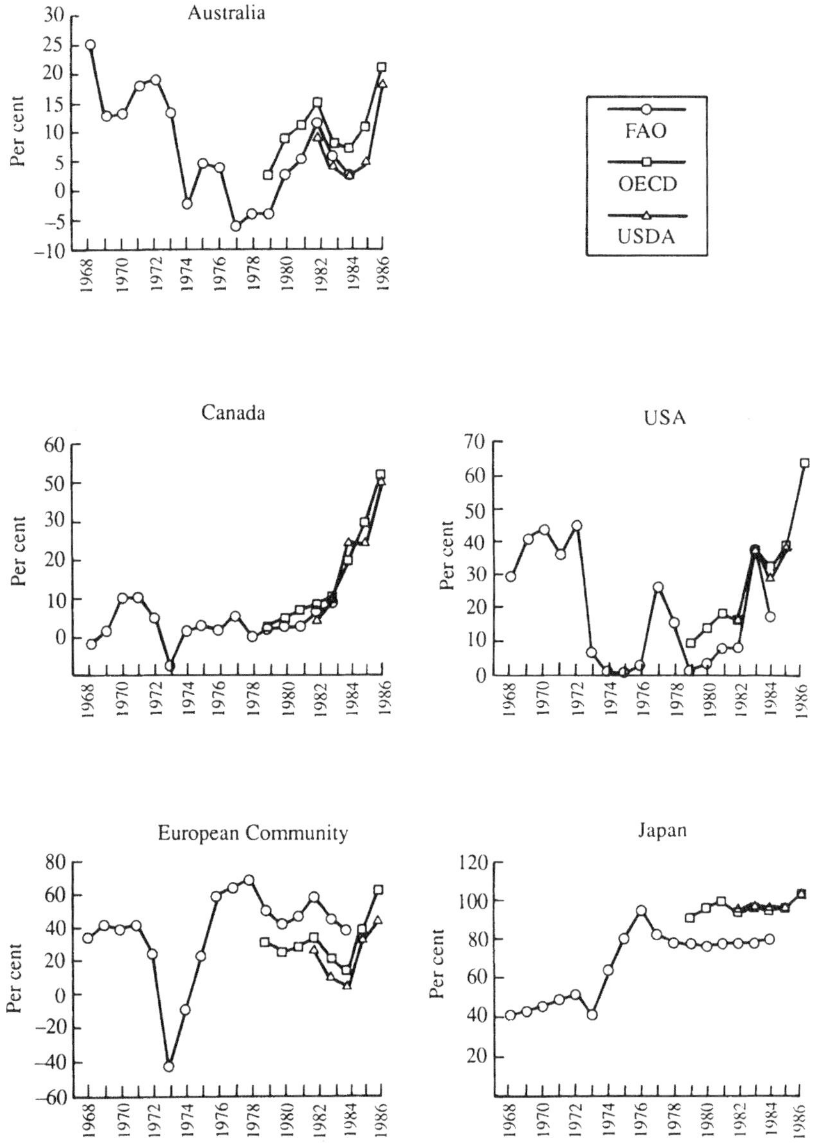

FIGURE 1 *Comparison of PSE Estimates: Wheat*

normally attributed to agricultural policy and not susceptible to modification in a negotiation on agricultural trade.[13]

The fact that transfers from various policies were aggregated in the PSE has led to it being labelled an 'income' measure. It is not necessarily the case that a dollar transferred to farmers under various types of programmes win have the same impact on farm output. Income support can be 'decoupled' from output levels; it can be tied to some form of acreage control; it can be linked with the use of specific input; and it can be given in the form of subsidized research and extension programmes, which may have a less immediate impact on output. The path from PSEs to output and trade effects needs to be trod with care.

This distinction between income and trade measures was drawn out in the 1973 FAO study, where the PSE and CSE were treated as 'domestic performance measures' (along with budget cost, effective protection, and the cost per unit of transfer). The suggested 'trade performance measures' included the tariff equivalent, the foreign exchange displacement, the trade volume effect and the impact on world price levels. Trade volume effects were used in the IAA progress reports in 1977 and 1979, but in later years only the PSEs were reported. The OECD took the PSEs and CSEs and fitted them into a multi-country trade model to get trade volume and world price impacts, glossing over the income/ output distinction. The USDA study does not make any claim that the PSE calculations accurately reflect trade effects, although later work in USDA has built such measures into a multi-country trade model.

The similarity of the methods used in the three institutions should lead to comparable results. Differences that exist will tend to be of policy coverage and of judgement on the impact of particular policies. Figure 1 shows the estimates for PSEs for one commodity, wheat, for the countries and over the period for which comparison is possible. In general, results of the three different studies are rather similar. In particular, the directions and magnitudes of changes from year to year are consistent in most cases. The FAO estimates are below those of OECD and USDA for Japan, and above for the EC.

CONCLUSIONS

The notion that the effect of farm support policies can be measured is not new to economists: its emergence in the arena of international negotiations is however fairly recent. Measurement of policy impacts always presents a challenge to distil the essence of a government action from the mass of detail in legislation and the complexities of national markets. An appropriate measure for one purpose may be less than useful for another. The policy focus may also differ; sectoral trade talks may need a measure which captures sectoral policy effects, whilst national policy discussions might include consideration of macroeconomic impacts.

This pragmatic view of measurement leads to the conclusion that economists should always be pushing for more complete ways of capturing policy effects – both the costs and the benefits. But they should not be surprised if their efforts are used selectively. The most general protection measures – the effects of all policies on factor incomes from a general equilibrium model – may be useful in certain institutional settings. Partial measures –nominal protection rates and price gaps – may also serve a purpose. At present there seems to be a need for a flexible, reasonably comprehensive, easily-explained measure of the level of support given by output-increasing national support policies. The PSE (or TDE) seems to meet that need; it will be interesting to see whether the political process makes use of this new-found knowledge.

NOTES

[1]To be exact, world and domestic prices have to be expressed at an equivalent level, that is, the producer or consumer level. Since producers and consumers may be affected by different policies and because of different marketing margins, the NRP will usually differ between producers and consumers.

[2]More precisely, the NRP is equivalent to that part of the tariff which is non-redundant. If there is 'water' in the tariff, the NRP is below the tariff.

[3]Complications in empirical work, though, usually arise from heterogeneous product qualities and difficulties of defining the appropriate border price equivalent of domestic price. Moreover, in special cases (in particular where the country is self-sufficient) there are even conceptual ambiguities (see Corden, 1971, pp. 21–7). The same complications apply to most of the other measures mentioned below.

[4]The classical textbook exposition of the concept of the ERP is Corden, 1971. For a summary of the history of this concept see Appendix I of Corden's book.

[5]Particular problems arise when the non-protected value added is negative.

[6]Another element which could be included at this level, though not quite systematically, is special sectoral treatment with regard to direct taxes (for example, income tax privileges for agriculture). However, tax concessions are usually excluded from both ERP and DRC calculations.

[7]Corden, 1971, pp. 106 ff., has used the terms 'net protective rate' and 'net effective rate' in this context.

[8]It would appear that under normal conditions the (true) general-equilibrium-adjusted rate of protection always tends to be less than the rate of protection measured in the traditional partial framework.

[9]A recent study has suggested the terms 'adjusted protection rate' for the case of single-country liberalization and 'real protection rate' for the case of global liberalization (Parikh *et al.*, 1986, p. 2/9).

[10]In the following we refer only to PSEs since CSEs play less of a role in the current policy debate.

[11]Budget expenditures were also used extensively in the FAO studies to calculate the price effect. Estimating the average per unit export subsidy on the basis of annual expenditure on such subsidies may be better than trying to calculate the appropriately weighted average of a variable export subsidy over the period of a year.

[12]The OECD study included expenditures given at the sub-national level (and the national level, in the case of the EC). These were excluded from the FAO measure largely on grounds of data availability.

[13]The attempt to qualify the impact of macroeconomic policies on agriculture is, of course, invaluable in the context of national decision taking. Recent work at the World Bank has increased our knowledge of these issues (Krueger, Valdes and Schiff, 1988).

REFERENCES

Corden, W.M., 1971, *The Theory of Protection*, Clarendon Press, Oxford.

FAO, 1973, *Agricultural Protection: Domestic Policy and International Trade.* C 73LIM9, Rome.

FAO, 1975, *Agricultural Protection and Stabilisation Policies: A Framework for Measurement in the Context of Agricultural Adjustment.* C 75LIM2, Rome.

GATT, 1958, *Trends in Agricultural Trade: Report by a Panel of Experts*, Geneva.

GATT, 1962, Committee II, *GATT Programme for Expansion of International Trade: Trade in Agricultural Products*, Second and Third Reports of Committee II, Geneva.

Haszler, Henry, and Parsons, David, 1987, 'The Price Adjustment Gap and World Agricultural Policy Reform'. *Quarterly Review of the Rural Economy*, Vol. 9, No. 2, June.

Hathaway, D.E., 1987, *Agriculture and the GATT: Rewriting the Rules*, Institute for International Economics, Policy Analyses in International Economics No. 20. Washington, DC.

Krueger, A.O., Schiff, M. and Valdes, A., 1988, *Measuring the Impact of Sector-Specific and Economy-wide Policies on Agricultural Incentives in LDCs.* Mimeo.

Miller, G.,1986, *The Political Economy of International Agricultural Policy Reform*, Australian Government Publishing Service, Canberra.

OECD ,1987, *National Policies and Agricultural Trade*, Paris.

Pearson, S.R., and Monke, E.A., 1987, *The Policy Analysis Matrix: A Manual for Practitioners*, Pragma Corporation, Washington, DC.

Stoeckel, A.,1985, *Intersectoral Effects of the CAP: Growth, Trade and Unemployment*, BAE Occasional Paper No. 95, Canberra.

Tangermann, S., 1986, *Escalation of Barriers to International Trade of Agricultural Products–a Research Survey and Illustrative Case Study for Cocoa and Soya*, Paper prepared for FAO, Commodities and Trade Division. Göttingen.

Tangermann, S., Josling, T.E. and Pearson S.R., 1987, 'Multilateral Negotiations on Farm Support Levels: The Role of PSEs'. *World Economy*, Vol. 10 pp. 265–81.

USDA/ERS, 1987, *Government Intervention in Agriculture: Measurement, Evaluation, and Implications for Trade Negotiations.* Staff Report No. AGES861216, Washington, DC.

Chapter 7

Of Models And Measures

Some Thoughts on the Use and Abuse of Policy Indicators

Tim Josling*

Introduction

There has been an unusual surge in the use of policy indicators in recent years. Much of this has come from the inclusion of domestic policies in trade negotiations, both at the bilateral (U.S.-Canada) level and at the multilateral (GATT) level. Negotiating and codifying particular quantitative aspects of national policy is often convenient. But the demand is also evident for ways to capture the essence of national policies for purposes of evaluation and analysis even where no negotiations are involved. The growth of multicountry models has led to the need for variables that capture the essence of a national policy without the unnecessary detail. I want to take this opportunity to explore these two different uses of policy indicators and try to indicate what characteristics make such indicators useful. I shall conclude that we may need to rethink the way in which we calculate such policy indicators. At present, we are in danger of confusing ourselves as a profession and not helping those who seek our advice.

What Makes a Good Policy Indicator?

One can define a policy indicator as a number which can be used to convey information about the level, impact, or effectiveness of a policy

* Professor, Food Research Institute, Stanford University, Stanford, California. Lecture given in acceptance of the IATRC's first Minnesota prize for distinguished trade policy contributions.

instrument or set of instruments. A large number of possible indicators illuminate some aspect of policy and the choice among such indicators should depend upon the use to which it is to be put. As economists, we have developed and quantified a number of these measures. Sometimes we use these as inputs into our own analyses of markets; they become the policy variables in our models. On other occasions, policy administrators, the media, and industry groups look to us for quantitative indicators that sum up the level, impact, or effectiveness of policies. The issue is whether we are meeting that twin demand.

To be useful to an administrator or trade negotiator, a policy measure should have certain features. It should be comparable over time, across commodities, across policies, and across countries; easily understood and interpreted; noncontroversial; easily measured and replicable; and reasonably accurate. A measure that does not allow comparisons gives little information for the policymaker, even if it is simple to understand, noncontroversial, and easy to calculate. A good, comparable measure which is easily understood can probably withstand a little controversy. The ease of measurement is perhaps of less direct interest to the policy administrator, though replicability might be an issue in international discussions.

To be desirable for use in economic analysis, the criteria for an indicator are almost entirely reversed. Ease of measurement (and finding a convenient source for the data) is the most crucial aspect, followed by its professional respectability and lack of controversy. Ease of understanding (by noneconomists) is of little moment, and comparability will not usually be an issue for use in a specific model.

How well do our indicators meet this dual task of monitoring policy and representing it in economic models? My answer would be "not too well." We tend to separate model building and scenario construction on the one hand from policy monitoring and indicator calculation on the other. As a result, our indicators are based on inadequate empirical foundations and our models use simplistic policy inputs. This generalization is not, however, inevitable. Measures can be both input into and output from models. Models and measures should be working together to add to our understanding of policy. We can improve our contribution to policymakers by rethinking the way we make use of both models and measures in the process of policy monitoring and advice.

Types of Indicators Available

To make this argument more concrete, let us look at a few of the policy indicators in use in both economic modeling and policy description. Perhaps the most widely used is the nominal rate of protection, which is usually defined as the domestic price relative to an appropriate international price. This definition seems to fit the main requirement for an indicator of the level of a policy in a trade model in that it can be used in place of a tariff. It is both replicable and respectable and relatively easy to calculate. Although on the surface easy to understand, it does suffer from problems of interpretation in situations of world price instability. Moreover, any measure which uses world prices suffers from low credibility outside an academic environment. The nominal rate of protection (NRP) fares badly on the criteria of comparability; only in a world of tariffs and producer subsidies does the NRP have much informational content as a comparative indicator of policy levels or impacts.

As a reaction to this, policymakers have resorted to using simpler measures such as budget outlays as indicators of the extent of policies. Comparability is, at least superficially, rather good, as is comprehension. The economist might argue that a dollar spent on different programs can have very different effects, but in a zero-sum budget situation, program costs may indeed be the key policy variable. Economists have tended to react differently to the inadequacy of relative price measures, trying to make them more informative. The concept of value-added (effective) protection was devised to get around some of these problems and has had a good run in the trade literature, but as a policy indicator for administrators and the media, it has been a flop.

A more elaborate set of economic indicators has found favor in the development literature, based on the analysis of social profitability. Best known among these measures is the domestic resource cost (DRC), which indicates the social opportunity cost of resources used per unit of social value added. The DRC acts as an indicator of comparative advantage (low numbers indicating less cost incurred to add the same value to traded inputs) and as a proxy for social profits (the difference between social value added and social resource cost). Its value as a policy indicator has been extensively explored by Monke and Pearson (1989), in what they style as a policy analysis matrix (PAM). The contribution of different types of policies (output, input, and factor market) to correcting divergences between private and social costs is clearly identified in the PAM. Any measure which involves calculation of social costs is bound to be both controversial and empirically challenging. But the reward is an indicator that attempts to capture the most fundamental aspects of policy, their cost to society.

Economists working on developed country agriculture have taken a different tack. Perhaps because of the greater availability of data and econometric estimates at the market level, the emphasis has been on the analysis of costs and benefits using Marshallian partial-equilibrium measures. This approach has led to such policy indicators as the economic cost of transfer to farmers, the ratio of the producer surplus gain to the net economic cost.[1] More recently, with the interest in international ramifications of farm policies, a new set of indicators has been added. These indicators measure the international externality of farm programs such as the effect on the income of one country's farmers of support to those of another country.[2] Heavily model-based, these indicators are not easily replicable and may be somewhat controversial. They do, however, have that element of communicability that is essential to a good policy measure.

Yet another set of measures has emerged, largely as a result of work done by OECD and USDA's Economic Research Service. Their estimates have been regularly updated since 1987 (OECD, 1987, and USDA/ERS, 1987). The general set of measures are proxy indicators that translate various policies into an "equivalent" level of another policy. The tariff equivalent is the most venerable of these and has obvious value in trade matters. The producer subsidy equivalent (PSE) together with its kin, the consumer subsidy equivalent (CSE), have been widely used in recent years as policy indicators in the agricultural area.

Equivalent-type measures rely for their usefulness on the comparability and comprehension of the instrument chosen as the proxy. A PSE turns everything into producer subsidies on the assumption that such subsidies both have an intuitive meaning and are comparable across countries, commodities, policies, and time. Because of their nature as proxy measures, these policy indicators do not in themselves either require or generate information on what would happen in the absence of the policy

---

[1] For an early example, see Josling (1969). For more rigorous treatment, see Gardner (1983).

[2] A powerful use of such measures is found in Roningen and Dixit (1989).

under scrutiny. Thus, they are different in kind from most of the other measures mentioned above. The NRP requires an estimate as to what prices would be like without protection; the ERP does the same for value-added. The DRC and net social profit calculations also imply knowledge of the conditions in a situation without the policy. This knowledge is necessary to be convincing as a measure of the contribution of that policy to social profit. Recasting a mix of policies as a subsidy equivalent makes no claim about what would happen in the absence of such subsidies.[3] The calculation is correct or incorrect depending upon whether a subsidy would truly have the same effect, not whether the no-policy scenario is correctly specified.

The Debate on the Use of Subsidy Equivalents

The recent interest in subsidy-equivalent measures has stimulated a small literature on the desirability of the use of PSE-type indicators in policy descriptions and in trade negotiations. The general conclusion of this debate seems to be that as quantitative indicators of policy levels (that is, how high protection is in various countries and over time), the information imparted by the PSE has been useful. At the least, it has cured the impression that each country's agricultural price is either so complex or so different that it cannot be compared with those of others. Indeed, policy comparisons may be too easy now; the very real quantitative difference among policy instruments may not show up in the quantitative proxy, however technically correct that proxy is.

Economists, however, have been quick to point out that PSE's do not capture the net transfer to producers as a result of policy.[4] A subsidy payment includes the amounts transferred to input suppliers, rental payments, and transfers to foreign consumers through terms of trade changes. A relatively small part might stay with the farm family. As indicated above, the PSE does not try to indicate the impact of policies on net income; it merely compares them with a subsidy. If a subsidy overstates the transfer, so will the subsidy-equivalent. If a tariff overstates

[3] That is not to say that implicit with/without policy comparisons are not useful in calculating the PSE. To add up all the effects of various instruments, calculating the effect of each (relative to its absence) and adding them up is useful. But, the definition of a PSE is not based on knowledge about the no-policy situation.

[4] This point has recently been forcibly made de Gorter and Harvey (1990).

the net benefits from import protection (as it will), then a tariff-equivalent will do likewise. This constraint clearly limits the direct use of PSE's in the welfare analysis of farm policies.

The use of quantitative indicators for international negotiations has also been subject to scrutiny. The criticism, for the most part legitimate, has focused on two aspects of the PSE. The first is the implied link between income effects and output effects. All support policies generate somewhat different types of income flows; some might depend on input use, some on resource retirement, and others may be tied directly to output. Any measure that ignores these differences would misrepresent the output impact of policy. In Hertel's phrase, "the mix matters" (Hertel, 1987). The second aspect has been the implied link between output and trade effects. Policies can have different trade effects and yet similar output effects. The neglect of consumption effects is a common problem in trade policy. Why else would one encourage tariffs but discourage domestic subsidies? An uncritical use of PSE's as indicators of trade impacts would be open to this criticism.

The reaction to this debate of those of us who welcomed the increased quantification of policies and the opportunity to negotiate down the level of support in industrial-country agriculture was ambivalent. On the one hand, the weaknesses of using a simple policy measure to capture trade effects were apparent. On the other hand, the prospect of countries actually discussing quantitative reductions in all price support programs rather than haggling over the symptoms on an ad hoc basis was appealing. Criticism of the details of the measure could risk losing both baby and bathwater. Modifying the measure itself to improve its fit is better, keeping its clear advantages as an indicator of support cuts.[5]

This approach of modifying the measure on a seemingly ad hoc basis was clearly disturbing to the case for using the indicator in trade talks. Without a well-defined method, countries could play games with the calculations. And yet the definition of the method turned into a mininegotiation. Special interests began to take sides on the issue of the producer subsidy equivalent, aggregate measure of support, subsidy measure unit, and trade distorting equivalent (PSE/AMS/SMU/TDE), depending upon whether its use would help or hurt their cause. As the United States backed away from its use, the EC began to embrace it, or

[5] This view is taken in Tangermann and others (1987).

was the causality reversed? Doubts on the way in which the PSE had been calculated in the U.S.-Canada free trade agreement also added to the confusion.[6] Whether the PSE has added much to the arsenal (as opposed to the lexicon) of trade negotiations as we thought 3 years ago is unclear.

A New Approach to Policy Indicators

What are the lessons for our professional work and in particular for our work on policy indicators? I believe there has been widespread confusion over the meaning and interpretation of policy indicators such as the PSE which have made our work less useful to outsiders. I want to suggest a new approach which could help clarify some of the confusion still clouding the area. The approach starts with the notion of fixing the definition of a measure rather than its composition. This idea should appeal to us as economists. The consumer defines the product and its characteristics; the producer tries to meet those needs at a reasonable cost. The market signals the success of the venture. In this case, there are two "consumers," the policymaker and the modeler. Both should define the product, rather than the process by which it is created. How to create the product is the business of the profession.

Compare this with the present situation. Policy measures are defined by the formulae or techniques embodied in their generation. Both nominal and effective rates of protection are calculated from a formula. There are manuals that guide people down the path of social profitability analysis and partial equilibrium welfare calculations.[7] Such manuals are premised on the assumption that there is a "correct" way to calculate policy measures. This assumption clearly has benefits; assessing different protection estimates is easier if one knows that the same formulae have been employed. But the cost is that the interpretation is left to the decisionmaker. The chorus of cautionary statements that emerged from the profession when it became clear that the PSE might be used in trade negotiations is evidence of our legitimate concern. The problem was not with the PSE per se; other measures would have raised the same problems. The concern was that the measure might be misinterpreted. Fixed-definition measures would not prevent professional controversy, but

[6] This controversy triggered a GAO (1991) report.
[7] A recent and excellent example is Tsakok (1990).

they would channel it into discussions as to how best to calculate the indicator, leaving the interpretation of the indicator reasonably transparent.

To illustrate this proposition, consider a PSE as a "generic" measure of the following type:

PSE_{gen} = the subsidy which is equivalent to a set of policies.

As such, this definition is not workable for an empirical measure; instead, it defines a class of such measures. The three underscored parts of the statement have each to be further defined. The subsidy can be per unit, lump-sum, or any other form of readily identifiable transfer that has a specific interpretation. This subsidy can be equivalent in several different dimensions, such as farm income, farm output, asset value, net trade, farm employment, or the income of farmers abroad. The set of policies also can range from a single policy instrument to all government measures, both in agriculture and outside. Thus, many possible specific PSE's can use combinations of these definitions, each with its own correct interpretation.

The notion of a fixed-definition indicator is to prevent any problems of interpretation. Consider a few "fixed-definition" indicators that might be of interest in the context of policy reform:

1 - The budget cost of substituting lump-sum payments which leave the net income of farmers unchanged, following the removal of a policy.

2 - The per unit subsidy which would give the same output as the current policy mix.

3 - The direct producer subsidy which would have the same trade volume effect as the current policy mix.

Indicator (1) above is unequivocal. It is by definition the budget cost of such payments. Indicators (2) and (3) are similarly transparent in interpretation. The uncertainty comes in the calculation, not the interpretation. Estimating the budget cost may indeed be difficult. To do so, one needs a model of farmer behavior more sophisticated than encompassed in a partial equilibrium supply curve. Thus, such a model is needed to understand the effect of policy whether or not an indicator is calculated. The model becomes more useful to policymakers because it generates the indicator that has been chosen for its relevance. The indicator becomes more useful because its definition is predetermined.

The three fixed-definition indicators listed above can be measured by specific PSE's. One could call them iso-income, iso-output, and iso-trade PSE's, respectively. No one would knowingly ask for an iso-output PSE as an indicator of the compensation required to offset the removal of price supports. No one could argue that the iso-trade PSE did not capture the different trade effects of diverse policy instruments; it does so by definition. The use would determine the measure, which would be custom-built rather than off-the-shelf.

What about the demand for policy indicators as inputs into models? These too can be customized. A trade model will usually require a fairly simple representation of domestic policy instruments. These often take the form of domestic supply and demand response to policy prices. In such cases, a measure such as an iso-output PSE (and the comparable consumer measure) will be appropriate. Transfers not tied to output or to input use would be excluded. By contrast, a world market model with no explicit domestic behavioral functions would require an iso-trade PSE to represent the relationship between world and domestic prices as a proxy for the actual set of trade-distorting policies. The model will operate "as if" the actual policies were included.

Doesn't this need ask a lot of our ability to derive these measures? Yes, but our ability is in any case limited by our understanding of the relationship between policy variables and economic impacts. In effect, we must use this understanding to improve the quality of our policy indicators. At present, models and measures compete for the eye of the policymaker. Models are constructed to answer particular scenario questions or sets of questions. Measures appear to offer a shortcut, a way to get policy answers without the full-blown model. But each measure (NRP, ERP, DRC, PSE, and so forth) contains its own implicit model. An ERP can be calculated only if we make assumptions about what value-added would be without output and input protection. Those assumptions include an informal model linking domestic price to world markets (usually that world market prices will hold in the absence of domestic protection). A PSE contains the result of a considerable amount of informal modeling of the transfers inherent in the various program instruments. My suggestion is to make that modeling apparent. Make the measures more sophisticated and accurate by harnessing the information included in the models. Instead of competing for the policymakers' attention, the two activities would be complementary.

The implications of this can be seen by referring to the fixed-definition indicators discussed earlier. An iso-income PSE would require a sophisticated model of farm behavior. But such models exist and are used to examine the implications of changes in present program details. Simulating the replacement of some or all of the instruments currently used with a lump-sum payment which keeps net income to the farm family unchanged would seem a straightforward task. The iso-output and iso-trade PSE's are in principle easy to calculate from current models. But as models progress, the measures should keep pace. Models that include economywide feedback effects are refining our knowledge of policy impacts. A computable general equilibrium model would seem invaluable for estimation of a number of policy indicators. Hence, a CGE-based PSE would be a logical extension of recent trends in modeling.

Conclusion

Models and measures should be seen as complementary aspects of economic analysis in support of policy advice. At present the two, as often as not, appear to be competing. Measures are seen as largely descriptive in nature and subject to misinterpretation or misuse. Where the measures require analysis, it is usually of an informal kind, with implicit models rarely specified. These descriptive statistics have found a limited place in modeling but are often considered to be a poor substitute for "policy detail." My suggestion is to think of measures as having specific definitions tied to their use and not their method of calculation. Competition would be among economists trying best to calculate the measure, rather than among marginally different measures, none of which is clearly focused on the problem. Models would be harnessed to provide sophisticated calculations, to supplement the current back-of-the-envelope methods. The measures would in effect be stylized output from the models, which in turn would allow better assessment of model strengths and model differences. Policymakers would be more likely to take seriously the output from a profession where analysts strove to refine and improve the product to meet consumer demand, rather than engage in internecine quibbles about which product the consumer should be offered.

References

Gardner, B. (1983) "Efficient Redistribution throughout Commodity Markets," *American Journal of Agriculture Economics,* 65: 225-34.

de Gorter, H., and D. Harvey. (1990) *Agricultural Policies and the GATT: Reconciling Protection, Support and Distortion.* IATRC Working Paper. International Agricultural Trade Research Consortium.

Hertel, T. (1987) *The Mix Matters: Using PSE's to Negotiate Reductions in Agricultural Support.* West Lafayette, IN: Purdue University.

Josling, T. (1969) "A Formal Approach to Agricultural Policy," *Journal of Agricultural Economics,* 20 (2): 175-96.

Monke, E.A., and S.R. Pearson. (1989) *The Policy Analysis Matrix for Agricultural Development.* Ithaca, NY: Cornell University Press.

Organization for Economic Cooperation and Development. (1987) *National Policies and Agricultural Trade.* Paris, France.

Roningen V. O., and P. M. Dixit. (1989) *How Level Is the Playing Field? An Economic Analysis of Agricultural Policy Reforms in Industrial Market Economies.* FAER-239. U.S. Dept. Agr., Econ. Res. Serv.

Tangermann, S., S. Pearson, and T. Josling. (1987) *International Negotiations on Farm Support Levels: The Role of PSE's.* IATRC Working Paper. International Agricultural Trade Research Consortium.

Tsakok, I. (1990) *Agricultural Price Policy: A Practitioner's Guide to Partial Equilibrium Analysis.* Ithaca, NY: Cornell University Press.

U.S. Department of Agriculture, Economic Research Service. (1987) *Government Intervention in Agriculture: Measurement, Evaluation, and Implications for Trade Negotiations.* FAER-229.

U.S. General Accounting Office. (1991) *Agricultural Trade: Determining Government Support Under the US-Canada Free Trade Agreement.* GAO/RCED-91-63.

Part II

Domestic Policies and the Structure of International Markets

GOVERNMENT PRICE POLICIES AND THE STRUCTURE OF INTERNATIONAL AGRICULTURAL TRADE*

Tim Josling
University of Reading

Farm policies of developed countries have repercussions on the structure of world markets and on the performance of the world food system. A simple model is developed which links such policies to stock levels, food aid, and non-commercial demand. This model is then used to examine some of the recent suggestions for improving conditions in agricultural markets, leading to the conclusion that a combination of more flexible domestic price objectives and co-ordinated stock policies could improve the level of world food security.

Introduction

Two issues in international policy in the realm of trade in temperate zone agricultural products have persistently captured the attention of economists. The first is the influence of national domestic policies on the international location of production. Much of the literature in this area concentrates upon the implications for trading patterns of policies aimed at supporting and stabilising domestic prices. The concepts used relate to the measurement of the effects of protection on levels of imports and exports and hence, by implication, the consequences of reducing or withdrawing such protection. The second issue, brought into focus again by the events of 1972–74, is the ability of the trading system to maintain satisfactory levels of food consumption particularly in those countries where average levels of nutrition are at best barely adequate and which consequently suffer most hardship from shortages. Analysis of these problems has centred around the usefulness of reserve stocks and the management of these stocks to maintain consumption levels.

These two issues have, of course, their institutional manifestations. The question of trade distortions has been the preoccupation of the G.A.T.T., which has been concerned with the advantages that trade liberalisation can confer on countries in terms of lowering the resource cost of producing basic foodstuffs. Despite the interest of some developing countries, in particular those with exportable surpluses of temperate zone commodities, in trade liberalisation, the political battle-lines have been drawn between importer and exporter developed countries. Since the poorer food importers have probably on balance benefited from competitive oversubsidisation of advanced country agriculture, even though it may have encouraged them to ignore desirable investment in their own farm sectors, it may not be too surprising that they have not taken a great interest in the debate about domestic farm policies and trade patterns. The question of

* I am grateful to Ronald Tuck, Chris Ritson, and Alex McCalla for their constructive comments on a draft of this paper.

'world food security', on the other hand, is of prime importance to such countries, and those organisations which they see as catering more specifically for their needs, the F.A.O. and the U.N.C.T.A.D., have shown concern for the question of the performance of the trading system.

My intention in this paper is to try to bridge the gap between these two issues. I shall avoid explicit discussion of institutional and political questions, not because such considerations are unimportant but because I believe that the first step towards understanding such institutional matters is the development of an analytical framework into which political negotiations can be placed. More specifically, I will try to illustrate the way in which national farm policies in developed countries do more than just alter the location of production of temperate zone foods, and that the question of the performance of the system in providing reasonable levels of food security is organically related to the way in which developed country policy problems are resolved.

The first section of the paper discusses briefly the background to these issues: the second section introduces a form of analysis which is intended to throw light on the interaction between government policies and the structure of the trading system, and a concluding section looks at some questions of international policy in the light of the analytical framework to illustrate the thesis that the problems of domestic farm protection and world food security cannot be separated.

Problems in international trade policy

It may help to review briefly the set of problems to which this paper is addressed, even though broad generalisations hide the complexity of individual issues. Until the 1930's the main protective instrument used by governments with respect to their domestic farm sectors was the tariff. In this sense, commercial policy in agricultural and manufacturing sectors was superficially similar, but the importance of such protection was influenced by the pattern of trade of each individual country. Thus in agricultural exporting regions such as North America and Australasia the industrial tariffs stimulated the development of domestic manufacturing but were of limited value in maintaining profitability in agriculture. Agricultural importers, by contrast, found little difficulty in maintaining the size of their farm sectors but struggled to expand markets for their industrial exports.* The contrasting interests in trade liberalisation that this engendered are still apparent today.

The depression of the 'thirties' required much more extensive involvement in market management than was possible under a tariff system. As part of the wider assumption of responsibility for economic management, governments began to intervene in domestic agricultural markets – led in this case by the exporting countries. Such domestic policies required a measure of control over international trade. These trade policies in agriculture became to complement, reinforce, underwrite and facilitate domestic programmes of price support and market guarantees in a way which has shaped the nature of international discussions on such policies throughout the last forty years.† The major temperate zone agricultural markets have effectively escaped the process of de-escalation of trade restrictions negotiated for industrial goods through the G.A.T.T.

This is not to indicate that the policies themselves have remained intact, but to emphasise the primacy of domestic objectives in their formulation. These objectives themselves have changed along with the conception of the nature of the

* For a discussion of the history of agricultural protectionism see McCalla (1969).

† A discussion of the rise of the 'new-protectionism' is to be found in F.A.O. (1973); Warley (1976) gives a more detailed account of recent G.A.T.T. discussions.

problems of the farming and food sector. Concern with rural depression and its macro-economic consequences gave way to the need to increase productivity in agriculture and then to worries about the resource adjustments, in particular in the labour market, implied by such productivity increases. More recently, doubts about continuity of food supplies and generally concern with inflation has added a new dimension to the debate. Whilst importing countries found that the control of imports itself gave a powerful weapon for the attainment of such domestic objectives, exporting countries found the strain, in particular in budget cost, to be formidable. Supply control programmes, initially conceived as price support measures became necessary to limit the impact of farm productivity on national treasuries. Such countries felt that they were being obliged to shoulder the burden of adjustment of both their own and importing country agricultures and renewed diplomatic pressure for trade liberalisation. However, when prices, for a variety of reasons by now well documented, rose sharply in the early seventies, exporters found new instruments in the form of export controls and taxes to contain domestic price rises and it was the turn of the importing countries to complain about the trading system and to search for remedies in international negotiations.*

Developing countries have a variety of interests in the market conditions for temperate zone products. At one extreme, a few countries have export capacity and hence an interest in market access and strong prices; somewhat more countries produce goods such as sugar and oilseeds whose market is directly affected by temperate-zone production and consumption patterns. But the largest group are importers of staple foods to the extent made possible by their export earnings, and this dependency is likely to increase in the years ahead.† But whereas the availability of the fruits of high technology agriculture in temperate areas has played a crucial part in maintaining and improving nutritional levels, the vulnerability of such countries to sharp rises in the price of food imports has been cruelly demonstrated in the last five years. If they lack the purchasing power to maintain imports, consumption levels are threatened; if they continue to import then general development aims are thwarted, and debt burdens increased; if they attempt to cushion the impact of price rises on their urban populations then they may require massive consumer subsidy programmes outside the scope of their fiscal base to finance. Though they may share the same problem as more affluent importers, their ability to cope with such a problem is circumscribed.

Since the basic problems are well-rehearsed, why should I suggest the need for a fresh analytical approach? My concern is basically that as economists we have yet to link these problems together in a way which allows an evaluation of the merits of solutions proposed by various bodies both national and international. Economists have tended to concentrate on the implications of government intervention in the domestic agricultural sector, and by extension the impact on world trade patterns, by superimposing the various instruments that governments use on a freely operating competitive market.‡ We tend to be disdainful of those who claim that 'there is no world price' or that 'world market conditions give little guidance to domestic policy considerations'. Yet until we know more about how world prices – which surely exist – are indeed determined, we are in a poor position to provide a convincing basis for improved domestic decisions. And a knowledge of

* The changes in national objectives of farm policies are discussed in Josling (1974); for an analytical view of the 1972–74 world food 'crisis', see Johnson (1975).

† This trend is documented in the assessment of the world food situation, produced for the World Food Conference (W.F.C., 1974) and by more recent studies such as I.F.P.R.I. (1976).

‡ The observation that our models tend to assume competitive conditions where they do not exist has been made by a number of writers. Among those who have attempted to rectify the situation are McCalla (1966) and, somewhat earlier, Farnsworth (1956). My contribution is intended to follow up these specific studies in a more general way.

how such prices are influenced by conditions such as poor harvests and low stock levels in turn is essential for a proper analysis of initiatives to improve the international trading system. To classify academic work on trade policy in agricultural goods as either 'protection-measurement' or 'optimal reserve estimation' may be a little oversimplified, but my intention is not to decry such work but to highlight the link between such studies, through the analysis of the effect of government policies on international market structure.*

A 'government intentions' model

The conventional starting point for analysing the impact of policies on interaction markets would be to postulate a 'free' market and then introduce policy instruments sequentially. The instruments would normally be converted into some 'tariff equivalent' and standard techniques used to estimate trade effects. But suppose we start at the 'other end': assume that governments can manipulate markets as they wish; draw out the implications of these government 'intentions'; and examine the role of the market as a residual or constraint on such government action. If the exercise leads to a satisfactory interpretation of the structure of the international market, then it carries with it some potentially useful conclusions as to policy interactions. Conceptually, these results should be identical to those which follow from a full 'traditional' analysis: my point is not so much that one approach is superior to the other in terms of final results, but that the questions that are raised on the way to the results are themselves of interest, and focus attention on neglected areas of study.

My starting point is that governments are concerned with the levels of domestic prices at which farm goods sell within their countries, and the wholesale or retail price of food products. They have at hand an impressive armoury of instruments to secure these domestic price objectives. Although it is easier (for me) to think of these price objectives as being obtained by a system of variable trade taxes and subsidies, the model includes implicitly decisions taken by countries with extensive state trading systems or rigid quota arrangements. The level at which domestic prices are fixed is decided by a complex of political and economic factors specific to each country. Assume initially that goverments are entirely successful in maintaining a domestic price level of their own choosing. At that price level, a certain quantity of the product in question will be produced and another quantity consumed: the external view of each domestic market will be a particular predetermined quantity of goods available for export or required in the import market. This is illustrated in Figure 1. Taking the case of a single importer buying from a lone exporter, the 'world market' in any particular time period is represented merely by a fixed quantity of imports demanded and of exports supplied. Only by chance will these quantities be equal: we might refer to the differences between such export and import volumes as 'policy-induced' surpluses or shortages. In Figure 1(a), import quantity (M) is that which will sell in the importer's markets at the domestic price of P_m and this is less than export volume (X), which is the quantity which exporters would put on the market at their own domestic price (P_x). In Figure 1(b), import intentions exceed exporter supplies and a potential 'shortage' exists. This construct needs some elaboration before we can use it further. Figure 1(a) (and its counterpart, 1(b)) represents the juxtaposition of two national market situations. The vertical axis represents a predetermined domestic price, which is assumed (though this is not necessary) to be different in each of the two countries. Strictly speaking no functional relationship is illustrated with respect to these domestic prices: (M, P_m) and (X, P_x) are pairs which satisfy domestic intentions. In practice, there will be a function underlying these points representing different

* Among other attempts to link government behaviour with international price movements are Johnson (1975), Hillman (1975), Harris and Josling (1974), and F.A.O. (1975).

Figure 1 'Policy induced' surpluses or shortages arising from fixed domestic price policies

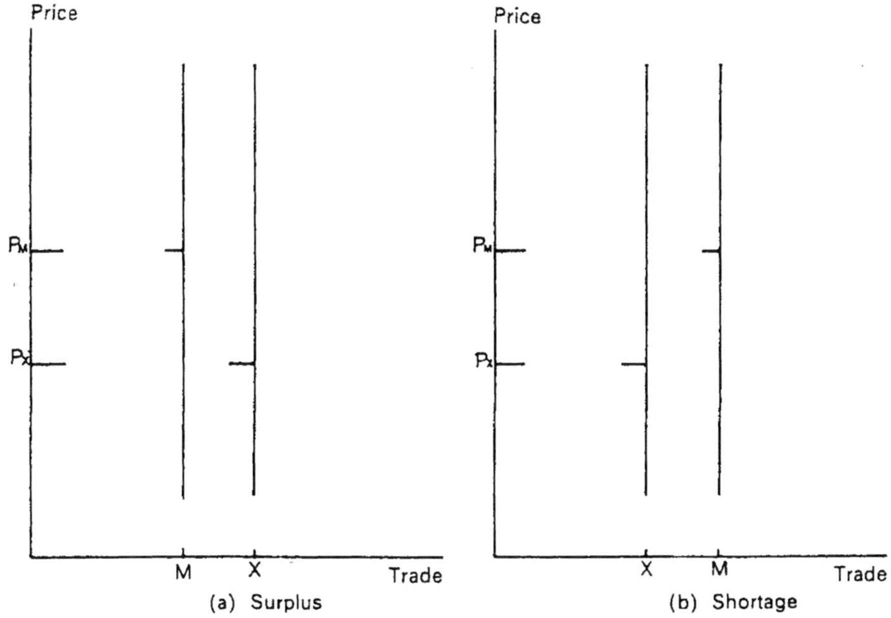

price objectives and consequent import and export quantities. These underlying functions will be introduced later. The vertical lines drawn in Figure 1 have a different interpretation: to the exporter, the line at M represents a completely inelastic import demand schedule in that the quantity imported does not vary with the price at which exports are offered. Similarly, the line at X represents a quite inelastic export supply function implying that the quantity available is not influenced by the price that the importer is prepared to pay.

In order to introduce the function of stock or reserves in their proper place, the quantities X and M should be interpreted as being the current production of exports and use of imports in the two countries: actual trade volumes will include transfers of such stocks among countries, but it is assumed that the domestic price target is linked with production and consumption patterns only over the period in question. It may be easier to think of all stock accumulation and release as being performed by governments, though it is only strictly necessary to assume that private storage agencies 'obey the rules' so as not to undermine domestic price targets.

One thing is clear from Figure 1: it does not help us to define a 'world price'. The situation can be thought of as an acute case of 'market failure'. There is no instrumentality which reconciles import requirements and export availabilities. It implies a disequilibrium, or rather an inconsistency caused by irreconcilable domestic price objectives. It is not even a complete model in that nothing is explained. But it does highlight a significant problem. The resolution of the policy inconsistency illustrated in the diagram is at the heart of the questions of relative adjustment burdens, domestic programme costs, international diplomatic tensions, world price determination, optimal reserve policies, and the performance of the trading system.

To illustrate this contention, it is necessary to distinguish between two cases: the first is where there are only two countries involved in trade in the good in question, or where all the countries involved can be aggregated into two groups called 'importers' and 'exporters' which have similar policy aims within these groups; the second is where there are other participants in the market not characterised by fixed domestic price objectives or with economic systems which allow them to divorce trade flows from the effects on the internal market. Let us consider the 'closed' system first. A relatively trivial sub-case is where the product is not storable. In this situation, imports and exports (as defined above) have always to be equal. The situation illustrated in Figure 1 may be the intention of the governments concerned, but they will be disappointed. Unless they change their domestic price objectives, produce will go unsold (1(a)) or import desires unsatisfied (1(b)). Suppose by coincidence that X and M are equal *ex ante*, so that the two policy objectives appear consistent. Even in this case the 'world price' is not determined. It can be above P_m, below P_x or between the two. Additional information would still be needed to yield a solution. The introduction of relative bargaining power might seem to help, but even this may not be enough. The implication of presenting one's trading partner with a completely inelastic import demand or export supply curve is that one is relinquishing any market power that one might otherwise possess. The situation postulated is of countries deliberately denying themselves international bargaining power by virtue of their domestic price imperative. Sooner rather than later, one suspects, the domestic objective would in this case yield and a more aggressive trade policy emerge.

The most interesting case of the 'closed' system is when the good can be stored. At least in the short run, the qualities X and M can diverge in that carryover from year to year enables the situations in Figures 1(a) and (b) to alternate. The 'world price' is still indeterminate in the sense that it will be bounded in surplus periods by the willingness (of either importers or exporters) to buy up stocks, and in times of shortage by the price at which those stocks are released. But even these bounds are influenced by the degree of collusion among importers and among exporters. An exporter cartel, for instance, might be able to drive the price up further in times of shortage, just as co-operation among importers could preempt this power by purchasing reserves in times of surplus. If over time the 'surpluses' and 'shortages' did not offset each other, market power would be determined by whether stocks built up or were steadily exhausted. The inconsistencies would reappear, and policy changes in one or more countries would be inevitable. Once again, by paradox, the ability of countries to exploit their world market position is circumscribed by their devotion to domestic price objectives. It is more satisfactory to build into the policy model an explicit stock function. This can be done simply, by postulating that as with any asset more will be released from stocks the higher is the current price. The function itself will of course depend on storage costs, price expectation, and interest rates – but it is sufficient for present purposes to hold these constant. Thus the behavioural function:

$$C_t = C(P_t)$$

where C_t is the stock or carryover from year t to year $t+1$, and $C' < 0$; and the identity:

$$C_t + X_{t+1} = C_{t+1} + M_{t+1}$$

together give the determination of world prices missing in the earlier formulation as represented by Figure 1.

This situation is illustrated in Figure 2, where the carry-over function (C) determines the trade price level in a surplus year. Under these conditions, stocks are increased by $(C_1 - C_0)$: if surpluses persist, world prices will be lower in the next year, as the right hand axis (and hence the C function) moves to the right by this additional amount. In a year of shortage, stocks fall: persistent shortages would exhaust stocks and M would again be limited by X. Such a stock function will of course exist in a free-trade model, where exports and imports are responsive

Figure 2 World price determined by carry-over function, in turn determining next-period stocks

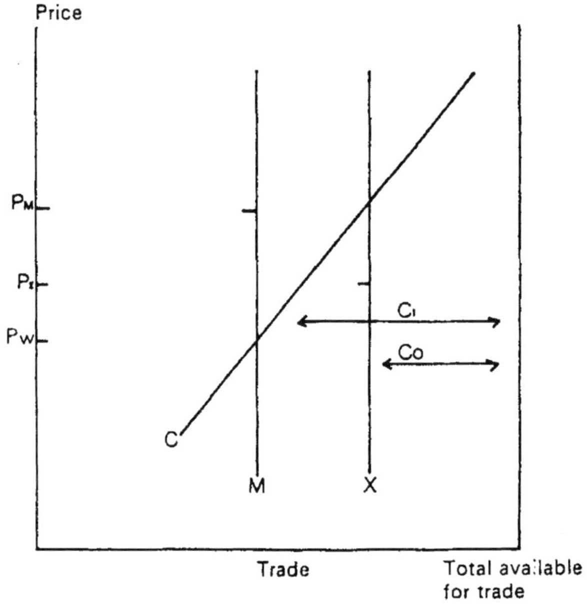

to prices on world markets. The reason for introducing it in this 'policy' model is to indicate *both* that world prices can be determined and determinate in a model where trade flows themselves do not respond to such prices, *and* that stocks as such do not remove the policy inconsistencies. The problem still remains: if export supply exceeds import demand then stocks will accumulate.

Incorporation of a carry-over function is important for another reason. In Figure 2, the level of stocks is represented as a steadily declining function of price. But it is precisely the 'shape' of this function which determines the stability of the market represented by the model. Some alternative functional forms will indicate this. Figure 3 gives four functional forms for the decision to hold stocks into the next time period. In 3(a), the function is unresponsive to price. A special case of this is when the C and M lines coincide: 'someone' is prepared to hold as stocks everything which is not bought for use by importers, irrespective of world price levels, and to release from stocks the quantity $(M\text{-}X)$ when shortages occur. Such a naïve stocks function will of course break down if M were to exceed $(X+C_0)$, since C_1 cannot be negative. But more importantly, this functional form does not help to give a market clearing price. We would again have to resort to domestic policy changes in order to establish such a price. But such a 'dead-stock' is not without its relevance, as we shall see when discussing recent policy initiatives. The function represented by 3(b) goes to the other extreme. Stocks are freely traded at a particular price. Certain domestic farm policies operate on this basis. It ensures a world market price and puts the impact of all instability of output and inconsistency of policy decisions on the level of stocks. Such a 'pure' price-related stocks function again has analogies in international discussions. It translates the basic problems of international price determination into one of fixing the price at which stocks will be bought and sold. Unless the vagaries of weather exactly offset the policy inconsistencies, stocks will either steadily accumulate or gradually disappear. To put all the burden on stock adjustments is clearly not a long run recipe for stability, though it makes world prices predictable over the short term.

Figure 3 Four different carry-over functions

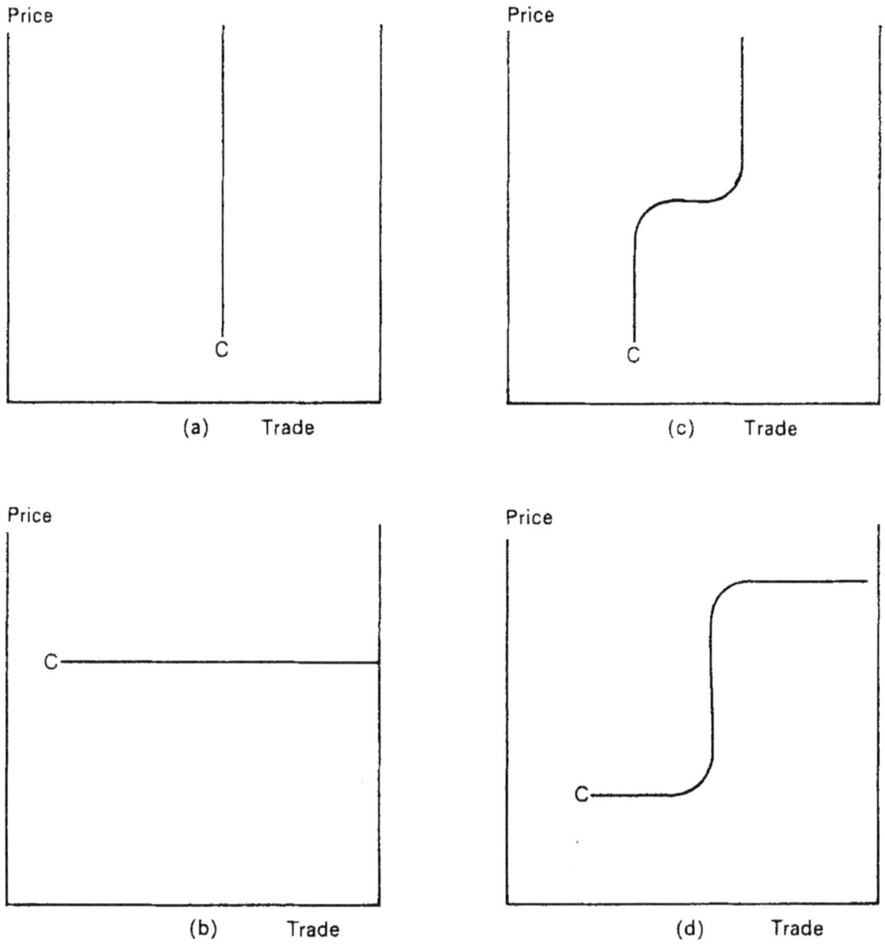

The functional form illustrated in Figure 3(c) combines the problems and possibilities of both the two extreme carry-over decision rules. At high world prices, stock demand becomes inelastic with respect to the price level and exacerbates such price increases: at low prices, stocks again reach a limit and do not alleviate the price fall. In between, like the egg balanced on its pointed end, there is stability of prices. In one sense, this stock policy is 'rational': capacity is limited and stock costs rise when such limits are approached, whilst at the same time some minimum 'pipeline' stocks would seem to be necessary for the transaction of normal commercial business even when the opportunity costs of holding such stocks are high. But whether a carry-over function of this type does stabilise world markets will depend on the behaviour of the *M* function relative to the *C* function: periods of stability are likely to be broken by wild price fluctuations as stocks become less responsive to high and low prices. Situation 3(d) is the reverse: general price uncertainty over an intermediate range is replaced by relative price stability at extremes, with stocks taking up the slack. The stock manager may not like this functional form, but it could perform better in terms of world food security.

So far the argument has run in terms of a closed system of importers and exporters. But now suppose that not every country suffers from the handicap that its trade policy has to bolster domestic objectives. If these 'liberated' countries were important enough in trade terms, they would have the ability to set prices, though those prices would tend to be highly variable if they had to absorb fluctuations in output elsewhere in the system. As a special case of such price setting, consider what might be termed 'non-commercial demand'. For the moment, let us repress the carry-over function, in order to discuss the alternative way of determining the model, and hence the world price.

Non-commercial demand, in the sense in which I use it here, is a willingness of certain countries to take goods off the market at a price lower than that which would obtain if the market were operating reasonably freely. For our purposes, it can be thought of as an infinitely elastic demand at a price below the exporter domestic price level. It represents the 'buying-up' of surpluses in a predatory fashion in the case of central-plan countries, or the acceptance of surplus disposal by developing countries under various food aid programmes. Figure 4 represents the intrusion of this non-commercial demand (N.C.D.) as a 'deus ex machina' to set the world price in times of surplus. The 'concessional' element of food aid is represented in Figure 4(a) by the difference between this world price (P_w) and the dotted line below it, the actual price to the recipient. If it is in fact the recipient price which is fixed (by the value of such aid to developing countries) then P_w could be in turn determined by the willingness of legislatures in donor countries to foot the bill (H) for such aid. (Depending on the accounting procedure adopted, the 'aid' cost could include the degree of export subsidy (I) needed additionally to move the surplus into aid channels). The non-commercial or food aid demand has come to the rescue of the commercial system by containing the accumulation of policy induced surpluses. But when the situation changes to one of 'shortages', N.C.D. loses the price determining function, and the cost of food aid becomes prohibitive: if exporter stocks went as food aid the cost would be represented by area J in Figure 4(b) and the commercial market would remain unsatisfied. Further price rises would presumably follow, increasing the aid cost. Since it is traditionally the budget appropriation which limits such food aid costs, recipient countries find such flows dwindling as world price rises.

To recapitulate the arguments of this section:

(a) if major commercial markets are effectively determined not by world trade prices but by domestic price objectives, the world trading system is put under strain,

(b) the world price can be established by a number of devices, including the existence of predatory demand, food aid, and stock functions,

(c) the performance of such a trading system is likely to be unsatisfactory if output shows marked variability and if this does not happen to offset policy inconsistencies,

(d) stocks functions can help in the short run, but their place in the system is not just to even out production fluctuations but to absorb the instability generated additionally by the policy inconsistencies.

(e) if these policy inconsistencies persist then eventually the domestic objectives themselves will come under pressure.

International adjustment mechanisms

There has been no shortage of suggestions as to how to improve the performance of world markets for temperate-zone agricultural products. If the analysis of the previous section is to be useful it must sort out those proposals which are sensible

Figure 4 The importance of non-commercial demand in world price determination: (a) commercial surplus; (b) commercial shortage

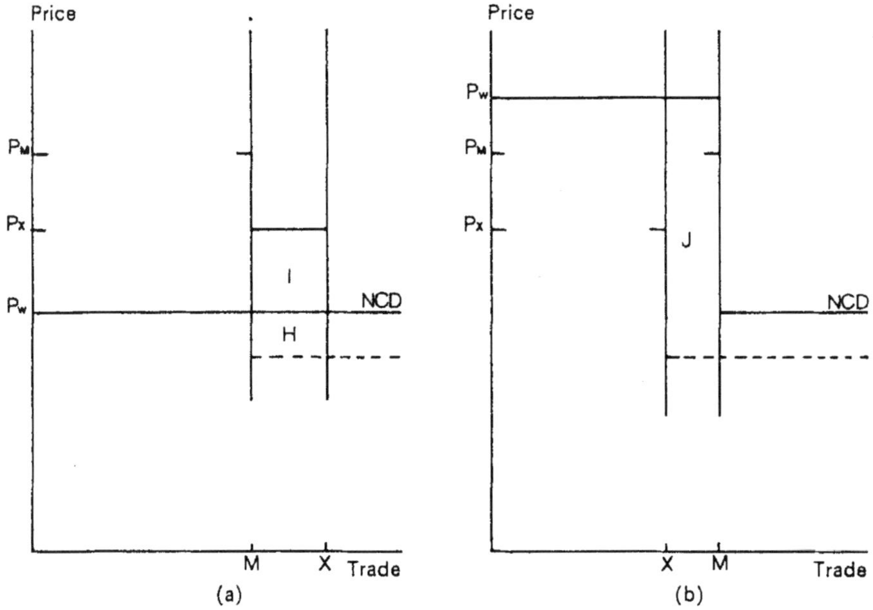

from those which avoid or exacerbate the problems. My task in this section is to examine some of the proposals in the light of the previous analysis. I shall deliberately avoid the institutional background to the proposals as such, and concentrate on their apparent implications. Many of the proposals are 'additive', but I shall treat them individually. I shall deal with them under five headings: price fixing at an international level; price harmonisation among countries; bilateral deals, including food aid targets; stocks arrangements; and trade liberalisation, implying an increase in the price responsiveness of trade flows rather than the reduction of levels of protection *per se*.

(*a*) *International price fixing*

Price bands have been a common feature of a succession of international commodity agreements. For our purposes it is necessary to point out that an international agreement to trade within a particular price band relies on the ability and willingness of governments to adopt policies which allow the price to settle within that band. If the price changes or puts constraints on these national policies then clearly it has an impact on the market. It may, for instance, prevent exporter competition when prices are low and limit exploitation of market shortages in periods of high prices. But the instrumentality is not so much the price band itself but the change in national behaviour. If exporters respect a price floor, then the effect is as if they had colluded to fix a minimum price. If economic and political conditions are such that collusion is possible, there would seem to be no reason to analyse the situation as an initiative to improve world market performance when in reality it is merely the institutional blessing of the international community to an exporters' cartel. Similarly with respect to maximum trade price levels: either exporters are prepared to forego potential price advantages in times of shortages – perhaps for the sake of the collusive benefits in surplus periods – or else they are not. It is difficult to see importers having the market power to dictate a maximum price, but such a price does presumably protect them against exporters' market power if those exporters choose to respect it. The main point is that price bands do not of themselves correct imbalances in the market or eliminate policy inconsistencies. They may alter the collusive behaviour of countries; they may change national price decisions (of which more later), they will if effective limit government liabilities on subsidy costs; they can alter implicitly the stock or carry-over function insofar as countries are willing to make adjustments to keep within the price band. But they do not ensure tranquility in the market unless countries take appropriate actions of their own. It would seem more logical to consider those actions themselves which would lead to a *de facto* price band than to start with the band as a policy and hope that the appropriate actions follow.*

(*b*) *National price harmonisation*

The aim of trying to reconcile differences in national price objectives seems at first sight to get close to the problem. It has two manifestations: the harmonisation of levels of protection (either nominal or effective) as such, or the linking of domestic prices to some 'reference' price. Such a reference price could itself have the function of a minimum trade price (as discussed above) but it is probably neater to separate these two functions. Unfortunately, our model (of trade volumes fixed by the implications of autonomous domestic price objectives) suggests that such harmonisation does not necessarily remove the 'policy-induced' surpluses or deficits. Figure 5 shows the possible problems of such an approach. Unless, by chance, policy prices are harmonised at an 'equilibrium' level, surpluses and shortages will persist. Prices are harmonised at level P_h, presumably based on some compromise between P_m and P_x; imports increase to M' and exports to X'

Figure 5 Price harmonisation, at Ph, in (a) surplus, and (b) shortage conditions

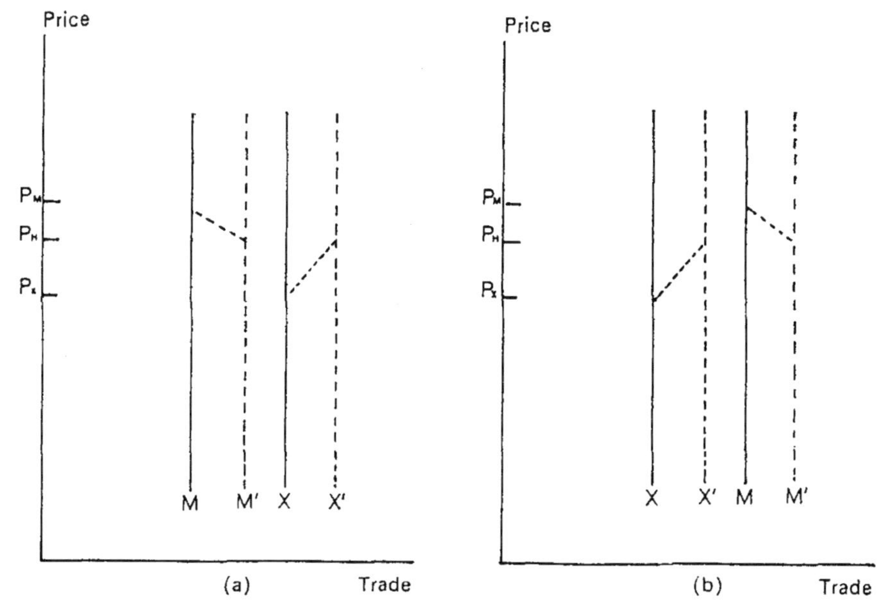

* At the risk of introducing specific institutions, it could be pointed out that successive International Wheat Agreements which have needed price bands have relied as much on collusive behaviour by exporters as by the collective restraint of all market participants. This was the thrust of the McCalla (1966) argument which has never seriously been disputed. For a discussion of the Agreements see F.A.O. (1970).

in both surplus and shortage situations. Quantity response may differ: indeed the only hope of such a position restoring some order in the market is if in the 'new' balance of policy surpluses and shortages happens to cancel out over time the output fluctuations due to weather. But even then, no price mechanism has been established: the carry-over function is still needed to determine a trade price, which can be above or below P_h. Harmonising nominal degrees of protection and negotiating similar support prices are analytically alike if protection is related to a reference price. Equalising nominal degrees of protection with respect to a fluctuating world price will tend to destabilise the whole system further. Equalising *effective* protection could have any variety of implications depending on farm production structures: in any case it has no logic in terms of world market flows.* It is *within* economies that harmonisation of effective rates is legitimate: they have no particular merit as indices of international action.

(c) Bilaterals and aid commitments

A number of countries have been attracted to bilateral agreements as ways of securing supplies of foodstuffs or of ensuring access to markets. Contrary to the prevailing view (including, until recently, my own) bilaterals as such have no particular relevance for market stability. This result holds generally, and not just in the present fixed-trade-volume model. Figure 6(a) will make this clear. To take a sub-part of M and X and negotiate its price (P_b) separately from the world price has no effect on total trade volumes, nor on their response (if any) to price. Once again, world price will be determined by some other factor, such as a carry-over function. The terms of the bilateral contract can either be for a quantity at a fixed

Figure 6 (a) Bilateral deals, and (b) food-aid quantity targets, in surplus conditions

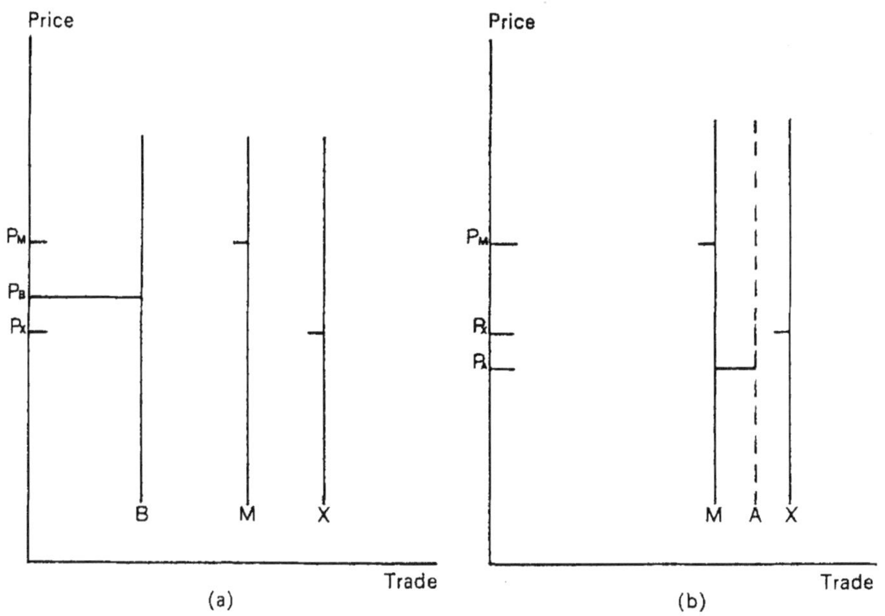

* The harmonisation of effective rates of protection has been advocated by, among others, Johnson (1973): to be fair, he would presumably see this as a step towards reducing and eventually eliminating such protection, whereupon the measure used for such negotiations becomes irrelevant. For a discussion of protection in the context of international negotiations, see F.A.O. (1973).

price or at the world price. In the former case the difference between the world price and the bilateral price will merely determine who wins from the deal. If the loser decides not to honour the commitment, again no harm is done to the total market – just to good trade relations. Exceptions to the 'irrelevance' of bilaterals may occur if the existence of the bilateral is tied to output or demand decisions in one or other country (which then requires a different analysis) or when the amount covered by bilaterals exceeds current export availability, which may influence the distribution of release from stocks.* But even in this latter case, arbitrage among importers would tend to remove this effect.

The case of the pre-fixed quantities of food aid is somewhat similar. In Figure 6(b) the aid quantity is added onto commercial demand for imports. The aid price may be fixed, but aid volumes no longer play their part in determining world prices. Whereas this might be eminently desirable from the viewpoint of the recipient, in the present context it tends to *destabilise* the market further, just as does a 'dead-stock' policy of reserve holding. By extension, tying non-commercial demand to particular quantities by means of bilateral agreements also makes world price formation more difficult. The stocks function becomes the only one of our price determining factors still able to reconcile national policies.

(*d*) *International and national stocks agreements*

We have suggested that stocks policies already exist and that in the case of easily storable commodities these have an important function in addition to that of evening out variations in supply. The management of these policies either through international agreement or through the intervention of a supranational agency has been proposed and explored many times in the last two years.† Our model suggests certain constraints on such policies. Some of these were mentioned above when dealing with market price determination. The dilemma is to get the right balance between fluctuating levels of stock holding and fluctuating levels of price. If greater price stability is the objective then stock levels must bear more of the instability than in the past. Two mechanisms have been suggested: price triggers which indicate buying or selling decisions from stocks, or quantity triggers which indicate when further accumulation or release is called for to stabilise supplies.‡ Figure 7 attempts to show that the two mechanisms are similar if the basic objectives are comparable. Assume that a price band is established between P_u and P_l, to be maintained by stock changes. Assume further that there already is a carry-over function, C, that is responsive to price. Since shifts in the export availability shift the right-hand axis in Figure 2, it is convenient to suppress such changes and represent them instead by variations in the C function relative to imports, M. In Figure 7, C represents a 'shortage' when prices would be generally high. To keep prices down to P_u, an additional release of stocks of 'a' must be made. Between P_u and P_l no stock changes are called for over and above those indicated by C'. Below P_l, additional stocks of 'b' are purchased. Clearly, quantity triggers could do the same thing: if stocks were adjusted by releasing 'a' and buying 'b' prices would be kept within the band as before. Import levels would be stable and price changes contained. But this represents an 'active' stocks policy, buying more when stocks are high and releasing more when stocks are low. The 'quantity' that triggers stock changes is not the existing quantity of that stock but the quantitative

* If bilateral *trade* agreements also carry with them policies of domestic supply quotas or fixed consumption levels, then the 'bilateral' problem becomes a special case of the general fixed-trade-volume model.

† Among the academic offerings on this subject, see papers by Sinha (1976), Abbott (1976), and Josling (1974). A report prepared for F.A.O. (1975) dealt with many of the problems of such stockpiles.

‡ This discussion is germane to present negotiations in the G.A.T.T. and the I.W.C., and is developed in Josling (1977).

Figure 7 Price triggers and quantity triggers for a storage policy within a commodity agreement

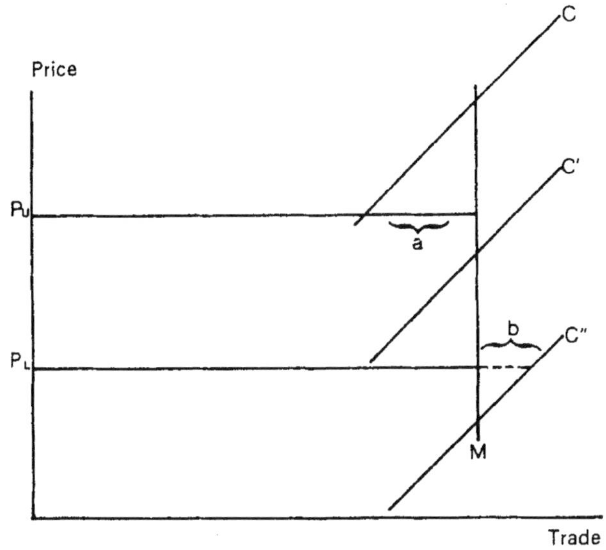

estimate of surpluses and shortfalls which can then be alleviated by such management of reserves. It is, for instance, quite distinct from a third approach which would run a stocks policy on the basis of a 'desirable' carry-over of some fixed proportion of consumption. Such a trigger which tied purchase and release to a target stock volume would exacerbate price instability. The point may sound elementary, but a number of policy initiatives have had just a stock target in mind.*

(*e*) *Trade liberalisation*

The premise of the model has until now been that countries fix domestic prices which in turn determine trade volumes. Attempts at trade liberalisation have not had great success in agriculture in the past. Whereas one might rule out straightforward trade liberalisation as being of academic rather than political interest, the element of trade liberality which is crucial to world market stability is not the removal of trade barriers *per se* but the linking of domestic price targets to international conditions. The initiatives with respect to co-ordination of stocks discussed above give some limited hope that countries may be prepared to modify their domestic prices towards some price range so long as they were (a) convinced that other countries were participating actively in the stabilisation process, (b) that there were tangible gains to themselves in terms of price stability, and (c) that the 'burdens' as perceived by legislatures were reasonably equally shared between importers and exporters.

The concept of exporter and importer adjustment is illustrated in Figure 8. Again we can dispense with the export schedule by incorporating it in the slope of the *C* function with respect to the *left*-hand axis: extra supply will increase total availability and hence if the supply is positively related to price then the carry-over function itself will tilt relative to the import curve. Thus in Figure 8(a), exporters

* Whenever the question of reserves is posed as 'what is the optimal level of stocks' rather than 'how should stocks be managed', there is the danger of falling into the trap of advocating destabilising stocks.

Figure 8 (a) Exporter adjustment, and (b) importer adjustment in the presence of a storage policy

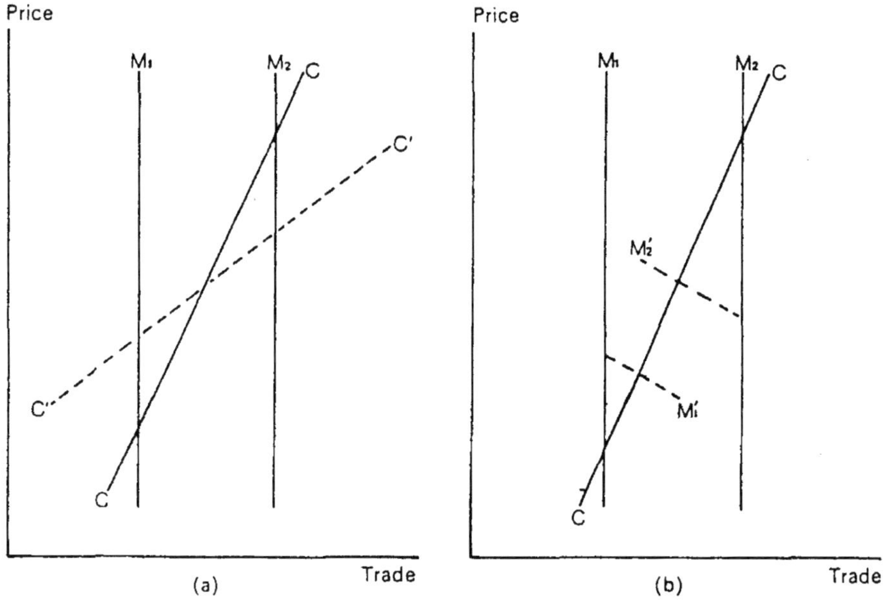

are deemed to make cut-backs in supply at low prices and increase availability at higher prices. This enhances market stability, as shown by the prices where C and C' cut the M line. There are various ways in which this can occur without serious injury to domestic producers in exporting countries. Demand for grain for livestock feed, for instance, in exporting countries tends to be reasonably price elastic: food grain availability therefore does respond to price even when producer wheat prices are fixed. It is not difficult to think of ways of enhancing this effect. Figure 8(b) shows the way in which importers could liberalise their own policies to aid market adjustments. In low price years additional demand (M_1') will tend to raise price and in high price periods a reduction in import demand will keep prices from rising, as M_2 flatten to M_2'. Ultimately, the stability of the market depends on a combination of a sensible stocks policy and a willingness of countries to make adjustments even at the expense of their own domestic stability.

Conclusion

My conclusion is twofold. In terms of the usefulness of the model, it seeks to highlight at the expense of some exaggeration, the possible consequences for the world market of inconsistent domestic objectives. To start with the government objectives and work backwards to a well functioning market does not in itself presume support for those objectives. A policy model of this type puts emphasis on the impact that governments have on the way a market operates, and draws the implications for market performance. It enables various proposals for market reform to be examined against the background of the underlying government objectives. In terms of the world of current policy problems, my conclusion is that economists need to put more emphasis on the analysis of such problems and their remedies in order to evaluate fully their implications. The profession has tended to lag behind the policymakers and administrators to the extent that meaningful analysis is lacking on matters of urgent concern.

References

Abbott, P. C. (1976). Developing Countries and International Grain Trade (unpublished Ph.D., dissertation, M.I.T., 1976).

F.A.O. (1975). *Food Reserve Policies for World Food Security: A Consultant Study*, ESC:CSP/75/2, Rome.

F.A.O. (1973). *Agricultural Protection: Domestic Policy and International Trade*, C73/LIM/9, Rome.

F.A.O. (1975). *Agricultural Protection and Stabilisation Policies*, C75/LIM/2, Rome.

F.A.O. (1970). *The Stabilisation of International Trade in Grains*, Commodity Policy Studies, No. 2, Rome.

Farnsworth, H. C. (1956). International Wheat Agreements and Problems, 1949–56, *Q. J. Econ.* **66,** 217–248.

Harris, S. and Josling, T. (1974). Can World Commodity Prices be Explained? *National Westminster Bank Quarterly Review*, August, 29–40.

Hillman, J. S. (1974). Negotiations on Trade-Disruptive Measures. In Henrichsmeyer, W. *et al.*, *Trade Negotiations and the World Food Problem*, Trade Policy Research Centre, London.

International Food Policy Research Institute (1976). *Meeting Food Needs in the Developing World*, Research Report, No. 1, Washington.

Johnson, D. G. (1973). *World Agriculture in Disarray*. London: Macmillan.

Johnson, D. G. (1975). *World Food Problems and Prospects*, American Enterprise Institute for Public Policy Research, Washington.

Johnson, D. G. (1975). World Agriculture, Commodity Policy, and Price Variability, *Am. J. agr. Econ.* **57** (5), 823–828.

Josling, T. E. (1974). Agricultural Policies in Developed Countries: A Review, *J. agric. Econ.* **25,** 229–264.

Josling, T. E. (1974). Towards our International System of Grain Reserves. In Henrichsmeyer, W. *et al.*, *Trade Negotiations and the World Food Problem*, Trade Policy Research Centre, London.

Josling, T. E. (1977). *Agricultural Negotiations in the Tokyo Round*, Trade Policy Research Centre, London.

McCalla, A. (1969). Protectionism in International Agricultural Trade, 1850–1968, *Agricultural History* **43,** 329–343.

McCalla, A. (1966). A Duopoly Model of World Wheat Pricing, *J. Fm Econ.* **48,** 711–727.

Sinha, R. (1976). World Food Security, *J. agric. Econ.* **27,** 121–135.

Warley, T. K. (1976). Western Trade in Agricultural Products. In Shonfield, A. (ed.), *International Economic Relations of the Western World, 1959–1971, Vol. 1: Politics and Trade.* R.I.I.A. and O.U.P.

World Food Conference (1974). *Assessment of the World Food Situation*, E/CONF/65.3, Rome.

Résumé

LES POLITIQUES OFFICIELLES DES PRIX ET LA STRUCTURE DU COMMERCE AGRICOLE INTERNATIONAL

Les implications de la politique intérieure agricole des pays développés sur le commerce des produits agricoles de zone tempérée se répercutent à leur tour sur la structure des marchés mondiaux et sur le fonctionnement du système mondial des approvisionnements alimentaires.

Un modèle simple est élaboré, qui relie ces politiques intérieures aux niveaux des stocks, à l'aide alimentaire et à la demande non commerciale, et qui sert ensuite à examiner certaines des récentes propositions visant à améliorer les conditions sur les marchés agricoles, pour arriver à la conclusion qu'une conjonction entre des objectifs de prix intérieurs plus flexibles et des politiques coordonnées en matière de stocks pourrait améliorer le niveau de sécurité mondiale dans le domaine de l'alimentation.

Zusammenfassung

DIE PREISPOLITIK DER REGIERUNGEN UND DIE STRUKTUR DES INTERNATIONALEN AGRARHANDELS

Die Implikationen inländischer Farmpolitiken entwickelter Länder für den Agrarhandel haben Rückwirkungen auf die Struktur der Weltmärkte und auf den Ablauf des Weltlebensmittelsystems. Ein einfaches Modell wird entwickelt, das solche Politiken mit den Vorratsniveaus, der Lebensmittelhilfe und der nicht kommerziellen Nachfrage verbindet. Dieses Modell wird dann benützt, um einige der neueren Vorschläge zur Verbesserung der Bedingungen auf Agrarmärkten zu prüfen, wobei gefolgert wird, dass eine Kombination flexibler inländischer Preisbestrebungen und koordinierter Vorratspolitik das Niveau der Sicherheit der Weltlebensmittel verbessern könnte.

4 Domestic Agricultural Price Policies and Their Interaction through Trade

TIMOTHY E. JOSLING

INTRODUCTION

In recent years the interrelatedness of national policy decisions on agriculture has become particularly apparent. In agricultural markets, one country's policy helps to set the market for another country's goods. Combinations of such policies together determine in large part the structure of world markets and the short-run performance of those markets. The export markets for such products as sugar, dairy products, and meat are to a large extent dominated by the activities of governments concerned with their own problems of rural incomes. Similarly available supplies are determined as much by these domestic policies as by the free play of markets. In the world grain market, price stability is sacrificed in times of production variability as each country seeks to shelter its own farmers and consumers from the effects of fluctuating harvests. Attitudes toward such price-support and domestic-stability policies become very defensive in the context of international negotiations, as governments attempt to separate domestic from international pressures.[1]

In the light of these well-documented interactions through trade, the study of agricultural policies necessarily involves explicit attention to the international dimension. In the analysis of policy alternatives, the structure of the product market is of prime importance. If that market is itself a reflection of the policies of others, knowledge of

IMPERFECT MARKETS IN AGRICULTURAL TRADE. McCalla and Josling, eds. © Allanheld, Osmun (Montclair, N.J.)

those policies becomes significant. This applies whether the policy concerned is developing country food-supply security, export promotion programs, farm income-support measures, or price stabilization schemes. An understanding of the way in which policies impinge on each other is a key aspect of the analysis of such policies. The object of this essay is to explore some of these policy interactions with the intention both of illustrating the problems which arise in agricultural markets as a result of the dominance of policies and of suggesting analytical approaches to allow a fuller incorporation of government policies in sectoral trade models. The discussion can be illustrated with the aid of a partial equilibrium, comparative static representation of a "typical" temperate-zone agricultural product market, though some qualifications will be necessary in discussing more general equilibrium and more dynamic policy interactions.

LINKAGES AMONG DOMESTIC FARM POLICIES

Although it is not possible here to explore in full the variety of interactions among national policies, a simplified example may illustrate some of the main problem areas. Assume that two countries have policies where each establishes a fixed domestic price level (P_I in the importer and P_{II} in the exporter) and makes deficiency payments to bridge the gap between these levels and world market prices. On the assumption that these two countries (or groups of countries) make up the whole of the world market for this good, the impact on the trade position is as illustrated in Figure 4.1. Domestic supply in each country will be determined by the guaranteed price level and will not be directly influenced by world prices, whereas consumption is free to react to the prevailing market price.[2] In Figure 4.1 (world market), the import demand curve (D_m') will be kinked at the internal price in the importer, and a similar discontinuity and change in slope at the exporter's domestic support price will be evident in the export supply curve (S_x'). The budget cost of the deficiency payments will be the quantity supplied in each country multiplied by the respective price difference, (P_I − P_w) and (P_{II} − P_w), where P_w is the policy-distorted world price. This world price is in itself a combination of the impact of the two policies. The importer policy, in the absence of any policy in the exporting country, would have depressed the world price from P_f (under free trade) to P_a. Similarly, the exporter policy alone would have lowered world price from P_f to P_b. The two policies together reinforce the drop in the world price to P_w and, in addition, make it more sensitive to supply shifts in each country.

This rather straightforward but by no means trivial example of policy interactions highlights certain features of markets dominated

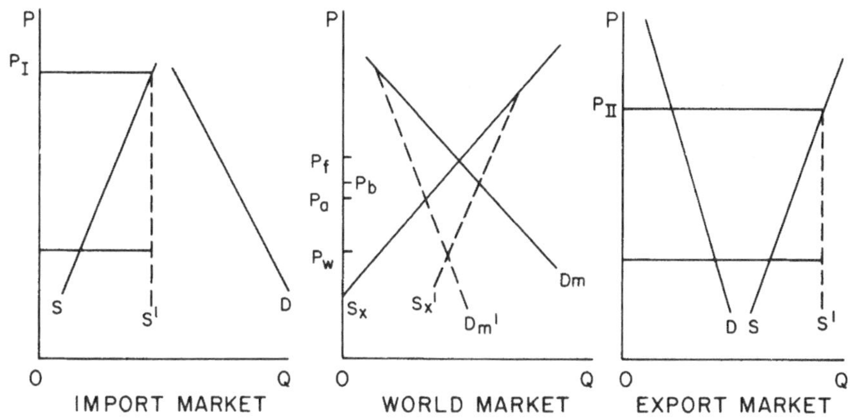

Figure 4.1 Policy interaction: deficiency payments in both importer and exporter.

by such national price-support schemes. It makes clear that such policy interactions need not involve any overt trade measures. This aspect, the international implications of policies relying on purely domestic instruments, has become more familiar in recent years with the examination in political as well as academic circles of nontariff measures influencing trade patterns. As the use of "direct" methods, such as producer subsidies, to correct perceived internal distortions has the cautious blessing of economic theory, the tendency has been for academics to view deficiency payments in a more favorable light than tariffs, levies, quotas, and export subsidies. But justification of direct subsidies, even if possible on welfare grounds, clearly does not make such policies immune from scrutiny with respect to their international impact. The "European" view of U.S. farm policies—that the present system of making payments to producers of the major crops is an effective subsidy to U.S. exports which, therefore, should be discussed along with the more overt subsidies paid by the European Economic Community (EEC)—takes advantage of this fact.

This example also illustrates the importance for market structure of policy interrelationships. Any policy which sets a price for domestic producers that does not respond directly to world price changes—as with policies that fix consumer prices or trade prices—in effect reduces the slope of the trade "curve" exhibited by that country. The fixed-price nature of farm policies has been the object of considerable comment in recent years with respect to the fixed trade prices (threshold prices) of the EEC, but the implication extends to U.S. target price policy and other similar schemes. In the face of production variations, world prices are made less stable whenever domestic prices are made more stable. This fundamental linkage bedevils all attempts to negotiate agreements to foster international price stability; the unstable nature of the markets is largely a result of policies with substantial domestic appeal which are unlikely to be relinquished at the bargaining table.[3]

Another consequence of price instability arising from fixed-price policies shows up in program costs. In each country, domestic production increases will increase budget costs both at home and abroad and likewise for decreases in output. The stability of budget cost in one country is, therefore, a function of the stability of production in both. Though this is true even in the absence of fixed-price policies, the effect is enhanced by the steeper slopes of the excess demand and excess supply curves. Budget cost instability, a major problem in the management of developed country policies, can be even more serious for developing countries. Consumer prices are similarly destabilized by fixed producer prices, a factor significant to governments concerned about inflation in a world where retail prices seem reluctant to fall with raw material costs as easily as they rise. Since cattle are "consumers" of grain, livestock cycles are also closely affected by transmitted instability.

A slightly less obvious implication also follows from the effect on the trade curves: the degree of potential market power of each country is increased. The gap between marginal import cost and world price is increased. The gap is increased, enhancing possible monopsony rents, as is the divergence between marginal export revenue and price, encouraging monopoly behavior. In other words, supply control by the exporter becomes more profitable (under certain conditions relating to the importer price level and the import demand elasticity) as does import control by the importer (depending on the corresponding exporter parameters). Thus, the structure of markets is determined by the interaction of policies; and the choice and effectiveness of domestic policy instruments in one country is constrained and influenced by others in the same market.

The effect of these policy interactions can also be expressed as a transfer. The importing country will gain on the terms of trade from its own policy as the world price is depressed (from P_f to P_a in Figure 4.1) by its own subsidy policy. It will also gain from the terms-of-trade impact of the foreign country policy (P_a to P_w). Looked at from the viewpoint of the exporting country, it incurs losses on the terms of trade from both its own and its partner's subsidy policy, as shown by the fall in the world price from P_f to P_b and P_b to P_w, respectively (Fig. 4.1). The importer's taxpayers are effectively paying to consumers in both countries a part of the transfer intended to go to their own farmers; in addition, the exporter's taxpayers join in the act by subsidizing additional production and, hence, lowering world price still further. In effect, taxpayers in both countries are paying to farmers a subsidy which also benefits consumers, with the net transfer among countries reflecting their respective balances of production and consumption activity. These international transfers may be considered arbitrary to the extent that they are not clearly related to any purpose. They are implemented through the trading system (in this case without overt trade barriers) and represent hidden, yet obvious, linkages among policies in different countries. The direction of these transfers is important in discussions of international agricultural policy, as is their instability in times of market shortage.

Nothing in this illustration is likely to be surprising to practitioners of policy who spend a fair proportion of their time concerning themselves with the impact of the policies of their competitors and customers and a significant amount of energy in negotiating, either formally or informally, to offset the adverse implications. A scholar of trade policy could also say with justification that juxtaposing two simple policies gives few results which are not intuitively obvious. But it remains true that much academic work on domestic and trade policies in agriculture ignore important elements of the nature of the market in which those policies act. The structure of markets, as circumscribed by the concatenation of domestic policy measures, should be the starting point of any such analysis.

The example given above, with two producer subsidies tied to fixed domestic prices, is indeed a relatively straightforward case, primarily because both countries have retained control over their producer price levels through their willingness to pay the subsidies. As far as the domestic producers in each country are concerned, the demand which they face is both perfectly elastic at the guaranteed price and unrelated to the output levels or policies of their countries. They are perfectly insulated as long as farm program budgets are expansible. This battle of the treasuries is vulnerable where policy prices get out of line with world market conditions. The importer, in particular, has options open which are more attractive to finance ministers while they retain control over farm prices.

Assume that the importer, consequently, institutes a variable-levy mechanism to replace the deficiency payment in order to save budget costs.[4] The import demand curve now takes a vertical dive at the internal price level [Dm^2 in Figure 4.2(a)], indicating that world prices do not influence trade volume below that price. The levy represents the difference between the fixed importer price, P_I, and the new level of world price, P_W'. Several features of the interrelationship change with the new policy. First, to the importing country the depression of world prices by policies no longer has a budget cost; instead, it

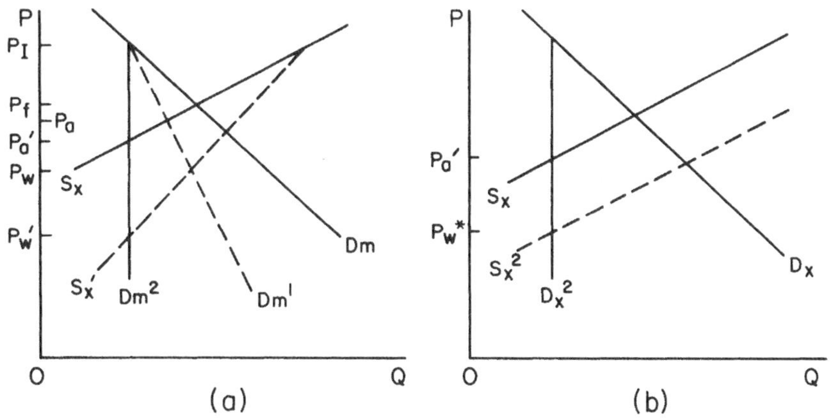

Figure 4.2 Policy interaction: introduction of levies and export subsidies. Panel (a) variable levy-importer: deficiency payment-exporter. Panel (b) variable levy-importer: export subsidy-exporter.

generates levy receipts. Second, the terms-of-trade loss to the *exporter,* as a result of its own policy, increases.[5] In other words, the levy policy "exploits" the exporter's deficiency payment, capturing more from the foreign taxpayer for the importing country government. Third, an increase in production by the exporter will now have a positive rather than an adverse budget impact in the importing country. The importer now has a sure mechanism for capturing the natural bounty of a good harvest in other countries, as well as productivity increases, sharing them with consumers in the exporting country. Fourth, increases in production in the importing country have a less-adverse impact on the budget and could even increase levy revenue, if the foreign supply were inelastic. Morever, increases in domestic price levels may have little budgetary effect, as the larger per unit levy works to offset the smaller trade volume. Such considerations make it difficult to give up a variable levy system once it is, as in the case of the EC, firmly established.

The impact on world price stability of the variable-levy policy is, of course, more pronounced than with a deficiency payment system. A fixed consumer price level has joined a fixed producer price, ensuring that neither is directly responsive to world price changes. The comments made above with respect to the induced instability in world markets of the deficiency payments system hold *a fortiori* for the levy. Exporter budget costs are destabilized further in the face of variable import levies, as are their consumer prices and livestock cycles. In addition to not allowing foreign production instability (through prices) to impact on the importer's domestic markets, their domestic production instability is exported in its entirety. On the other hand, the profits from exporter supply control increase. The Achilles heel of the variable levy is the fact that *if* export volume or price can be controlled, the entire levy receipts are potential income for the exporter. This in itself has major significance for the marketing policy of exporting countries in those products where levy systems are employed by the importers.[6] Coordination of exporter policies may, however, be made more difficult, even if more profitable—as countries compete against each other for a particular volume of trade in import markets.

The notion of international transfers through policies can be extended to this example. Taxpayers in the exporter pay their producers, while consumers in the importing country pay their government through levies and their producers through higher prices for domestic output. The consumers in the exporting country gain from both payments, with taxpayers in the importing country also benefiting from the system. In national terms the importing country benefits through the terms of trade, though at a resource cost arising from the production and consumption distortions. These transfers, in conjunction with the instability impacts described above, give the international dimension of agricultural policies much of its flavor and make the variable levy, in particular, a major irritant in discussions of agricultural trade.[7]

An extreme case of such a transfer can be seen if the exporter decides to offer a per unit export subsidy to maintain producer prices rather than a deficiency payment. In Figure 4.2b, the export supply schedule (as seen by the importer) moves down to S_X^2. Since no more produce can enter the importing country, the effect is merely to dilute the world price (from P_a' to P_W*) to the benefit of the importer exchequer and to the cost of the exporter government. Domestic prices in the exporter could not rise, as this would generate unsalable surpluses. One domestic price-support instrument has, in effect, to be dropped from the exporter's armory. A variable export subsidy, designed to support a fixed domestic price, is also ruled out on even stronger grounds. If the domestic price is set at a level above that which generates the quantity which can be sold in the importing country, surpluses will accumulate and world prices collapse.[8]

It is clear that the variable-import levy has a significant impact on the structure of world markets and limits the actions of other countries. It increases the potential gains from the exercise of monopoly power but also intensifies the competition among exporters. It renders of doubtful value any export subsidy policies although these can be used to change market shares for various exporters. It ensures that domestic production instability is "exported" and that world price variations (below the domestic price level) are not reflected in domestic decisions. It thus increases world price instability both through the negation of trade volume response to such price changes and through reduced incentives to hold domestic stocks. But concentration on this policy instrument should not be taken to imply that all the "blame" for international tensions can be placed on those countries employing such levies. It was suggested above that quota systems had similar impacts on world markets. Indeed, any country that can choose the volume of imports—whether by quotas, through state trading, or as part of central economic planning—will have a strong tendency to adjust those trade flows with more than one eye on domestic market conditions. Leaving aside the case where the absolute amount of foreign exchange available for imports is the limiting factor, as could be the case with some developing countries, imports are bound to be used to impart a degree of stability on the domestic market with the aid of implicit import taxes and subsidies. To put it another way, it is very doubtful whether consumers in countries where trade is controlled by government agencies can expect to be the beneficiary of the transfers noted above, which come about as a result of farm subsidies and trade restrictions in other countries. The variable levy is a convenient example of an importer policy with widespread external implications, but it is only a specific instance of a general point.

One further example may help to reinforce this argument. Suppose that governments in both importing and exporting countries hold stocks and that these are managed in such a way as to attempt to hold prices within a band by buying at the lower and releasing at the higher price level. Assume, also, that "normal" prices are within the bands of both countries but that these bands themselves differ. Figure 4.3 shows one possible combination, with price triggers higher in the importing country than in the exporter. It will be obvious that policies justaposed in this way will not be viable. If good harvests cause prices to drop to the importer buying trigger, then that country will accumulate stocks to restore market balance. But then, as prices rise, the exporter stock-release trigger has no significance because no stocks have been accumulated in that country. Prices will continue to rise until the importer release trigger is reached. The country with the higher buying-in price will effectively set the range over which prices can vary. Other price combinations and less extreme specifications of stock functions could be explored. The simple example again gives a simple message: one country's stock policies rely for their efficacy on what other countries are doing in this regard.

The linkage between stock policies and price policies is also important. Suppose that an exporter has a stock policy designed to keep

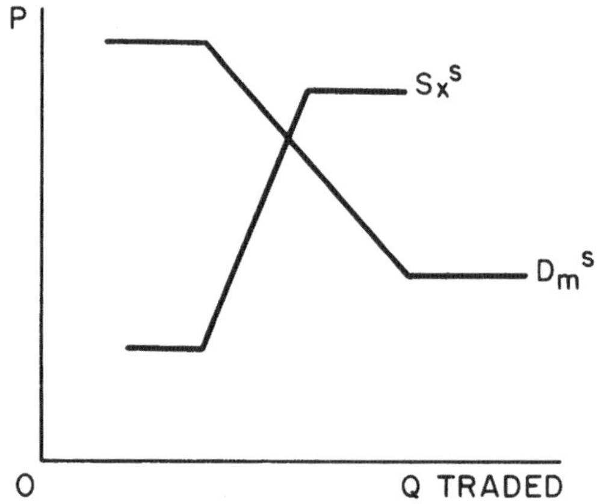

Figure 4.3 Import demand and export supply in the presence of stocks policies in both countries.

prices within a certain band, but the importer has only a trade policy of the variable-levy type. The three policy price decisions—accumulation and release prices in the exporter and import price in the importer—are clearly related. An increase in the importer's threshold price necessitates a lowering of either the upper or the lower price trigger (or both) for the exporter, if the reserve scheme is not to overaccumulate stocks. The exporter is, in effect, stabilizing within a range the importer's levy receipts, making exporter stock policies popular in importing countries even when there are no domestic price implications; but the importer essentially controls the level at which such stabilization occurs. Such problems of interdependence have arisen in connection with the stock policies of grain exporters, which would rapidly become too expensive if not consistent with the market outlets in importing countries.

IMPLICATIONS FOR NATIONAL POLICY INVESTIGATION

The premise of this chapter is that these various policy interactions are significant enough to warrant their careful inclusion in research on national agricultural policies and international agricultural markets. The previous section considered a class of policy interrelationships through trade in a simple two-country model. This discussion needs to be put in perspective lest the model itself take over the role of defining the problem. In this section the perspective is that of national decision-making on agricultural policy and the type of research support needed to clarify choices and evaluate options. The next section will discuss the separable issue of international market analysis.

Decisions on national agricultural policies range from occasional discrete choices as to the type of program, through the setting of price levels, usually once each year, to the administrative operation of these policies on an ongoing basis. The basic policy choices are determined in large part by such factors as the objectives of the government, the place of the agricultural sector in the economy, and the trade balance in particular products. Price levels within that program will reflect production costs, budget expenditure, foreign exchange flows, consumer sensitivities, and the like. Policies, once established, adjust to unexpected developments and pressures at home and abroad. Each of these three types of policy decision is effected by similar policies in other countries, though in somewhat different ways; and each requires specific research input. A brief indication of some of the issues under the first two headings is all that can be attempted here; the question of research on policy management is a topic of its own, involving different techniques and imposing a further set of requirements on the research design.

Basic decisions on agricultural policy do not come lightly or frequently. The United States is perhaps the only major country which has a regular process for review of policy instruments as each successive Agriculture Act expires. In spite of this, a large amount of academic writing on domestic policy is indeed on the comparison of systems of support. This is particularly true in Europe where the prevailing mechanisms of the common agricultural policy (CAP) are constantly under discussion in academic circles and plans for reform are numerous. Policy design is emphasized in teaching where courses in agricultural policy commonly include comparative analyses of subsidy and trade policy systems.[9]

Governments retain their "inefficient" policy tools despite the wealth of such analysis and the plethora of alternative solutions to policy problems. The exploration of the international dimension of these policies may help to explain why they persist and why they take certain forms.[10] This involves recognizing the role of governments as actors in an arena larger than their own national borders. It extends the common perception of international trade in agricultural products as being plagued by the unpredictable externalities of national farm policies. The forces at work may be neither unpredictable nor truly external to the decision process. It suggests that one needs to look at sets of policies in particular markets in order to evaluate the scope for national decision. Rather than collapsing all overseas policy effects into a single function—the demand for an export good or the supply of an importable product—this approach emphasizes the simultaneous or sequential nature of policy decisions. "If we do X, then our trading partners will probably do Y. . . ."

The examples of the previous section undoubtedly overdraw the mutuality of farm policies and their interactions. A two-country case with terms-of-trade changes that show up on a diagram (or can be seen at the back of a classroom) will exaggerate the impact that one country has on another in a market where many countries participate. The "small-country assumption" in policy studies may indeed be appropriate for many questions in agriculture. The case for due recognition of policy interactions nevertheless rests on the fact that a small group of countries—including the United States, Canada, Australia, the EEC, Japan, the U.S.S.R. and Brazil—have, through their policies in the agricultural field, a major influence on each other and on the markets for such traded products as meat, dairy products, wheat, feed-grain, sugar, oilseeds, fruits, and rice. The small-country assumption has to be treated with caution in any discussion of these products and countries.

The analytical challenge in this area is to incorporate as endogenous factors those aspects of the policies of major governments likely to respond to international conditions and to place them in a framework which makes explicit the international transmission of pressures on policy.[11] Problems of information and interpretation make such a prescription ambitious and perhaps account for the reason so few studies attempt the task. The value of such an integrated policy approach suggests, however, that this work should not await a perfect data base.

The second aspect of policy decisions mentioned above is that of price-setting. Although connected with the choice of policy instruments, decisions on prices are made much more often than those on policy design. The question of policy interaction is of interest in this case, not so much because certain types of policy are appropriate or otherwise in themselves, but because the price levels at which those policies are operated have an interactive aspect. Once again, a small-country policy assumption will be appropriate in many cases where the impact of one national decision on other countries is small and where that country can subsume the policy price decisions of others as part of the economic climate in which it trades. For the major countries, it is plausible to look at policy prices as a set of interrelated decisions in which each of these countries plays a part but cannot ignore the consequences of its own actions on those of other participants. The fact that governments are generally unwilling to admit to domestic interests that their price options are contingent upon those in other countries is not in itself a reason to dismiss such linkages.

Just as the conceptualization of national policies as a set of related actions requires that the factors shaping them be identified, so the idea of national policy prices as being not independent of each other requires that the forces which influence those price levels be explored. The lists of relevant variables for each country will be different, but most of these lists would include the structure of farm incomes relative to the nonfarm population, the budget cost of policies, the consumer price level and its significance, the foreign exchange position, farm cost considerations, investment policies, and the general level of inflation. Since budget costs, producer and consumer prices, and foreign exchange variables are often linked through trade to policies in other countries, depending on the policies employed, the "system" as a whole should at least be specified before examining individual parts.[12]

One development in recent years has given an additional dimension to the question of policy price levels. The higher rates of inflation among industrial countries, the disparities among such rates, and the consequent movement of currencies against each other have led to the threat of major divergencies in farm prices under price-support systems. Exchange rates—themselves part of an interdependent monetary process—add a further dimension to the farm policy interactions. The structure of trade markets influences the incidence of exchange rate changes, reflecting the degree to which governments allow monetary influences to impinge on farm and food prices. The ubiquitous fixed-price policies, cited earlier as leading to lower sensitivity of trading patterns to world price movements, are the main instruments for insulating domestic markets from currency changes; these prices are set in domestic currencies and adjust slowly to the external value of those currencies.[13] If the policy device is of the variable-levy or variable export-subsidy type, the direct impact of exchange rates on trade patterns is nullified, implying a consequently greater burden of adjustment on other sectors and other markets. Policies which preset producer and consumer prices in other ways—including those in most developing countries, all central-plan economies, and many industrial nations—have similar, though sometimes less-marked, impacts on exchange rate adjustment. This process is ripe for further empirical study.

IMPLICATIONS FOR INTERNATIONAL TRADE RESEARCH

If the full understanding of the implications of various national price-support policies requires investigation of their interplay through trade, it follows that research on trade itself must also take these policies into account. Such research is usually aimed at two sets of questions: (1) the performance of the trading system, including the stability of markets, the incidence of costs and benefits from trade, and the overall efficiency of international markets, on the one hand; and (2) the behavior of trading prices and the potential size of markets for public and private investment and marketing decisions, on the other.[14] All of these issues require, in principle, detailed information on and analysis of national policies mentioned above. Market performance will depend largely on the type of market structure generated by the external face of farm policies, whereas future market developments (in price and quantity) will depend largely on the more-dynamic aspects of price-level changes and exchange-rate impacts. Even if one were to hold (counter to the argument in the previous section) that national policy decisions for farm programs on both the design and the price levels are independent of each other, an understanding of their impact upon trade is still essential. The fact that these policy factors are rarely built into models of world markets illustrates the considerable conceptual and empirical difficulties of such a prescription.

The impact of farm policies on market stability has indeed been explored for the wheat market, stimulated by the recognition that the price rises of 1973 could hardly have been the result of a minor setback in world output the previous year.[15] Similar attention is needed to markets other than wheat and to the impact of central-plan and developing countries on this process. In addition, the transmission of cycles in the livestock sector presents a phenomenon at present not fully understood. The relatively small number of countries which trade the major livestock products would seem to make a study on policy interactions feasible.[16] The link between international grain market instability and livestock trade patterns is similarly unclear at present.

The international transfer of policy costs and benefits arising from policies was illustrated earlier. Although one might wish for trade negotiations to be centered on questions of global efficiency, in reality they have as much to do with such transfers as with "pure" resource allocation. Intergovernmental discussions on agricultural trade barriers provide an opportunity for countries to adjust these implicit transfers when they become too large or when they are perceived to move in the wrong direction. Broad statements of principle favoring trade liberalization or expansion serve to provide consistency among *ad hoc* positions on individual items on the agenda, but the "who benefits and who loses?" approach to negotiations is more fundamental than the overt philosophical motivation. Consequently, research into such transfers offers more hope for an explanation of trade talks than the exploration of free trade solutions. Such a transfer approach also has merit in examining the position and interests of developing countries in agricultural trade.

Lest this conclusion appear unduly cynical, it should be acknowledged that questions of efficiency in resource use have a more-fundamental importance even than intergovernmental transfer games. Happily, these games are played against the backdrop of constraints and opportunities of the wider economic system. The actual loss in real income from the totality of agricultural policies in the world may be significant, but it is probably in the nature of a once-and-for-all loss resulting in more expensive farm products and a lower output of nonfarm goods. The system may not be efficient, but it is not necessarily getting worse. These statements are themselves testable and require that the performance of the trading system be monitored overtime.

That the ability to predict future agricultural trade prices is invaluable in making both public and private production and marketing decisions is not contentious. The argument of this chapter is that an understanding of the mutual dependence of farm policies is a useful part of the process of refinement of such predictions. If government policies could be "made endogenous" in prospective models, then the common assumption used in many of these exercises—that there be no change in government policies—could be relaxed. The question is whether or not the policies themselves are the reasonably predictable outcome of a set of (national and international) pressures or are the consequence of inscrutable domestic political forces.[17] To take the mystery out of farm price and policy decisions is a reasonable object of research in this area. The benefits may well accrue to those in, say, developing countries who may not, in fact, participate in the arena of international farm policy discussions but who are, nevertheless, profoundly influenced by their outcome.

SUMMARY

The argument here is that an appreciation of the nature of the interaction among farm policies, notably those that support prices by internal marketing measures or by trade interventions, is useful for both domestic policy research and that concerned with agricultural trade. The counterargument would be that although policies influence trade, they are essentially independent. The development of the theory of commercial policy has indeed generally assumed independent national decisions.[18] In a number of cases, independence of policies may be realistic; but the dominance of a small number of countries in trade in temperate-zone commodities and the concern that each of these countries shows with the policies of others suggests that a measure of interdependence exists. A study of this aspect of policy requires that the nature of the policy linkages through trade be investigated and formalized and that the determinants of the policies themselves be explored. So far, this line of development appears only spasmodically in the literature, despite the large volume of analytical work on agricultural policies themselves and the revival of interest in questions of agricultural trade. The behavior of policy-dominated markets, the structure of such markets, and the implications for domestic and international decisions should be subjected to closer examination.

APPENDIX

The text discusses a simple example of policy interactions. This appendix is intended to develop somewhat further the graphical approach to this question. Although the interaction of national policies influences both domestic policy choices and the structure of international markets, separate treatment of these two aspects emphasizes the different perspective of national and international concerns. As an illustration of this, assume that the key objective in domestic price policy can be condensed to the level and stability of prices to domestic producers under conditions of variable production at home and abroad. The impact of policy sets on such budget costs and the like can be handled in similar ways. A convenient concept, implicit but rarely explicit in policy analysis, which exemplifies directly the producer-impact of price support is the *demand schedule that faces domestic producers.* The essence of trade is that it unties this schedule from the consumer demand in that country. The consumer demand becomes only one determinant, along with foreign demand and supply, in influencing the demand for domestic output.

This schedule is derived in Figure 4.4 for the exporter market by examining producer prices as domestic supply shifts. This line, D_P, is flatter and (over the relevant range) lies above D_C, the consumer demand in that country.[19] Policies which flatten the slope of D_P still further increase producer price stability (but not necessarily income stability), and those policies that raise this curve afford protection. Figure 4.5(a) illustrates the impact of a number of domestic price policies on this producer's demand curve. The resulting curves are numbered to correspond to the different policies as follows:

1. no domestic price policy
2. fixed export subsidy or producer subsidy
3. fixed domestic price through variable export subsidy
4. stock policy with buying and selling triggers
5. export quota (with quota rents retained by government)
6. deficiency payment (open ended)

This menu of policy choices would be sufficient to illustrate the situation under free-trade conditions in other countries; but price

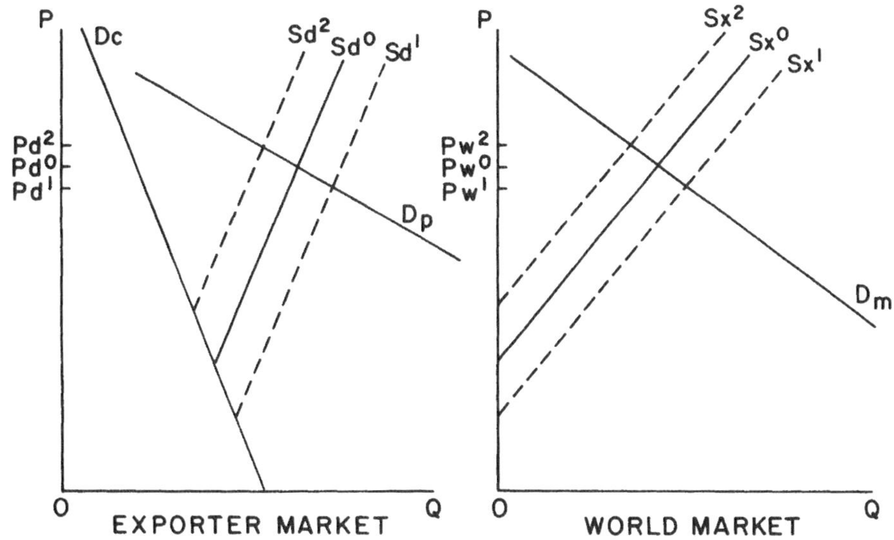

Figure 4.4 Impact of changing production levels on producer price. *Note:* Supply levels S_d^0, S_d^1, S_d^2 generate corresponding export supply curves S_x^0, S_x^1, S_x^2, which in turn determine world price and domestic producer price levels. D_p is the resulting demand curve for domestic production, tracing the producer price at each level of domestic supply.

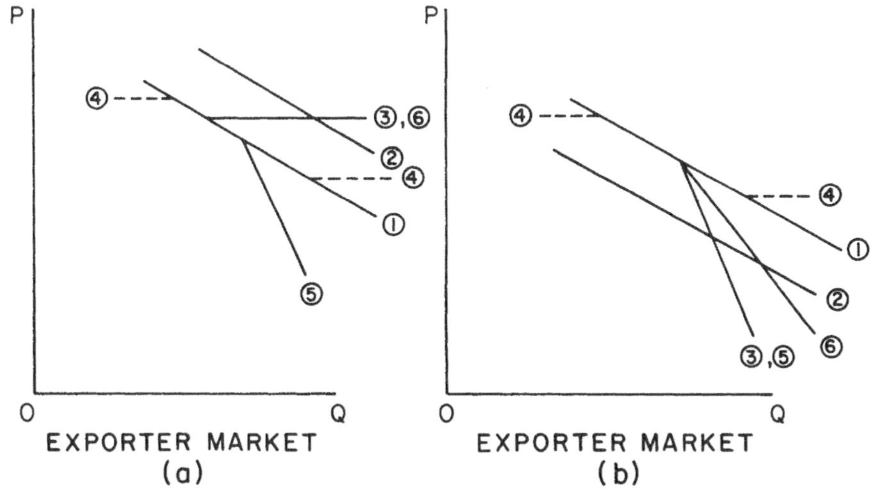

Figure 4.5 Impact of (a) exporter policies and (b) importer policies on the demand curve for domestic production in exporting countries. (Policies described in the text are identified by number.)

policies *abroad* also shift this demand curve. Figure 4.5(b) illustrates some of the impacts of importer policies on the exporter producers. The importer policies considered are analogous to those considered for the exporter:

1. no domestic price policy
2. fixed import tariff
3. fixed domestic price through variable import levy
4. stock policy, with buying and selling triggers
5. import quota (with quota rents retained by government)
6. deficiency payment (open ended)

The net effect of the combination of policies on exporting-country producers can thus be determined by the double shift of the D_P schedule. With the proviso in the text that effects which look significant in a two-country diagram may actually be small in a multicountry world, it is clear that both sets of policies potentially impact on the level and stability of producer prices. Similar constructs would demonstrate possible impacts upon consumer prices (through the total supply facing domestic consumers) and on the budget, foreign exchange position, and real income. The full interactive system would take all these and other variables into account. The effect on the demand for domestic production is used here purely as an example of these interrelationships.

If, by contrast, one were to emphasize not the internal impact on domestic producers but the implications for trade of domestic policies, then the appropriate analytical devices would be the import demand or export supply curves. How these reflect different policies is fairly straightforward and well known. Figure 4.6 elaborates on some of these policy shifts, both (a) for the exporter policies, and (b) for those of the importer. The numbers refer to the same policies as listed above. To incorporate policies for each (important) country in an analysis of trade in a particular commodity may be tedious, but it is nevertheless essential. Along with the policy "reaction"—in particular, the parameter governing the choice of policy prices—such knowledge gives a reasonable approximation of the structural parameters of the world market. Random disturbances, behavioral changes by countries, and modifications to price policies can thus be examined in a consistent framework.

ACKNOWLEDGMENTS

This paper benefited from the comments of Alexander H. Sarris, Alex F. McCalla, Jimmye S. Hillman, Roger Fox, and other Workshop participants.

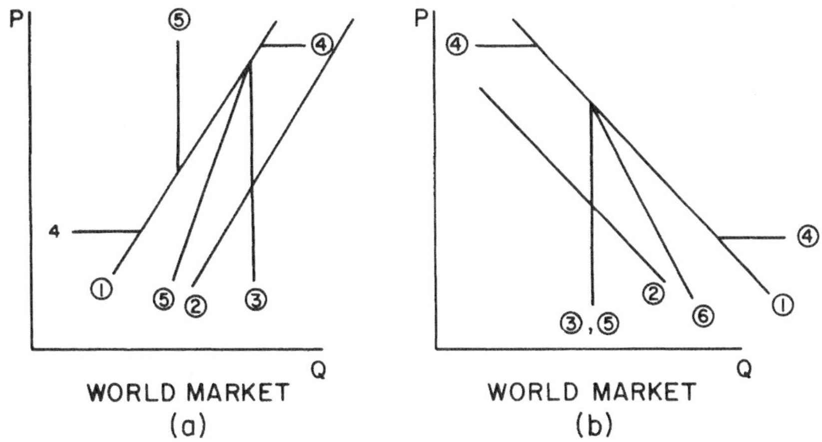

Figure 4.6 Impact of (a) exporter policies on export supply schedule and (b) importer policies on import demand schedule.

NOTES

1. The implications for international agricultural policy are discussed in Josling [5]. This present essay concentrates on the national policy issues created by interdependence among farm programs.

2. For market prices below P_I and P_{II}, the respective domestic supply schedules become completely inelastic as shown by S^1. The demand curves are not altered by the deficiency payment policy.

3. The cost of such domestic stability policies is conveniently measured by the cost of the additional reserves needed to offset their impact on world prices. Unfortunately, those countries have the most internal price stability will tend to have less need for reserves—a significant obstacle to the negotiation of "equitable" sharing of the cost of holding stocks.

4. Such a change was, in fact, made during the 1960s in the United Kingdom. Deficiency payment costs had become large and unpredictable. The fact that the change was also consistent with modifications which would eventually become necessary when the United Kingdom joined the EEC was a bonus. The EEC, by contrast, started its CAP with trade measures; the difficulty of moving to deficiency payments is chiefly one of budget cost.

5. In Figure 4.5(a), the price fall due to the exporter policy increases from $(P_a - P_w)$ under importer deficiency payments to $(P_a' - P_w')$ under importer variable levies.

6. This was pointed out some years ago by Abel [1] in the context of market discrimination policies for U.S. exports. It is behind much of the appeal for more government participation in the marketing of grain evident in recent years. It gives an additional incentive for exporter collusion in concentrated markets as discussed in McCalla and Schmitz [8]. The attitude of the EEC toward such exploitation of the levy policy has been ambivalent. At times the EEC has appeared to welcome the prospect of world prices being raised to and stabilized at their internal levels despite the loss in levy receipts.

7. Essentially the same transfers will be occasioned by an import quota *auctioned* to the importing firms or agencies by the government. Auctioning quotas to the exporting

country, however, would make the international transfers direct rather than indirect and would have the additional advantage that such transfers would be paid in foreign exchange. The analogy with a quota system makes clear that the difference in the value of trade at world prices and at domestic prices in the importing country (quota rents or levy receipts) is "up for grabs." The variable levy captures this rent for the importer unless the exporter counters with an export tax to bring the offer price to the importer's threshold price level or controls the quantity of export sales.

8. The variable export subsidy will cause the export supply curve to become vertical at prices below the domestic support price. It is clear that, in combination with a similarly kinked import demand curve, no market equilibrium exists at low prices in the absence of stock accumulation or surplus disposal outside the commercial market. The wheat market of the late 1960s came close to such a collapse before the expansion of developing-country import markets and those of the central-plan economies provided an outlet for Canadian and U.S. exports. For a fuller discussion of such market failures, see Chapter 8, this volume.

9. Much of this research and teaching gives particular attention to the impact on net welfare of the country concerned. The conclusions are relatively straightforward: the "best" policies aim directly at the source of the problem to which they are addressed. Income support, crop insurance, mobility subsidies, rural education, improved marketing at the farm level, and assistance for structural adjustment are, in general, favored by this approach. Import levies, quotas, export subsidies, and the gamut of price-fixing schemes rank poorly on the scale.

10. To look for explanations of policies at the international level is not in itself to deny the importance of strong political interests in each country which undoubtedly act as a conservative force in perpetuating farm programs.

11. Examples of policy topics that would benefit from this approach include the role of the government in the marketing of U.S. grain, the options for revision of the EEC cereals regime, the implementation of a livestock stabilization program in the United States, the development of an EEC or Japanese grain storage policy, and the impact of EEC enlargement to include Spain, Greece and Portugal. Similar topics could be added in the area of central-plan and developing-country policy.

12. It should be clear that this goes further than acknowledging that one country's policy price influences its net exports or imports of a particular commodity. This is only the first step in the chain of implications considered here.

13. The European Community (EEC) provides an interesting example of the policy dilemma in a period of rapidly changing exchange rates. Despite the existence of a common policy, member governments chose to peg policy prices in local currencies when exchange rates began to diverge a decade ago. This was done by using special "green" rates of exchange to convert from common to national prices. What started as a buffer against abrupt changes in exchange rates developed into a system which gave member countries limited control over their national farm-price levels by choosing whether or when to change their green rates. The resulting divergence in prices within the EEC, with West German prices at times reading 40 percent above those in the United Kingdom, provides a neat example of the influence of economic factors on policy prices. For an explanation of EEC price divergences over this period see Heidhues, *et al* [2]. For a discussion of the development of the green rate system in the European Community, see Josling and Harris [7].

14. In the context of international agricultural policy, these topics are dealt with more fully in Chapter 8, this volume. The present concern is with the possible analytical approach to these research topics.

15. Among the authors who identify national policies in the role of a major destabilizing influence are Johnson [3], UN [10], Shei and Thompson [9], Johnson, Grennes, and Thursby [4] and Josling [5].

16. The role of the U.S.S.R. in international beef and butter markets would make an interesting topic for analysis. It is a plausible hypothesis that the Soviet Union has played a major part in stabilizing these markets and "rescuing" exporting countries when other outlets have been cut off, in the process benefiting from huge transfers from taxpayers in other countries.

17. The decomposition of policies into objectively measurable pressures does not in itself make the task of choosing assumptions simpler as one is likely to end up with a greater number of assumptions to make. If policies are linked, however, then many of these assumptions can be made consistent among countries—exchange rates, inflation, and so on—and any simultaneities among policies can be taken into account.

18. The main exception to this statement is the consideration of tariff retaliation. Two large countries each attempting to adopt an optimal tariff may end up in a worse position than if they had foresworn their monopoly or monopsony power in the market. The discussion of agricultural policies includes an element of retaliation, although for motives much more complex than the capture of monopoly rents.

19. A similar derivation for the demand facing importing country producers (not shown) would also be flatter than domestic consumer demand but would lie below it over the relevant range.

REFERENCES

[1] Abel, M. "Price Discrimination in World Trade of Agricultural Commodities." *Journal of Farm Economics* 48 (May 1966): 194–208.

[2] Heidhues T., et al. *Common Prices and Europe's Farm Policy.* Thames Essay No. 14, Trade Policy Research Centre, London, 1978.

[3] Johnson, D. Gale. "World Agriculture, Commodity Policy, and Price Variability." *American Journal of Agricultural Economics* 57 (December 1975): 823–28.

[4] Johnson, P., T. Grennes, and M. Thursby. "Devaluation, Foreign Trade Controls, and Domestic Wheat Prices." *American Journal of Agricultural Economics* 59 (November 1977): 619–27.

[5] Chapter 8, this volume.

[6] Josling, T. "Government Price Policies and the Structure of International Agricultural Trade." *Journal of Agricultural Economics,* 28 (1977):261–76.

[7] ———, and S. Harris. "Europe's Green Money." *Three Banks Review,* March 1976.

[8] Chapter 5, this volume.

[9] Shei, S. and R. Thompson. "The Impact of Trade Restrictions on Price Stability in the World Wheat Market." *American Journal of Agricultural Economics* 69 (November 1977):628–38.

[10] UN F.A.O., Agricultural Protection and Stabilization Policies, C75/LIM/Z, Rome, 1975.

8
Price, Stock, and Trade Policies and the Functioning of International Grain Markets

Timothy Josling

Food security is greatly influenced by the structure of the distribution system. Although the nature of the underlying structure and the policies that have been suggested to improve it will only change slowly, it seems worthwhile to explore in some detail the reaction of the world wheat market to shocks on the production side, particularly its impact on supply stability in developing countries. The relevance of the issues becomes apparent in periods of scarcity, but the policies need to be operative before such events propel the issue into prominence.

The Fundamentals of Market Stability

Market instability arising from inevitable production fluctuations can be explored by means of a simple conceptualization. Imagine a market for a staple food crop with naturally induced production yield fluctuations from a relatively static land area. All production moves either into consumption or into storage. If there is some "carry-in" from previous years then total availability (new production plus carry-in) must equal consumption plus carry-out. This ex-post identity for a closed market holds equally for changes from year to year. Variation in production levels must show up as offsetting changes in consumption and/or stock levels. The identity is also retained when put in value form, ignoring, for the moment, government activity. Producer receipts and revenue from stock sales will equal expenditure plus the cost of stock renewal—defined appropriately to reflect the two sides of the same set of financial transactions. Table 8.1 records these identities.

Because the world as a whole is a "closed system," even this basic identity has some merit in organizing one's thoughts about stability. First, it becomes clear that there is a significant limitation to government policy in this area. If instability in production exists, its implications cannot be willed away. Either stocks or consumption (or both) must vary. The extent of trade liberalization, commodity price agreements, food aid, and the like are all essentially powerless to alter the reality. They "merely" influence the distribution of changes within and between the categories of consumption and stocks.[1] This approach highlights the obvious but nevertheless fundamental observation that only by reducing production instability itself can other variables in the system be made in aggregate more stable. If instability has a net social (global) cost—which is presumably

Table 8.1 Basic Market Identities

a) Closed system: volume identity		
Production Carry-in		Consumption Carry-out
Total Available	=	Total Used
b) Closed system: value identity		
Producer receipts Revenue from stock sales		Consumer spending Cost of stock purchases
Total Receipts	=	Total Expenditure
c) Open sub-system: volume identity		
Production Carry-in		Consumption Carry-out
Imports		Exports
Total Available	=	Total Used
d) Open sub-system: value identity		
Producer receipts Revenue from stock sales		Consumer Expenditure Cost of stock purchases
Import costs		Export revenue
Total Receipts	=	Total Expenditure

true if the unstable element is yield, implying similar resource costs for large and small harvests—then the returns from stabilizing production may be substantial even if all of the mechanisms for distributing instability are of debatable merit.

The value identity for the closed system also has some intuitive relevance for approaching the instability problem. The difference between revenue from stock sales and spending on stock replacement can be thought of as the cash-flow position of the storage sector.[2] If storage activities require an injection of cash, then producer receipts are enhanced relative to consumer spending. If producer receipts vary with output, then either stock financing or consumer spending (or both) will vary accordingly. Steady profits over time from storage reduces producer receipts relative to consumer expenditure, at least in the absence of government activity to offset these effects.

The closed system can itself contain closed subsystems. The implications hold for each of the parts of the system. Many agricultural markets in the world are essentially closed, whether by policy or natural isolation. This has the immediate implication that they are "responsible" for making internal adjustments to production variability. Many countries, for example, rarely use trade to counterbalance their own production changes. Food insecurity, in these conditions, is basically the outcome of the choice between stock and consumption changes. Such closed markets are, however, unaffected by instability in other areas. It would be worthwhile, though not attempted in this chapter, to identify sources of instability according to their degrees of isolation. No amount of manipulation at the level of international commodity markets will bring stability to an isolated region with negligible market links to the outside world. But these regions themselves may have in some cases fewer instability problems than if more fully integrated with commercial life.[3]

The more traditional security and instability questions relate to open subsystems of the world market, where trade is an option. Table 8.1 also presents the simple identities in this case. Variability in production levels must now be balanced by a combination of changes in stock levels, consumption, and trade balance. The value identities also hold where stock changes are those on the domestic market rather than speculation on transactions overseas. The individual country can thus make use of trade as a device to stabilize, for example, consumption levels, even though that option is not open to the world at large. Economic, if not necessarily political, logic would suggest that such stabilizing trade flows represent an improvement in "security."

Trade possibilities may appear to reduce the need for national stocks. But to complete the picture, the implications for the rest of the market must be considered. Extra imports into one country must be matched by changes in either stocks or consumption (if production is predetermined in a particular year) in other countries. Thus, in the world as a whole, production variations must still show up either as stock or consumption changes even if trade were unhindered. The major impact of trade flows in this respect is to influence the distribution of such changes. The advantage is that production variability is "shared" among countries; the major disadvantage is the other side of the same coin, that such adjustments will be required of a country even if its own production does not vary. The ambivalence of trade policy arises from the conflict between these stabilizing and destabilizing influences of trade flows on individual countries. In the present context, the implication of the simple identity approach is that the question of trade flows is logically distinct from that of stock adjustments in the trading system as a whole. For instance, if the degree of trade liberalization, or the extent to which countries will allow trade flows to vary, is itself otherwise determined, then the question of adjustments within that trade structure is still relevant.

This analysis suggests that a straightforward approach to assessing the overall level of world food security is to explore what has, in fact, happened in the past as a result of instability in production. As mentioned above, the "closed economy" case reflects the situation in the world as a whole. One would expect therefore, given adequate data, that one could plot the relationship between global production variations on the one hand and changes in total consumption and stocks on the other. Consumption series for both specific and aggregate food groups tend to be more stable than those of production—implying that stocks do vary in a stabilizing way. The more significant question is how such instability is distributed. In which countries do stocks or consumption or both vary in response to world production changes? Unfortunately, the data to explore this crucial question are not readily available. Stock data are published only for a small number of countries and convincing consumption series are not much easier to find. Trade and production series, presumably the two most reliable of the basic market data sets, do not in themselves clarify this issue.

An Illustration: the Wheat Market

Since the object of this chapter is to elaborate a framework for approaching these issues, no attempt will be made to fill this empirical gap. However, a convenient illustration of this approach is given by one set of relationships, that between developed countries, the Soviet Union, and developing country food importers in the market for wheat. Table 8.2 shows the variation from year to year in production, consumption, and stocks for selected developed countries (SDCs) and the USSR and, for comparison, the net imports by developing market economies. Production varies considerably in both the major developed countries and the Soviet Union. Changes in consumption are more modest, as one might expect both from low price elasticities of demand and also from various policies designed to offset the impact of food prices on inflation. The stock figures represent the change relative to the previous year in the amount by which stocks increased or decreased.

Thus, for instance, in 1969/70 developed countries suffered a decrease in production from the previous year of about 8 million tons, and increased consumption by 5.5 million tons. The stock accumulation, the difference between carry-out and carry-in, dropped by 17 million tons—implying a release of reserves relative to a continuation of the previous year's stock "policy." This resulted in a 3.5 million ton increase in the trade surplus. In this case, changes in stock decisions absorbed the production fall and the consumption increase, and released an extra amount of wheat for export.[4]

The downturn in Soviet production in 1972/73 was met

Table 8.2 Change Over Previous Year in Selected Variables, Wheat, 1969/70 - 1976/77

	1969/70	1970/71	1971/72	1972/73	1973/74	1974/75	1975/76	1976/77
				(million tons)				
Selected developed countries[a/]								
Production	-8.4	-16.1	17.2	-2.4	12.1	2.6	5.2	12.3
Consumption	5.5	-0.1	2.3	0.4	-2.6	-1.4	-2.3	7.3
Stock increase	-17.4	-18.0	15.1	-17.0	11.9	8.1	2.7	10.7
Trade surplus	3.5	2.1	-0.2	14.2	2.8	-4.1	4.8	-5.8
USSR								
Production	-13.5	19.8	-0.9	-12.8	23.8	-25.9	-17.7	30.7
Consumption	7.7	7.4	-7.5	4.8	-3.0	-1.9	-9.6	4.6
Stock increase	-21.0	11.0	11.0	-1.0	12.0	-25.0	3.0	20.0
Trade deficit	0.2	-1.4	4.4	16.6	-14.8	-1.0	7.4	-6.1
Less developed countries[b/]								
Net trade deficit	1.0	2.4	1.9	0.4	4.4	2.9	2.6	-4.1
SDCs & USSR								
Net trade surplus	3.3	3.5	-4.2	-2.4	17.6	-3.1	-2.6	0.3

a/ Includes Australia, Canada, Japan, European Community, and the United States.

b/ Developing market economies, as classified by IFPRI.

effectively by a reduction in developed country accumulation stock (primarily in the United States) and a consequent increase in trade between these countries. Only a small net decrease in the surplus available for other countries was noticeable. The next year, 1973/74, an exceptional harvest in the USSR allowed stock rebuilding and a reduction in imports. Stocks also responded in developed countries to higher production, but the result was still an increase in the trade surplus over the previous year—even without Soviet demand. The net surplus (SDCs and the USSR) thus increased significantly.[5]

The relatively high degree of food security for the developed countries and the USSR is evidenced by the small consumption changes on a year-to-year basis. From the viewpoint of other countries, the extent to which stock policy changes offset production fluctuations in this situation determines the external impact through trade. Over the period as a whole, changes in the export surplus have been relatively small. There does, however, appear to be a difference between the market economies and the USSR with respect to the incidence of production changes. In the developed market economies, production and consumption changes have the same sign in only three of the eight sets of year-on-year changes shown. By contrast, in the Soviet Union production and consumption move together in five of the eight years. Thus it does appear that the link between domestic production and consumption is weaker in the SDCs, indicating again a potential destabilizing force in world markets. The actual impact on other countries has to take into account stock changes. From the table it would appear that stocks changes carry the same sign as do production variations in every year for the SDCs; net exports vary with production changes in only two of those eight years. For the Soviet Union, stock changes follow production variations in six years out of eight, whereas the net trade balance for wheat varies with production in seven of these years.

The picture, then, is one of developed market economies running domestic policies that appear to obscure price signals to the users and consumers of wheat in part through stocks policies that reflect strongly the changes in production. Such production variations do not appear to be imposed on overseas markets. The stocks are responsive to trade demands as well as to changes in consumption. The question for food security in other countries is to what extent this responsiveness is enough to provide a positive stabilizing influence. The Soviet Union, although holding stocks that vary somewhat with domestic production, uses the trade system to make up much of the harvest variability while imposing on its own consumers more variation in availability than do the market economies.

This example illustrates that questions of food security on a world-wide basis can be phrased in terms of the basic relationships between production, consumption, trade, and stocks for the major countries or groups. With more complete data on stocks and trade, it would be possible to trace the impact of supply variations at a global level on individual country consumption patterns. Introducing production, consumption, and trade values would lead to further conclusions on the incidence of instability. Clearly the incidence of instability is itself determined in large part by the activities of governments.

National Policy Options and Instability

The discussion of the previous section suggests an approach to policy options to deal with food insecurity both at a national and international level. If one retains the assumption that instability in production is the underlying cause of insecurity then it is possible to frame the question in the following way. Given that this instability will have implications for variables throughout the system, which subset of those variables should be made more stable and which, by implication, should be allowed to become less stable? The answer will clearly differ among countries and may change over time. It is also true that one country's answer will be contingent upon the resolution in other countries. Moreover, a collective agreement may not correspond to the individual choices of any nation separately. Nevertheless the various types of solutions can be illustrated.

For this, it is convenient to turn again to the value identities given in Table 8.1 but now to introduce government action in a more explicit manner. For any subpart of the global market, production value, import cost, and revenue from stock sales will equal consumption expenditure, export revenue, and stock purchases. The trade deficit or surplus on this commodity will therefore show up as cash flows on stock transactions and the difference between producer income and consumer spending. Once again this constrains the system and connects the various objectives and concerns that governments might have. So as not to leave the government sector impotent, assume that it can intervene with import taxes and export subsidies to change the private cost of trading. The identity now includes import tariff revenue as a part of import cost and export subsidy payments as a part of trade receipts. The difference between these two amounts represents a surplus or deficit to the government account. This difference must therefore equal the sum of the private sector surplus (or deficit) and that of the overseas trading account. Thus while the government cannot interfere with the volume identity (even if it participates in the stocks function), it can, by running a surplus or deficit on account of this commodity, influence the private storage cash flow, the trade balance, and the gap between current consumption expenditure and producer receipts. These relationships are reproduced in Table 8.3. For completeness, government tax and subsidy policies on the domestic market have been included: many of these items will of course be zero in any particular instance.

For an individual country, and in particular a developing country without a large, grain-consuming livestock sector, the first imperative of a food security policy is presumably to stabilize food consumption levels. This may conveniently be done by stabilizing food prices—indeed this latter objective may become an aim in itself. If food demand itself does not change then stable prices will control food expenditure and, more importantly, prevent the transmission of instability to nonfood markets. Control of food prices could be accomplished by adjusting trade barriers, as would occur automatically if import levies and subsidies were tied to the difference between world and (stable) domestic price levels. More usually, control will be through state purchasing and distribution of imports and possibly the domestic crop. We would expect two implications to follow from these devices. First, the incentive for domestic stockholding would be much reduced as prices on the internal market were stabilized.[6] Second, the foreign trade balance (in this product) and the government program cost will have to absorb the instability arising from production either at home or abroad.

If the instability occurs abroad, the foreign exchange and government revenue accounts may move together: an improvement in the trade balance (other import costs and export revenue remaining constant) will coincide with an increase in the government surplus (assuming no change in taxation and other government programs). Similarly, an increased deficit on external account may be linked with a similar deficit in the budget. If, however, the instability is in domestic production, government deficits may coincide with foreign exchange surpluses and vice versa. These impacts are made more severe by the depressing effect on private stockholding, since government-owned stocks would have to take up some of that function.

Similar problems arise with respect to developed countries, though the emphasis is more likely to be on stabilization of consumer prices than on consumption quantities per se. Those countries that allow private trade to conduct much of the business of marketing and storage will tend to use border taxes and subsidies to control prices. Central-plan countries and those with a structure of state trading will absorb instability directly into the government account. The end result will be similar, with the willingness to allow instability in the budget and the foreign exchange account being the quid pro quo for domestic price stability. Precisely the same problems arise with respect to stabilizing producer incomes, though it is much more normal for policies to aim at preventing rapid changes in producer prices, leaving incomes to fluctuate broadly with production variations.

If countries find that consumption-stability policies destabilize foreign exchange flows and government accounts, it follows that attempts to make these items more stable will clash with consumption objectives. For developing countries with a small tax base and severe payments constraints, this dilemma may be harsh. In the light of domestic production variations and a fixed amount of foreign exchange for use to purchase imports, domestic consumption can only be stabilized by stockholding extensive enough to cover all production changes. The private sector is unlikely to find such arbitrage profitable and govern-

Table 8.3 Market Identities and Sector Accounts

Value identity for open sub-system, with government.[a/]

Receipts	Expenditures
Private sector receipts	Private sector expenditures
Producer receipts	Consumer expenditure
Revenue from private stock sales	Cost of private stock accumulation
Government sector receipts	Government sector expenditures
Import tax receipts	Export subsidy costs
Producer tax receipts	Producer subsidy costs
Consumer tax receipts	Consumer subsidy costs
Sales of government stocks	Cost of government stock accumulation
Foreign sector receipts	Foreign sector expenditure
Import cost in foreign exchange	Export revenue in foreign exchange
Total Above Receipts =	Total Above Expenditure

a/ Value identity for a closed system is as above, but without the foreign sector.

ment costs will be high and erratic. Moreover this dilemma is evident also when world prices vary, as government stocks held when world prices rise will have a high opportunity cost and those held when prices fall will represent a more costly supply source than imports. Consumer price changes may be forced on a country simply because its fiscal and foreign exchange accounts cannot take the strain. In this respect, developed countries are more likely to be able to pursue single-minded consumption stability policies.

Developed Country Policies and Stability

This discussion of national policy choices is well illustrated in the chapters drawn from the Conference that deal with the situation in individual developing countries. The types of policy choices faced by developed countries differ in degree rather than kind. Since developed country policies have not been discussed in detail in the previous chapters, it may be appropriate to consider them here—both as illustration of the types of policy response to instability and with respect to their implications for world food security. As suggested above, the primary focus of developed country policies has been on the extension of mechanisms designed primarily to protect producers from price fluctuations to include a degree of protection for consumers against inflation. The mechanisms have included export taxes and embargoes on one side and import and domestic subsidies on the other.

The results of such policies have been widely noted. They have the effect of achieving domestic stability at the expense of world markets and hence of other countries. The analysis of this chapter suggests that the role of stocks is crucial in this process. If adequate stocks are held, then impacts on other countries through trade of the domestic policies can be offset. Unfortunately, countries with stable domestic prices are unlikely to carry large stabilizing stocks unless such reserves are a conscious part of government policy. Importers, in particular, have no reason to store significant quantities unless they fear physical supplies may be unavailable. Japan and the European Community, among developed countries, have been particularly reluctant to engage in extensive stockholding of grain.

In the present context, the reaction of each individual developed country government is probably less important to a discussion of world food security than is the total impact of these countries together. If the net result of policies, both with respect to farm income and consumer food prices, is to exacerbate price swings by increasing supplies when prices are low and reducing them when prices rise, then an important obstacle to food security has been identified. A straightforward test is possible, using results from the study mentioned in Footnote 4. Table 8.4 summarizes the implied impact of the farm and food policies of the major developed countries on the wheat market in recent years.[7] For each country studied, an estimate was made of the likely production and consumption

Table 8.4 Policy-Induced Trade Volume Effects, Selected Developed Countries, and Stock Changes: Wheat, 1967/68 to 1976/77

	1969/70	1970/71	1971/72	1972/73	1973/74	1974/75	1975/76	1976/77
				(million tons)				
Trade volume effect[a/]								
in SDCs	13.3	13.4	13.2	13.7	1.9	-4.6	-1.0	5.2
Change in stocks								
in SDCs	-2.8	15.3	0.2	17.2	5.3	-2.8	-5.6	-16.3
Change in stocks in USSR[b/]	19.0	8.0	-3.0	-2.0	-14.0	11.0	8.0	-12.0
Total stock and policy								
effect in SDCs	10.5	28.6	13.4	31.0	7.2	-7.4	-6.6	-11.1
Total effect including								
USSR stock change	29.5	36.7	10.4	29.0	-6.8	3.6	1.4	-23.1
Change from previous year[c/]		7.2	-26.3	18.6	-35.8	10.4	-2.2	-24.5

a/ Trade volume effect of policies as defined in text.

b/ Positive numbers refer to stock rundown.

c/ Change in total stock and policy effect: positive numbers indicate an increase in supplies due to stock and policy changes.

volume that would have been generated in the absence of the major price support programs. Production impacts were assumed to follow policy changes by one year, with consumption effects instantaneous. Stocks policies were defined as variations from a constant (or zero) level of stocks, even where such stocks were not under direct government control. A positive "trade volume effect" can be interpreted as the additional trade surplus in wheat generated by policy-induced production and the accompanying reduction in consumption due to price supports. This trade volume effect became negative during 1974–1976, as a result of policies designed to hold down domestic prices.

The rationale for adding stock changes to these policy impacts is to indicate whether these had the effect of offsetting the policy impact or of reinforcing such policies. Increasing stock levels at times of high prices accentuates the effect of domestic stabilization policies on world markets: when markets are adequately supplied, such stock accumulation removes from the market the extra net exports implied by price supports. If these net stocks-plus-policy effects are reasonably constant, the impact on world markets is confined to resource allocation rather than stability. The notable feature of the last few years, as illustrated in Table 8.4, is the extent to which this "total" policy effect switched from generating extra supplies in the period up to 1972/73 to creating extra demands on the market in 1973/74. Comparing these two years alone, one can see from the table that the price policies were "responsible" for the effective removal of nearly 12 million tons of wheat from the market: adding stock changes in the developed countries to this increased the figure to 24 million tons, and including Soviet stocks as well gave a total market "squeeze" of nearly 36 million tons.[8]

This total stock-and-price-policy impact reached its peak in 1972/73, with an estimated 31 million tons of wheat generated by stock rundown and price policy surpluses. By 1974/75 the corresponding figure was –7.4 million tons, with price policies reducing net availability and stocks beginning to be accumulated once again. The table also shows these total figures as changes from the previous year. Over the two-year period 1972/73 to 1974/75 the total policy impact was a reduction in net availability of 38.4 million tons. This should not be taken to mean that nearly 40 million tons was in fact held off the market: rather that with no price support policies in these countries and with constant stock levels the situation on world markets would have been the same as if 40 million more tons of wheat had been available over these two seasons.

Though this figure is considerable when seen in the context of the wheat market over these years, it should be interpreted with care. The charge cannot be sustained that the developed countries "created" a shortage by means of stock and price-support policies. In the absence of those policies it appears that wheat prices would have been somewhat higher over the period up to and including 1973/74, when the actual world price reached $170 per ton. Stock release and price protection in that year were still generating perhaps 7 million tons "extra" wheat over the situation that might have held if there were free markets and constant stocks in developed countries. Since 1974/75, wheat prices would have been somewhat lower in the absence of developed country policies. The high price in 1973 was not "caused" by the policies as such, but the change in prices from those prevailing before 1972 would have been much less, as they would have started from a higher base, and the duration of the "crisis" would have been diminished.

This can be put in another way. The Soviet purchase of 14 million tons of wheat (net of exports) in 1972/73 came at a time both when stocks were adequate and price-supported surpluses existed. The opportunity afforded by the intervention in the market of the USSR as an importer was welcomed by those countries with stocks and with expensive domestic programs. Soviet stocks had already been run down in previous years. Without the developed country stock release, market prices in 1972 would have risen considerably. But this action rebounded the next year. The Soviet Union built up stocks from a good harvest, more than absorbing the further stock depletion in the SDCs and their remaining surplus production. The net effect of Soviet and SDC stocks policies (and price policies in the SDCs) was to reduce supplies by nearly 7 million tons in 1973/74. Again it is the difference between this effect and that in the previous year that indicate the impact on price changes. This difference is nearly 36 million tons between 1972/73 and 1973/74. Coming at a time when developing country production was down (and when the cost of other imports, notably energy) was sharply up, this "squeeze" on the market was clearly a major reason for a 70 percent increase in the average export price over the year. The impact on prices in 1974/75 would have been worse if the Soviet Union had not released 11 million tons from stocks, indicating a combined stock-and-policy effect of an additional 4 million tons, an improvement of 10 million tons over the previous year as far as other countries were concerned.

This leads to the conclusion that developed country policies inadvertently exacerbated the problems in this period which arose from production variability. Stocks policies did not offset the impact of domestic policy changes. Instead they tended to reinforce these changes, moving in the same direction in every year from 1970/71 to 1975/76, inclusive. This is at the heart of the problem. For world price stability, stocks have to accumulate when domestic policies are generating overproduction until such policies can be changed, and have to be run down when domestic price stability objectives dictate that an increase in home supplies is necessary. Over the first half of the decade, policies were not responding in this fashion. Stocks were released onto markets as a way of exporting domestic overproduction and were accumulated just when consumption was higher and production lower than would have been the case under freer markets. This is the major impact of domestic policies on world market price stability.

These results illustrate the interrelationships that are crucial to an examination of food security. They indicate that even though stocks policies may over time appear to offset actual production changes and hence minimize the transmission of production variations (as in Table 8.2, above), a closer look suggests that they often reinforce the tendency of policies in domestic markets to shift the burden of instability or to avoid the "importation" of such instability from abroad. The international discussion of food security must grapple both with the problem of aggregate instability in production and with the mechanisms that operate to shift the burden of such instability onto markets that may be less able to cope with their effects.

International Policy Alternatives

International schemes and initiatives regarding the problem of instability in markets have not been lacking. Support at a political level for any particular scheme has been less forthcoming. Three broad approaches have been discussed in recent years. The first is to increase the level and/or the price responsiveness of stocks in the system. This has taken several forms including financial and technical assistance in the construction of storage facilities in developing countries, coordination of stock management among governments, and the ownership of reserves by an international body. The second has been to increase the variability of consumption in developed countries, again by various means ranging from abstinence during scarcity to reform of domestic farm and food-price policies. The third has tackled the problem from a financial viewpoint, advocating some form of payments aid or food aid to alleviate foreign exchange problems. Each of these approaches has its own characteristics of political attractiveness, of economic impact, and of the distribution of costs and advantages. In keeping with the aims of this chapter, none of these will be discussed in detail here. But the analysis of the preceding pages may help to put them into perspective.

The stocks option has its own attractions. At a domestic level, adequate stocks appear to give a degree of autonomy over food supplies that may be missing when resort to world markets must always follow poor harvests at home. Even discounting the fact that stocks will seem much more desirable in high price periods, the recent interest shown by countries in increasing storage capacity would indicate that this aspect of marketing may have been neglected in the past. Storage policies could also have an important role in some cases of reducing (or capturing for the government) the arbitrage rents of various "middlemen." In addition, they can facilitate the development of internal distribution systems and provide more stable seasonal supplies. But as a food security instrument greater reserve levels as such have their limitations. Since holding and managing stocks is expensive, a general attempt at the international level to impose an undue burden on developing countries in the form of increased stockholding may be regressive. The profits from stockholding for an individual importing country, particularly if its market is small in size, are derived from speculating against world market price changes. The amount of information needed and the ability to move into and out of stocks as conditions dictate place limits on the wisdom of such a policy, but such a strategy will not always require substantial physical holdings of grain by the country concerned. Other alternatives are available that might give the same degree of security at a lower cost.

What is true for the individual small country may not be the case for the large grain trader. Two situations can be distinguished. The large importer of grain may feel constrained to carry reserves if there is the likelihood that greater-than-average purchases will push up the import price considerably. The marginal import cost might be high relative to the marginal cost of grain from storage—an economic justification for the political feeling that supply security can be enhanced by stocks. The same arguments with respect to internal transportation and marketing as mentioned above hold a fortiori for the geographically large and populous developing country. The significant grain exporter will have other motives for holding reserves, in particular to retain credibility as a supply source. In this sense, exporter reserves assist the food security objectives of importing regions. As was indicated by the analysis above, for any given set of trading conditions the ability of developing (and developed) importing countries to use trade rather than domestic stocks to offset production variability rests on the existence of variable stocks elsewhere in the world and in particular in the developed exporting countries. Other countries have a direct interest in the way these exporter stocks are managed.[9]

Much of the discussion of reserves has recently revolved around the international coordination of stock policies. This gives rise to the question as to whether such coordination brings benefits over and above those arising from the existence of stocks held under national initiative. There is a strong presumption that just as private stocks within a country may be inadequate from a national point of view so national stocks may not be sufficient from an international perspective.[10] This arises from the fact that a risk shared is a risk reduced. A government may wish to indemnify private traders from large losses (possibly in return for a share in abnormal profits). Similarly trading partners may wish to bear some of the risks to individual countries in return for greater security. But, as one would expect, the negotiation of such a system has proved to be difficult, as each participant has pressed for a higher degree of risk taking and cost bearing by the others.

The second kind of solution to instability is to increase consumption adjustments in developed countries. The analytical approach of this chapter suggests this as a direct alternative to the manipulation of stocks in terms of evening out production variability. State trading and central plan countries can adjust world market purchases, should they wish, to avoid putting strain on available supplies in times of world shortage. They could increase imports when supplies are more than adequate. In doing so, their own foreign exchange costs might be made more stable. Countries that rely more on the price mechanism—whether or not distorted by trade barriers—for deciding on imports would be expected to allow price changes to stimulate consumption adjustments directly. The somewhat weaker mechanisms of moral suasion and voluntary abstinence have also been suggested. There are two problems with the consumption adjustment approach. First, it clashes with strong stability motives in these countries not just in terms of the consumer price level but also with respect to the cyclical behavior of the livestock sector. Secondly, it does not entirely solve, though it might somewhat alleviate, the foreign exchange problem of developing country importers. Nevertheless, this approach does bring into the open the interrelationship in the world food economy between developing and developed country policies. The extent to which such policies can be reconciled in this way determines the need for other measures such as stock management and foreign exchange facilities.

The various plans that address the foreign exchange problem come under two headings. The first group relates foreign exchange assistance directly to developing country import patterns. It envisages either a set of financial transfers linked to the variability of food import costs designed to improve the balance of payments of the importer and reduce that country's budget burden, or an additional line of credit to enable commercial imports to be paid for at a later date. It will be apparent from the analysis above that this type of solution is of a different nature than those involving stock and consumption adjustments. It does not in itself address the problem of global variability. To the extent that it allows countries to continue and strengthen policies that insure domestic consumption it increases the need for (and the profitability of holding) stocks. It aggravates the global adjustment problem and, without more flexible stocks or adjustments in developed country consumption, tends to destabilize prices. Such comments are not meant to reflect on the merits of these schemes but merely put them into perspective. Their objective is to reconcile the conflict noted earlier between the interest of a country in maintaining consumption patterns and stabilizing prices and the uncomfortably destabilizing implications of this for the foreign exchange account. They enable countries to participate in trade to a greater extent. Combined with more flexibility in stocks or with developed country consumption adjustments, they allow for both international stability and domestic food security; alone, they might promote the latter at the expense of the former.

The second group of foreign exchange-related policies is analytically similar, though with different connotations. Concessional food sales, both bilateral and multilateral, might be considered as the "traditional" approach to world food security. The recent emphasis has been to attempt to untie the link that has existed between food aid flows and domestic farm policies. Food aid that is dependent upon erratic surpluses in developed countries is not considered to be a sound basis for food planning in developing countries.[11] Food aid should therefore be made more directly a function of developing country needs, such as result from domestic harvest fluctuations. A guarantee of supplies to cover such needs would ensure that the developing country could avoid holding large domestic reserves—either of grain or of foreign exchange. The stocks necessary to underwrite such an "insurance" policy would presumably be held by the exporter, and the impact on global security would depend on whether the net change in stock flexibility was adequate to allow greater consumption stability. A policy of this type therefore has implications for the commercial as well as the concessional market. Again, as with more direct import-assistance schemes, the greater level of consumption stability engendered by the policy, or the reduction in recipient stock level changes, will impose a somewhat greater burden on the rest of the trading system in terms either of consumption adjustment or stock management. The objective—to remove some degree of security cost from the developing country—must be met by assuming corresponding responsibilities elsewhere in the market.

What is important to the importer or food aid recipient is the implicit price level: the degree of concession in the aid, relating to conditions of payment as well as nominal price. A lower import price is tantamount to reducing foreign exchange costs for a particular import volume, but does not necessarily reduce foreign exchange costs if import quantities are elastic with respect to price changes. This depends on the way in which the importing government disposes of the food aid on the domestic market. The difference between this type of policy and that concerned directly with foreign exchange cost is that concessional sales have a price effect, at least for the government concerned. The granting of a line of credit or the transfer of compensatory finance would be expected to have a more general impact on the economy and on trading patterns as a whole. One might say that nonfood security is enhanced by such policies. The price effect of concessional sales will have such a wealth effect too, but its more direct impact will be on the decision as to how much of the favored foodstuff to import.

The intent of this chapter is to raise questions and suggest a structured approach to food security problems. The main argument has been built around a simple set of identities regarding trade volumes. Such elementary observations seem occasionally to be overlooked. There has been a tendency for some commentators, for instance, to view the variability of stocks levels per se as a cause for concern, leading to suggestions that governments stabilize stock levels either individually or collectively. This is tantamount to insuring that consumption be made as variable as production. Happily, governments have resisted the lure of stock-level stabilization. But international discussions on the appropriate level of stocks to be accumulated under particular stability and security schemes suggest that the paramount need for stocks to vary is not universally recognized. The relationship between stock management, price stability, and trade is complex: the link between production, consumption, and stock quantities involves only basic accounting identities. The policy questions thus revolve around the political desirability of imparting additional stability to particular magnitudes, such as consumption levels, and the use of various instruments to perform this task. The examination of such policies requires that the corresponding increase in instability in other variables also be discussed. If all stability schemes made clear the implication for the variability of other elements in the system, the economic and political nature of the choice would be that much clearer.

Notes

1. It is sometimes implied that because variability in world production is less than the sum of variations in each country, freer trade reduces the need for offsetting consumption or stock changes. This is misleading, if not actually false. Aggregate production changes imply the same aggregate stock and consumption changes irrespective of the degree of freedom of trade. But whereas with no trade one country might be forced to consume (or store) less while another was consuming (or storing) more in a particular year, with trade these changes would be unnecessary. This is the sense in which trade influences the distribution of instability but not the total magnitude.

2. This is, of course, not the same as the "profit" from storage in that year arising from the difference between acquisition and sales prices of stocks (adjusted for costs and forgone interest). But over a period of years cash flows and gross profits will equate. In the present context, cash flow is emphasized mainly because of its relevance in discussions of the funding of reserve programs.

3. This situation is quite distinct from the other types of market isolation, arising from fixed domestic prices and variable trade barriers, as discussed below. A closed submarket "exports" none of its instability, whereas a price-unresponsive submarket "exports" all of its instability. The closed submarket "imports" no instability, whereas the fixed-price market absorbs instability in foreign exchange and government sector accounts without adjusting trade volumes. The implications for the world market as a whole differ considerably.

4. The concept of a change from the previous year of the level stock accumulation may seem unduly obscure, but its relevance is confirmed by the identities in Table 8.1. It is not sufficient to combine the actual stock change in a particular year with the production and consumption changes to obtain the trade surplus change. In 1969/70 for example, stocks actually increased by 2.8 million tons. But this did not imply a drop of 16.7 million tons in the export surplus. It was the difference between the stock increase of 20.2 million tons in 1968/69 and the 2.8 million tons in 1969/70 that effectively "released" 17.4 million tons to enable consumption to rise by 5.5 million tons, trade by 3.5 million tons, while production was down by 8.4 million tons relative to the previous year. The data presented here are from Josling (1980).

5. As developing market economies appeared to take only an extra 4.4 million tons of this surplus, the remainder presumably went to replenish reserves in countries not included in the table and to meet any higher import requirements that they may have had that year.

6. Some speculation on overseas trade might still be possible, but apart from the foreign exchange benefits of any profits this will not be relevant to the domestic market.

7. No attempt was made to estimate USSR policy impacts, though stock changes are included in Table 8.4. The difficulty in estimating Soviet output and consumption in the absence of government policies is obvious in a country where no clear market price mechanism is established. Since it is very likely that the effect of Soviet policy is similar to that in countries where farm support systems operate through market interventions, the figures in the table undoubtedly understate the impact on markets.

8. Soviet stock rundown in the next year (1974/75) more than offset the continued pressure from the developed countries on the wheat market.

9. Some of the most important developments in policy in recent years have, in the present context, been changes in internal stocks and reserve programs of major exporters and in the price conditions for their accumulation and release.

10. The differing attitudes of economists as to the appropriate management of stocks provides a further illustration of divergencies in objectives rather than a contest of alternative research methods. Stocks held for economic motives, matching a cost and a rate of return, may be very different in size and behavior from those designed to provide a particular path of prices or adequate to ensure a certain level of consumption. Added to the diversity of private, public, and international objectives, this makes the definition of an optimal stocks policy as much a political as an economic exercise.

11. In the light of the analysis of the relationship between production,

consumption, and stocks presented above, this criticism has to be modified somewhat. Farm product surpluses are not a readily identifiable item in the market balance identity: they are subsumed in the relationship between consumption, stocks, and trade. Thus the analysis of consumption, stocks, and trade changes incorporates concessional flows as well as those on commercial terms. Aid appropriations might be more forthcoming when commodities are in surplus and governments may make use of aid channels to divest embarrassing stocks. But the net availability of a commodity for export is not in itself changed by the existence of food aid outlets, just as the import requirements of developing countries per se are not related to the existence of surpluses. Surpluses will be disposed of somewhere, through trade or aid, and developing country governments will attempt to satisfy import needs on the best available terms. The natural ex-post link between food aid and surpluses does not seem to warrant excessive international concern.

References

Josling, Timothy. "Developed Country Agricultural Policies and Developing Countries Food Supplies: The Case of Wheat." *IFPRI Research Report No. 14.* Washington, D.C.: IFPRI, April 1980.

Part III

Disciplining Domestic Policies through the GATT and WTO

6

The GATT: Its Historical Role and Importance to Agricultural Policy and Trade

Tim Josling

Introduction

The multilateral trade system is facing its most significant challenge in recent years. The attractions of bilateral or regional trade pacts have been given a boost by the European Community's (EC) imaginative initiative to "complete" its internal market by the end of 1992. There is renewed talk of Pacific Rim trade associations. The U.S./Canada Free Trade Agreement, though not without its problems, has shown that like-minded countries can put together a package of trade liberalization in a relatively short period of time. Unilateral commercial diplomacy has also proved seductive, particularly in the U.S. Congress, where the temptation for one country to set rules and act as judge and jury is being encouraged by the "Super 301" provisions of the 1988 Omnibus Trade Act.

All this is taking place against the backdrop of a remarkably wide-ranging set of negotiations in the General Agreement on Tariffs and Trade (GATT)–the Uruguay Round. If successful, the GATT will have extended its influence to include trade in services and international aspects of property rights and investment policies. It will have strengthened its rules on nondiscrimination in government purchasing contracts, overhauled its dispute-settlement mechanism, and forged ties with the multilateral monetary and financial institutions. Among its most ambitious tasks, however, is to revise the rules of agricultural trade, making them apply with greater force and clarity to domestic agricultural policies. If this can be achieved, the Uruguay Round will rewrite the book on agricultural trade policy and influence farm product markets for years to come. But success in the Uruguay Round is by no means assured, and an outright failure could lead more people to agree with Lester Thurow that "GATT is dead," or with Susan Strange, who has stated that "if GATT were to slip below the water of Lac Leman, no one would notice."

The implications of success and failure are the subject of Professor Runge's chapter, "Prospects for the Uruguay Round in Agriculture." The task of this chapter is to provide some background to the GATT, and to the Uruguay Round negotiations in agriculture. An attempt will be made to stick to the historical perspective, with the understanding that "history" includes the comprehensive proposals of October to December 1989.

The GATT

The General Agreement on Tariffs and Trade has been described as an orphan among international institutions. It was negotiated in 1947 as a commercial code of conduct, part of a broader International Trade Organization (ITO). The treaty setting up the ITO (the Havana Charter) was never ratified by the U.S. Congress, who considered the charter's sweeping authority over trade policy too restricting on its own actions. The GATT slipped through on a technicality, as the U.S. president has authority to negotiate and conclude "executive agreements" in the trade area.[1] Though there have been recent suggestions that the ITO be revived, GATT has held up remarkably well as a low-key, small-secretariat institution with a limited and provisional mandate in international affairs.

The GATT provides a set of rules which the "contracting parties" agree to observe; acts as a forum for the negotiation of changes in trade barriers; and provides a means of settlement of disputes. The basic propositions embodied in the GATT are plainly liberal in intention, emphasizing the mutual benefits of freer trade, outlawing export subsidies and quota restrictions in most cases, and encouraging mutual reductions in bound tariffs. The GATT preaches nondiscrimination among member states, granting market access on the basis of "most-favored nation" status to all other contracting parties—subject to defined exceptions for customs unions and developing countries. It allows for the settlement of disputes, for compensation for the impairment of benefits, and ultimately for trade sanctions against violators of the agreement. Though originally oriented largely toward western industrial countries, its membership has now expanded to ninety-six nations, and includes many developing countries and some central European economies. Seven rounds of negotiations have been successfully completed since the inception of the GATT, which have led effectively to a low-tariff system for manufactured products in developed-country markets. The eighth such round, the Uruguay Round, has been underway since September 1986.

Agriculture in the GATT

From the beginning, agriculture proved a problem area for the GATT system of more liberal trade. Quantitative import restrictions on agricultural goods were excluded from the agreement's strictures against nontariff restrictions on trade (Article XI), provided that the country in question practised supply control. Variable levies are not presently mentioned in the GATT, and hence fall outside the GATT disciplines.[2] Primary products were explicitly excluded from the general prohibition on export subsidies (Article XVI). Although other parts of the agreement do require that governments manage their domestic agricultural policies so as not to harm the legitimate interests of others, and oblige governments to consult on agricultural trade problems, these provisions have been rarely applied. Waivers were frequently sought to exempt particular agricultural policy actions from the GATT code. Most notable among these derogations was the waiver granted to the United States in 1955, which effectively removed the major elements of U.S. agricultural policy from international scrutiny.[3] This insistence by the U.S., as the guiding force in the early years of GATT, that domestic policies should not be subject to international limitations, has severely hampered attempts to liberalize trade in farm products. More recently, the tacit acceptance by most countries of the Common Agricultural Policy (CAP) of the European Community, even though its major instruments have uncertain legality in the GATT, has reinforced the notion of the primacy of domestic policy in international trade discussions.

One measure of the unsatisfactory nature of agricultural trade rules is the number of complaints brought in the GATT in this area. Since 1976, there have been nineteen occasions when a GATT panel has been appointed to look into an agricultural trade complaint, out of a total of thirty-two GATT cases over this period. Twelve of these nineteen complaints involved objections against the EC, and included products ranging from pasta and wheat flour to poultry, citrus, beef, apples, sugar, and animal feed. Two reasons stand out as to why the EC is so often cited by trading partners: the widespread use of targeted export subsidies (refunds), relatively unconstrained by spending curbs; and a switch from deficit to surplus in many products, unaccompanied by a sufficient reduction in support prices to take account of that change. As a consequence, EC export (and import) policies have been under attack in the GATT for two decades. But the impact of these actions on the CAP has been minimal. Indeed, until recently, it has been difficult to find any examples of domestic policy changes stemming directly from GATT rulings.[4]

Previous Negotiation Rounds

The ineffectiveness of the GATT regulations in dealing with illiberal elements of national agricultural policy has not prevented the incorporation of agricultural discussions in the recent GATT rounds of trade negotiations. Though domestic policies have (until now) been kept off the agenda, a modest degree of liberalization has been achieved through the reduction of tariffs and the establishment of tariff-free quotas for certain products. A number of agricultural tariffs were "bound" in the Dillon Round of trade talks (1960-1961), when the newly formed European Community negotiated the necessary changes in member-state duties on imports from third countries. Some of these commodities, such as soybeans, high-protein meals, and cassava, later became big-ticket items in international trade—much to the discomfort of EC policy-makers and to the credit of the GATT.[5]

The isolation of agriculture from the GATT began to change in the mid-1960s. The U.S. became convinced that it had a comparative advantage in agricultural products, and that this profitable trade was being hampered by protection in other countries. In the Kennedy Round (1964-1967), a major discussion about the nature of agricultural trade policy took place, with the United States arguing for a return to the GATT notion of a market-oriented trading system, and the European Community generally favoring managed markets through commodity agreements. This philosophical difference was never solved, and echos of it are still evident today.

At one stage in the negotiations, the EC proposed a temporary binding of support levels, relative to negotiated reference prices (the "montant de soutien" proposal), but this was rejected by the United States as perpetuating rather than removing the protectionist policies in importing countries. Finally, an "agricultural component" of the Kennedy Round was put together, which included in particular an International Grains Arrangement (IGA) (1967), a modified version of earlier International Wheat Agreements. The market stabilization provisions of the IGA had a short life, as surplus grain production soon pushed prices below the established minima, and grain-producing countries proved unwilling to hold either exports or domestic output in check.[6]

In the next round of talks, usually known as the Tokyo Round, which concluded in 1979, agriculture again appeared high on the agenda. The underlying issue was still the extent to which agricultural trade should be subject to the same rules as trade in manufactured goods. Should markets be free or managed? Should domestic policies be the subject for negotiations? Should export subsidies be banned or otherwise controlled? Should quantitative trade barriers be phased out? And, should importers be able to shield their markets from disruption? Disagreements on these fundamental issues persisted through the Tokyo Round, and prevented any substantial progress toward liberalization. Some quantitative restrictions were relaxed (in particular by Japan), and two commodity agreements were concluded (for dairy products and for meat), neither endowed with the instruments to stabilize markets. At the same time, talks proceeded on another International Wheat Agreement, once more serving as an agricultural "component" in the round, though in reality the product of a separate set of negotiations. It suffered a worse fate than the IGA: it proved unpopular with developing countries and never saw the light of day.

One development of the Tokyo Round, the attempt to refine the rules governing export subsidies and countervailing duties, held out some promise for agricultural trade. The Subsidies-Countervail Code obliged countries to avoid export subsidies that lead either to an "inequitable" share in world markets or undercut prices. However, the implementation of that code, through the challenge within the GATT of certain practices (such as the EC's export refunds), has not been successful. Interpretation of such concepts as an "equitable" market share lead inevitably to conflicts and can render meaningless the spirit of the original agreement.[7]

Whether the GATT can improve its effectiveness in dealing with agricultural issues is being put to the test in the current GATT round of negotiations, the Uruguay Round, which includes agriculture as a centerpiece. How far this initiative can proceed depends upon whether the countries concerned, particularly the EC and the U.S., have confidence in a multilateral mechanism for resolving trade issues in agriculture.

Lead-up to the Uruguay Round

International agencies have little influence over domestic policies under normal conditions, but every now and then political and economic circumstances conspire to produce a demand for the product of the international bureaucracy. The period from 1982 to 1986 was such a time. The EC and the U.S. watched as their agricultural spending rose almost out of control; the U.S. lost much of its market share painfully accumulated over the 1970s; and even Canada began to reverse a trend toward more liberal policies. Both the GATT and the Organization for Economic Cooperation and Development (OECD) were at hand to offer solutions to the problems. Their initial responses were characteristically different. In November 1982, the GATT Council established a Committee of Trade in Agriculture (CTA) to look into the ways in which agricultural trade could be better handled within the GATT framework. Many of their proposals, tabled in November 1984, addressed the issue of the way in which existing GATT articles and codes could be applied more effectively. Particular attention was given to the implementation of Article XI, which allows quantitative restrictions on agricultural imports under certain circumstances, and Article XVI, which condones export subsidies for primary products.

Meanwhile, a parallel activity was going on in the OECD. Agricultural policies in OECD member countries have been studied by the secretariat in the past and have been discussed in the Agriculture Committee. But unlike macroeconomic policy, where such discussions of national policies have led to a degree of coordination, OECD discussions of agricultural policies have rarely gone beyond the descriptive. The OECD ministerial meeting in May 1982 gave the secretariat a mandate to undertake "an analysis of the approaches and methods for a balanced and gradual reduction in the protection of agriculture . . . an examination of relevant national policies and measures which have a significant impact on agricultural trade . . . [and] an analysis of the most appropriate methods for improving the functioning of the world agricultural market."[8] This initiative, known as the Trade Mandate, was to be supervised jointly by the Committee on Agriculture and the Trade Committee. This joint committee reported the results of its study to the Ministerial Council of the OECD in May 1987.

The OECD interpreted the mandate in an appropriately broad way, and looked at the whole range of domestic agricultural policies. Building on a quantitative measure of farm support used previously in the Food and Agricultural Organization (FAO), the OECD calculated Producer Subsidy Equivalents (and Consumer Subsidy Equivalents) for several member countries. Though countries with high levels of protection were less than enthusiastic with this attempt to quantify the effect of support policies, the Trade Mandate report represented a milestone in the discussion of agricultural policies and trade. In what constituted an important political development, details of national policies were openly discussed for the first time in a quantitative framework, and trade impacts were examined in an even-handed way. Subsequent decisions to update the calculations have suggested that countries find them useful as information for improved policy decisions. [9]

The OECD ministers, in May 1987, confirmed their commitment to trade negotiations, but went further in advocating changes in domestic programs toward a greater market orientation. The ministers called for concerted efforts to reform domestic farm policies, with the long-run aim of allowing market forces to determine production patterns. Although short-term palliatives, such as supply controls, were accepted as useful, and adjustment assistance was considered desirable, the emphasis was on liberalization. Income objectives were to be dealt with in ways that did not distort trade patterns or impose undue costs on other countries. High-level encouragement for this process came from the Tokyo Summit in 1986 and the Venice Summit in 1987. The Toronto Summit in 1988 confirmed the importance of progress in this area of international cooperation, and urged a comprehensive framework for the agricultural talks.

The Uruguay Round

The GATT effort culminated in the launching of the Uruguay Round in September 1986. The Punta del Este Declaration opened up the way for negotiations on all agricultural programs that influence trade in farm products. The section on agriculture called for "greater liberalization" and "more operationally effective GATT rules and disciplines" regarding all "measures affecting import access and export competition." It was made clear that the measures referred to include domestic policies as well as border measures. The inclusion of domestic support policies represented a new departure, which recognized that domestic policy reform provides the key to progress in agricultural trade relations.

The 1987 Proposals

Countries were invited to submit by the end of 1987 their ideas for the conduct of the negotiations, and their proposals for the implementation of the aims of the Punta del Este Declaration. The responses were more far-reaching than most observers expected, and much more imaginative than in previous rounds. It looked almost as if governments were eager to negotiate over policies they had so long held sacrosanct. The U.S. responded first, tabling a proposal in July 1987; the Cairns Group and the European Community followed with their own proposals in October 1987, together with a separate paper by Canada (even though it is a member of the Cairns Group). By early 1988 two more proposals had been introduced, one from Japan and another from the Nordic Countries (Sweden, Finland, Norway, and Iceland). Papers by Korea and by a group of developing countries (Egypt, Jamaica, Mexico, Morocco, and Peru), together with declarations from India, Nigeria, and Switzerland, were also tabled.

The U.S. proposal called for the elimination of "all policies which distort [agricultural] trade" over a ten year period. Certain domestic policies would be exempt, as only having a small impact on production and trade. These would include domestic food assistance programs, international food aid, and any "safety net" farm income programs not linked to the level of production. The Cairns Group shared the U.S. view of a liberalized agricultural market, but added a preliminary stage—a freeze in present subsidy levels. The EC paper appeared more concerned with short-term market imbalances, but agreed that a reduction in support prices was necessary over the long run. At the other extreme, the Japanese position implied that trade problems were the fault of the exporting countries, and that domestic policies were not subject to international negotiation.

Negotiations on domestic policies pose a tricky problem for the comparison of trade effects. The variety of measures used make the process less than transparent. In this respect, the OECD work fitted in well with the GATT aims. All the major proposals, except for Japan's, supported the use of an aggregate measure of support (AMS), based on the OECD's Producer Subsidy Equivalent (PSE), though most countries suggested that this be modified to take into account supply control, and the EC wanted the measure to consider changes in the exchange rate as well.[10] This technique of using an AMS held out the prospect of giving a clear focus to the liberalization aspect of the agricultural talks similar to that of a tariff-cut target in other areas. Countries would be free to modify policies in their own way, subject to the limitation that the overall level of support be reduced according to the agreement.

Discussion of these proposals took place during 1988, in the GATT meetings in Geneva. Seven meetings of the Agricultural Negotiating Group were held between February and November. In addition, the group set up technical working parties to consider the issues of the use of an AMS and of sanitary and phytosanitary regulations. The major participants also spelled out their own proposals over the year in additional papers. The Cairns Group introduced the notion that, in addition to the freeze in support levels, countries should agree to a two-year "down payment" on longer-term reform. This would ensure that policy changes were started during the negotiations, rather than awaiting their conclusion. The EC elaborated on its own short-term proposals, but declined to spell out what they had in mind for the longer-term reform. For much of the year, the U.S. stuck to its position that no short-term action was required, other than an immediate start on the long-term program. By the end of the year, the U.S. indicated its willingness to talk about short-term measures, so long as the goal of long-term elimination of support had been agreed upon. The EC found this position unacceptable, claiming that it went far beyond the mandate of Punta del Este.

Lack of agreement on the longer-term program for agriculture threatened the timetable for the Uruguay Round as a whole. The Midterm Review, held in December 1988 in Montreal, was intended to endorse at the ministerial level the progress so far, and set the agenda for the remaining two years of negotiations. In the event, the Montreal meeting broke up with no agreement on agriculture, and several agreements that had been reached on other issues were put on hold. The GATT director-general was asked to try to find a compromise on this (and some other outstanding issues) in order to allow the round to continue. A compromise framework for negotiations was finally agreed upon on April 7, 1989, in Geneva, to complete the Midterm Review.

The Midterm Agreement

The April agreement did not resolve the many issues that had separated the negotiating positions of the major participants, but it did provide a framework for their eventual resolution. Equally as important, it mandated a timetable for the workplan, which instilled some urgency and discipline into the negotiations. The main provisions of the agreement were a short-term commitment to freeze policy prices, a decision to substantially reduce support levels over a period of years, and an obligation to discuss revision of GATT rules governing agriculture, including those dealing with plant and animal health regulations and food safety. Countries also agreed to specify to what extent developing countries would be expected to accept all the obligations of the GATT rules.

The short-run program called for a two-year freeze in support levels, import access barriers, and national prices (in nominal terms), and registered an "intent" to reduce protection in 1990 by an unspecified amount. Policy prices had been edging downwards since 1986 in the EC, the U.S., and Japan, as a reaction to high budget costs and low world prices at the time. It is not clear whether or not the freeze has had a major impact on this trend. On the other hand, the freeze does appear to have helped guard against an upsurge in domestic prices in response to the higher world prices of the past year.

The second element of the April agreement was long-term reform in agricultural policies. Countries agreed to negotiate a "substantial, progressive reduction in agricultural support sustained over an agreed period of time." The time period remains to be decided, and the level of reductions was not specified. The U.S. appeared to accept that its goal of zero trade-distorting support within ten years was not going to be agreed to by others. Also still to be agreed upon is the mechanism for achieving this reduction. The two main candidates are negotiations on specific policies, including conversion to tariffs, and negotiations of commitments on an aggregate measure of support. It now seems likely that both will be used in various ways during the negotiations.

The third element in the April agreement was for changes in GATT rules. Two rules in particular have been notably significant in agricultural trade. Article XI specifies conditions under which quantitative trade barriers are allowed. Among these exceptions is one for situations where domestic supply is also controlled by quantitative means; some countries would like this exception removed. Participants in the negotiations seem to agree that it is time to get rid of the exceptions and waivers (though the negotiating value of relinquishing a waiver has yet to be tested), and to clarify the status of "grey area" import measures.

Article XVI allows export subsidies on primary products, although stipulating that countries should "seek to avoid their use." Countries have not taken this advice, and even with the negotiation of a Subsidies-Countervail Code in the Tokyo Round, the problem has proved intractable. Moreover, many domestic policies act as indirect subsidies to exports, including U.S. deficiency payments for grains. No consensus has emerged on how to deal with export and domestic subsidies by changing rules. An outright ban on this type of subsidy has been suggested, but the EC views this as both impracticable and inequitable. Constraints on the level of export subsidies may be possible, and the quantities exported with the aid of such subsidies could be limited. With firm world prices, these agreements could be workable. Whether they would be sustainable at a time when world prices were depressed, as happened in 1986, is much less certain.

Less dramatic than support reduction and export subsidies, but still important for agricultural trade, is the area of sanitary and phytosanitary regulations (SPR). The Punta del Este Declaration made special mention of the need to "minimize the adverse effects that sanitary and phytosanitary regulations and barriers can have on trade in agriculture." Behind this apparent agreement, the different approaches to the problem are still to be reconciled. The U.S. view emphasizes the need to base domestic regulations on internationally agreed standards, and to recognize the equivalence of different regulations (i.e., those that provide substantially the same protection to the consumer). The EC has been less explicit on such matters, and has argued for the negotiation of a "framework of rules" governing harmonization of standards. The need for equivalence is not fully accepted, and the EC also places less emphasis on the scientific basis for international regulation. The Cairns Group also favors a negotiation on a long-term framework based on strict justification for protecting human and animal health. It recognizes the value of equivalence where harmonization is not possible, but the unwillingness of Australia to sign the Standards Code has left it difficult for the Cairns Group to support the U.S. position more fully.

The Comprehensive Proposals

Under the timetable of the Midterm Agreement, countries were to present their ideas for a package of reforms, including the reduction in support and the changes in GATT rules, by the end of 1989. In October, the U.S. presented the first of these "comprehensive" proposals, which builds upon earlier papers but contains considerably more detail on the implementation of reforms. The proposal itself is organized by category of policy instrument–import access, export subsidies, domestic subsidies, sanitary and phytosanitary barriers, and distinctive treatment for developing countries. As discussed above, the three negotiating methods under consideration are changing GATT rules, reducing support by an AMS, and negotiating on specific policies and commodities.

The U.S. comprehensive proposal places a heavy burden on negotiating changes in GATT rules. Import access is to be tackled by getting rid of all nontariff import barriers. Tariff quotas would protect export interests over a ten-year transition period, and other safeguards are designed to prevent too rapid an increase in imports. Specific levels of tariffs, along with the amount of the tariff-rate quota, would be negotiated. Quantitative restrictions would be removed by the end of the transition, thus eliminating the need for the current waivers and exceptions. Export subsidies would also be removed (over a five-year period) and the GATT rules changed accordingly.[11] For domestic subsidies, a set of regulations would define those that are prohibited (i.e., those that reward farmers on the basis of current output) and those that are permitted (i.e., those that are effectively decoupled or only indirectly linked to output). Domestic subsidies falling between these two categories would be "disciplined" by negotiated reductions in the level of support afforded by such policies. New procedures would be developed to strengthen notification, consultation, and dispute-settlement obligations for sanitary and phytosanitary trade barriers.

Countries would need to present and agree to sweeping changes in domestic price-support programs, each being locked in to a ten-year program of domestic policy reinstrumentation. The U.S. originally pushed for the use of an AMS, as a way of capturing the totality of agricultural policy instruments in one comparative figure. When it became clear that a zero target for the protection level was not feasible, concern grew that countries might try to evade the trade implications of support reductions by shifting policies. It was feared that reductions in the AMS might not be translated into visible trade gains. Though many of the these concerns can be met by the appropriate definition of the AMS, the feeling grew that it would be desirable to deal with specific policies to enable exporters to target priority importer practices. The AMS finds only a minor role in the U.S. proposal, as a way of measuring these policies that fall neither into the prohibited nor the permitted list. These policies, largely input and investment subsidies that are not tied to particular commodities, would be subject to a phase-down over a period of years.

The Cairns Group tabled its own comprehensive proposals for the agricultural negotiations in December 1989. Like the U.S. plan, the Cairns Group emphasized import access and the control of export subsidies. Members also advocated conversion of nontariff measures to tariffs, and stressed the need for bringing all import measures under GATT coverage. For export subsidies, the Cairns Group proposal argued for a freeze and a progressive phase-out of these programs. They also suggested that the "option" of converting export subsidies to food aid should be made less attractive by limiting this type of aid to outright grants of food. The Cairns Group sees a somewhat larger role for the AMS than does the U.S., but treats it essentially as a scorecard to keep track of progress obtained by specific bargaining. The Cairns Group proposal on the reform of domestic policies is slightly more flexible than that of the U.S., allowing somewhat more choice of domestic policy instruments.

The EC "global proposal" showed perhaps the most willingness to bend from their previous position.[12] They reluctantly conceded that tariffication, in a modified form, could replace the present levy system on EC imports, and a careful reading between the lines suggests that a similar modification could be applied to EC export subsidies. So long as equivalent concessions were available on the main policy instruments of other trading partners, one could envisage a significant modification to EC policy following from such an agreement. The main thrust of the EC proposal is not, however, on changes in instruments. To the EC, negotiations on specific policies means attacking the CAP; by contrast, AMS negotiations would move some of the focus back onto the U.S. and Canada, who proved to have surprisingly high PSEs in 1986 and 1987. And an AMS negotiation might allow the EC to spare some sectors, and even to achieve an element of "rebalancing" in its policy. The EC is now the main enthusiast for an AMS approach.[13] Whether other countries will shift their own positions to accommodate the EC on this issue remains to be seen.[14]

Impacts of GATT on National Policies

The changes in national farm policies needed to improve both the domestic performance and the international acceptability of farm programs will not be easy. They will require significant skill in international negotiations and considerable political will at home. "Success," in some countries, requires that traditional forces that opposed these changes, and that have been able to block them in the past, be persuaded to remove their opposition. The Uruguay Round cannot dictate domestic farm policy change; any attempt to do so would condemn it to failure. But the round cannot ignore domestic policies and concentrate solely on trade rules or the exchange of trade concessions. Such tinkering with the symptoms has been a major part of the problem in the past. What is now possible is an outcome that *assists* the process of domestic reform, just as the trade problems themselves will be reduced by such reform.

It now appears possible that the Uruguay Round negotiations on agriculture could end in agreement which would:

a) specify a substantial reduction in the levels of support under farm programs;
b) encourage the reinstrumentation of policies toward more decoupling in domestic subsidies;
c) promote some recoupling of domestic markets with world market conditions (such as through tariffication);
d) restrain export subsidies, even if not removing them altogether; and
e) modify GATT rules to encourage and underpin these developments and to ease the resolution of any conflicts that may arise in the future.

Observers of the process tend to fall into two camps. One group, who might be called the "realists," consider the agricultural negotiations in the

Uruguay Round largely an exercise in illusion, a game played by trade officials at the periphery of agricultural policy. Whatever comes out of the round, they feel, will amount to minor changes in the trade rules and some collective but empty encouragement to domestic policy reforms. The chances of major farm policy changes being agreed upon in Geneva are remote; to pretend otherwise is fanciful at best and possibly even dangerous. It flies against all the experience of recent history and ignores political realities. Under such a "realistic" interpretation, the U.S. and the EC should not look to the GATT to reduce trade tensions. Some hard bargaining on a bilateral basis could yield results, but essentially the solutions lie in domestic politics and initiatives.

History and political logic is so firmly on the side of this interpretation that it seems foolhardy to argue otherwise. But there is another more "optimistic" interpretation of current events that is worth passing consideration. Suppose that special-interest politics and middle-class entitlement programs have now become less attractive to politicians. Imagine agricultural price policy becoming identified with transfers to wealthy families and with the degradation of the environment. Add a sense of frustration over agricultural trade squabbles from those in charge of commerce and commercial policy. It is not inconceivable that the GATT round under these circumstances could play a nontraditional role. The tail of trade policy could for once wag the domestic-policy dog. A bold agreement in the GATT could essentially dictate the framework for domestic policies for the next decade.

If the realist interpretation is proved correct, then the unimportance of the GATT in agricultural trade will have been confirmed. Once again, negotiations will have failed to find the elusive formula that allows domestic policies to run under internationally agreed rules, rather than bending international rules to fit domestic policies. There may be enough of an agreement to allow the Uruguay Round to be counted a "success" without, at the same time, challenging the dominance of domestic policies. Some deals could be struck that promised exporter constituencies greater access without seriously constraining domestic support. In such a case, the underlying problems will remain so long as the instrumentation of those policies, and the general level of support, is unchanged. Domestic pressures will work slowly to move support away from surplus-generating measures, but without external disciplines the temptation to resort to passing the burden to other countries will be irresistible. If world market demand were to become weak, then all the problems of the early 1980s will return. A scramble for markets will push up program costs and set in motion another cycle of reform.

The optimistic scenario offers a short cut to this process. By constraining domestic policies within effective GATT rules, countries would incur much greater risks when running policies that offer excessive protection to agriculture. Domestic policies would run up against these constraints and adapt more quickly. Trade conflicts would not disappear overnight, but they would take place in a framework of rules and obligations. This attractive scenario could just be enough to persuade negotiators to defy history and challenge political reality. If that were the case we could look back to the Uruguay Round as a turning point in international cooperation. The GATT would then truly have a role to play in agricultural policies and markets.

Notes

1. The establishment of the GATT and its legal constitution is described in McGovern (1986).
2. For a fuller discussion of the treatment of agriculture in the GATT see Hathaway (1987) and Hartwig, Josling, and Tangermann (1989).
3. The waiver allowed quantitative import restrictions, under Article 22 of the Agricultural Adjustment Act, to be used even in the absence of domestic supply control.
4. This situation may now be changing. Recent panel rulings on US sugar, EC oilseeds and Canadian dairy policies, each appear to have inescapable implications for a change in domestic policy.
5. It is ironic that the most notable agricultural "achievement" of the GATT, to bind EC duties on oilseeds and cereal substitutes, came in an otherwise unsuccessful round of negotiations, which ended with little agreement on liberalization of trade.
6. In the nonagricultural area, the Kennedy Round proved a significant success, with an across-the-board cut of 50 percent in bound tariffs.
7. For a discussion of the experience with Article XVI and the Subsidies Code, see Hartwig, Josling, and Tangermann (1989).
8. OECD (1987).
9. For a fuller discussion of the OECD work see Sanderson, Warley, and Josling (1990).
10. For a discussion of the use of an AMS in trade negotiations, see Hartwig, Josling, and Tangermann (1989).
11. The U.S. proposal also calls for the removal of the clause that allows export restrictions in time of domestic shortage.
12. Tangermann (1990) makes the point that the U.S. has considerably hardened its line on the reinstrumentation of domestic policies, while abandoning its goal of a zero level of trade-distorting support. The EC position has moved some way to meeting U.S. requests on changes in domestic policy, perhaps more than the rhetoric of the proposal would suggest. However, the EC also appears to have made such policy changes contingent upon agreement to "rebalancing" protection among sectors.

13. The EC has labeled its measure a Support Measurement Unit (SMU). It is essentially the OECD PSE corrected for supply control and measured using reference prices and exchange rates rather than current world prices.

14. The extent of the "common ground" between the proposals is explained in Bredahl, et al. (1990).

References

Bredahl, M., et al. *Report of the Task Force on the Comprehensive Proposals for Negotiations in Agriculture.* IATRC Working Paper No. 90-3 (1990).

Cohn, Theodore H. *The International Politics of Agricultural Trade.* Vancouver: University of British Columbia Press, 1990.

GATT. *Submission of the United States on Comprehensive Long-Term Agricultural Reforms.* Geneva: GATT, 1989.

———. *Comprehensive Proposal for the Long-Term Reform of Agricultural Trade: Submission by the Cairns Group.* Geneva: GATT, 1989.

———. *Global Proposal of the European Community on the Long-Term Objectives for the Multilateral Negotiation on Agricultural Questions.* Geneva: GATT, 1989.

———. *Negotiating Group on Agriculture: Submission by Japan.* Geneva: GATT, 1989.

———. *Ministerial Declaration on the Uruguay Round.* Geneva: GATT, 1986.

———. *United States Proposal for Negotiations on Agriculture.* Geneva: GATT, 1987.

———. *European Communities Proposal for Multilateral Trade Negotiations on Agriculture.* Geneva: GATT, 1987.

———. *Japanese Proposal for Negotiations on Agriculture.* Geneva: GATT, 1987.

———. *Proposal of the Nordic Countries.* Geneva: GATT, 1987.

———. *Final Text: Mid-Term GATT Review.* Geneva: GATT, 1989.

Hartwig, Bettina, Timothy Josling, and Stefan Tangermann. *Design of New Rules for Agriculture in the GATT.* Report to NCAP, Washington, D.C.: Resources for the Future, 1989.

Hathaway, Dale E. *Agriculture and the GATT: Rewriting the Rules.* Washington, D.C.: Institute for International Economics, 1987.

Josling, Timothy E. *Agriculture in the Tokyo Round Negotiations.* London: Trade Policy Research Centre, 1977.

McCalla, Alex. "The History of Agricultural Protectionism." *Journal of Agricultural History* (April 1971).

McGovern, Edmond. *International Trade Regulation: GATT, the United States and the European Community.* Exeter: Globefield Press, 1986.

Moyer, H.Wayne and Timothy Josling. *Agricultural Policy Reforms: Politics and Process in the EC and the USA.* Ames: Iowa State University Press, 1990.

OECD. *National Policies and Agricultural Trade.* Paris: OECD, 1987.

Sanderson, Fred H., T.K. Warley, and Tim Josling. "The Future of International Agricultural Relations: Issues in the GATT Negotiations." In Fred H. Sanderson, ed. *Agricultural Protectionism in the Industrialized World.* Washington, D.C.: Resources for the Future, 1990.

Tangermann, Stefan. "Options and Prospects: A Feasible Package." Department of Agricultural Economics and Business, University of Guelph, 1990.

Warley, T.K. "Implications for Canadian Agrifood." Department of Agricultural Economics and Business, University of Guelph, 1990.

———. "Western Trade in Agricultural Products." In Andrew Shonfield, ed. *International Economic Relations of the Western World 1959-71: Politics and Trade*. London: Oxford University Press/RIIA, 1976.

GJAE 59 (2010), Supplement
Perspectives on International Agricultural Policy – In Honor of the Retirement of Professor Stefan Tangermann

Reflections on the Exceptional Treatment of Agriculture in the WTO

Betrachtungen über die Sonderstellung des Agrarsektors in der WTO

Tim Josling
Stanford University, California, USA

Abstract

The GATT gave special treatment to agriculture by allowing quantitative import restrictions when domestic output was also controlled, and made an exception to the ban on export subsidies by allowing them for primary products, subject to somewhat weak and imprecise conditions. Both were concessions to the operation of domestic farm policies in developed countries, primarily the US and the UK and later Canada and the EU, and full advantage was taken of these legal exceptions. Subsidies in general had been treated leniently in the GATT with merely the obligation to notify if they impacted upon exports. Domestic subsidies for agricultural products had significant impacts on both imports and exports and were seen to be a significant part of the trade problem, but operated under minimal constraints. So the exceptional treatment of agriculture in the GATT had led to a dysfunctional trade regime.

The Uruguay Round faced up to the inchoate conditions on world markets and the deterioration of trade relations that these exclusions allowed. The Agreement on Agriculture (URAA) specifically banned quantitative restrictions on imports, except those introduced to guarantee access and banned new export subsidies, capping and reducing existing expenditures on the programs and the volumes that could be subsidized. Domestic subsidies that were deemed to be most trade-distorting were capped and modestly reduced. The Doha Round would, if completed, eliminate export subsidies, severely limit the ability to provide trade-distorting support, and reduce the bound tariffs by a considerable extent.

The URAA was negotiated at a time when the US and the EU were the main players in the agricultural policy space and it represented a way of disciplining trade to avoid conflicts and reduce protection. Domestic policies were reformed in a way that was consistent with the URAA constraints. If the Doha Round is successful, most of the special provisions for agriculture will no longer be needed. But at that stage the URAA may inadvertently hamper the process of developing trade rules that meet new challenges.

Key words

WTO; GATT; agricultural trade; exceptionalism; normalism

Zusammenfassung

Der Agrarsektor erfuhr im GATT eine Sonderbehandlung, indem quantitative Einfuhrbeschränkungen im Falle der Beschränkung der heimischen Produktion erlaubt wurden. Zudem wurde der Agrarsektor vom Verbot für Exportsubventionen ausgenommen: Sie wurden für Primärprodukte unter relativ schwachen und unpräzisen Bedingungen erlaubt. Dies waren Zugeständnisse an die Gestaltungsmöglichkeiten inländischer Agrarpolitik in Industrieländern, und die rechtlichen Ausnahmeregelungen wurden vor allem von den USA und dem Vereinigten Königreich, später auch von Kanada und der EU, intensiv genutzt. Subventionen wurden im GATT im Allgemeinen nachsichtig behandelt: Es bestand lediglich eine Notifikationspflicht, wenn sie sich auf die Exporte auswirkten. Inländische Subventionen für Agrarprodukte hatten allerdings häufig starke Auswirkungen auf den Außenhandel, dennoch gab es kaum Beschränkungen für ihren Einsatz. Somit resultierte die Sonderbehandlung des Agrarsektors im GATT in einem weitgehend dysfunktionalen Handelsregime.

Die Uruguay-Runde beendete die weitgehende Regelungsfreiheit des Weltagrarhandels. Mengenbeschränkungen auf Importe wurden im Agrarabkommen (URAA) von wenigen Ausnahmen abgesehen ausdrücklich verboten. Für die Ausgaben für Exportsubventionen sowie die subventionierten Exportmengen wurden Obergrenzen eingeführt und sukzessive reduziert. Die am stärksten handelsverzerrenden inländischen Subventionen wurden ebenfalls beschränkt und reduziert. Im Falle eines Abschlusses der laufen-

GJAE 59 (2010), Supplement
Perspectives on International Agricultural Policy – In Honor of the Retirement of Professor Stefan Tangermann

den Doha-Runde würden Exportsubventionen ganz unterbunden, die Möglichkeiten für handelsverzerrende inländische Subventionen stark eingeschränkt und die gebundenen Zollsätze erheblich abgesenkt.

Das URAA wurde zu einer Zeit verhandelt, zu der die USA und die EU die wichtigsten Akteure in der agrarpolitischen Landschaft darstellten. Es eröffnete die Möglichkeit, Außenhandel zu regeln, um Konflikte zu vermeiden und den Außenschutz zu verringern. Inländische Politiken wurden gemäß den Beschränkungen des URAA reformiert. Wenn die Doha-Runde erfolgreich ist, werden die meisten der Sonderbestimmungen des URAA für die Landwirtschaft nicht mehr gebraucht werden. An diesem Punkt könnte das URAA unbeabsichtigt die Entwicklung von Handelsregelungen, die den neuen Herausforderungen gerecht würden, behindern. Viele der Bestimmungen des URAA waren als Übergangsregeln wichtig, es stellt sich aber die Frage, an welchem Punkt wir uns vom URAA lösen sollten und welches Regelwerk wir stattdessen brauchen.

Schlüsselwörter

WTO; GATT; Agrarhandel; Sonderstellung

1 Introduction

Agriculture has, in almost all multilateral, bilateral or regional trade agreements, been accorded special treatment. This exceptional treatment reflects a number of factors, most of which can be traced back to the special attention afforded by developed country governments to their farming sectors in the post-war period. This attention had been manifested by substantial tariff protection for many staple commodities and by price supports implemented by the state in buying up, storing and often exporting surplus products with subsidies. In many cases the state became the main buyer of farm commodities: in all cases governments set up specific departments and agencies to assist, regulate and oversee the agricultural and food sectors. This special treatment reflected a range of concerns of an economic, political and social nature, all embedded in historical narratives, that open markets could not be trusted in the agricultural and food sectors. Agriculture was seen as somehow "different".[1]

Perhaps the most striking example of exceptional treatment in trade agreements emerged from the Uruguay Round of negotiations under the General Agreement on Tariffs and Trade (GATT). The Marrakesh Treaty setting up the World Trade Organization (WTO) contained an Agreement on Agriculture (URAA) that established detailed rules for domestic farm support policies as well as for import tariffs and export subsidies. No other sector of goods trade, with the temporary exception of textiles, has its own set of rules in the WTO.[2] The URAA was arguably necessary as a way of disciplining the exceptional treatment of agriculture in developed countries. To the extent that it has succeeded it is reasonable to raise the question of whether or not it is still needed. In any case the future of the special treatment of agriculture in the WTO hinges on the way in which the URAA develops over the next decade or two.

Exceptionalism in trade rules and high protection go together. Limited market access will tend to make the application of trade rules to the sector more problematic. And if the high protection itself is a reflection of the political importance of the sector then the same forces that maintain the favored position at home will make sure that it is not undermined by trade agreements abroad. It follows that reducing the degree of exceptionalism in trade rules can only be attempted after some degree of "reform" in domestic policies.[3] This domestic reform allows for the negotiation of lower tariff barriers that in turn constrain the scope for trade-distorting subsidies at home. Once protection levels at the border have come down sufficiently, and a modest safeguard system together with some form of direct payments or income insurance has been introduced, the threat to domestic producers from im-

---

1 It should be said that in historical terms agriculture has been treated rather badly by governments, who have seen the sector as backward and a source of labor and troops rather than a pillar of the economy. The wool trade in Western Europe was a counter-case, where wealth and prestige was based on an agricultural product. Assistance to agriculture (as opposed to status for landowners) appears to be a late nineteenth century phenomenon.

2 The Agreement on Textiles and Clothing (ATC), also a part of the Uruguay Round outcome, established the conditions for phasing out textile quotas and hence for its own demise.

3 The term "reform" is of course context-sensitive. In this paper it will be used in its post-1985 sense of changes to domestic agricultural policies that emphasize protection by modest tariffs at the border and the move away from heavy intervention by governments on the domestic market to stabilize and raise prices. It commonly is associated with the introduction of direct payments targeted at the farm household as compensation for reducing policy prices. In this context, such reform makes it easier to "reform" the trade rules as discussed below.

GJAE 59 (2010), Supplement
Perspectives on International Agricultural Policy – In Honor of the Retirement of Professor Stefan Tangermann

ports should be significantly reduced. Trade agreements can then be negotiated on the traditional basis of a balance of interests and an exchange of concessions without blocking threats from sectors determined to hang on to their border protection.

This progression was indeed at the root of the URAA. In the decade from the mid 1980s to the mid 1990s it appeared that several developed countries (and many developing countries) were moving down the path to domestic policy reform. The depressed state of world markets for agricultural products was causing budget problems for both the EU and the US: dumping surpluses onto the world market exacerbated the situation and led to many irritating trade conflicts. Latin American countries had begun to reduce their own level of protection as a part of structural adjustment programs. New Zealand and Australia began to implement reforms that essentially reduced the need for agricultural protection by lowering the manufacturing tariffs that were adding to farmers' costs. Only Japan and a handful of non-EU countries in Western Europe held on to the high levels of protection and resisted reform. So the concord between the EU and the US at Blair House in November 1993 represented an agreement to go ahead with significant restraints on domestic programs in the Uruguay Round, made possible by reforms undertaken or contemplated in Brussels and Washington.

Today the situation is very different. The US and the EU are much closer together, both in terms of the style of farm programs and their aspirations for global trade rules. The EU has dramatically changed its policy and moved to the type of "tariffs and decoupled subsidy" regime that fits in well with the URAA, though still under an umbrella of high tariffs. The US took two steps forward in the 1996 Farm Bill by abandoning market intervention and decoupling some payments but took one step back in 2002 when some price-triggered support was reintroduced and another step sideways in 2008, with the perpetuation of the 2002 programs but with a tentative introduction of a whole-farm insurance option for arable farmers.

But the biggest difference has been that the range of countries that have taken an active interest in agriculture rules in the WTO has widened. The rise of the influence of developing countries, and in particular the emerging trade powers of Brazil, China and India, in the direction of the trade system has already had profound implications. These countries have an active interest in agricultural trade and have policies that are somewhat different from those of the EU and the US. An US-EU deal no longer is a sufficient condition for closing the Doha Round: indeed it was just such a deal that in August 2003 sparked off the creation of the (agricultural) G-20 and led to the deadlock in the negotiations at the Cancun Ministerial. The implications of the change in the balance of influence in the WTO are already being felt. An agricultural component in the Doha Round will have to be supportive of the aspirations and sensitivities of developing and emerging economies. The historical background to "exceptionalism" may be less relevant.

This paper provides some reflections on the creation of the URAA as the emblem of exceptional treatment of agriculture in the trade system and on its future. On the one hand it did bring agriculture explicitly within the disciplines of the WTO. But it did so in a way that may well make it more difficult in the future to remove the special provisions and achieve full integration of agriculture in the trade system. So the question that one must ask is whether the URAA is still fulfilling its purpose of bringing discipline to agricultural trade? Or was it useful in a limited period when new rules were needed to extricate the trade system from the *cul-de-sac* of the prevailing tensions over EU and US farm policies? What relevance has the URAA to the current agricultural and food trade system? How suited is the URAA to the issues facing developing countries? Would it be better to work towards its removal, much as the ATC engineered its own demise?

2 Exceptionalism in the GATT

It was of course no accident that the GATT, the somewhat shaky pillar of the post-war expansion of trade, reflected the ideas of the time on the way on which trade rules interacted with domestic policy concerns in the area of agriculture. The backdrop was the way in which governments in the developed countries viewed their role in the regulation and promotion of domestic production. The rules governing agriculture in the GATT, and later the WTO, have deep roots in domestic farm policy.

2.1 The Domestic Roots of Exceptionalism

The special treatment of agriculture within the postwar trading system clearly owes its place to the political sensitivities of the sector in the major countries of Western Europe and North America. Several scholars have examined the historical development of agricultural trade policies in Nineteenth Century Europe

GJAE 59 (2010), Supplement
Perspectives on International Agricultural Policy – In Honor of the Retirement of Professor Stefan Tangermann

and noted the emergence of high levels of protection at certain times of economic stress (TRACY, 1964; SWINNEN, 2010). The opening up of the agricultural markets in the last half of that Century was followed in the 1880s by a flood of imports from the New World and Australia as well as from Russia. A widespread agricultural depression in Europe led to severe restrictions on trade. Ideas of the need to protect domestic farmers spread across Western Europe. Jules Méline in France and Otto von Bismarck in Germany influenced not only tariff policy but also established a philosophical tradition that has been the inspiration of autarkic agricultural strategies to this day.

The US has also undergone periods of protectionism where agricultural imports have been sharply restricted to aid domestic producers, but as an exporter of temperate zone products it has generally supported open markets. This began to change in 1929 when a legislative attempt to protect farmers from falling prices escalated into a sweeping across-the-board tariff increase for all products - the infamous Smoot-Hawley tariff of 1930 (IRWIN et al., 2008: 6). Later in the 1930s, policies were developed to boost rural incomes through control of supplies, both domestic and foreign, and agricultural trade policy became a tool of market management. These developments led to powerful coalitions in Congress and a close relationship between commodity producers, program administrators and rural politicians – the so-called "iron triangle" (GOLDSTEIN, 1993). Though certain political ideologies favor agriculture, one has to conclude that agricultural exceptionalism in the US is more the product of strong regional interests in the maintenance of support "entitlements" than a general feeling that agriculture is the backbone of the state and the economy.

The ideational roots of obsessive domestic support for agriculture are explored in a recent book by DAUGBJERG and SWINBANK (2009). The phrase "agricultural exceptionalism" and its relative "agrarian fundamentalism" are used in political science to indicate the notion that the agricultural sector has some particular characteristics that set it apart. It has been identified as one of the factors behind prevalence of the "State Assisted Paradigm" for the sector, which characterized the policy set in most industrial countries for much of the Twentieth Century. But perhaps as important as the ideational nature of the exceptional treatment was the institutional manifestation of these notions. The formation of ministries of agriculture in the 1930s and 1940s is an important part of the story. Ministries also collect and disseminate information about the sector. Many entered into a corporatist relationship with farm groups. These factors virtually ensured that international negotiations on agricultural trade rules would be difficult and confrontational. This was the background to the treatment of agricultural trade in the GATT.

2.2 Agriculture's Place in the Early Stages of the GATT

The history of the special treatment of agriculture within the GATT has been told in detail elsewhere (JOSLING et al., 1996). The treatment of agriculture in the GATT reflects the place of the sector in domestic politics in the early post-war period. Discussions about the post-war trade system can be traced to the US/UK talks in 1942 on the Lend-Lease program and the Atlantic Charter (IRWIN et al., 2008). At first it seemed that agricultural trade might be treated in a similar manner to trade in manufactures in the post-war economic framework, a position initially taken by the UK. But this proved too controversial. The level of government involvement precluded that action. The US had introduced price supports for main farm products in 1933, and linked these to quantitative restrictions. Open markets for imports seemed impossible under such conditions. And the enthusiasm of the UK was ambiguous. By 1944 they abandoned the notion of a full integration and instead proposed a plan for a multilateral convention on trade in food products that would be appended to the convention on commercial policy (IRWIN et al., 2008: 53). They argued that control over food imports would likely be needed in the post-war economy: besides the UK had an empire that supplied it with foodstuffs, so lower tariffs on imports from other countries would have reduced the degree of preference that the Commonwealth enjoyed rather than lowering domestic prices. Even Canada, with a predominantly export-oriented agriculture, had begun building a raft of parastatal marketing agencies and was not willing to see their effectiveness reduced. So the architects of the GATT decided to avoid controversy and introduce special treatment for agriculture.

Besides an unwillingness to challenge the emerging domestic farm programs of the framers of the GATT, another theme runs through the discussions of the period. The main agricultural problems revolved around commodities, so it was "obvious" that the solutions lay in coordinated intervention in commodity markets. Though only two international commodity agreements existed at the time of the GATT (for

GJAE 59 (2010), Supplement
Perspectives on International Agricultural Policy – In Honor of the Retirement of Professor Stefan Tangermann

wheat and sugar) the negotiators went out of their way to leave the door open for this type of market management. One prominent supporter of international commodity agreements was John Maynard Keynes, who considered a system for commodity price stabilization to be an important part of the emerging architecture for the post-war economy. The enthusiasm for commodity price stabilization schemes continued through the 1970s, and could well return under conditions of uncertainty.

2.3 GATT Rules and the Articles XI and XVI

How did drafters of the GATT resolve the issue of countries wanting to keep autonomy for their domestic policies? The General Agreement on Tariffs and trade (GATT) does not in general differentiate trade rules by sector or product group.[4] The GATT referred to all goods trade and thus included agriculture.[5] Agricultural goods are also not defined in the GATT, but special provisions for agricultural or fisheries products, primary products and commodities are found in several places (TANGERMANN, 2002). These specific provisions each act in the direction of giving domestic farm policies more scope than those in other sectors of the economy.

This "GATT Exceptionalism" is centered on two articles: those dealing with import quotas and export subsidies.[6] In addition, the issue of commodity agreements is addressed in the GATT text, though not as fully as in the stillborn Havana Treaty. Import quotas are restricted by Article XI (General Elimination of Quantitative Restrictions) to certain specified circumstances. One of those circumstances relates to cases where agricultural programs restrict domestic supply: their effectiveness is clearly enhanced if imports can be quantitatively controlled as well. Article XI:2(c)(i) allows quotas to be applied to imports under those conditions, a concession not provided for other sectors in which similar conditions might apply. HUDEC (1998) notes that this "exception" did not in fact prove so easy as might be imagined for importers to implement in a way that stood the test of a challenge. The frustrated exporters facing such quotas brought disputes to the GATT Council charging the importers with improper use of this article. But in all sixteen such cases the panels involved found that the importers' use of Article XI as a defense was inadequate (TANGERMANN, 2002: 259). This GATT article does not seem to have been particularly helpful in regulating quantitative restrictions on imports. In any case, much of the controversy over Article XI was sidelined when the US requested and was granted a waiver in 1955 that allowed that country to use quotas in defense of domestic programs even when those programs did not control production. After that, countries felt less pressure to respect either the letter or spirit of Article XI.

The emergence of the European Economic Community (EEC, later the EC and then the EU) in the late 1950s posed a different problem: the CAP import regime for cereals and (*mutatis mutandis*) for other products had chosen a variable levy rather than a fixed tariff or a quota to protect against low priced imports. Though effective for avoiding the impacts of low and fluctuating world prices it was resented by exporters as undermining price competition in the EEC market. The clarification of the status of the "grey area measure" was never fully resolved, and it continued to be a point of contention until elimination of such variable levies in the URAA.

Export subsidies had begun to be used in agricultural markets early in the post-war period, and were considered necessary as a way of relieving pressure on domestic markets. The restraints on export subsidies (and domestic subsidies that might increase exports) in the GATT Article XVI were initially weak: essentially obliging countries to notify other countries that may be affected (BARTON et al., 2008). A stronger version was introduced in 1955 that banned export subsidies for all but primary goods. For these products the provisions are more lenient, obliging notification as before but adding a requirement that subsidizing countries should not capture more than an equitable share of the market. This infamous Article XVI:3 proved impossible to implement, and an attempt to supplement it in the Tokyo Round with an explicit Subsidies Code did little to help. As with challenges

[4] There is one exception to this generalization: GATT Article IV is entitled "Special Provisions Relating to Cinematograph Films".

[5] This point was emphasized by HUDEC (1998) who was correcting the misapprehension that agriculture was not fully included in the GATT rules.

[6] The significance of Article XX (General Exceptions) to agriculture has long been recognized: import restrictions are allowed in support of certain policy objectives, including avoiding threats to human, plant and animal health. Health and safety regulations commonly increase the cost of trading agricultural and food products and exporters have suspected that they are on occasions used to protect domestic producers. But for convenience this Article is not discussed here as it is not strictly a part of agricultural exceptionalism.

GJAE 59 (2010), Supplement
Perspectives on International Agricultural Policy – In Honor of the Retirement of Professor Stefan Tangermann

to Article XI, sixteen cases were brought, but only one panel actually found a country in violation of Article XVI. As TANGERMANN (2002) concludes, of the two special exemptions, that relating to export subsidies for primary products proved the more important from the point of view of giving legal coverage for agricultural policies.

3 Exceptionalism in the WTO

The exceptional treatment of agriculture in the GATT figured prominently in the discussions that lead up to the Uruguay Round, as well as becoming a major issue in the Round itself and in the URAA that emerged from the negotiations. The question that has persisted since that time is whether the URAA was a necessary step in the incorporation of agriculture fully in the provisions of the GATT? Or did it, by setting up a parallel system of agricultural rules that can occasionally differ from those for manufactured goods, perpetuate special treatment?

3.1 Agriculture and the Uruguay Round

The "Waterloo" for the agricultural exceptionalist argument came in 1986, at the start of the Uruguay Round. Prior to that time the EU had been insisting that the issue of domestic policies could not form a part of the negotiations. It was a key intervention by some small countries like Colombia and Switzerland (the "Café-au-lait group") that resolved the issue. The result was the inclusion of some ambitious objectives in the Punta del Este Declaration (GATT, 1986) that launched the Round but these were set in the context of an exceptionalist framework. Agriculture was to be included though in its own negotiating group. More importantly, domestic agricultural policies were for the first time to be part of the agenda for the Round. The final outcome needed the agreement on all groups as a package (the Single Undertaking) to allow for trade-offs among sectors.[7]

The Agricultural Negotiating Group had plenty of ideas and analysis on which to build. The GATT had set up a Committee on Trade in Agriculture in 1982. The OECD had followed suit with a Committee on Trade and Agriculture, which mandated its Secretariat to explore ways of reconciling domestic farm policies with more open trade rules. The GATT Committee on Agriculture produced a detailed report that included, among other things, that a conversion of non-tariff barriers to tariffs would be a constructive move. The OECD showed that it was possible to develop quantitative indicators of domestic support along with market access and export subsidies. Initial proposals for the Uruguay Round talks on agriculture explored the idea of using such a comprehensive indicator to act as a basis for support reductions. This would indeed have been a radical departure and would have reinforced the separate nature of agriculture – unless the notion was extended to other sectors where domestic market interventions were prevalent. By 1988 the idea of a comprehensive indicator was abandoned in favor of having separate obligations on three elements: market access; export competition and domestic support. What we know as the URAA emerged from a 1990 "Chairman's Draft" and the 1991 "Dunkel Draft". The comprehensive measure had been reduced to a way of calculating the amount of trade-distorting domestic support.

The URAA proved to be a watershed in the history of agricultural trade and domestic policy. DAUGBJERG and SWINBANK (2009) consider it the end of agricultural exceptionalism for practical purposes. They argue that this historical perception was replaced by a new idea that they call "agricultural normalism", the notion that agriculture can be covered by the same trade rules as other goods. The Agreement in effect cemented the shift in domestic policies from the State Assisted paradigm to a Market Liberal paradigm, as appeared to have been gaining ground in the period after 1985 (SKOGSTAD, 2008). Indeed, it was the MACSHARRY reform of the CAP (lowering support prices and paying compensation payments unrelated to production) that allowed the EU to conclude a deal with the US at Blair House that limited export subsidies and put domestic support into colored boxes.

It is unquestionable that the URAA made a remarkable stride toward bringing agricultural trade more explicitly under GATT rules. New rules were added and reductions in trade barriers and distortions were agreed. The URAA formed a comprehensive framework for the regulation of measures that restrict trade in agricultural products (WTO, 1995). Market

[7] DAUGBJERG and SWINBANK (2009) argue that the Single Undertaking was needed to allow the EU to participate actively, as it knew that within the agricultural talks it would be on the defensive. Success in other areas of trade would be needed for the EU Commission to agree to any concessions on agriculture. Later the Single Undertaking served a different task by obliging the developing countries to sign on to the whole UR package or be left on the roadside.

GJAE 59 (2010), Supplement
Perspectives on International Agricultural Policy – In Honor of the Retirement of Professor Stefan Tangermann

access rules included the conversion of all non-tariff import barriers (quotas and restrictive licenses) to tariffs (Article 4.2). Hence Article XI:2(c) was no longer needed, as quotas were no longer allowed. A footnote to Article 4.2 specifies some of the non-tariff measures that are now prohibited, including variable levies. Moreover, it was agreed that tariff levels were to be bound and that tariff-rate quotas (TRQs - quantities that can be imported at a zero or low tariff) were to be established to maintain market access as "tariffication" took place. A Special Safeguard (SSG) was introduced triggered by either price or import quantity changes.

Domestic support was defined to include payments to farmers in addition to the transfers from consumers through administrative price systems. These included deficiency payments, direct income supplements, and subsidies tied to research and extension, conservation compliance and other programs that benefited farmers directly. These elements of domestic support were put into three categories, which have become known as the Amber Box, the Blue Box, and the Green Box. Amber Box measures were those tied to output or input prices or to current output levels. The Blue Box contained subsidies that were tied to supply control programs: such subsidies were regarded as less obviously output-increasing. There was no reduction obligation for Blue Box policies, but such subsidies were restricted to payments based on fixed acreage and yield or paid on a maximum of 85% of production (Article 6.5). Green Box subsidies were defined (in Annex 2) as those unrelated to price and output ("decoupled") and included research and extension, payments designed to compensate farmers for the cost of compliance with environmental regulations and domestic food assistance programs. Both the general criteria (that they be provided from public funds and not act as price supports) and the specific criteria for each type of subsidy identified have to be met. Those subsidies that qualified as Green Box payments were not constrained, though they had to be notified.

The domestic support commitments were implemented by means of a calculation of the Total Aggregate Measure of Support (AMS) (Article 6) for the base period. This included market price support given by administered prices (calculated by a price gap relative to a reference price), non-exempt direct payments, and other subsidies. These were to be reduced by 20% (in aggregate) relative to the base period (1986-90), subject to exemptions including the Blue Box and Green Box subsidies and a *de minimis* amount of 5% of the value of production for non-product specific subsidies and 5% of the value of the output of an individual commodity for product specific payments. The reduction commitments were applied to the Base AMS to give the annual commitment levels included in the country schedules, and each year the Current Total AMS is compared to this commitment.

The rules regarding export competition included a prohibition on new export subsidies (Article 8) and a reduction of existing subsidies by both volume and expenditure. A list of export subsidy practices that are covered is given in Article 9.1. Following the agreed modalities, country schedules were drawn up that provided for reductions relative to the base period of 36% by expenditure and 21% by quantity subsidized. In addition, rules were made more explicit with regard to food aid (Article 10.4) and countries agreed to negotiate limits on export credit guarantees (government underwriting of sales to purchasers that might lack creditworthiness) (Article 10.2). So Article XVI:3 of GATT no longer is needed to discipline export subsidies, as they come explicitly under the constraints of the URAA.

In the context of multilateral trade rules, the URAA introduced exceptionalism in a permanent rather than transitory way. As TANGERMANN (2002) points out, the WTO includes an agreement that regulates agricultural trade and domestic policy in much more detail than the GATT articles that relate to trade in goods. While the URAA removes many of the exceptions in GATT Articles XI and XVI it does so by creating a new and separate set of rules for trade in agricultural goods. It is difficult to argue that agricultural policy should lose its place as a matter of national, cultural and social identity when it is treated more leniently than other sectors in trade rules.

A comparison with textiles is striking. In that case the issue was not so much the special provisions in the GATT but the fact that the prohibition on quotas in trade (Article XI) had been deliberately ignored by countries who set up a series of international agreements (not under the rubric of international commodity agreements but more akin to voluntary export restraints) to divide the main import markets among suppliers. The latest one, the Multi Fibre Agreement (MFA) was up for renewal during the Round. The Uruguay Round established an Agreement on Textiles and Clothing that set a timetable for the expansion of the MFA quotas and their transformation into global quotas and then to a tariffs only system. The ATC abolished itself when this conversion to tariffs was complete.

GJAE 59 (2010), Supplement
Perspectives on International Agricultural Policy – In Honor of the Retirement of Professor Stefan Tangermann

Two questions can be distinguished in assessing the role of the URAA in agricultural exceptionalism. The first is one of tactics: was it easier for those who wanted to eliminate the special treatment of agriculture in Articles XI and XVI and tighten up disciplines on subsidies to do so with a new Agreement, as opposed to modifications of the offending articles themselves? Obviously this was the implicit assumption behind the decision to negotiate the URAA. But it may have reflected the view that the importer policies that the exporters were concerned with had to be regulated very specifically, with detailed rules, notification, and schedules for reduction. This judgment seems in hindsight to have been correct. It is the comprehensive nature of the notifications of export subsidies and domestic support that made it difficult, if not impossible, for countries to hide their trade-distorting programs. The notifications themselves in effect saved the alternative step of extensive litigation in the dispute settlement process. Amendments to Article XI might have been possible as an alternative to including market access in the URAA, but the details of tariffication and the specification of TRQs and the Special Safeguard also suggest that a sector-specific approach was desirable.

Another question is whether the distinction between market access, domestic support, and export competition which emerged particularly after the Montreal Mid-term Review in 1988, was a sound way to define the agricultural agenda. The main proposals by governments certainly made a distinction between market access and export competition as rules (i.e. addressing the Article XI and XVI special treatment provisions) but the adoption of domestic support as a separate item for discipline with its quantitative basis (the AMS) somehow divorced from the protection given by tariffs and export subsidies was a much less defensible decision. Initially the proposals tabled in 1987 from the US, the EU and the Cairns Group (and Canada) moved towards the notion that domestic support be thought of as a combination of benefits to producers through border measures and subsidies (on products or inputs). But concerns about the possibility that policy makers in importing countries might keep up high "administered prices" even when the bound tariff was reduced (through control over the supplies on the domestic market) persuaded negotiators from the exporting countries to insist on a "belt-and-braces" strategy, disciplining both market access and the "market price support" element of the AMS, calculated from the administered price. As discussed below, this has largely been ineffective.

3.2 WTO Disputes

Exceptionalism shows its face in the legal side of the WTO activities. Agricultural trade accounts for a small and declining share of global merchandise trade.[8] But its share of trade disputes is large and shows few signs of declining.[9] For the first fifty years of the GATT/WTO multilateral trade system one could have put this down to imprecise rules and inadequate enforcement mechanisms in that sector (JOSLING et al., 1996). With the introduction of the Uruguay Round Agreement on Agriculture (URAA) much of the ambiguity was removed, but this did not stem the flow of disputes. Indeed, the strengthened legal provisions of the Dispute Settlement Understanding (DSU) gave encouragement to complainants to attempt to settle long-standing disputes that had eluded the weaker GATT dispute settlement process.

Many dealt with market access issues, in part over the interpretation of the new obligations. More recently, agricultural disputes have challenged the scope for domestic and export subsidies, under the Agreement on Agriculture and the Agreement on Subsidies and Countervailing Measures. In the absence of an agreement in the Doha Round one might expect these conflicts to intensify, as countries attempt to use litigation to achieve what might otherwise be gained through negotiation. And if the Agreement on Agriculture does become revised in a successful Doha conclusion, there will certainly be several more issues that will need to be resolved through the DSU.

Market access issues were the most important in the early days of the WTO, as countries explored through the DSB the practical implementation of the new rules and the agreed schedules. The process of tariffication was fairly smooth, and the introduction of the SSG also was without major problems. However, the establishment of TRQs did lead to several conflicts, as one might imagine in cases where government decisions had immediate commercial impact. The success in limiting trade-distorting subsidies has been somewhat more elusive. Export subsidies that were included in the schedules in general caused few disputes, in part because the limits were well above actual levels. But panels examining country policies unearthed several policies that acted as export aids

[8] Agricultural exports now make up 8% of global exports. For further discussion of the recent WTO agricultural cases see JOSLING (2009).

[9] Of the 367 requests for consultations made to the Dispute Settlement Board, 100 have primarily been about agricultural trade, a share of 27%.

GJAE 59 (2010), Supplement
Perspectives on International Agricultural Policy – In Honor of the Retirement of Professor Stefan Tangermann

within the terms of the WTO but had not been notified as such. Thus the major challenges to domestic farm programs in the EU and the US came from other exporters complaining that the export subsidy restrictions were being circumvented.

Cases brought against particular types of domestic support have been infrequent. With inconclusive debates in the Committee for Agriculture and without the guidance of panel reports, countries were able to largely decide for themselves whether particular policies were consistent with the definitions of the Green and Blue Boxes, and hence not subject to reductions. As long as countries were way below their limits on domestic support it was not a priority to challenge the notifications themselves. But the jump in funding for the 2002 US Farm Bill caused a rethinking of this situation, with the possibility that the limits may have been breached if notifications had been erroneous. The statement of the US-Cotton panel that some of the expenditures that the US had claimed as "green" may have been mislabeled turned this possibility into a contestable proposition.

The current case brought by Canada and Brazil, challenging the level of US farm subsidies as notified under the categories used by the URAA, illustrates that ambiguity still exists.[10] On the one hand, it is a remarkable case, which could clarify the somewhat fuzzy nature of the domestic support "boxes". On the other hand, it refers to past notifications that were alleged to wrongly classify certain subsidies. So the remedy in the event of a successful challenge is presumably to oblige a re-notification by the US of its domestic support for several historical years. But the US could well argue that in the current period of high prices, support levels are already well below the limits set in the schedules even with re-notification. So it would not be clear what the US could do to make amends: changing current policies would not be an appropriate remedy, and compensation for past violations is not contemplated in the DSU.

This does not drain the interest away from the case. The re-classification of direct payments in the US away from the Green Box in a revised notification would indeed be a small prize for competing exporters. But add the possibility of a new set of limits in the Doha Round, and the case becomes critical. If the Doha Round succeeds in reducing allowable trade-distorting subsidies (as calculated by the Aggregate Measure of Support, or AMS), the allocation of subsidies to these boxes becomes sensitive. The prospect exists that the major driver of change in US farm policy could indeed be the WTO dispute settlement process, and the decisions on the classification of subsidies. That could also set up some controversy over the role of WTO rules when they clash with powerful political interests.

3.3 WTO Doha Negotiations

Article 20 of the URAA mandated (the start of) further talks on agriculture to begin by the year 2000. These talks, part of a "built in agenda" that included some service sector negotiations, did indeed start (approximately) on time, but were soon to be incorporated in the Doha Development Agenda (DDA, or Doha Round) that was launched in November 2001. The assumption was made that more progress could be made and more ambition contemplated with trade-offs possible among sectors. It is not clear, with hindsight, that this assumption was well-founded: though agriculture-only talks have always been considered to be doomed to failure, a simple continuation of UR cuts in agriculture together with some attractive progress in services may well have been possible early in the decade.

Agricultural exceptionalism permeates throughout the DDA because the structure of the URAA was taken as the basis for the Doha discussions. Once again, agricultural issues are negotiated in a separate Committee, reflecting the locus of interest and expertise but perpetuating the exceptional character of the sector. The notion of a Single Undertaking was again endorsed and so agriculture is an essential part of the final package. The fact that agriculture requires separate treatment even when the Article XI and XVI anomalies have been removed is mainly a reflection of the incomplete nature of the URAA. The rule changes were accompanied by some reductions in the levels of protection and support, but agreeing on the rules was a multi-year task itself, and the liberalization aspect was in large part put off to the Doha Round. So the choice of the structure of the URAA as a framework for the liberalization phase was perhaps inevitable. The Doha Round was needed to complete the task of getting agriculture into a position where it can be fully incorporated (like textiles) into the GATT rules and procedures. The problems facing the Doha Round are much the same as those discussed in the Uruguay Round, only this time there is a greater sense of reality.

[10] The two cases brought by Canada and Brazil (DS 357, 365, respectively) have been merged. The complaint is that US exceeded its Total AMS limits in several recent years.

GJAE 59 (2010), Supplement
Perspectives on International Agricultural Policy – In Honor of the Retirement of Professor Stefan Tangermann

This gives rise to the question as to whether agricultural exceptionalism has not in fact been thrown a lifeline by the URAA? It may be much easier to prevent agricultural normalism if agricultural trade falls under its own set of rules. Or, to put it another way, the URAA was once the mechanism that agricultural exporters hailed as a means to get rid of quantitative trade barriers, curb export subsidies and shift countries toward less trade-distorting domestic support. It may end up as a means for protectionist importers to slow down the process of tariff cuts, maintain a quota system for imports of sensitive products and promote a complex categorization of domestic support that acts as a distraction to shelter new and more elaborate subsidies.

Exceptionalism manifests itself in many ways in trade negotiations. Without an Agreement on Agriculture there would not be a plethora of coalitions focused on one or more aspects of the talks. Of course, the country positions that underlie such groups would still be manifest in particular ways, but the existence of the G-20 that began as a reaction to the 2003 US-EU joint proposal on agriculture reflects the strength of feeling that surrounded the question of domestic support and the determination that it should be cut back in the Doha Round. Few issues could have cemented the disparate interests of the G-20 as effectively as agriculture. Similarly, the G-33 of developing countries that are the main protagonists for the Special Safeguard Mechanism in the Doha Round would not have been as cohesive if the issue were (say) being dealt with as an interpretative paragraph attached to the Safeguards Agreement.

Perhaps more fundamental are the national actors, the ministries of agriculture that act as the repositories of knowledge and wisdom about farm policies. In the developed countries, in particular, representatives from the agricultural ministries have traditionally been in command of negotiating positions on agriculture. This clearly narrows the flexibility of trade-offs among sectors: it is possible that without the direct involvement of agricultural officials and without the narrow focus of negotiations on agricultural rules the scope for reaching agreements might be expanded. Of course, one would expect pressure from special interest groups at home to keep agricultural officials involved in trade talks, but that in itself is an indication of the extent to which the "special treatment" of agriculture is beneficial to producer interests.

Finally, the separation of the agricultural talks from those in other areas leads to the concept of achieving a balance between, in the case of the Doha Round, manufacturing and other tariffs, liberalization of trade in services, and agriculture. This promotes agricultural exceptionalism. It would indeed be interesting to have a trade round where legitimate agricultural interests have to compete with the items that other sectors might wish to place on the agenda.

4 The Future of Exceptionalism

So what is the future of the exceptional treatment of agriculture in the WTO? Clearly, further agricultural tariff reductions in future rounds would bring protection into line with that for manufactured goods. This would imply very little room for domestic price policies and lock countries into developing agricultural programs that do not require border interventions for their effectiveness. Two problems would survive: the TRQs, which are a prominent aspect of agricultural exceptionalism, and the Special Safeguards (SSG and SSM) which again have no direct counterpart in other sectors. The problem with TRQs is that they set up incentives for their continuance: exporters who sell within the quota get a benefit that they may not wish to give up. Importing governments see TRQs as one of the few instruments (since tariff rates are bound) to control import levels. And in the context of regional and bilateral trade agreements the ability to grant access through TRQs to partner countries is useful. But is this the direction in which the trade system is heading?

4.1 A New Domestic Policy Context?

Perhaps the key issue is the future domestic policy mix for agriculture used by the major trading countries, including the emerging nations, and the trade rules that will be necessary to prevent negative impacts on other countries and on the trade system. The type of domestic policy that is encouraged by the URAA is one based on modest tariffs (zero for bilateral and regional trade partners, and for agricultural products not domestically produced, and at a comparable level to manufacturing tariffs to avoid negative real protection) and an effective safeguard against import surges and sharp price swings. Domestic subsidies would be decoupled from prices or production and thus be compatible with the Green Box. No export subsidies would be used. So the significance of the URAA is to constrain policies that do not conform to this "model".

GJAE 59 (2010), Supplement
Perspectives on International Agricultural Policy – In Honor of the Retirement of Professor Stefan Tangermann

The farm policies in the US and the EU have in fact moved in this direction, as noted above. But changes in the last few years have cast some doubt on the continuation of this trend. The US has begun the process of deliberation for the next Farm Bill, expected in 2012. Among the issues are the choice between crop insurance and whole-farm revenue assurance and the future of the direct payments. These latter policies seemed to be tailor-made for the Green Box. But it is possible that the direct payments may be phased out and the funds used for other parts of the program: paying farmers in good years and bad is not politically attractive. The US has almost no Blue Box programs, but makes extensive use of "non-exempt direct payments" (i.e. not green or blue) and non-product specific AMS payments (those related to many crops). With these two categories liable to be squeezed in the Doha Round the question is what will be the types of policies that will replace them? The EU has embraced presumably Green Box payments of the Single Farm Payment and Single Area Payment schemes. But there is the possibility that pressure could rise for some counter-cyclical programs as employed in the US. The EU has also almost abandoned Blue Box payments, and with a Doha Round completion would have little flexibility for policies that did not fit in the Green Box. Again, the search is on for a politically acceptable way of making traditional payments to farmers without exceeding WTO limits.

One such candidate is the encouragement of biofuels, as a way of both reducing dependence of fossil fuels and in developing a "new use" for farm products. Corn in the US and oilseed crops in the EU have certainly boosted farm incomes by increasing demand. This poses a dilemma for the URAA: currently very few of the subsidies that have been necessary to build up the biofuels market have been notified as agricultural support, though some have been reported to the WTO as non-agricultural subsidies (JOSLING et al., 2010). In fact, the notion of a subsidy that increased the size of the market for and agricultural product was in itself somewhat of a novelty. Both domestic producers and foreign suppliers stood to gain, directly or indirectly. The effect was similar to a control over domestic output, which had rarely been the basis for a trade dispute.

The price spike in 2007 and 2008 threatened to change this traditional notion that trade rules were to protect the exporter from the actions of an importer. Exporters that restricted output (as the US had done for several decades, through the conservation reserve and acreage control programs) were now accused of jeopardizing food security. Similarly, those that restricted exports directly were taken to task for withholding supplies from poor consumers. So a "new" set of issues has surfaced on the agricultural agenda relating to food security and price stability, the latter having taken a back seat since the 1970s. It is not clear that the Agreement on Agriculture has much to offer in these matters.

Another issue of considerable relevance to domestic farm policy is the wider range of interests involved in policy discussions and decision-making. This has subtle impacts on the issue of exceptionalism. If the domestic policies are under the control of agricultural ministries, with close relations to production agriculture, the trade mandates are going to be relatively uncomplicated. But many ministries (particularly in the European Union, where the responsibility for most agricultural and trade issues has been ceded to the Union level) have changed their names and embraced a number of rural causes that often inconvenience farmers and raise their costs. Under these circumstances it is by no means certain that exceptionalism is embraced at home and therefore may be nuanced in trade talks. Add to that major questions such as the role of agriculture in climate change mitigation strategies and the picture looks very different from that of 1986.

4.2 New Actors on the Scene

There is no disagreement over the rapidly rising influence of emerging countries on the world trade system. Countries such as India, China, South Africa, Egypt, Brazil, Chile and Argentina have taken an active interest in the WTO in the past few years. But in emerging countries the jury is still out as to what type of trade system these countries will favor and what parts of the present system they will find less than useful. Developing countries as a whole have in essence captured the agricultural trade agenda: the G-20 in particular has become a more active participant in that area than the US and the EU. But this raises as many questions as it answers. Countries such as Brazil would favor a trade system that had low tariffs for agricultural products and no subsidies for developed country farmers. As a competitive supplier of a number of products the possibility of expanding both south-north and south-south agricultural trade is appealing. But it is not so clear that India has the same view: small scale producers may need protection from the larger

GJAE 59 (2010), Supplement
Perspectives on International Agricultural Policy – In Honor of the Retirement of Professor Stefan Tangermann

scale agricultural farm sector in Brazil perhaps even more than from US competition. China has aspirations as a major exporter of farm products but also needs to ensure that rural areas with less productive farm sectors do not suffer too much from open markets. So the EU-US rivalry of the post-war period may be repeated among developing countries in the future.

Recent estimates by BRINK (ORDEN et al., 2011: chapter 2) indicate that in the post-Doha period the ability of developed countries to use trade-distorting policies will have been drastically curtailed. But the same is not true for large developed countries, who will be allowed to spend up to 10%of the value of their agricultural production on such support, even though they had "zero" bound AMS commitments. In fact, most of the allowable trade-distorting domestic support will be in those countries. So if the trend noticed by ANDERSON (2009) materializes, emerging countries (unless competitive exporters with relatively small home markets such as Brazil) may increase their protection levels. They have some flexibility in raising tariffs, but the more likely path is to spend more public funds assisting their rural sectors. In other words: they could resist the progressive opening of markets and develop their own agricultural policies. They would be moving away from the policy direction envisaged in the Agreement on Agriculture.

Presumably, the benign transition from domestic reform to full incorporation of agriculture in trade agreements development works best, if all (interested) countries are at a similar stage in the (cyclical or secular) path of agricultural protectionism. The prospect of developing countries moving toward more protection just as the developed world was embracing open markets would put strain on the Agreement on Agriculture as well as the concept of exceptionalism.

4.3 The Future of the URAA

Where does this leave the URAA? Is it a necessary part of the architecture of the WTO? Or has it served its purpose? What would be missed if it were to be phased out in the next decade or two? What would be involved in such a phase-out so as to preserve its positive aspects? What are the benefits of such an approach? Or is the URAA valuable as a permanent part of the WTO even when its primary task has been accomplished?

Clearly, the answer to these questions depends on the outcome of the Doha Round and on the behavior and intentions of the major trading countries. Assuming that an agreement along the lines of the December 2008 Draft Modalities is reached, much of the current URAA, and the associated schedules of commitments, could be phased out. These parts of the URAA would no longer be needed as a part of the WTO rules and much of the monitoring would no longer be necessary as part of the procedures.

With respect to the market access provisions in the URAA (Articles 4 and 5) certain aspects of the URAA would need to be retained but could be incorporated as amendments to the GATT (94). The tariffication provisions of the URAA are no longer needed, even in the absence of a Doha Round agreement. All non-tariff measures are now converted into tariffs and a revised Article XI would prevent their reappearance. The revisions would incorporate the improved definitions agreed in the Uruguay Round. In particular, Article 4.2 of the URAA would be needed to be incorporated in Article XI to be specific as to which non-tariff barriers were prohibited. As the WTO members have already agreed to this provision, no negotiation should be needed.[11]

The "exceptional" existence of TRQs as a way of ensuring minimal access to markets where tariffication was introduced in the Uruguay Round, and when Special Product status is called for in the Doha Round, will need to be handled in negotiation. A rapid elimination of TRQs is unlikely to be agreed: they are too useful as a way of controlling liberalization. However, they also constitute a major distortion in the way that some agricultural products are traded. The situation is similar to that involved in phasing out the textile quotas. The first phase could be the expansion of the TRQs on a progressive basis over a number of years and a continued effort to make their distribution on a non-discriminatory basis. The end-point would be the elimination of TRQs. The URAA in its present form seems to inhibit this change.

Some provision for agricultural safeguards would probably need to be preserved: developing countries consider an SSM to be an essential element of the trade system. On the other hand the SSG will be on its way out if there is a conclusion to the Doha Round (WTO, 2008). So the SSM could be added to the Agreement on Safeguards also agreed in the Uruguay Round. The provisions can be limited to developing countries and become a part of the effort to respond to the concerns of these countries.

---

11 A temporary waiver may be needed for countries that still make use of the "rice provision" (Annex 5 of the URAA) to put off tariffication.

GJAE 59 (2010), Supplement
Perspectives on International Agricultural Policy – In Honor of the Retirement of Professor Stefan Tangermann

How much of the content of the Export Competition part of the URAA needs to be kept? If export subsidies are eliminated in the Doha Round, along with other forms of export enhancement (the subsidy element export credit guarantees, the beneficial treatment of state export agencies, and the provision of food aid that directly competes with commercial sales) then agriculture has lost its specificity in this regard. None of the Articles 8-11 would be needed (though, if necessary, the provisions in article 11 regarding subsidies in incorporated products could be addressed by a footnote to Article XVI or the SCM Agreement).

And what about Domestic Support (Articles 6 and 7 of the URAA)? This was a novelty introduced in the URAA and does not have a counterpart in trade in other products. But the experience with the monitoring and disciplining of domestic support has been mixed. It is not clear which parts of Articles 6 and 7 really do discipline domestic support. A forthcoming study (ORDEN, et al., 2011) delves into the details of the notifications of domestic support in several major countries, both developed and developing. The picture is one of inconsistent (and tardy) notification of support levels. But more worrying is that the support levels themselves are easily manipulated by changes in notifications that have little to do with changes in policy as it affects production. The major problem is with the reporting of Market Price Support, a critical part of the AMS. Taking administered prices (which in several cases have been changed with no impact on producers) and fixed reference prices (which relate to the 1986-88 base period) and multiplying the difference by "eligible quantities" which can vary from the amount purchased by the government to the whole of production gives a figure that has no resemblance to the level of incentive to producers. In other words: a key part of the constraints on domestic support have virtually no meaning.

Of course, it would be retrogressive to give up the monitoring and control of domestic support. But subsidies already have to be notified to the SCM Committee, and many agricultural subsidies are already included. A coordinated notification process may serve a better purpose for improving transparency.

Does one need the boxes of the URAA at all? They certainly seemed to help in constraining domestic farm programs. But if the AMS allowances for developed countries have been reduced to where trade distortions are minimal then what is needed is a way to prevent them from increasing and a way of relating them to the SCM. The Green Box definitions could be incorporated in the SCM by means of defining which types of agricultural programs are considered "specific" subsidies and which are covered by the definitions of "non-actionable" subsidies. This would presumably require the current Green Box to be split between programs that are in effect ways of providing for public goods and those that give specific benefits to particular producers. These latter subsidies would be actionable in that other countries could challenge them as causing serious prejudice to their economic interests.

The Blue Box could be jettisoned without any great loss in control of subsidies: it was a convenient device for getting an agreement between the US and the EU in the Uruguay Round: it is rapidly dropping out of use as fewer governments attempt to control domestic production. The AMS would be kept only as a way of monitoring subsidies that would be actionable. But the MPS part of the AMS would be dropped and the *de minimis* provisions could also fall by the wayside. If non-product specific support was ruled to be non-specific under the SCM then that too would no longer be monitored.

One article of the URAA stands out as useful and underused. Article 12 contains weak disciplines on export prohibitions and restrictions. "Due consideration" and advance warning should be given by developed country exporters before restricting agricultural exports. How unfortunate, that a provision that would be welcome by so many developing countries has remained on the back shelf of the Doha talks even at a time of high prices. It would seem both practical and politically acceptable to package this clause, with some more mordant language, with some other elements to constitute a "food security" obligation. This would seem a more widely defensible example of special treatment in trade rules.

This thought-experiment is intended not so much as a proposal, but as a way of taking stock of how much the Agreement on Agriculture really contains that is essential as a separate part of the trade rules. If the politics were right, the trade system could survive and prosper without the Agreement on Agriculture, however convenient it was in 1995.

5 Conclusion

Exceptional treatment of agricultural products in the WTO has been a function of the political difficulties of constraining domestic farm policies, the legacy of the GATT articles that appeared to allow quantitative import restrictions and export subsidies, and the high

GJAE 59 (2010), Supplement
Perspectives on International Agricultural Policy – In Honor of the Retirement of Professor Stefan Tangermann

levels of protection for the sector in many industrial countries. It is manifest primarily in the URAA that specifies in considerable detail the ways in which domestic and trade policies should be disciplined. It is perpetuated by the institutional arrangements in each country that reflect the "differentness" of agriculture and this spills over into trade negotiations. Agriculture plays a role in the balancing of concessions in trade agreements as well as having to strike an internal balance.

This exceptionalism will no doubt survive as long as these conditions exist. But it is useful to consider them in the broader context of trade rules. Bound tariffs are the norm in all sectors, with few exceptions: in that sense agriculture still has a little way to go but is essentially in line with manufactured trade. The remaining special treatment would be the TRQs, which would still be an agriculture-specific element of the WTO until they could be eliminated. Export subsidies are banned in other areas of commerce, and will be eliminated for agriculture after the Doha Round. Domestic subsidies are now covered by both the SCM and the URAA, with the constraints on trade-distorting support being of little value. Incorporating a relatively small number of paragraphs into the SCM and the Agreement on Safeguards would seem to replicate the current situation – or rather that in the post-Doha period.

What benefits might one get from phasing out the Agreement on Agriculture? This would plausibly improve the pace of trade negotiations, though the difficulty of reducing sensitive agricultural tariffs would not be avoided. The agenda for such future talks would certainly be simplified. Trade-offs will always have to be made within the governments that take part on the talks. At present, the trade-offs are often delayed while the special negotiators for agriculture discuss more and more arcane ways of achieving balance within the sector. Non-agricultural parts of the negotiations often have to wait until the agricultural portfolio is almost completed to get the "level of ambition" that needs to be matched in other areas. Most commentators agree that "agriculture only" talks are unlikely to be successful, as trade-offs are not present, but by the same token if agriculture were totally integrated the possibility of such give-and-take among national interests would be made easier. If the Agreement on Agriculture is becoming more of an empty shell, reflecting its use as a valuable transitional device, now might be a good time to think about eliminating it. Then, exceptionalism really would have taken a step backwards.

References

ANDERSON, K. (ed.) (2009): Distortions to Agricultural Incentives: A Global Perspective 1955-2007. Palgrave Macmillan, London and World Bank, Washington DC.

BARTON, J.H., J.L. GOLDSTEIN, T. JOSLING and R.H. STEINBERG (2008): The Evolution of the Trade Regime: Politics, Law and Economics of the GATT and the WTO. Princeton University Press, Princeton.

DAUGBJERG, C. and A. SWINBANK (2009): Ideas, Institutions and Trade. Oxford University Press, Oxford.

GATT (1986): Ministerial Declaration on the Uruguay Round. GATT Doc. MIN. DEC. (20 September). Geneva.

GOLDSTEIN, J. (1993): Ideas, Interests and American Trade Policy. Cornell University Press, Ithaca.

HUDEC, R.E. (1998): Does the URAA Work? Agricultural Disputes after the Uruguay Round. Working Paper 98-2. International Agricultural Trade Research Consortium, St. Paul, MN, USA.

IRWIN, D.A., P.C. MAVROIDIS and A.O. SYKES (2008): The Genesis of the GATT. Cambridge University Press, Cambridge.

JOSLING, T., S. TANGERMANN and T.K. WARLEY (1996): Agriculture in the GATT. Macmillan, London, UK.

JOSLING, T., D. BLANDFORD and J. EARLEY (2010): Biofuel and Biomass Subsidies in the U.S., EU and Brazil: Towards a Transparent System of Notification. IPC Position Paper, September 2010. International Food & Agricultural Trade Policy Council, Washington DC, USA.

JOSLING, T. (2009): Agricultural Trade Disputes and the WTO. In: Hartigan, J.C. (ed.): Trade Disputes and the Dispute Settlement Understanding of the WTO: An Interdisciplinary Assessment. Emerald Press, Bingley, UK.

ORDEN, D., D. BLANDFORD and T. JOSLING (2011): WTO Disciplines On Agricultural Support: Seeking a Fair Basis for Trade. Cambridge University Press, Cambridge.

SKOGSTAD, G. (2008): Internationalization and Canadian Agriculture. University of Toronto Press, Toronto, Canada.

SWINNEN, J.F.M. (2010): Agricultural Protection Growth in Europe, 1870-1969. In: Anderson, K. (ed.): The Political Economy of Agricultural Price Distortions. Cambridge University Press, Cambridge.

TANGERMANN, S. (2002): Agriculture on the Way to Firm International Trading Rules. In: Kennedy, D.L.M. and J.D. Southwick (eds.): The Political Economy of International Trade Law: Essays in Honor of Robert E. Hudec. Cambridge University Press, Cambridge.

TRACY, M. (1964): Agriculture in Western Europe. Praeger, New York, USA.

WTO (World Trade Organisation) (1995): The Results of the Uruguay Round of Multilateral Trade Negotiations: The Legal Texts. World Trade Organisation, Geneva.

– (2008): Revised draft modalities for agriculture. TN/AG/W/4/Rev.4, 6 December. World Trade Organisation, Geneva.

PROF. TIM JOSLING, PHD
The Europe Center
Freeman Spogli Institute for International Studies,
Encina Hall, Stanford University
Stanford, CA 94305, USA
e-mail: josling@stanford.edu

13

Competing Paradigms in the OECD and Their Impact on the WTO Agricultural Talks

Tim Josling

Evidence exists of an emerging new paradigm in U.S. agriculture that emphasizes the ability of the sector to compete both with other sectors in the domestic economy and with overseas competitors. But a rival new paradigm has been gaining significance in Europe that stresses the public-good nature of agriculture and the inability of the sector to earn satisfactory incomes just by providing agricultural commodities. A third paradigm points to the nature of agriculture as increasingly one stage in an integrated supply chain that crosses borders in a global food system. The current WTO talks on agriculture will provide an opportunity for these paradigms to compete for the setting of international trade rules.

INTRODUCTION

The premise of this book is that a paradigm shift in agricultural economics is underway that is reflected in a new view of the nature and causes of "the farm problem." Essentially, this new view holds that U.S. agriculture has become a sector able to compete with others for resources without government price support, and able to compete on world markets without recourse to subsidies. Luther Tweeten is a major proponent of this view, and several of his writings describe the new paradigm and its domestic implications.

I focus on two aspects of this issue. First I cast the paradigm debate in the context of the OECD countries as a whole rather than just the United States. I argue that the discussion becomes more interesting if one asks whether a common paradigm exists in industrial countries and, if no common paradigm has existed in the past, has a "paradigm convergence" taken place in the last 15 years? Second, I look at the implications for trade policy discussions of having different paradigms "competing" in the international arena, specifically the WTO agricultural negotiations. Or, alternatively, if a convergence in paradigms is indeed under way, how does one negotiate among countries that are in a different phase of this paradigm shift?

The thorny question of the definition of a paradigm shift I leave to others.[1] For the purposes of this chapter, I assume that a policy paradigm is a common set of ideas that guide attitudes and justify policies. The paradigm provides a model that serves as a mental testing ground for policies. A paradigm shift is therefore a replacement by one such model with another, either suddenly or over time. Farm policies will tend to change as a result of this paradigm shift, subject to bureaucratic inertia or political entrenchment. Policies will therefore change at different speeds in different countries depending on specific conditions even if a common paradigm shift has occurred. Lagging policies are common in agriculture, because the ability to change policy instruments to respond to events is often limited by both political and institutional factors. Policy reform is the process of changing policies in response to a paradigm shift in the face of those forces that would defend the status quo.

No one would deny that farm policies in developed countries have changed markedly over the past two decades. The nature of these changes, however, seems still to be in doubt. Some have claimed that an irreversible policy reform has indeed occurred in response to a paradigm shift; others that the changes in these policies have been more along the lines of a natural evolution, reacting to structural, economic, and political forces but retaining their essential characteristics.

This debate is not just a matter of semantics and perspective. If a nonreversible change in policies has indeed taken place, then recognizing that change is crucially important for our understanding of the future relationship between the government and the agricultural sector. Moreover, the nature of the change has implications for trade policy as well as for domestic farm programs. In particular, the WTO process of trade liberalization is premised on a continuation of domestic policy reform. Some who argue for an irreversible shift also conclude that the relationship between domestic and trade policy has itself changed. Domestic policy change, at least in the OECD countries, has in effect been locked in by the WTO and the Uruguay Round Agreement on Agriculture. This effectively makes the case for a new "trade paradigm" for agriculture, in which the nature of world markets is no longer merely a residual of all the autonomous domestic policy decisions but is endogenous to the domestic policy process. This view rests on the notion that the Uruguay Round on the one hand constrained policy choice but on the other expanded the scope for such choice by providing new instrumentalities.

However, if the argument that a significant change has occurred in the underlying view of agriculture and of the relation between trade and domestic policy is found to be weak, then the prospects for further progress in the current agricultural trade negotiations are correspondingly dim. If all is "business as usual" in farm policies, then the implications for both domestic and trade policy as well as for the development of global agricultural markets are rather sobering. This chapter explores the question of whether a significant shift has occurred in agricultural policies in the OECD countries that can usefully be described as the result of a paradigmatic shift. But in the process, the issue is raised of whether the relationship between domestic and trade policies has changed, and hence whether the prospects for further trade policy reform have been thereby enhanced.

PARADIGM SHIFTS AND POLICY REFORM

The idea of a new paradigm for agricultural policy was explored explicitly by Coleman, Skogstad, and Atkinson (1997). They argue that a change has occurred from a state-assisted to a market-liberal paradigm. In the former paradigm, the state considers that the agricultural sector contributes importantly to realizing national policy objectives and that special support is required to enable that contribution to be maximized. In the latter paradigm, the sector is treated much like other sectors of the economy. Competitive markets should be the main source of income for commercial farmers, though public programs can still exist in areas where the market is inadequate. To Colman, Skogstad, and Atkinson, paradigm shifts can come slowly over time, rather than in a Pauline conversion of politicians to a new faith. They find some evidence of shifts of this nature but recognize that the process was by no means complete.

Tweeten has also argued strongly for the emergence of a new paradigm. His "new economic paradigm" for (U.S.) agriculture is characterized by the idea that agriculture is no longer the backward, noncompetitive sector that it once was thought to be (Tweeten forthcoming; Tweeten and Zulauf 1997). Such a sector was thought to require government assistance to deal with the triple jeopardy of weather and disease, concentration in upstream and downstream activities, and a chronic tendency toward overproduction. Instead, the sector (or that part of it that produces the bulk of the output) is now recognized as competitive both with other sectors or the economy (generating roughly comparable return on resources) and on international markets (at least when not facing undue foreign subsidies). Again, government programs are limited to correcting for externalities, particularly in the environmental area, and perhaps to helping farmers manage risk.

If paradigms are the bundle of ideas and analytical concepts with which we approach farm policy, what can we say about policy reform? The conditions under which one would expect to see a significant shift in policy include dissatisfaction with existing policies and instruments and broader ideological and political climate change. Ample evidence exists of such policy reform in many countries, both inside the OECD and outside. This reform has been towards less manipulation of the commodity price level and towards more use of direct payments to farm families. Early signs of this shift in developed countries were the adoption of commodity-based deficiency payments in place of price supports so that consumer demand could respond to market prices. These deficiency payments over time have become increasingly decoupled from present production levels to reduce the incentive to overproduce. The decoupled payments have in some cases been targeted to various environmentally friendly farming practices. Revenue and crop insurance schemes have also been introduced to act as a stabilizing device for rural areas, though these can become incentives to produce when subsidized by governments.

Underlying these changes in farm policy are fundamental trends in the sector itself. Advances in technology and rapid structural change in agriculture increase yields, but domestic market growth is slow in most OECD countries. After the domestic market is satisfied, the protection at the border against competing foreign goods is no longer adequate to maintain farm prices. The traditional options facing policymakers were to control supply, an unpopular solution with farmers and agribusinesses; to store the surpluses against the next period of shortage, which may not come in time; to export with generous subsidies, thus distorting other countries markets; or to lower farm-support prices, with or without paying compensation to those who were disadvantaged. Until the mid-1980s, most countries tried a combination of supply control and surplus disposal, with some attempts to constrain price increases.

The situation began to change in the period after 1985, as countries both adjusted their domestic policies and then later incorporated new trade rules into the Uruguay Round Agreement that reinforced the domestic policy changes. The shift occurred because the old policies were clearly inappropriate in a more open world economy and a less regulated domestic market. Commodity price intervention rewarded farmers according to their output of the product, regardless of the state of the market. Farm output and structures responded to the policy signals rather than consumer demand, and agriculture became dependent upon further government assistance to dispose of surpluses. Moreover, environmental groups began to point out that farming systems geared to high price policies were creating problems for the water supply, for worker safety, for public health, and for the preservation of plant and animal species. Targeting payments to the farmer has the advantage of being more direct, involves less distortion in production incentives, can be tied to environmental standards, and allows the consumer to choose more freely among competing products.

Similarities were apparent in the ways in which countries attempted to change policies. Orden, Paarlberg, and Roe (1999) have framed the reform strategy in U.S.farm policy (and by implication in the European Union as well) as the choice among four options: a "cutout" is a quick termination of price supports without compensation; a "buyout" is a quick termination with compensation; a "squeeze-out" is a slow reduction in price supports without compensation; and a "cash-out" is a slow, compensated cut in prices (Orden, Paarlberg and Roe 1999, 8). In the terminology used in this chapter, a buyout and a cutout are likely to be clear evidence of a reform, though not too many cases exist in the U.S.and the EU where such options have been tried. A squeeze-out is the traditional way in which poorly performing policies get modified, when the forces for change overcome the bureaucratic inertia and the power of vested interest. Calling such changes "reform" may not make much sense. A cash-out has been the instrument of choice in the policy adjustments of the 1990s, both in the United States and in the EU, because it weakens opposition to the squeeze. Whether a cash-out necessarily is evidence of policy reform is debatable, and indeed is at the core of the debate on whether policy trends are reversible. But instruments such as cash-outs clearly are a convenient way of making the transition to a reformed policy if that is indeed what is intended.

But those claiming policy reform cannot be too complacent. Several policies have remained essentially unchanged in the face of significant shifts in the performance of agricultural markets. This is particularly true for policies toward commodities that have enjoyed special status in political circles, the "sacred cows" of farm policy. One could call these policies evidence of "policy lag." It is the tension between policy reform and policy lag that conditions the prospects for further trade liberalization in the WTO and in regional trade agreements.

POLICY CHANGE IN THE OECD COUNTRIES

Much of the discussion of paradigm shifts and policy reform has focused on experience in the United States. But other countries have been grappling with the same problems and many of them have experienced more pronounced policy changes. In fact, the period since 1985 has been one of remarkable change in domestic agricultural policy in most parts of the world. This change was most apparent in the developing and middle-income countries of Latin America, where the overhaul of agricultural policies was part of a package of economic policy changes induced by a combination of external pressures and shifting notions of the role of the state (Williamson 1994). Little doubt exists that both a paradigm shift and a policy reform took place in these countries. Moreover, the two were closely related. Changes in the set of ideas about the role of agriculture in development, as well as those about the linkages between macroeconomic policy and farm policy, were an important precursor to the policy reforms (Krueger et al. 1992). Domestic reforms then allowed countries to bring agriculture into the trade-policy reforms, generally involving the removal of nontariff barriers and the setting of low fixed tariffs against imports. In retrospect, the remarkable fact is that politicians in these countries did not shy away from the inclusion of agricultural markets in the overall reform of economic policy. In most cases, difficult decisions had to be made in the face of opposition from rural constituencies. This agricultural reform implies either a compliant political system that was unable to stop the "technocrats" from adopting the reform measures or a general, if reluctant, acquiescence that such reforms were worth a try.

In the major industrial countries, however, agricultural policy reform came only reluctantly in the period up until 1990 and with a great deal of domestic opposition. The farm policies in these countries had become so entrenched that they seemed almost to be immune from paradigm shifts and external pressures. Among the developed countries, the lead in the policy reform race was taken by New Zealand in 1985. Facing a deepening economic crisis, the new Labor government took a bold approach to economic reform, introducing monetary stringency, deregulation of the economy, and trade liberalization. The reform included a sweeping overhaul of the agricultural programs that had become unwieldy and ineffective.[2] The programs that were cut included the price-support schemes for livestock products, subsidies on capital and on the use of inputs, and tax breaks for landowners. In addition, many of the marketing boards that had been set up as government-sponsored monopolies lost their market power. The wheat and poultry industries were deregulated, and a partial deregulation of the liquid (town) milk sector occurred (Sandrey and Reynolds 1990).

The programs that had been removed were of rather more recent origin than the farm policies of the United States, Europe, or even Japan. The lessons were perhaps more applicable to a middle-income country with favorable agricultural prospects but with a counter-productive mix of agricultural policies giving inappropriate signals to an otherwise competitive farm sector.[3] However, in practical terms, successful agricultural policy reform gave New Zealand a new authority in international discussions of farm policies, as being willing to make dramatic policy changes of the sort being suggested to others.

Some other high-income countries also underwent radical reforms of agricultural policy, following the lead of New Zealand. Australia made a significant step toward reducing market price support for a number of agricultural products in 1988 (OECD 1988, 86). Administered prices for wheat were eliminated and the domestic market deregulated in 1989 (OECD 1991, 115). A process of tariff reduction for sugar was begun in 1991 (OECD 1991, 150), though parastatal marketing of domestic production was allowed to continue. In 1992, the federal support for milk was reduced and an end to export subsidies for dairy products was announced (OECD 1992, 118). Despite some marginal backsliding, market price support in Australia is now minimal—running at about 7 percent of farm output (OECD 1999, 99).

But for every reform in the 1980s, many more examples exist of reform delayed and watered down. The Common Agricultural Policy (CAP) of the European Union was perhaps the most resistant to change. In an account of reform attempts of the 1980s, Moyer and Josling (1990) had to stretch the definition of reform somewhat to include the 1984 and 1988 changes in the CAP. They spent much of their effort explaining why the CAP had survived pressures that might have been thought to be enough to lead to change. U.S. farm policy did change somewhat more noticeably in the direction of "reform" in the 1981 and 1985 farm bills, but again at a pace dictated by domestic political resistance from the agricultural sector. Serious policy lags were clearly predominant on both sides of the Atlantic, even while New Zealand was paving the way toward reform.

The experience of most industrialized countries in the 1980s falls somewhere between the radical shifts of the developing countries and New Zealand and the snails-pace incrementalism of the United States and the European Union. Canada offers a good example of such a country with an ambivalent record over this period. New instruments were introduced that emphasized such elements as crop insurance and direct payments at the expense of open-ended price supports. But supply control still dominated the import-competing sectors, and the export industries still benefited from federal subsidies and state marketing. Japan began to move away from the tight control of internal markets and imports, but only in those sectors in which domestic production was not adequate to meet demand. The basic laws governing agricultural policy still mandated a search for higher degrees of self-sufficiency in spite of new paradigms that defined food security in terms of the availability of food on international markets and the ability of countries to pay.

The situation changed quite appreciably in the 1990s. The 1992 changes in the European Union's Common Agricultural Policy (CAP) and the 1996 farm bill in the United States represented very significant shifts in direction for farm policy and qualify as "reform." Whether one can attribute the reforms to a paradigm shift is less clear. The MacSharry reforms of 1992 were deliberately aimed at preserving the CAP. As Agriculture Commissioner, Ray MacSharry had as his primary objective to put the CAP on a more stable footing, and a compensated price-drop for cereals and oilseeds was a way of removing some of the pressure not only from abroad but also from domestic critics. The connection with the GATT talks has been discussed elsewhere in detail (Coleman and Tangermann 1997) but the causal link between CAP reform and a paradigm shift is more indirect. The nature of the CAP is that it represents a bargain among countries as well as a farm policy for the European Union. Change can come about as a result of changes in the terms of the bargain just as much as a shift in the model of agriculture. Or, to put it differently, each country in the European Union has its own version of the paradigm, and the CAP is a reflection of the bargaining process within the European Union as much as of a coordinated and consistent European view of the appropriate role of government in agriculture.

The U.S. farm bill debate did have elements of "new thinking" in it, but the final bill owed more to a careful calculation by its supporters that it would generate larger returns to farmers than any feasible alternative (Orden, Paarlberg, and Roe 1999). The two agricultural superpowers seemed at last to be following the lead of the smaller exporters and the middle-income countries in adapting their agricultural policies to the new global realities. However, the end of the decade of the 1990s brought indications of backsliding as the United States, along with other countries, tried to protect their farmers from low world prices.

In other parts of North America, agricultural policies began to change somewhat more rapidly. Canada dropped its rail subsidies for western grains in 1995 (OECD 1995, 26) and converted quotas to (rather high) tariffs for sensitive import products such as dairy goods and poultry meat. But tying this development to a conversion to the liberal cause is difficult. The changes were forced on Canada by the exigencies of international trade pacts, NAFTA, and the Uruguay Round Agreement on Agriculture rather than being domestically generated through a revision of orthodoxy. In Mexico, a stronger case can be made that a paradigm shift led to the dramatic reform of agricultural policy that was put in place in 1994, when the PROCAMPO program instituted direct payment in place of high price supports for a number of crops, including maize and beans (OECD 1994, 81). Two years later, Mexico launched another initiative, Alianza para el Campo, which helped farmers purchase capital goods and provided technical assistance (OECD 1996, 59). A constitutional amendment (*ejido* reform) helped to free the land market, and the radical trimming of the role of the main parastatal, CONASUPO, liberalized the domestic market. These changes were not mandated by NAFTA and the WTO, though they made compliance with the terms of these trade agreements very much easier.

In Japan, one of the more reluctant reformers, agricultural policies also began to change significantly in the 1990s. Pressure from the United States had already led to the conversion of quotas to tariffs for citrus and beef imports. The Uruguay Round speeded the process and led to further tariff cuts. The law that mandates the role of the government in agricultural markets was modified in 1996 in the direction of privatization, in particular in the sensitive rice market (OECD 1996, 54). Direct payments were introduced the next year, under the New Rice Policy (OECD 1997, 72), though these instruments have been used more sparingly in Japan than in many OECD countries. As a result, the task of bringing down domestic prices has hardly begun.

Perhaps the most surprising convert to the new paradigm was Sweden, long considered, along with Norway and Finland, to be a bastion of high-cost protected agriculture. In 1991, the government introduced the New Food Policy that included the immediate phasing out of internal price supports, intervention buying, and export subsidies (OECD 1991, 177). However, this liberal policy survived only a couple of years, because by 1993 Sweden had to reintroduce intervention and export subsidies as a part of its entry into the European Union (OECD 1993, 155). Norway, relieved of the obligation to adopt the CAP by its decision not to join the European Union, also began to drift toward direct payments and lower prices (OECD 1993, 152) but with nothing of the abrupt policy shift of its Swedish neighbor. Even

Switzerland, long known as having among the highest levels of agricultural protection in Europe, began in 1992 the process of switching from high price supports to the use of direct payments (OECD 1992, 150). In 1998, this shift was accelerated by a new policy framework (AP 2002) that linked these payments to environmental standards (OECD 1998, 142).

COMPETING PARADIGMS OF OECD AGRICULTURE

Can one conclude from the active period of farm policy reform in the 1990s that all the major OECD countries have evolved a broadly similar view of agriculture and its policy environment? Such a conclusion is almost certainly premature. The extent to which OECD countries have embraced the model of a market-oriented farm sector differs greatly across countries. It is difficult to argue that Japan and Korea, though actively discussing policy reform at home, have fully abandoned either the rhetoric or the policy manifestations of the "old" paradigm of an agriculture that needs support for national objectives that transcend commercial viability. Debate in Norway and Switzerland is still based on the premise that agriculture is basically an uncompetitive sector, hampered by climatic and physical limitations and competing unsuccessfully with an affluent nonfarm sector for labor and capital. The lively debate in the European Union on farm policy reform is certainly not predicated on an efficient sector that can duel with the United States, Canada, and Australia for market shares in emerging regions. It is therefore necessary to examine in more detail what might be other "competing" paradigms of agriculture in the OECD countries. The old paradigm may be on the way out, but that does not necessarily imply that the same new paradigm is being embraced in all OECD countries. In fact, three competing paradigms appear to be vying for the title of successor to the old view of agriculture as a sector in need of support. These are identified in table 13.1, together with the policy objectives and instruments implied by the paradigm. In addition, the implications for trade rules are suggested, as well as the implicit or explicit paradigm for the nature of the world market.

The Dependent Agriculture Paradigm

To highlight the changes inherent in the adoption of each of the three new paradigms, it is useful to briefly characterize the "old" view of agriculture as a dependent sector unable to compete either internally with the nonfarm sector for resources or with other agricultures overseas (table 13.1). The major role of the OECD governments was to find and secure markets for farm products. Over time, this role expanded to managing, through domestic production quotas, the quantities produced. Farmers themselves were in general left to focus on the production of commodities. The implicit social compact was that the government would provide border protection, buy surpluses, and assist with exports if they were in excess of the unsubsidized sales possible on world markets. Such surpluses frequently emerged, as technical change tended to outstrip demand growth. Support for this paradigm came from the mainstream farm organizations and from first-stage processors, whose profits appeared to be linked to the level of domestic production. Even countries that were major exporters of farm products subscribed broadly to the notion that agricultural market supports were necessary for a viable rural sector.

The trade policy implications of such a view of agriculture were patently obvious for years. Trade rules could not be allowed to get in the way of the management of domestic markets. In particular, Articles XI and XVI of the GATT were designed to ensure that agriculture was relieved of some of the disciplines applied to other traded goods.[4] Moreover, the GATT waiver granted to the United States in 1995 and the choice of the ambiguous "variable levy" and "export restitution" instruments by the European Union in 1962 made it clear that countries were not prepared to submit their policies to international discipline. Behind this determination to keep trade rules weak in agriculture was a particular view of the functioning of world markets. Commodity prices were seen as low and unstable, and not a sound basis for domestic policy. This view of a market characterized by chronically weak world prices became self fulfilling, as interventionist policies promoted surpluses that came up against insulated markets.

The Competitive Agriculture Paradigm

The main feature of the competitive agriculture paradigm is the view that the sector can stand on its own two feet (table 13.1). Government policy is defined in this paradigm as performing the twin tasks of giving the competitive farmers a "level playing field" on which to compete while simultaneously putting a safety net under those who cannot play on that field. Eventually the noncompetitive farmers will leave the sector. Supply control is not only unnecessary but also undesirable: Why handcuff a competitive sector and give the market to others? Policy instruments include decoupled payments for when a transition is needed from the previous policy. Emphasis is switched to such issues as risk management and low "safety nets" in lieu of price support. Such policy directions generally have the support of large farmers and their organizations as well as of agricultural traders and processors.

Table 13.1. Four Competing Paradigms of Agricultural Policy in the OECD

	Dependent	*Competitive*	*Multifunctional*	*Globalized*
Nature of Agriculture	Low incomes Not competitive with other sectors Not competitive with other countries	Average incomes Competitive with other sectors Competitive in world markets	Incomes from farming inadequate Producer of under-rewarded public goods	Farmers as part of supply chain Manager of land and livestock resources Consumer-driven sector
Policy Objective	Government needed to find markets Supply control necessary	Move towards free market Relax supply control	Preserve countryside Keep family businesses viable	Establish quality and safety standards Fairness in contractual relationships
Policy Instruments	Border protection Surplus buying State trading Export assistance	Decoupled payments in transition Risk management Low safety-nets	Environmental subsidies Protection against "mono-functional" agriculture	Harmonization of regulations and standards Competition enforcement Protection of intellectual property
Main Supporters	Farm organizations First-stage processors	Larger farmers Agricultural processors and traders	Small-farm groups Farmers in remote areas	Retail stores Specialty farms Food processors
Trade Policy Aims	Avoid restrictive trade rules	Market access Remove export subsidies Constrain domestic support	Moderate pressure on agriculture Allow subsidies under trade rules	Strengthen intellectual property rules Harmonize SPS and TBT rules Ensure competitive conditions
World Market Paradigm	World market unstable Prices depressed and no basis for domestic policy	World market stable and reliable if domestic policies are reformed World prices best guide for domestic policy	World market reflects "mono-functional" agriculture Prices inadequate for supply of public goods	"World market" is often intra-firm sales Instability and uncertainty created by government intervention

This trade-friendly paradigm has been accompanied by (and perhaps reflects) a shift in the composition of the groups that have political influence in agricultural policy (Josling 1999). This is in part connected with the move away from commodity-based support systems. If the government supports the price of a commodity by restricting imports, subsidizing exports, buying up surpluses, or taxing substitute products, then it usually needs to work through the processing sector or the wholesaler to implement the policy. Sugar policies are operated largely through sugarbeet factories and cane refineries. Dairy policy is implemented through the dairies and creameries that take delivery of farmers' milk. Grain policies involve storage and shipping of cereals through merchants and middlemen. Oilseeds policies involve oils and meals from the crushing activities as well as just seeds and beans. When the basis of farm payments is the output of commodities, some coincidence of interests occurs between the processor and the farmer. When the farmer gets paid compensation bonuses on the basis of historical hectarage and regional yield, the processor has less interest in the profitability of the domestic producer and is more willing to import the raw material and look for the cheapest source of supply.

Moreover, the "decoupling" of support from output has in turn had a profound impact on the range of trade policy choices in the sector. It essentially means that a country can recast its trade policy for agricultural goods to be consistent with that for nonagricultural goods. Shifting from price supports to income insurance schemes, for instance, gives the possibility of relaxation of import regulations. One is substituting financial instruments for physical commodity market intervention, generally at lower cost. Similarly, production constraints previously needed to limit government payments on export subsidies would no longer be needed if the compensation payments to farmers were not influenced by market price. The decline of commodity programs liberates trade policy, just as the de-linking of price from income liberates social and environmental policy.

In the absence of externalities in commodity markets, a major role of governments is to run a trade policy that supports the competitive parts of agriculture along with a policy to improve competition at home. This implies that governments agree to restrictions on their ability to intervene in markets in exchange for agreements by others to do the same. Market access needs to be improved by tariff reductions; export subsidies should be removed because they grossly distort world markets; and domestic support payments that escape the disciplines imposed at the border have to meet certain criteria. This is essentially the set of rules that emerged from the Uruguay Round. In other words, the competitive paradigm is enshrined in the Agreement on Agriculture. The implicit world market paradigm that supports this domestic view of a competitive agriculture is of a sector that is essentially stable if domestic policies are reformed.

The Multifunctional Agriculture Paradigm

The primary challenge to the new market-oriented paradigm has come from Europe. In recent years, farm politicians in many European Union members have adumbrated a "paradigm" of their own, that of a "multifunctional" agriculture sometimes referred to as the "European Farming Model" (table 13.1). This argument is often dismissed as merely a mixture of political posturing for position at the WTO and of the repackaging of some bland facts about the significance of farm activities in rural areas. But it is also the case that real differences in perception exist between Europe and (say) the United States about the place of agriculture in the modern economy. Population density and farm size are not unrelated to the political (and economic) relationship between agriculture and other sectors. One does not have to be a closet protectionist to recognize that Holland has a serious problem of groundwater pollution, or to acknowledge that Austrian meadows give pleasure to millions of town dwellers in winter and summer. The question is whether these differences show up as nuances of an essentially similar agricultural model or whether they lead to incompatible policy sets that in turn constrain the reform of the international trade system?

The main characteristic of the "multifunctional" paradigm is that agriculture is viewed as a provider of public goods in addition to, and in many ways more important than, its role as a producer of raw materials for the food industry (table 13.1). The market for commodities inadequately rewards the farmer for such public goods as a pleasant-looking and environmentally friendly countryside, or a stable social infrastructure built on small towns and villages. Appropriate instruments for policy in such an agriculture include environmental payments, either as a reward for providing the public goods or as compensation for the loss of market share to those whose costs are lower as a result of not having to provide those public goods. Support for this view of agriculture comes predominantly from small farmers and those in remote areas. So far, no consensus seems to exist among environmental groups that this is a good way to formulate policy toward the environment: Presumably there is the potential conflict of interest if the total sum that society wishes to devote to environmental stewardship is constrained.

One key question is what are the trade policy implications of a multifunctional view of agriculture? It is often argued that multifunctional agriculture needs protection from the lower-cost supplies from those countries whose agricultural sectors are not asked to bear the burden of countryside preservation, rural development, or societal stability. This is based on a "world market" view of a European agricultural system handicapped by small-sized units and by demands and regulations imposed by a crowded continent, and therefore unable to meet the challenge laid down by the sparsely populated "new world" suppliers. Far from being competitive, border measures are still needed for the viability of such an agriculture. But one can also argue that providing additional public goods through the taxing of private goods at the border is inefficient. In other words, the issue is not whether but how to give the support. And the support could well be given in a way that does not spread the burden to others.

Not all countries in the European Union, or farmers in any one country, fully accept the notion of a multifunctional agriculture. Many European farmers also see themselves as part of a competitive core and have begun to question the restrictions that the CAP has put on them in the name of saving them from "unfair" competition from abroad. This view is particularly prevalent in the United Kingdom, Denmark, and Sweden. It is also possible to argue that the European Commission is using the multifunctional argument for domestic consumption to set up something that can be defended at the bargaining table without having to support the continuation of export subsidies and high tariffs. If multifunctionality means paying producers directly for the amenity value of their farming or their care of animals rather than through distorted prices for output, then the concept is not so inconsistent with the competitive paradigm.

The Global Agriculture Paradigm

As if to escape from the choice between the competitive and the multifunctional agricultures, a third "new" paradigm is emerging with very different implications for trade relations and domestic policy. The main feature of this paradigm is that agriculture is seen as one stage in a global supply chain stretching from chemical and biological input suppliers to retail stores and niche markets (table 13.1). In fact, this view sees agriculture as the "land management" and "animal management" functions in the vertical supply chain. Several sectors of agriculture have gone a long way toward this model, such as pig and poultry farming as well as many fruit and vegetable activities. The emergence of transgenic crops, or rather the opposition to them, has begun to transform the cereal and oilseed sectors as well: The technology encourages the development of the contractual relationships along the chain, and traceability and liability have forced the supply chain to be more transparent.

This "global" agricultural model points policy in a very different direction. The prime role of government is to establish safety and quality standards and to make sure that contractual relations among the elements in the chain are fair and acceptable. Policy instruments are the harmonization of standards and the removal of onerous regulations. Protection of intellectual property and the maintenance of competitive conditions (but perhaps not too competitive!) are the counterpart to the removal of distortions from government price policy. Such a view of agriculture has some resonance within the sector, but its general acceptance will more probably come as a result of the increasing influence of retailers and food processors on the policy process (Josling 1999).

A distinguishing feature of this model is that it is consumer driven. This makes the old style agricultural policy mechanisms less relevant to the needs of the industry. The support of raw commodity prices in the market through the withholding of supplies or the buying up of surpluses effectively breaks the link between producer and consumer. Just as the market is getting more sophisticated and differentiated, the old-style policy sends the message to farmers to "produce low-quality goods for government stocks." Just when supply chains are being set up for the provision of goods to supermarkets, farmers are encouraged under the old policies to take land out of production and live on payments for keeping farmland idle. Clearly the vast expense of farm policy has not helped farmers to meet the challenges of providing for modern consumers. The farmers who have prospered are those who have taken advantage of the changed conditions and begun to service the differentiated market.

Changes in agricultural structures, along with the corresponding changes in the nature of world markets for agricultural products, give this new paradigm an interesting "trade" perspective. The key concept driving such a perspective is of a global market (or a small number of subglobal markets) cooperatively managed and regulated through trade agreements and other forms of accord. National markets cease to be relevant units unless they coincide with other market characteristics. "Countries" do not trade with each other; that is the function of firms. Much "international" trade is in fact transfers of products within a company. Trade policies such as tariffs and export subsidies are undesirable not so much because they distort the resource allocation of a country but because they get in the way of a business transaction among willing partners or branches of the same corporation. Under such a view of the world, market access is a right, subject to well-defined national restrictions, not a benefit to be granted by a government to friends and neighbors. The rules for the global marketplace would include competition laws (including outlawing export subsidies), health and safety regulations, and adequate intellectual property protections to encourage innovation. The scope for domestic action would be largely confined to local and national environmental regulation and rules related to social, health, and educational services that would be provided at the national level.

THE ROLE OF PARADIGMS IN THE WTO AGRICULTURAL TALKS

The Uruguay Round was, whatever domestic politicians may say, the first "global" negotiation on domestic agricultural policy. The completion of the trade negotiations in 1993 marked the first time that effective international constraints had been put on domestic agricultural policies. The Uruguay Round Agreement on Agriculture (URAA) put in place a set of rules that has already gone a considerable way toward shaping the development of such policies. Bound tariffs replaced nontariff import measures, export subsidies were curbed, and domestic programs were codified on the basis of their potential to distort trade.[5] Every significant agricultural policy since that time has been tailored to fit within the new rules.

The attempts at reform of national agricultural policies and the negotiation of modified trade rules in the period since 1985 have been mutually supportive. Though the United States and the European Union adhered steadfastly to the notion that their own domestic policies were not negotiable in trade talks, it was becoming increasingly clear that trade and domestic policies were intimately connected and that progress on one front required movement on the other front as well. Thus the saga of the Uruguay Round negotiations on agriculture formed an important backdrop to the process of domestic policy reform. Though changing trade rules and modifying domestic support are conceptually separate, the politics and the process are closely intertwined.[6]

The role of the competing paradigms identified previously in shaping the current WTO round of agricultural talks is likely to be crucial. The talks themselves are mandated by Article 20 of the Agreement on Agriculture, which sets up the next stage of trade policy reform. But Article 20 also allows for the consideration of "non-trade concerns" in the next step. The focus of much of the debate in Geneva since the start of the new agricultural round in March 2000 (and indeed before that in the lead-up to the Seattle WTO ministerial) has been on the scope that the phrase "non-trade concerns" offers to the proponents of multifunctional agriculture.

The Cairns Group, the most vocal and articulate proponent of the competitive paradigm and the associated view of stable and reliable world agricultural markets, clearly does not want to see multifunctionality enshrined in the WTO. The European Union member states, on the other hand, cannot go home to their electorates without being able to claim some "victory" in this area. Thus much of the real negotiating will be on such seemingly arcane topics as the definition of the green box and the future of the blue box. Should the green box contain some policies that have a positive production impact? At present, this appears impermissible. The Agreement on Agriculture sets up the "fundamental requirement" for support measures to be in the green box that "they have no, or at most minimal, trade-distorting effects or effects on production" (Uruguay Round Agreement on Agriculture, Annex 2:1). However, the "policy-specific criteria" set out in the same Annex states, with respect to environmental programs, that payments are allowed to the extent of the cost of complying with the requirements of the program (Annex 2:12(b)). The apparent conflict between the general and the specific criteria has not been tested in a WTO panel. But it would seem to be vital to the concept of multifunctional agriculture that incidental output effects (presumably, only increases would be of interest) be allowed. For the Cairns Group to swallow this argument, some clear trade-off in terms of market access and export competition would be necessary.

The fate of the blue box may also hang on the outcome of the dialog between the advocates of the competing paradigms. To the Cairns Group, the blue box is a temporary aberration hatched up by the United States and the European Union to avoid the issue as to whether payments linked to supply control were production enhancing. Now that the United States has moved away from supply control in the major arable crops, the only question might seem to be whether the European Union will follow suit. But the European Union and Japan argue that the blue box has been a useful "half-way house" for the transition from coupled to decoupled programs. To close this avenue could make it more difficult for countries such as Japan to reform their policies. And the United States has been reluctant to call for the elimination of the blue box, possibly because to do so would constrain future policy options. In effect, the blue box stands for an established mode of policy, the management of surpluses through supply control, which is out of tune with the competitive paradigm.

Meanwhile the advocates of a "global" view of agriculture will be constantly trying to introduce other elements into the discussion that appear to be outside the realm of the Agreement on Agriculture. They will not so much clash with the other two paradigms as try to move the agenda to consider these "new" issues. One key area would be that of investment policy, not fully covered in the Uruguay Round and unsuccessfully negotiated later in the OECD. Another area would be competition policy, for which at the least a global market should have some global rules. A third aspect of trade policy that is seen as important to this global, consumer-driven agriculture is the establishment of international norms (preferably science based, but certainly consumer credible) for certifying food safety. This, however, threatens to confuse and delay the discussions on market access, export competition, and domestic support. A fourth topic is the possible expansion of the scope for protecting "geographical indications," such as widely-recognized names for particular foods that denote their regional origin. The agricultural talks could well be slowed down by this "agenda creep," to the frustration of those who see the negotiations as being a simple continuation of the process started in the Uruguay Round.

CONCLUSIONS

Agricultural policy instruments in many OECD countries have changed within the last decade, with a convergence toward a set of less trade-distorting programs. These have emphasized targeting and decoupling, replacing the support of commodity markets by payments to farm families on a range of other criteria. In some countries, particularly the smaller exporters such as New Zealand and Australia, and in reforming developing countries such as Mexico, this has reflected a true paradigm shift, involving a sea-change in ideas about the role and scope of policy and the nature of the farm sector. In other countries, including the United States and Canada, the change has been less dramatic and the vestiges of the old policy and the old mental models about agriculture are still apparent. In general, the larger the country, the more resistant are political structures to accept the new paradigm.

In Europe, the old paradigm of a sector needing support is also giving way but is being replaced by one that emphasizes the role of agriculture in providing public goods such as environmental benefits. Other European countries, such as Norway and Switzerland, support this view. This position stands in contrast to that taken by Japan and Korea, where the view of agriculture still reflects more the old paradigm of an agriculture that needs support in order to provide adequate agricultural commodities for domestic consumption—an argument usually cast in terms of food security.

The European Union's multifunctional paradigm and the Japanese concern with food security could soon come to clash with the market-oriented view of agriculture promoted by the Cairns Group and the United States, leading to continued trade conflicts. The WTO talks will provide a ready forum for the articulation of the paradigm clash. The Cairns Group and the United States will be pushing for further reform of the trade rules, in effect trying to eliminate the "exceptions" for agriculture built in to the Agriculture Agreement. The "friends of multifunctionality" will be making sure that enough scope exists in those rules to allow the type of policy that rewards environmental stewardship and promotes agriculture that does not cross the line in terms of public perceptions of animal cruelty. The Japanese will insist that their ability to maintain the agricultural capacity that they consider necessary is preserved, and hope that attention focuses on the exporters for adjustment. Meanwhile, those already in the global supply chain will be pressing for tighter regulations on competition and intellectual property protection, as well as more harmonized standards. The question is whether these divergent demands can be made compatible. The next few years will tell.

NOTES

1. See in particular Orden's Chapter 3 herein and Coleman, Skogstad, and Atkinson (1997). The seminal article on the concept of a paradigm shift in economic policy is Hall (1993).

2. Assistance to agriculture had grown to about 10 percent of the total public expenditure. For a small economy dependent upon livestock export earnings, these subsidies imposed a heavy burden. The political conditions that allowed these reforms are discussed in Williamson (1994).

3. See Valdés (1994) for a discussion of the similarities and differences between the Chile and New Zealand experiences.

4. Article XI allowed quantitative restrictions in cases in which there was domestic supply control, and Article XVI implicitly condoned export subsidies for agricultural products (see Josling, Tangermann, and Warley 1996).

5. See IATRC (1997) for a more complete discussion of the Uruguay Round results and Josling (1998) for the need for further reform of the agricultural trade rules.

6. This interaction has been studied by political scientists, following Putnam (1988), as two-level games (Paarlberg 1997; Moyer 1993) and three-level games (Patterson, 1997) when the national politics of the European Union is involved. Coleman and Tangermann (1997) incorporate the role of secretariats in intermediating these games.

REFERENCES

Coleman, W., G. Skogstad, and M. Atkinson. "Paradigm Shifts and Policy Networks: Cumulative Change in Agriculture." *Journal of Public Policy* 16 (1997): 3.

Coleman, W. and S. Tangermann. "Linked Games, International Mediators, and Agricultural Trade." Paper presented at the IATRC Annual Meeting, San Diego, December 1997.

Hall, P. "Policy Paradigms, Social Learning, and the State." *Comparative Politics*, 25 (April 1993): 3.

International Agricultural Trade Research Consortium. "Implementation of the Uruguay Round Agreement on Agriculture and Issues for the Next Round of Agricultural Negotiations." IATRC Commissioned Paper No. 12, November 1997.

Josling, T., S. Tangermann, and T. K. Warley. *Agriculture in the GATT*. New York: Macmillan, 1996.

Josling, T. *Agricultural Trade Policy: Completing Reform*. Washington, DC: Institute for International Economics, 1998.

Josling, T. "Globalization of the Agri-Food Industry and its Impact on Agricultural Trade Policy." Paper presented to the conference on Agricultural Globalization, Trade, and the Environment, University of California at Berkeley, March 1999.

Krueger, A. O. "The Political Economy of Agricultural Pricing Policy: A Synthesis of the Political Economy in Developing Countries." In A. Krueger, M. Schiff, and A. Valdes, *The Political Economy of Agricultural Pricing Policy*. Baltimore: The Johns Hopkins University Press, 1992.

Moyer, H. W. "EC Decisionmaking, the MacSharry Reforms of the CAP, Maastricht, and the GATT Uruguay Round." Paper delivered to the Third Biennial Conference of the ECSA, Washington, DC, May 1993.

Moyer, H. W. and T. Josling. *Agricultural Policy Reform: Politics and Process in the EC and the US*. Harvester Wheatsheaf, Hemel Hempstead, 1990.

OECD. *Agricultural Policies in OECD Countries*, Paris: OECD, Various Years.

Orden, D. "The Soul of Farm Policy in the 21st Century." Paper presented to the conference on Challenging the Agricultural Economics Paradigm. Columbus, Ohio, September 2000.

Orden, D., R. Paarlberg, and T. Roe. *Policy Reform in American Agriculture: Analysis and Prognosis.* Chicago: University of Chicago Press, 1999.

Paarlberg, R. "Agricultural Policy Reform and the Uruguay Round: Synergistic Linkage in a Two-Level Game." *International Organization* 51 (Summer 1997): 3.

Patterson, L. A. "Agricultural Policy Reform in the European Community: a Three-Level Game Analysis." *International Organization* 51 (Winter 1997): 1.

Putnam, R. "Diplomacy and Domestic Politics: the Logic of Two-Level Games." *International Organization* 42 (Summer 1988): 3.

Sandrey, R. and R. Reynolds (eds.). *Farming without Subsidies: New Zealand's Recent Experiences.* MAF, New Zealand, 1990.

Tweeten, L. "Trade, Uncertainty, and New Farm Programs." Forthcoming in C. Moss et al., eds. *Agricultural Trade, Globalization, and the Environment.* Norwell, MA: Kluwer Academic Publishers, 2001.

Tweeten, L. and C. Zulauf. "Public Policy for Agriculture after Commodity Programs." *Review of Agricultural Economics* 19 (Fall/Winter 1997): 2.

Valdés, A. "Agricultural Reforms in Chile and New Zealand: A Review." *Journal of Agricultural Economics* 45 (May 1994).

Williamson, J. (ed.). *The Political Economy of Policy Reform.* Washington, DC: Institute for International Economics, January 1994.

Part IV

Trade Conflicts over Domestic Policies

Agricultural Trade Issues in Transatlantic Trade Relations

Tim Josling

1. INTRODUCTION

AGRICULTURAL trade relations between the US and the EC reached a low ebb on November 5, 1992, as the US announced the imposition of punitive tariffs on $300 million worth of agricultural imports from the EC. Specifically targeted was white wine, mainly from France and Italy. Two days earlier the 'last ditch' talks to settle the twin problems of EC oilseed subsidies, twice ruled illegal under the GATT, and the agricultural component of the Uruguay Round of trade negotiations had broken up without agreement. A last minute compromise had apparently been blocked by the President of the European Commission, causing the Agricultural Commissioner to resign his GATT portfolio. A delay in the application of the punitive tariffs allowed an additional set of negotiations. The 'lame duck' US administration quickly cut a deal with the EC Commission on November 20, on both the oilseed and the Uruguay Round issues, to the relief of the outgoing Agricultural Commissioner, who had returned as a negotiator, but to the consternation and anger of French politicians and farmers. The 'Blair House' Accord, as it is known, has been less than popular in the US, where it was widely seen as a desperate attempt to get a GATT agreement through before the Clinton Administration took office. The Uruguay Round still staggers from crisis to crisis, kept alive only by the realisation that failure would be bad for the prospects for economic recovery.

How did the future of the trade system become hostage to a dispute over a few hectares of soybeans? Is agricultural trade really that important to the US that other sectors must await resolution of these issues before enjoying their own trade

TIM JOSLING is Professor of Economics at the Food Research Institute, Stanford University, Stanford, California. This paper was presented at the Conference on 'Transatlantic Trade After the Uruguay Round', organised by the Centre for Research in Economic Development and International Trade (CREDIT), University of Nottingham, England, Monday April 26, 1993.

expansion? Are these endemic problems in agriculture so intractable that the world must watch as a few countries spar over farm trade issues? Will these problems persist in the future, or would a GATT agreement put an end to such quarrels? Are there better ways of dealing with agricultural trade disputes between the US and the EC?

This paper attempts to answer some of these questions. After a brief discussion of the trade philosophies of the EC and the US, and an account of the background to the agricultural conflicts, the issues of the completion of the Uruguay Round and the oilseeds dispute are explored. The argument then turns to other emerging areas of potential conflict arising from recent developments in trade. A final section suggests some modest ways of improving the situation.

2. US AND EC TRADE PHILOSOPHIES

Transatlantic trade problems are surrounded by rhetoric. In agriculture, the situation is complicated by the separate rhetoric of farm policy. This compound rhetoric would seem to indicate deep philosophical differences between the US and the EC, that show up as divergent trade and farm policies. These policies lead to trade tensions that cannot be lessened by commercial diplomacy. In case there exist some fundamental differences, it is necessary to address the issue of 'system clash', the mutual incompatibility of two alternative economic systems which prevents them from going too far in the direction of free trade.

It is easy to make the case that the US and EC have some fundamental differences in their respective approaches to trade in general and agricultural trade in particular. The last three US administrations have been adamant in their belief that the US is an open market, a place where the rest of the world can come and sell their goods without hindrance, whereas the other developed countries, Japan and the EC in particular, guard their markets with a mix of subtle and blatant trade barriers. The US economy itself is seen as more market-oriented and less directed by government policy. The 'big debate' in economic and trade policy in the US has been over the desirability of moving towards more management of the economy, through industrial policy and active trade policy, to better compete with the regulated economies of Japan and Europe. The success of Japan, in particular, is seen as a challenge to the notion that open markets and a 'hands-off' industrial policy are good for growth.

Of course, from outside the US, even as close as across the Canadian border, the picture looks very different. The US is indeed a relatively open economy, but with all manner of residual restrictions on commerce — even among states — and new protectionist measures emanating from every level of government. A fundamentally protectionist alliance of organised labour and a Democratic Congress was only kept at bay by elaborate free-trade rhetoric from the Republican

Adminstration and their allies in the business community. The trade remedy laws are strongly tilted in favour of US businesses, and act to scare off potential exporters. Harassment through state taxation laws and minor court decisions adds to this view of the US economy as hostile to trade.

Views on Europè also depend upon the location of the viewer. Is the EC the great experiment in a single, seamless market, open to foreign firms and products, as advertised by the Commission? Or is the single market a device to develop European competitiveness at the expense of overseas firms, and a way of consolidating at the Community level a range of protective devices? Within Europe, views on trade differ among countries. It is therefore easy to support almost any interpretation of the EC's liberalism.

The rhetoric of agricultural policy is equally confusing. Is the US the champion of free agricultural markets? Not so, say those who have to face Section 22-sanctioned quantitative restrictions, 'voluntary' export restraints, or compete with exports under the Export Enhancement Program (EEP). It is easy for a large exporter to preach free markets, and point the finger at importing countries. The EC often claims to be an 'open' agricultural market, importing more farm produce than any other region. But this does not ring true to the suppliers of cereals, dairy products, meat and sugar who face high and sometimes prohibitive import levies, or seem relevant to those competing with the EC's open-ended export restrictions.

Though political structures differ, and the domestic policies of farm support require a dose of 'we-they' system confrontation, the similarities between the EC and the US are more striking than the differences. The US-EC farm trade clashes are better seen as conflicts among similar systems, each of which would work better if only the others were to be modified. The tensions are a result of this unfortunate fact.

3. UNDERLYING CAUSES OF AGRICULTURAL TRADE DISPUTES

There is one over-riding explanation as to why governments have got into conflicts about agricultural trade.[1] They take on, through their agricultural policies, the responsibility of finding markets for domestic farm products. By and large, governments do not control output decisions: that is left to the millions of small and medium size family businesses that make up the farm sector. Sometimes governments attempt to bribe or coerce farmers to restrict output of various products, though often without notable success. On other occasions they allow the market to determine prices and 'top up' farm income with an extra payment. Very occasionally they give farmers payments related to income need or to environmental

[1] These arguments are explored further in Josling (1991a).

contribution rather than output. But the major thrust of farm support policies has always been the provision of 'markets' sufficient to maintain chosen levels of price. These 'markets' are often the creation of policies rather than of consumer choice. They are created by protection against imports; by state purchasing and intervention schemes; by export restitutions and enhancements (note the variety of pseudonyms for subsidies); and by taxing substitute products.

It follows that if more than one government is trying to create such an artificial market, then each will come into (potential) conflict with the others. Each such policy imposes a financial and administrative cost on the policies of all other governments. Some of these costs go unnoticed, as a part of the 'trading environment': others are made apparent and cause friction. What causes a particular potential problem to emerge as a conflict is in part a result of world market forces; in part a reflection of the political influence of particular producer groups; and in part a consequence of the policy instruments used. Conflicts will diminish if world market conditions 'improve' (i.e., prices increase, which reduces the cost of providing the artificial market); if political influence of producers groups diminishes (which may happen if the public loses sympthy with farmers); or if governments shift to other types of policies (such as direct payments or supply control).

US-EC trade conflicts reflect this clash of domestic farm policies. More often than not, the conflict pits US export interests against the Common Agricultural Policy (CAP) of the EC. The US has a strong belief in the capacity of its own agriculture to compete on level terms with other countries. It has maintained a consistent objection to subsidised competition from other countries who seek to use world markets to avoid domestic resource adjustments and hence prevent true competitiveness from emerging. The EC is singled out as a major player in the game of subsidised exports and high domestic market prices. As a result, the CAP has achieved a particular status in US agricultural policy circles as 'public enemy number one.'

This continued attack on the community is not without cause. The EC's Common Agricultural Policy (CAP) has been almost a caricature of a trade-distorting policy. The principal instruments developed in the late 1960s are the variable import levies applied at the border in such a way as to keep domestic markets stable, the intervention purchases which put a floor in the domestic market, and the variable export subsidies which operate to keep domestic intervention stocks at a reasonable level. Only for sugar was a quota system chosen, on a 'temporary' basis, though for some products protection came through fixed tariffs (as in sheep, fruits, and vegetables) and in some cases the intervention system was weak or absent (pigmeat, poultry and eggs and fruits and vegetables). Later, quotas were introduced for milk, and the intervention system for cereals and meat was weakened.[2] Despite

[2] See Moyer and Josling (1990) for a discussion of the stages of CAP reform over the 1980s.

these changes, the emphasis on border protection was a major contributing factor to trade tensions. By contrast, the US policy for cereals and oilseeds operated for years essentially at the farm and internal market level, until the growth in export subsidies in recent years.

The conflicts between the US and the EC in agricultural trade go back twenty-five years to the founding of the CAP in the early 1960s. Until recently, these conflicts looked as if they were under control. The sharpness of the conflict has increased in the past decade. The exacerbation of tensions since 1980 is a clear reflection of the emergence of EC agriculture as a major exporter in temperate-zone markets. The US has seen its exports to the EC diminish over the last decade, and has faced increasing competition in third country markets. EC exports have also penetrated the US domestic market to an increasing extent. During the 1970s, US exports rose rapidly. The United States had in place the capacity to meet the surge in demand from the USSR and from the developing world. European exports lagged until 1977 but accelerated with the generally favourable trade conditions until 1981. That year represented a peak for US agricultural exports, at $43 billion. Over the next few years, US exports declined dramatically, to a low point of $26.1 billion in 1986. EC exports stalled a little then recovered, and in 1986 were actually higher than those of the US. The EC, always touted as the 'largest import market' for farm products was temporarily the world's largest exporter. A recovery in US exports since 1987 has helped to restore somewhat the earlier balance.

The trend in overall exports sets the tone for US farm policy. The budget cost largely reflects the balance between domestic production and export demand. Escalation of budget costs over the 1980s was a major policy concern in the US as it was in the EC. In the 1970s, farm support costs stayed low — with buoyant export markets and firm prices. Support costs in the US took off in the wake of the drop in exports in 1982, coupled with the generous policy prices set under the 1981 Farm Bill. A drought-induced drop in production in 1983, coupled with the cost-shifting effect of the payment-in-kind (PIK) scheme, gave a temporary respite, but by 1986, expenditure had reached a peak of $25 billion. Indeed, as EC representatives in Brussels and Washington were quick to point out, US support costs exceeded those in the EC at that time. More recent developments have returned this relationship also to its more normal state.

The fall in US exports to the Community in the 1980s was primarily in the 'big-ticket' items of grains, non-grain feed ingredients and oilseeds and products. Corn sales were hard hit by emerging surpluses of barley in the EC and by the continued attractiveness of non-grain feed ingredients in livestock rations. Soybean sales were hit by increased oilseed production in the EC, which grew from 3.2 million tons in 1980/81 to 11.6 million tons in 1987/88. Domestic oilseed production then accounted for nearly one-half of the total EC oilseed use (USDA, 1989). More recently, other markets have been affected. Beef and variety meat sales to the EC from the US had reached over $100 million in 1988, when the ban on imported meat produced with hormones was introduced. Cotton sales fell away after 1985.

Added to the concerns about import access has been the intensified competition in third countries. This has been particularly true in the case of wheat. EC wheat production has more than doubled since 1962, largely as a result of yield increases (USDA, 1989). In the face of stagnant consumption, self-sufficiency was reached in the mid 1970s, and the EC emerged as a major exporter of wheat, capturing 15 per cent of the world market by 1987. The US share declined sharply in the 1980s from 48 per cent in 1981 to below 30 per cent in 1985 (ABARE, 1989a and 1989b). Whatever the true cause of this decline, the Community's generous export subsidies were held in part to blame. This experience led to a minor subsidy war, with the US using an Export Enhancement Program (EEP) to target export subsidies at markets lost to the EC. These EEP sales accounted for about 50 per cent of US wheat exports from 1985–1988 (USDA, 1989). The struggle for markets was particularly intense in the North African countries of Morocco, Algeria, Tunisia, and Egypt, which import large quantities of wheat and wheat flour. With the aid of considerable subsidies, the US was able to regain market shares in this region. The incident, however, left a mark on US-EC relations which perhaps exceeded its real significance.

4. CURRENT ISSUES IN AGRICULTURAL TRADE RELATIONS

The combination of weak world market prices and high budget costs put reform of the agricultural policies high on the domestic agenda in both the US and the EC.[3] Along with this domestic activity came a new awareness that trade policy changes could improve the world market environment in which the policy reforms were to take place. Higher world prices would make it easier to remove domestic support, and lessen budget exposure. But for any one country to take the initiative was problematic. What was needed was a multilateral forum for negotiating new trade rules for agriculture.

The start of the Uruguay Round of GATT negotiations, in September 1986, seemed to provide the opportunity to resolve many of the problems of agricultural trade. But imbedded in the context of a formal trade negotiation, US-EC conflicts began to take on an added significance. Agreement or disagreement could be seen to have wide-ranging implications for the trading system as a whole. Failure of the negotiations could lead major countries to lose confidence in multilateral trade arrangements. However, the agricultural stakes for the US and the EC are also high, since by mutual agreement domestic agricultural policies are 'on the table'.

[3] For background to the negotiations see Hathaway (1988), Josling et al. (1990) and Rayner, Ingersent and Hine (1993).

a. The GATT Round

Countries have traditionally taken the view that domestic agricultural policies, supported as they are by strong political interests at home, take precedence over the rules on international trade. The operation of these policies has given rise to persistent problems in international markets, with harmful effects on both developed and developing countries. The major development that makes the Uruguay Round different from earlier efforts to discuss agricultural trade is that these domestic policies are, at least in principle, subject to negotiation. Countries have expressed their willingness to discuss constraints on these policies which would make them more compatible with stable world markets.

The attempt to negotiate new rules for agricultural trade goes back to 1982, when the GATT set up a Committee on Trade and Agriculture. At the same time the OECD gave to its Secretariat a Trade Mandate, to examine the trade-distorting effects of domestic agricultural policies and to suggest ways to ease the trade problems in the sector. The OECD work proved important both for convincing governments that domestic policies were at the root of the trade problems (a fact which many had sought to ignore) and for illustrating the magnitude of support in a way that could be compared across countries (OECD, 1987). At the same time the GATT set up a committee to look at the same set of issues. This committee studied ways in which 'all measures affecting trade in agriculture would be brought under more operationally effective GATT rules and disciplines' (GATT, 1986). As was to be expected, the OECD focused on domestic policies and the GATT on trade rules. An added high-level political boost was given to both GATT and OECD initiatives by the Tokyo Summit of the heads of government of the largest seven industrial countries in May 1986.

The history of the Uruguay Round talks in agriculture is of the various methods suggested by countries to write new rules and to reduce levels of protection. In the initial salvo, in 1987, the US won high marks for originality and imagination, if not for political realism, by suggesting the elimination of all trade-distorting farm programmes in ten years. For the next year the talks were stalled on the question of whether such a drastic move was feasible or even desirable. The EC, among others, argued for a more gradual approach.

After finally getting an agreed form of words on the long-term objective ('substantial and progressive reductions') in April 1989, at the Mid-Term Review, the negotiators set about making concrete proposals. These proposals finally emerged in late 1989. By this time the US had decided that it was more important to change the types of policies used by countries to support prices than to merely reduce them. They introduced the notion of 'tariffication' of non-tariff import barriers, a ban on export subsidies, and a 'traffic light' system for domestic subsidies.

Meanwhile the EC had warmed to the idea of reducing protection levels overall, with no constraints on the type of policies used. They took over as the champion of the Aggregate Measure of Support (AMS). They reluctantly agreed to tariffication, with safeguards, so long as the US would accept taxes on non-grain feeds as a contribution to 'rebalancing' protection. The EC rejected any separate constraints on export subsidies.

The GATT Secretariat attempted in July 1990 to blend these ideas into one proposal, the de Zeeuw Draft. This draft looked to the EC rather too much like a victory for the US (and Cairns Group) position, and they declined to endorse the text as a basis for negotiations. The 'final' offers of the negotiators were still based on inconsistent approaches. After the negotiators had missed the December 1990 deadline for the conclusion of the talks, the EC finally agreed to the agenda in February 1991, and serious negotiations began. Anxious to bring the talks to a close, the GATT Director-General, Arthur Dunkel, put forward a text of a compromise in December 1991. At present, the negotiators are close to signing a slightly revised version of the Dunkel text, awaiting only a political push.

The main elements of the Dunkel Draft are as follows:

- tariffication of non-tariff trade barriers,
- reduction in tariffs by 36 per cent in 6 years,
- safeguards for importers (quantity trigger of 125 per cent, and price trigger),
- safeguards for exporters (minimum access opportunities of 3–5 per cent of consumption),
- reduction in expenditure on export subsidies of 36 per cent in 6 years,
- reduction in quantity of subsidised exports by 24 per cent in 6 years,[4]
- reduction of overall suppport, as measured by an AMS, by 20 per cent in 6 years,
- exclusion of 'green box' measures from the AMS,
- special terms for developing countries,
- agreement on sanitary and phytosanitary measures.

How well does this agreement match with the needs of a multilateral trade system? In general, these elements seem rather well suited to the task of bringing 'bulk' commodity, temperate-zone agriculture into the mainstream of trade policy. Tariffication gives a transparency to trade that is missing at the moment. Developing countries would know what barriers they face, and newly-marketised countries could plan their agricultural exports without fear of arbitrary exclusion from markets. Safeguards (quantity and price triggers) for importers are deemed to be necessary to encourage countries to 'try the waters' and the minimum access opportunity is apparently necessary to convince exporters that market access will

[4] The Blair House Accord between the EC and the US agreed to a 21 per cent reduction in the volume of subsidised exports.

be improved. Export subsidy reduction will be useful to avoid exports being pushed out of markets by EC and US subsidies. Domestic support reduction is less constraining, but guards against the possibility of having to compete with untargeted treasury payments in high income countries. Categorisation of policies gives useful guidelines for domestic policy change, in both developed and developing countries. Special and differential treatment is however largely a political device for avoiding the appearance of imposing policy change on developing countries: one hopes that most developing countries will revise their agricultural policy regimes more quickly than required by these rules. The new rules on sanitary and phytosanitary barriers should help resolve some of the problems in this area. Countries are encouraged to make use of internationally recognised standards and guidelines, and to base domestic regulations on sound scientific evidence.

This proposal contains so much that is an advance on the situation before 1986 that it would represent a major turning point in the regulation of international trade in agriculture. It does not however, represent a situation of free trade in agricultural products: the cost of changing the rules has been to give up some degree of liberalisation. Reducing by 36 per cent tariff rates which were very high in 1986–88, still leaves a considerable amount of protection. Reducing export subsidies by 36 per cent in expenditure and 21 per cent in volume would not end such subsidies. The reduction of overall support by 20 per cent, designed to constrain domestic (non-border) measures is not very tough, though it could be significant if world prices drop, but the elimination of non-tariff import barriers is of considerable value, and should make trade much more transparent.

It is, in fact, a selling point of the agreement that few changes will be needed in domestic policy. The Commission has argued strenuously that the reform of the CAP already imposes constraints on EC agriculture that will make it possible to live within new GATT rules.[5] The US Congress is in no mood to write too many restraints on US farm policy, which is after all deemed to be more liberal than that of trading partners. The GATT agreement would be most useful as a backstop, to preventing backsliding of policies which are undergoing reluctant reform.

b. The Oilseeds Dispute

Certain agricultural markets have provided the lion's share of trade conflicts. The longest-running battle is over soybean exports to the EC. The US received a concession from the Community in the Dillon Round that the tariff on soybeans

[5] There is some evidence to support this view. See Tim Josling and Stefan Tangermann (1992). The French government maintains that yield increases will vitiate many of the output reductions arising from CAP reform.

and meal would be bound at zero.[6] This one action has turned out to dominate more than any other the next twenty-five years of trade and trade relations. To the EC it was a concession easily made, since trade was fairly small in those commodities and domestic production almost non-existent. Low tariffs on imports of oilseeds in any case favoured the domestic crushing and refining sectors. To the US it seemed like a useful concession, but the US was generally unhappy with the outcome on other products. It carried out of the Dillon Round 'unsatisfied negotiating rights' to be used in later trade talks.

What followed is well known. High wheat prices set for the new CAP (a political compromise which was made to satisfy German rural interests) drove feed demand to corn — much of it imported from the US. When grain prices were harmonised in the EC under the so-called silo system (moving corn prices up to meet the higher wheat prices), feed compounders switched to non-grain feeds. The pressure was particularly strong in Germany and the Netherlands, where 'green' exchange rates ensured higher cereal prices than in other parts of the EC. Compounders found that a mix of soybean meal and cassava chips (from Thailand) made an excellent substitute for corn, barley, and wheat.[7]

Soybean sales to the EC boomed over the 1970s and continued high when EC corn market imports slowed down. The hole in the dike was letting in a flood of imports. Later, when the EC entered into a bilateral agreement with Thailand on a limit to cassava imports, other starchy feed ingredients such as citrus pulp, maize germ meal and distillers dried grains began to be used to replace cereals in feed rations — many imported from the US. Corn gluten feed, a by-product of the corn wet-milling process in the US, became the ingredient of choice in the 1980s.[8] The EC classifies all these starchy products as 'cereal substitutes': the high protein meals are, of course, better considered 'cereal complements'.[9]

The conflict has simmered for years on three fronts. The EC proposal to institute a fats-and-oils tax, often rejected by the Council of Ministers but never quite abandoned by the Commission, is seen in the US as a scarcely disguised tax on soybean imports. The fact that the tax would apply to domestic as well as imported oils cuts little ice. The fats-and-oils tax to be effective would undoubtedly have to reduce consumption of soybean oil, benefiting the market for butter and perhaps olive oil. US opposition to the tax has been made abundantly clear, and this has perhaps influenced the member states (the UK and West Germany) that have consistently opposed it within the EC.

[6] The concession was actually negotiated in the Article XXIV (6) negotiations which preceded the Dillon Round proper.

[7] For a discussion of these developments in the EC feed sector see Schmidt and Gardiner (1988).

[8] The wet-milling of corn is used to produce high fructose corn syrup (isoglucose), a substitute for cane and beet sugar, and ethanol, used as an additive to gasoline.

[9] The distinction is not always so clear. At times feed ingredients high in protein have been used for their carbohydrate content.

The attempt in 1985, to limit imports of corn gluten feed from the US — following the 'success' of the voluntary export restraint agreement with Thailand — also received a rebuff from the US. Why enter voluntarily into an agreement to limit a booming export market when the open market was due to a firm commitment in GATT?[10] At least, if the negotiations were undertaken in the GATT, the US could have expected to be offered compensation. Unilateral action of this kind was ruled out of the question in Washington.

The third 'front' of this conflict has been the growth of oilseed production in the EC promoted in part by subsidies to crushers who use domestic oilseeds (and pay at least a minimum price). Production of soybeans has increased in Italy, rapeseed has become a popular crop in Northern Europe, and sunflower production has expanded in the south. The threat to US soybean exports did not go unnoticed. The American Soybean Association (ASA) lodged a complaint against the EC oilseed programme, and the US Administration successfully pushed for a GATT investigation of the case. The US view is that the EC is trying to promote the production of one of the few products that it has actually allowed in from abroad. The GATT binding is being avoided by the back-door method of subsidising production, and hence US rights under the GATT are being impaired.

The GATT panel has ruled twice on this complaint. The first time, they found that the way in which the EC operated its oilseed policy did indeed interfere with trade, over and above the bound tariff agreed in the GATT. The EC changed its oilseed policy, in effect bringing forward its 'reform' proposals by applying them to oilseeds in advance of other arable sectors. This was insufficient to placate the exporters, who argued that 'hectarage payments' still encouraged oilseed production. A second panel agreed with this assessment, and led to the crisis of November 1992.

The second GATT panel report became inextricably entwined in the Uruguay Round final stages. For the EC, the second panel appeared to be saying that the Community should either offer compensation to the US (and other suppliers) or change its newly reformed oilseed policy yet again. Reform would mean cutting even further the link between production and support (i.e., fully decoupling) in order to avoid the implication that exporter's rights were being impaired. But to do this for oilseeds would have implications for other products. The 'Green Box' could hardly hold the MacSharry price compensation payments if some part of these payments (for oilseeds) were deemed trade distorting.[11]

5. EMERGING ISSUES IN US-EC TRADE RELATIONS

These issues, of export subsidies, import access, and the trade impact of domestic

[10] The duty on corn gluten feed had also been bound at zero in the Dillon Round.

[11] See Alfred Friedeberg (1993).

programmes, have been around at least since the inception of the CAP. Meanwhile, agricultural trade itself has changed, bringing new issues to light. This section will consider two such 'emerging' issues in the area of US-EC trade relations. The first has to do with environmental health and safety regulations and the second the trend towards regionalisation of trade. But before discussing these issues, it is useful to make some distinctions between various parts of agricultural trade.

Many agricultural products are 'location based' tradeable goods, though less location-specific than minerals. Such agricultural trade tends not to have the characteristics of economies of scale and product differentiation mentioned above. The process of farming has relatively low economies of scale; sourcing out is rarely possible (except in the case of live cattle moving across the border for fattening); regulatory conditions vary, but not usually by enough to offset natural and climatic factors; and innovation rents are less common. Trade among countries in the main homogeneous ('bulk') agricultural products, such as cereals, milk and meat, is based in large part on different natural advantges, although with a heavy overlay of distortions arising from agricultural policies.

The 'bulk' products do not generally attract international investment. Increased exports of these commodities is of limited interest to most countries in the third world. Trade reform is of interest to most developing countries largely because of the disruptive effect that developed country farm policies have had on the level and stability of world prices. Any move to improve the functioning of such markets is likely to be beneficial, but the chance of inflows of investment to take advantage of scale economies in regional markets is more remote. The former Soviet Bloc, by contrast, has a vital interest in the export market for the bulk commodities, cereals, milk, and meat. These countries could well become the focus of international investment for this purpose if access into developed country markets were assured.

Trade in differentiated products, including fruits and vegetables, is now becoming much more important to developing countries. Unlike bulk commodities, producers of these commodities can develop comparative advantages by investment from abroad; they can build markets through quality and name recognition; and the overlay of government price support policy is less important in this trade. Government regulations regarding quality and safety standards are more significant. These new areas of agricultural trade are of increasing interest to both the developoing and the formerly central-plan countries.

The task is to integrate both the bulk and the high value-added sectors of agriculture and food into the new world trade order. This requires that there be an agreed set of rules for trade and for domestic policy which will allow countries to develop their potential. Most of the need for adjustment in the bulk, homogeneous products falls on continued internal support policy changes by individual governments, encouraged by multilateral negotiations. For the other products, this adjustment will also require the development of new rules, at the multilateral, regional or bilateral level to deal with investment, copyright law, harmonisation of health and safety regulations and the setting of standards.

a. Environmental, Health, and Safety Regulations

A recent trade conflict that illustrates well the future of trade relations in agricultural markets is that over beef imports. The EC is not a major market for US beef. Most exported beef goes to Japan, a market which seems to appreciate the grain-fed beef with the marbled texture produced on US feedlots. The US in turn imports considerable quantities of grass-fed manufacturing beef from Australia and Central America, together with some cooked meat from South America. The EC has moved from being a steady importer of south American and Australian beef to one of the world's largest beef exporters. Beef imports are controlled by both a tariff (of 20 per cent) and by variable levies, to protect the domestic market price. However, beef is still imported under a number of schemes for preferential access, such as levy-free quotas and tariff-free quotas. The US has a levy-free quota for high-quality ('Hilton') beef, accounting for some $10 million annual sales. But much more important has been the growth in the market for 'variety meats,' comprising beef offals used in making pies and sausages in Europe. This market had reached $100 million, and provided a valuable outlet for beef byproducts not commonly used in the US. It is this trade that was threatened by the import ban.

In December 1985, the EC decided to ban the use of anabolic hormones in livestock production. The ban followed rising consumer concern over the health effects of such hormones, spurred by the well-publicised incidents in Italy involving the use of a synthetic estrogen, Diethylstilbestrol (DES). DES has been banned in the EC (and the US), but consumer confidence in the safety of cattle feeding and in the ability of the regulatory authorities to control such practices was shaken. The hormone ban, applicable at first to domestic production and then extended to exporting countries in January 1989, was ostensibly a reaction to this consumer pressure. The US reacted to the loss of the trade in beef and offals by imposing a 100 per cent tariff on an equivalent value of EC exports to the US. An EC counter-retaliation was announced, but has so far not come into force, pending the outcome of bilateral negotiations.

It is in the nature of new technology that it brings problems as well as benefits to mankind. Agricultural technology is no exception. The chemical industry has provided agriculture with an impressive array of products to enhance yields and control pests and diseases. At times of surplus, such yield-enhancing technologies add to the strain of adjustment and make harder the task of running farm policies. Several types of agricultural chemicals carry with them negative externalities in the form of groundwater contamination and other environmental hazards. It is natural that governments should exhibit some ambivalence toward such chemically based technologies. But an equally tricky problem is posed by a new set of technologies related more to biology than chemistry.

For several decades, agricultural progress has centred around improvements in crop yield. There are signs that many of the most interesting technologies of the 1990s will be in the area of animal production. Conventional research in animal production was largely focused on breeding by selection and on improved feeding practices. Bio-technology has opened up several other possible lines of advance. Some of the most immediate possibilities have to do with the genetic engineering of micro-organisms to increase the production of naturally occurring substances. These substances include growth hormones and other valuable products. Commercial production and sale of such products poses a particular challenge to policy.[12]

As if the increased output from biotechnology were not enough, policymakers face an additional problem associated with the acceptability of food products from biotechnology. In part reflecting the general shift toward a healthier diet, consumers seem to be questioning the safety of several new techniques of agricultural production and food marketing. Governments are reacting to this concern by revising food legislation and standards. As laboratory instruments get more sophisticated, technicians can detect even smaller amounts of harmful substances. This adds to the fears of consumers, whether founded or not, and leads to an even longer list of suspect food items. The products of biotechnology generally fall in this category of foods that are 'guilty until proved innocent.'

The food industry is not always to blame for these heightened concerns. Many food-related illnesses have been linked to poor food handling by retailers and by the consumers. Anxious to consume only 'natural' foods, many consumers have avoided products with 'preservatives,' without at the same time improving their own methods of inventory control in the food closet or refrigerator.

This leaves government with an uncomfortable dilemma when it comes to food standards. Pressure from consumer groups (and environmental lobbies) tends to lead toward more regulation and the banning of substances with even minimal health risks. On the other hand, such tighter regulation goes against the trend towards less government intervention in business and consumer affairs. Moreover, exporters will see such regulation as a form of protectionism.

The beef trade conflict mentioned above is a good example of this dilemma. The Commission claims to have been reacting to consumer concerns about the health hazards of hormone-treated beef. The US view of the beef hormone ban sees the Commission's actions as essentially of a protectionist nature, bowing to pressure from cattle producers and being concerned with the build-up of intervention stocks of beef. Not that anyone doubts that there have been consumer concerns over the health effects of hormone use in cattle, but as yet there is no credible scientific evidence that hormone treatment of beef cattle, under proper conditions, leaves any harmful residue in the meat sold to consumers. The US Food and Drug

[12] For a concise review of the agricultural uses of biotechnology see John W. Longworth (1987).

Administration tests artificial growth hormones before approving their use in livestock production, and the USDA has a test programme to check for chemical residues in meat. Therefore in the absence of protectionist motives, the role of public authorities in the EC could have been to educate consumers on the matter, and to make sure that (both domestic and foreign) producers followed accepted practices.[13]

The whole issue of the role of government in shielding consumers from small or imagined risks is under review in both the EC and the US.[14] A 'liberal' approach to standards would be to legislate for full disclosure on labels along with regular inspection of food production and handling facilities. The regulation of food content would be confined to clear cases of consumer safety, rather than imposing a strict 'risk averse' consumption strategy on consumers. Indeed, this is the intention of the EC Commission in their Directives to complete the 'internal market' by the end of 1992 (Gray, 1990). But this has come under pressure from those who favour a more interventionist approach, with the implicit threat that such action might be taken at a national level. Nor is this centrifugal threat confined to the Community: the US has also recently introduced legislation to improve food labelling in part to forestall the proliferation of diverse state regulations. There is the possibility that this legislation will prove to be even more restrictive to trade than that of the EC.

Two such issues which seem destined to precipitate such problems in the future are the use of BST as a growth stimulant in cattle (and the related product PST in pigs), and the use of irradiation of food. BST (bovine somatotropin) is a naturally occurring hormone in cattle. Experimentation has revealed that milk yields can be increased by 15–25 per cent by the feeding of additional BST to dairy cattle. Biotechnology had made it possible to produce the hormone in large quantities at a cost which makes its use profitable. There are no obvious side-effects, either to the cow or to persons drinking the milk. There are, however, all-too-clear side-effects on farm policy. The EC Commission, concerned at the prospect of different regulations springing up in each member state, has been considering whether to allow the use of BST in the Community. The licensing of such a product would normally require the Commission to consider the safety and efficacy of the product, along with its reliability. However, in this case the Commission has considered the introduction of a 'fourth criterion', that of economic and social need. As the social value of additional milk in the EC is presently rather low, such a criterion

[13] A recent example of such a response is the case of the outbreak of Bovine Spongiform Encephalopathy (BSE) in the UK. First Germany and then France tried to ban UK beef exports. The Commission has taken a 'scientific' approach to the problem and sought to reassure consumers that there is no health risk involved in beef consumption.

[14] For a discussion of the issue in the context of pesticide residues in food, see Archibald and Winter (1989).

would presumably have militated against licensing BST.[15] In the event, the Commission has postponed a decision on the use of BST for three years, until the results of further studies are available.

The US Food and Drug Administration has also yet to pronounce on the acceptability of BST. In the US there is somewhat less concern about the impact on budget cost of higher milk yields. There is, however, a fear that the technology might benefit large dairy farmers rather than those with fewer cows. Largely for this reason, the dairy producing states of Minnesota and Wisconsin have recently banned the sale of milk from BST-treated cows. The 'fourth criterion' is clearly not the exclusive preserve of the EC.

Though one would assume that there is a loss to the economy from the repression of known cost-reducing techniques, it is not easy to see consumer pressure for its use. The story of PST (porcine somatotropin) is somewhat different. Addition of extra PST has led to impressive live-weight gains in pigs, improving feed efficiency. But it has also been shown that the fat content of the meat is reduced. This leads to the interesting possibility that the product, a leaner cut of pork or slice of bacon, may have considerable consumer appeal and be difficult to dismiss on health grounds. PST has not yet been developed on a commercial scale, and its use is a few years away.

b. The Growth of Regionalism

The other 'new' issue facing agricultural trade relations stems from the growth of regionalism in world trade. In the past, agricultural trade relations have not been much affected by free trade areas (FTAs) and other trading blocs. In fact, agriculture has often been left out of FTAs. This may not be a possible solution in the future, if these arrangements take on greater significance in national trade policies.

There are four reasons to include agriculture in the provisions of an FTA: exporters will want access to import markets; food cost differences could distort economies; the food sector will tend to remain national, as a result of different raw material costs and regulations; and it is not GATT legal to exclude agriculture. There are only two reasons to exclude agriculture: domestic agricultural price policies require protection at the border; and negotiations are likely to be complicated by domestic farm policy considerations.

Experience with free-trade areas shows how seriously countries have taken these problems. In the Belgium-Luxembourg Economic Union (BLEU) 1922, Luxembourg farmers had to be granted special subsidies to compensate for having to compete against the low-cost Belgian farmers. When the Netherlands joined

[15] On the other hand, as a cost-reducing technology, one could argue that it is precisely in those areas where costs exceed value that such a technology is needed.

the union, to form the BENELUX Union in 1948, it was the Belgians who asked for, and got, special protection against efficient Dutch farmers. In the formation of the European Economic Community (EEC) in 1957, at the Dutch insistence, agriculture was treated just like any other product, except that it had a Common Policy to keep the internal market protected.[16]

In the treaty establishing the European Free Trade Association (EFTA) in 1960, agriculture was left out at the insistence of the British, who did not wish to weaken preferences for the Commonwealth (Canada, Australia and New Zealand in particular). The EFTA-EC bilateral trade agreements (1973), again left agriculture out, as no EFTA preferences were being eroded by accession of Denmark and the UK to the EC. In the recent negotiations to establish the European Economic Area (EEA), agriculture has been largely left out of the EC/EFTA internal market agreement, to the chagrin of the Spanish. A series of preferential quotas is included which only serves to highlight the current fragmented nature of the market.

In North America, CUSTA (1990) included agriculture in the tariff-cutting activity, but not in the non-tariff barrier removal.[17] Neither the US nor Canada thought of the other as a big potential market, and the GATT Round seemed to be taking care of agricultural trade issues. The NAFTA (1992) includes provision for bilateral (US-Mexico and Canada-Mexico) access for agricultural products, because Mexico wanted better access into the US and Canadian agricultural markets, and *vice versa*. Perhaps only the Closer Economic Relations (CER) Treaty between Australia and New Zealand fully incorporates agriculture, but that was made easier by the sharp reduction in the level of protection of the sector in New Zealand in late 1980s.

Intra-bloc agricultural trade problems arise for the same reasons as with the GATT: indeed, one can think of GATT as a near-global free-trade area. Domestic programmes require border measures to be effective; removing these border measures would make domestic programmes difficult to work. The problems are more serious when income support is coupled to output (i.e. given as price support). 'Producer coupled' programmes pose the worst problems. 'consumer coupled' programmes are less likely to be an issue. Movement to decoupled programmes will help.

One might think that policy towards third countries would not be affected by entering into a free-trade area (as opposed to a customs union). In fact, a free trade area poses serious problems for such policies. Independent third country trade measures lose effectiveness. Different tariff rates lead to trade deflection through the lowest tariff market: with homogeneous goods, one cannot rely on rules of

[16] In 1969 the Community introduced the 'green money system' which segmented the agricultural market by currency zone.
[17] The exception to this was the liberalisation of Canadian cereal import licensing.

origin to prevent such arbitrage. There will be a tendency toward uniform tariffs in the free-trade area.

Variable levies would lose their ability to stabilise domestic markets if partner countries had straight tariffs. Countries attempting to block the importation (or reimportation) of subsidised exports would find such imports coming through the back door. Third-country import quotas operating only in some member countries will become ineffective, as trade will come in through the non-quota countries: there will be a tendency to avoid quotas, or to make them FTA-wide. Subsidies on exports to third countries will become very expensive, as the export-subsidising country will be encouraging imports from partners (either for exportation or for domestic consumption). Rules of origin don't help much, if the volume of domestic consumption is large enough. Voluntary Export Restraints (VERs) become difficult to sustain, if a partner can import freely: the VERs would have to be renegotiated at an FTA level.

This problem is not just confined to trade policies: even domestic measures become less effective. Domestic supply control is weakened: domestic consumers could buy from partner supplies, and the price-raising impact of supply control would be lost. Domestic market stabilisation policies also become less effective: storage policies would end up by attempting to stabilise the whole of the new 'domestic' (i.e. intra-FTA) market.

The realities of arbitrage in an FTA imply three tendencies:

(a) exclusion of agriculture from the FTA provisions,
(b) movement toward uniform bloc policies (common policies), and
(c) change to policies relying on decoupled payments.

In this light, it is interesting to consider the linkages between the GATT approach and the FTA developments. Exclusion of agriculture from FTAs is not a long-lasting solution, and threatens to create the same conflicts within FTAs as it has in the GATT. Movement toward common bloc agricultural policies is a real possibility, which reinforces the need to have a strong GATT to referee the development of such policies. The movement toward decoupled payments would be made much easier by a GATT agreement along the lines of the Dunkel Draft, as the move to 'green box' payments would simplify the negotiation of FTAs. A favourable GATT outcome would make negotiation of these agreements much easier: in the NAFTA large parts of the GATT text, on the definition of acceptable subsidies, etc., could be included which would have to be negotiated separately if there were no GATT deal. In EC enlargement, one could envisage transition periods for tariffs and green-box payments, avoiding the confusion of policy harmonisation of previous enlargement exercises.

Trade blocs could therefore have both a positive and a negative impact on trade relations. In so far as they tackle internally the trade and policy problem, the situation is improved. If they merely add to the defensive nature of domestic policy, their effect is likely to be less benign.

6. CONCLUSION

Significant changes in attitudes towards farm policy and trade have occurred in the developed countries in the past five years. Take for example the EC. After a series of aborted attempts to reform the CAP dating from 1968, the budget crisis of 1986 finally forced serious reform in the policy. This started somewhat modestly with the stabiliser agreement of February 1988, but has come to a head with the MacSharry proposals of June 1991, a revised version of which was finally agreed by the Council in May 1992.

This EC reform plan is important on several levels. It reduces the market price for cereals and oilseeds to a level which is much closer to the world market price; it reduces the impact of the trade instruments (variable levy and export subsidy) on world markets; it reduces the tax on livestock and prepared cereal foods (but also reduces their prices accordingly); it removes the incentive to keep up yields above the level which would be appropriate at free-market prices; and it allows for better targeting of payments by means of conditionality.

However, it is not perfect. Set-aside provisions should be unnecessary if the policy is truly decoupled; provisions to keep land out of production should be made on other grounds, if at all. In addition, dairy policy reform was avoided at the last minute, and should be reinstated, and corresponding reforms for sugar and wine should be added in the next few years.

In the United States budget pressures have reduced price supports considerably since 1987, although real policy reform seems on hold until after the Uruguay Round, and some backsliding is possible (and actually mandated) if the Round does not come to a conclusion. Canada has been experimenting with income insurance schemes that are production-neutral, but has sought to defend its protectionist provincial marketing legislation from the influence of both the Uruguay Round and the newly-agreed NAFTA.

A GATT agreement will presumably help this process of reform of domestic policies, though the GATT discussion is no longer forcing the pace of reforms if it ever could have done so. A GATT agreement will be most useful as a backstop, to prevent backsliding, as the beginning of a process which can be continued, and as a push for those countries that are lagging in the process. Some specific aspects of a GATT agreement will make further domestic policy reform more easy. One major benefit of tariffication, for example, is the ease with which one can negotiate tariff reductions, and thus continue the process of reform through trade talks. But tariffication has other benefits. The level of export subsidy which a country can use to support the domestic price is effectively limited to the size of the tariff, if no non-tariff measures are allowed. In this way, countries will be obliged to use other ways of controlling surpluses. Unfortunately, some may opt for extensive supply controls, and hence go against the trend of domestic deregulation and liberalisation.

The requirement in a GATT agreement to classify domestic subsidies can provide another positive link between the GATT round and domestic reform. Defining sets of policies that are internationally permissible is a way of encouraging domestic policy reform along certain lines. These lines are generally constructive, emphasising targeting rather than open ended payments through the price system. As a spin-off, the need to aggregate the value of transfers to the farm sector paid in different ways has already provided a transparency to the policy process.

The changes that are needed to improve both the domestic performance and the international acceptability of farm programmes will not be easy. They will require significant skill in international negotiations and considerable political will at home. Success requires that traditional forces which opposed these changes, and that have been able to block them in the past, be persuaded to remove their opposition, or else be countered by others. The Uruguay Round cannot dictate domestic farm policy change. But the round cannot ignore domestic policy and concentrate on trade rules or the exchange of trade concessions. Such tinkering with the symptoms would have little lasting impact. What is needed is a trade reform outcome which *assists* the process of domestic reform, just as the domestic reform is needed to improve the trading system.

This suggests three criteria for success in the Uruguay Round negotiations on agriculture: the agreement should specify a substantial reduction in the levels of support given by farm programmes; the agreement should encourage the reinstrumentation of policies toward more decoupling income subsidies from output decisions and some recoupling of domestic prices with world market conditions; and the agreement should modify GATT rules to encourage and underpin these developments and to ease the resolution of any conflicts that may arise in the future.

The current GATT Round offers to improve trade relations between the US and the EC. By constraining domestic policies within effective GATT rules, countries will incur much greater risks when running policies which offer excessive protection to agriculture. Domestic policies will run up against the constraints and adapt more quickly. US-EC agricultural conflicts will not disappear overnight, but they will take place within a clearer framework of rules and obligations. This attractive scenario could be enough to persuade negotiators to come to an agreement in the Uruguay Round. But few would put the probability of a strong agreement very high. More likely is a continued period of tension, with both the EC and the US trying to interpret the terms of a weak agreement in their favour, at the same time accusing the other of bad faith. The prospects for a peaceful decade in farm trade do not look very bright.

REFERENCES

ABARE (1989a), *The 1988 EC Budget and Production Stabilisers*, Discussion Paper, No. 89, 3, Canberra.

ABARE (1989b), *US Grain Policies and the World Market*, Policy Monograph, No. 4, Canberra.

Archibald, S.O. and C.K. Winter (1989), 'Pesticides in Food: Assessing the Risks', in C.K. Winter, J.S. Sieber, and C.F. Nuckton (eds.) *Chemicals in the Human Food Chain*, Agricultural Issues Center, University of California.

Friedeberg, A.S. (1993), 'Solved or Shelved: The Oilseed Trade Conflict in Focus', (unpublished, March).

GATT (1986), *Recommendations: Draft Elaboration* (Committee on Trade in Agriculture, AG/W/9).

Gray, P. (1990), 'Food Law and the Internal Market: Taking Stock', *Food Policy*, **15**, 2.

Hathaway, D.E. (1988), *Agriculture and the GATT: Rewriting the Rules* (Institute for International Economics: Washington, DC, Report No. 20).

Josling, T. (1991a), 'Agricultural Trade Conflicts in the 1990s', in C.E. Barfield and M. Perlman (eds.), *Industry, Services and Agriculture: the United States Faces a United Europe* (AEI, Washington, DC).

Josling, T. (1991b), 'The CAP and the United States', in C. Ritson and D. Harvey (eds.), *The Common Agricultural Policy and the World Economy* (CAB International, Wallingsford).

Josling, T. and S. Tangermann (1992), 'MacSharry or Dunkel: Which Plan Reforms the CAP?' IATRC Working Paper No. 92-10, Food Research Institute, Stanford University.

Josling, T. et al. (1990), *Report of the Task Force on the Comprehensive Proposals for Negotiation in Agriculture*, International Agricultural Trade Research Consortium Commissioned Paper.

Longworth, J.W. (1987), 'Biotechnology: Scientific Potential and socio-economic Implications for Agriculture', *Review of Marketing and Agricultural Economics*, **55**, 3.

Moyer, H.W. and T.E. Josling (1990), *Agricultural Policy Reform: Politics and Process in the EC and USA* (Hemel Hempstead: Harvester-Wheatsheaf).

OECD (1987), *National Policies and Agricultural Trade* (OECD: Paris).

Rayner, A.J., Ingersent, K.A., and Hine, R.C. (1993) 'Agriculture in the Uruguay Round: An Assessment. *Economic Journal*, Vol. 103.

Schmidt, S.C. and W.H. Gardiner (1988), *Non-Grain Feeds: EC Trade and Policy Issues* (FAER No. 234, USDA/ERS, Washington, DC).

USDA (1989), *Western Europe: Agriculture and Trade Report* (USDA/ERS, Washington, DC).

6

Production and Export Subsidies in Agriculture: Lessons from GATT and WTO Disputes Involving the US and the EC

T. JOSLING and S. TANGERMANN

I. INTRODUCTION

The United States and the European Community have sparred over agricultural subsidies for the past 20 years.[1] Conflicts over domestic farm programmes have spilled over into a number of international trade disputes, in particular in the 1980s. Two complaints against the EC were brought by the US before the General Agreement on Tariffs and Trade (GATT) in 1981, protesting export subsidies paid on wheat flour and pasta; the next year saw another three complaints initiated by the US, on EC export and domestic subsidies on sugar, poultry and canned fruit. This was followed in 1983 by a complaint by the EC about US export subsidies on wheat flour exports, and in 1983 the US complained about EC production subsidies on oilseeds. The oilseed dispute dragged on until finally settled during the negotiations in the Uruguay Round. The Uruguay Round Agreement on Agriculture changed radically the treatment of farm subsidies in international trade rules. Since that time, relative peace has prevailed, though a 1997 complaint to the WTO by the US challenged the operation of EC export subsidies on cheese.

In this paper we attempt to draw some lessons from the history of trade disputes between the US and the EU over agricultural subsidies.[2] The history of the disputes has to be seen, of course, in the broader context of transatlantic disagreements over agricultural policy and of the intense commercial rivalry in the markets for temperate zone farm products.[3] Agriculture is widely (and

[1] For convenience the term European Community will be used even for the period since 1995 when the more inclusive term European Union would be more usual.

[2] Research assistance by Rachel Anderson is gratefully acknowledged.

[3] For a fuller discussion of the transatlantic tensions over agriculture see S. Tangermann, 'The Common and Uncommon Agricultural Policies—An Eternal Issue?' in O.G. Mayer & H.-E. Scharrer (eds), *Transatlantic Relations in a Global Economy* (1999).

correctly) considered the epitome of a protected and subsidized sector, with widespread use of export subsidies by several countries to move high cost produce on to world markets. Smaller exporters continually complain about the export subsidies of the EC and about the corresponding programmes operated by the US. Agriculture has certainly caused its share of trade tensions, but the nature of these disputes is of interest both in agricultural terms and as indications of how the GATT/WTO rules have been interpreted in practice. More particularly, the agricultural disputes indicate some interesting features of US-EU trade relationships and the pressures on trade diplomacy from domestic political actors on both sides of the Atlantic.

Surprisingly few of these tensions over agricultural trade have actually reached the stage of the adoption of the report of a panel. Many were settled bilaterally, some reached the panel report stage but the report was never adopted, and others were subsumed in broader ongoing trade negotiations. In a few cases, a subsidy war replaced diplomacy and resulted in an ad hoc accommodation. Therefore one question that must be considered is whether one might have expected more use of trade dispute mechanisms over the past 20 years to resolve transatlantic agricultural trade tensions? Have there been factors that limited the frequency of trade conflicts in the GATT? And has the emergence of the WTO, with its improved dispute settlement disciplines, provided the opportunity for more use of international processes for resolving transatlantic agricultural disputes? Or is the scope for such multilateral processes so limited that the transatlantic partners should be devising and using other channels of dispute resolution?

II. Frequency and Outcome of Agricultural Subsidy Disputes

The multilateral dispute settlement system has proved only marginally useful in settling the transatlantic disputes that have periodically arisen in the area of agricultural subsidies. To illustrate this proposition it is necessary to distinguish between disputes that were brought under GATT rules and those that have been brought under the more clearly defined WTO disciplines. The GATT dispute settlement process was tested to its limits in the 1980s by a succession of acrimonious agricultural subsidy disputes. Though some policies were indeed modified as a result of panel decisions, the record is not impressive. By contrast, the improved WTO dispute settlement mechanism has yet to be faced with a challenge to a major agricultural subsidy programme. The Uruguay Round Agreement on Agriculture both clarified the rules regarding agricultural subsidies and strengthened the procedure for settling disputes involving those rules. One might therefore have expected even more activity in this area since 1995. But the explanation of the outbreak of relative calm has largely to do with the inclusion of Article 13 in the Agreement on Agriculture, commonly known as the Peace Clause, which obliges countries to show 'due restraint' in bringing such actions. Other factors, such as the binding in schedules of levels of permissible subsidies, and the notification of subsidy levels to the Committee on Agriculture, have also had a significant effect.

A. US-EC GATT conflicts over agricultural subsidies

Though adjudicated under the 'old' rules and with weaker dispute settlement procedures, the GATT disputes still have significance in two respects: they illustrate well the frustrations that led up to the adoption of the WTO disciplines, and they give some clue as to what could happen if the Peace Clause is allowed to expire. In a classic discussion of trade disputes brought before the GATT, Hudec lists 207 such complaints over the period 1948–1990.[4] The list includes 20 agricultural trade disputes between the US and the EC. Many of these, however, were about market access rather than about subsidies.[5] Only seven such conflicts centred on agricultural subsidies, all of which occurred during the 1980s.[6] Of these seven, five related to export subsidies and two to domestic subsidy programmes. The two domestic subsidy conflicts proved to be the most 'successful'. In both cases, the US challenged an aspect of the domestic policy of the EU. In each case the panel decided in favour of the US, and the EC subsequently altered its domestic policy. The same cannot be said for the five export subsidy cases, four of which were challenges by the US to the EC export subsidy programmes and one was a challenge by the EC against the US export programmes. In three of these five cases a panel was never established. In the remaining two cases the panel was unable to find violation of the 'equitable share' rule embodied in Article XVI of the GATT, and in any case the panel reports were not adopted. Thus the key question is why the GATT articles proved so ineffectual in resolving the 'trade wars' that have been a feature of the agricultural trade landscape over the past two decades. A brief account of the significance and outcome of each of these cases is necessary before drawing lessons about the success or lack of success of the dispute settlement process in easing tensions between the US and the EC in the area of agriculture.

1. Domestic subsidy cases

Before the Uruguay Round, domestic agricultural subsidies were not accorded any special treatment. Article III:8(b) explicitly stated that 'national treatment'

[4] R.E. Hudec, *Enforcing International Trade Law: The Evolution of the Modern GATT Legal System* (1993).

[5] Though the market access conflicts are not directly relevant for the present paper, their importance should not be overlooked. The Chicken War of 1963 represented the first major challenge to the nascent EC from its main sponsor, the US. This highly visible trade conflict brought home the potential of the transatlantic partnership for discord as well as harmony. Twenty years later, the issue of tariff preferences for citrus imports from the Mediterranean countries again caused a major political rift at a time when support for EU policy toward its southerly neighbours was broadly in the strategic interest of the US.

[6] The Annex to this chapter contains a listing and brief description of these seven cases, along with a related subsidy case (wine) and the sole WTO case between the EC and the US that addresses agricultural subsidies.

should not prevent 'the payment of subsidies exclusively to domestic producers'. However, subsidizing countries had to observe certain precautions.[7] If the subsidy resulted in increased exports (or reduced imports) it should have been notified to the GATT, and if it had resulted in 'serious prejudice' to the interests of other countries there was an obligation on the subsidizing country to 'discuss the possibility of limiting the subsidization' (Article XVI:1). Moreover, a country negatively affected by another country's subsidy could have taken the matter to the GATT if it felt that it had suffered 'nullification and impairment' of the benefits expected from the agreement. Even if the subsidy itself was not illegal, 'non-violation' nullification and impairment (under Article XXIII:1(b)) could be cause for the subsidizing country to be required to remove the offending instrument.[8] Though GATT cases against domestic agricultural subsidies have not been common, they do have a special place in the legal history of transatlantic challenges to domestic farm policy.

The two domestic subsidy cases that were brought under GATT rules between the EC and the US in the area of agricultural trade demonstrated, at the least, that not all domestic agricultural policies are immune from challenge by outside suppliers. Though both disputes dragged on over several years, they did in the end lead to policy changes. In the case of EC subsidies to the canned fruit sector, subsidies were reduced under a bilateral agreement, and in the case of the EC subsidies paid to oilseed crushers for using domestic seeds a radical change in the Common Agricultural Policy (CAP) was instituted that eventually led to more widespread reforms for the cereal sector.

(a) Canned fruit (1981–85)

The conflict over the EC's subsidies to processors of fruit simmered for much of the 1980s. The US had complained in 1979 about the minimum import price for tomato concentrate, as well as the licence and surety deposits that were used to regulate imports into the EC. Other processed fruits competed with products from the US in third markets. The EC fruit and vegetable system supported prices of the raw product and then compensated processors for the higher cost of the raw materials. Though not one of the more familiar of the regimes of the CAP, the fruit and vegetable programme was well known in California and Florida to those that considered that the EC was unfairly favouring its own southern producers.

In March 1982, the US requested that a GATT panel be set up to investigate the EC subsidies.[9] The case was brought under the GATT Subsidies Code. The panel reported in November 1984, finding that the EC was in violation of their

[7] T. Josling, S. Tangermann & T.K. Warley, *Agriculture in the GATT* (1996) at 125.

[8] In addition, the country suffering from the effect of the subsidy could under certain conditions levy a countervailing duty on imports from the subsidizing country. Countervailing duties have been used in agricultural trade somewhat sparingly, with the exception of trade between the US and Canada, and will not be discussed further in this paper.

[9] Hudec, supra note 4, Case No 107.

GATT obligations in respect of subsidies to processors of peaches, pears and fruit cocktails (though not of dried grapes). The subsidy to processors was found to be larger than necessary to compensate for the extra cost of the domestic fruit. Accordingly, the EC's subsidy constituted 'non-violation nullification and impairment'. The panel suggested that the EC avoid action that distorted competition between the domestic and the imported canned fruit. But the panel did not find sufficient evidence of subsidies to growers of these products. The panel report was never adopted, as the EC blocked its consideration by the GATT Subsidies Committee. But, after protracted negotiations, a bilateral settlement was reached between the US and the EC (US-EC Canned Fruit Agreement, 1985) that reduced the scope and level of the subsidies to canners. The EC agreed to cut its aid to peach canners by 25 per cent in 1986–87 and to phase out processing aid to canned peaches in subsequent years.[10] With respect to canned pears, the US accepted the subsidy reductions already announced by the EC.

The bilateral accord was not, however, the end of the story. In August 1988, the US claimed that the EC had violated the terms of the US-EC Canned Fruit Agreement, and domestic pressure began to mount to retaliate against the EC if their subsidies on canned peaches and pears were not reduced.[11] The complaint was both that the US suppliers were being undercut in the EC market, by subsidized local production, and that EC canners were making inroads into foreign markets (specifically in Japan and Canada) traditionally supplied from the US. The US launched an investigation (under section 301) of the EC subsidies, and drew up a list of targeted products for retaliation.[12] The EC once again reduced its subsidies and the US action was suspended.[13] However, the canned fruit saga remained an issue just below the surface. A 1997 US State Department list of worrisome trade practices by the EU included the following observation:

> The United States and five other producing countries (Argentina, Australia, Brazil, Chile and South Africa) are continuing to exchange letters with the European Commission regarding the EU's internal support regime for canned fruit. These governments believe that the operation of the EU support regime for fresh peaches and pears has allowed EU fruit processors to unfairly undercut the domestic and export prices for canned fruit of the EU's trading partners. Despite the EU's claims of adherence to the letter of the 1985 U.S.-EC Canned Fruit Agreement, oversupply of the fresh fruit under the support regime may allow processors in certain Member States to ignore the minimum price requirements of the agreement. The industries in all five countries have been hurt by EU exports of cheap

[10] K. Featherstone & R.H. Ginsberg, *The United States and the European Union in the 1990s: Partners in Transition* (1996) at 177.

[11] Ibid at 178.

[12] Ibid. Under section 301, 'firms can complain about a foreign country's trade policies or practices that are harmful to U.S. commerce. The section empowers the USTR to investigate the allegations and to negotiate the removal of any trade barriers. USTR may also self-initiate investigations. Specific timeframes for conducting the investigations are specified by law. Section 301 requires that GATT's dispute resolution process be invoked where applicable and, if negotiations fail, to retaliate within 180 days from the date that discovery of a trade agreement violation took place.'

[13] The EU amended its regulation (Council Regulation 1277/84, OJ 1984 L 123/25) to limit the amount of aid.

canned fruit. Modifications in the overall fruit and vegetable production scheme may improve the situation, but it is too early to tell.

The fact that no dispute has come before the WTO suggests that both sides have had an incentive to keep this venerable dispute out of the headlines in recent years.

(b) Oilseeds (1988–93)

The oilseed case is in many ways the archetypal EC/US conflict over agricultural subsidies within the GATT. The US has held a dominant position as an exporter of vegetable oilseeds, particularly soybeans, in the post-war period, in many ways developing the international market for both the oilseeds themselves and the vegetable oil and high protein meal that result from the crushing of the seeds and beans. The market has generally expanded, with rather less domestic protection in the exporting countries than for cereals and considerably freer market access into the importing countries such as the EC and Japan. The EC had from the 1950s been an importer of soybeans, though the oils from such seeds competed with the tree oils (such as olive oil) from southern Europe and imported tropical oils from former colonies. The rapid growth in the importation of the seeds and beans led to the development of a major oilseed crushing industry around the major EC ports.

The import market growth was always a point of contention for European agricultural interests, who pressed continuously for a 'completion' of the CAP, to include protection for oilseeds and the exclusion of imported products.[14] But the GATT effectively precluded such a move. In the Dillon Round the EC had agreed to a zero binding for a number of oilseed products that were of limited interest to domestic producers.[15] For US export interests the preservation of the open access for soybeans became an over-riding priority for any trade talks.[16] For the EC, moving resources into oilseed production was a popular domestic option to counter the increased surplus of grains. Subsidies given to processors of domestic oilseeds seemed a convenient way of stimulating domestic production without having to 'unbind' the oilseed tariff, and such subsidies were initiated in 1966. This trade tension was exacerbated by the rapid development in the animal feed industry of lower-cost poultry and pig rations based on a mix of protein-rich soybean meal and starchy manioc chips, a perfect substitute for corn and barley whose price was kept artificially high by the CAP.[17]

[14] Later, the argument became transformed into a call for 'rebalancing' the CAP. See, U. Koester *et al, Disharmonies in EC and US Agricultural Policies: A Summary of Results and Major Conclusions*, Report for the Commission of the European Communities by the EC/US Study Group, Commission of the European Communities (1988).

[15] This binding was one of the more significant achievements of the Dillon Round, which in other respects provided little in the way of trade liberalization. See Josling, supra note 7, ch 3.

[16] US exports of oilseeds had reached $8 billion a year. The industry claimed that the EC subsidies were costing them around $1.5–2 billion each year. See Hudec, supra note 4, at 559.

[17] Later, corn gluten, citrus pulp and other 'junk' feeds began to enter the mix. These did nothing to help the trade conflict as they also were largely exported from the US. The trade conflict over corn gluten is not discussed here, as it relates to market access rather than subsidies.

The overt trade dispute began in 1988 when the American Soybean Association filed a section 301 petition with the US Trade Representative (USTR).[18] The complaint was brought to the GATT in 1988, when the US alleged that the EC had both violated Article III:4, by encouraging the use of domestic rather than imported oilseeds, and impaired the benefits that the US had expected from the duty-free bindings negotiated in the Dillon Round.[19] The EU argued that the US had been losing market share in part because of new competitive suppliers from Latin America. It resented the direct attack on a component part of the CAP. It resisted the establishment of the panel for two months and delayed the naming of the panellists for a further year. Finally, the panel met and reported in December 1989.

The panel found in favour of the US, that the EC subsidy to oilseed crushers was not a protected subsidy under Article III:8(b), and violated national treatment by favouring the use of domestic oilseeds over imports. Aid to the processors, even if given in a GATT-legal form, would have also constituted non-violation nullification and impairment, as it reduced the size of the market for imports.[20] The EC noted its reservations to the report but did not block it, and the report was adopted by the GATT General Council in January 1990.[21]

Subsequent to the oilseed ruling, the EC changed its agricultural policy instrument. In place of subsidies to processors based on the use of domestic oilseeds, it paid a hectarage subsidy to growers.[22] But this was not enough to satisfy the oilseed interests in the US. The panel was reconvened to consider the new EC policies, and found that though the EC had removed the violation of Article III:4, the effect was still to nullify and impair the benefits that the US might reasonably have hoped to get out of the Dillon Round bindings. The EC attempted to renegotiate the tariff bindings themselves, under Article XXVIII:4, but talks with the US did not reach a conclusion. In turn the US suggested binding arbitration, but the EC refused. The US requested authority to retaliate, under Article XXIII:2, but was rebuffed by the EC.[23] Instead, the US prepared for unilateral retaliation, and set a deadline for the introduction of prohibitive tariffs on $300 million worth of imports from the EC.

The oilseed dispute was working its way through the dispute settlement process at the same time that negotiators were trying to find a new set of rules to apply to agriculture in the Uruguay Round. This coincidence of timing led eventually to a resolution of the oilseed conflict. The bilateral discussions culminating at the Blair House meeting in November 1992 laid the groundwork for a solution. The EC agreed to limit oilseed production and the amount of subsidy afforded to domestic producers. But the significance of the conclusion to the

18 Featherstone & Ginsberg, supra note 10, at 195.

19 Hudec, supra note 4, Case No 179.

20 Ibid at 245.

21 Even in this case, the panel did not actually address the issue of what an acceptable level of subsidy or method of providing such subsidy would be. This task would be left to the Uruguay Round Agreement on Agriculture.

22 See Council Regulation 3766/91, OJ 1991 L 356/17.

23 Hudec, supra note 4, at 560.

oilseed conflict was that its resolution cleared the way for an agreement on the framework for the Uruguay Round Agreement on Agriculture. The existence of the talks had facilitated the conclusion of the GATT dispute, but the need to resolve the dispute had provided an opportunity for a 'package' deal that might not have been possible if each element would have been considered in isolation.

(c) Wine (1985–86)

A third subsidy case should be mentioned in passing, though its relevance to the other agricultural subsidy cases is somewhat remote. In 1985 the EC requested a panel to examine certain provisions of the US Wine Equity Act.[24] The contention was that in broadening (albeit temporarily) the definition of the wine industry to include growers, the US was opening the way for an increase in requests for anti-dumping or countervailing duty action under US trade law. EC imports had begun to penetrate the US market and domestic growers were known to be supporting this legislation as a way of countering what they perceived as subsidized trade from the EC.[25] A GATT panel reported that the new definition was indeed contrary to the GATT rules, that define the 'industry' from the point of view of anti-dumping and countervailing duties action as the producers of the product, not of an input to that product.[26] However, the adoption of the report by the Committee on Subsidies was blocked by the US, on the grounds that the expanded definition of the industry was in any case about to expire under the terms of the Act.[27] Thus the wine dispute petered out with little gained by either side.

2. Export subsidy cases

If some success can be found in the dispute settlement process in the case of domestic agricultural subsidies, the same cannot be said for export subsidies. The record is of almost total failure to apply any judicial restraint or discipline to the export subsidies in use for farm products. The issue of what constituted a subsidy was not seriously in doubt. But the permissive treatment of primary product export subsidies in Article XVI undermined any attempt to rein in these disruptive trade policies. And even the improved disciplines on subsidies carefully negotiated in the Tokyo Round Subsidy Code proved impossible to deal with in the reality of widespread subsidies to agricultural exports.

Export subsidies for primary products, in contrast to those employed in other sectors, were not prohibited in the GATT.[28] Such subsidies were legal as long as

[24] Ibid, Case No 137.

[25] Most of the wine being imported from the EC did not benefit directly from the CAP regime for wine, and certainly received no explicit export subsidies. But the support for the price of the lower quality bulk wines could have been argued indirectly to have helped EC growers to target the US market for quality and branded wines.

[26] Featherstone & Ginsberg, supra note 10, at 177.

[27] In addition, the action of blocking the adoption of the report was apparently to put pressure on the EC to settle two other cases of contested subsidies (pasta and wheat flour, as discussed below).

[28] Josling, Tangermann & Warley, supra note 7, at 118.

they were not used to gain 'more than an equitable share of world trade' in the product concerned (Article XVI:3).[29] This exception proved to be the Achilles heel of the GATT as far as imposing constraints on the farm programmes of the major exporting countries. In spite of several GATT cases testing the interpretation of the exception, subsidizing countries were rarely found to be in violation of their GATT obligations.[30] The root of the problem was the difficulty that panels had in imparting meaning to the phrase 'equitable share of world trade'. Though an early GATT panel, in 1958, had found that France had exceeded its 'equitable share' of world wheat trade when its exports doubled in a short period of time, displacing the exports of the complaining country, Australia, this was the only successful resort to Article XVI:3.

In an attempt to improve the precision of Article XVI, the Tokyo Round Subsidies Code elaborated on the definition of 'equitable share'. Four problems had bedevilled panels in their interpretation: the assessment of the relevant market in which to measure the share; the relevant quantities of exports to consider; the appropriate reference period to use; and the causality between the export subsidy and the market share.[31] The Subsidies Code was unsuccessful in resolving these problems.

The choice of the relevant market in which to assess an equitable share was never satisfactorily clarified. In the case of French wheat exports, the panel looked at the total world market, though it considered individual markets in assessing the 'damage' incurred by the plaintiff. But when panels considered EC sugar exports (further discussed below), they rejected the evidence that the EC had nearly doubled its overall market share and looked for cases where sales from individual exporting countries had been displaced by the EC subsidies. They found few such markets and took this as a reason to conclude that displacement could not clearly be established.[32] And even when such evidence of displacement seemed overwhelming, as in the case of wheat flour discussed below, the panel found that the market 'had changed considerably in size and nature over the period, and that the changes in market shares were such that cases of displacement . . . [were] not evident'.[33]

Defining the scope of the world market and the reference period also proved problematic for panels. Was food aid under concessional terms part of the world market? What about sales under bilateral agreements or even trade within regional trade agreements? And how might one define a representative period in cases where the subsidies had been in place for years? Or what period should

[29] The rules on export subsidies were added to the GATT in 1955, including the primary product exception.

[30] Josling, Tangermann & Warley, supra note 7, at 119.

[31] See Hartwig, 'Die GATT-Regeln fuer die Landwirtschaft: Eine Oekonomische Analyse ihrer Wirksamkeit vor dem Hintergrund der Streitbeilegung' (1992) 134 *Argrarwirtschaft, Sonderheft* 179–88 and Jestaedt, 'Europäisch-amerikanischer Streit um die Subventionierung von Agrarexporten', *RIW-Recht der Internationalen Wirtschaft*, October 1986/Heft 10, at 805–812.

[32] Josling, Tangermann & Warley, supra note 7, at 120.

[33] Ibid at 121.

be used when instability in markets and market shares made any concept of 'normal' conditions a matter of contention. The Subsidies Code made a valiant attempt to define a previous representative period as normally 'the three most recent calendar years in which normal market conditions existed'. However, that merely focused attention on what constituted 'normal' market conditions. But perhaps the greatest difficulty faced by panels in adjudicating export subsidy cases was to establish causality between the subsidy and the change in market shares. After the confidence of the French wheat case, panels appeared overwhelmed by the multiplicity of 'special factors' at work in the markets concerned.[34] As a result, definitive rulings in this area are scarce. The history of US-EC conflicts over export subsidies illustrates the difficulties faced by panels in interpreting the somewhat vague concept of equitable market share.

(a) Wheat flour (1981–86)

If the oilseeds case was prototypical of the conflict over the domestic subsidies paid under the CAP, the wheat flour case was the most significant and persistent trade conflict that focused on export subsidies.[35] The US and the EU (mainly France) had important positions in the market for wheat flour. The EC market share had increased from 29 per cent of world commercial exports in 1959–62 to 75 per cent in 1979–81, while the US share dropped from 25 per cent to 9 per cent over the same period.[36] EC export subsidies reached as high as 50 per cent of the world price in some years. The US milling industry filed a section 301 complaint in December 1975. Consultations under GATT Article XXII were begun in 1977 but adjourned for the duration of the Tokyo Round trade negotiations. The wheat flour complaint thus was waiting in the wings to test the newly-minted Subsidies Code that emerged from the Tokyo Round.[37]

The US initiated its complaint before the GATT under the Subsidies Code in December 1981.[38] The US claimed that subsidies had resulted in EC exports gaining more than an equitable share of world trade, in violation of Article 10:1 of the Subsidies Code. In addition, the US argued that these subsidies had displaced US exports and undercut prices (in violation of Article 10:3) and had 'nullified and impaired' benefits that the US could reasonably expect from the GATT and caused 'serious prejudice' to US exports, in violation of Article 8 of the Code.[39]

[34] Ibid at 122.

[35] It is not clear why the exception for primary products was implicitly extended to include wheat flour, which undergoes some processing (milling) before reaching the market. An interpretive note to Article XVI, section B explicitly defined the nature of commodities falling under the exception as a product 'in its natural form or which has undergone such processing as is customarily required to prepare it for marketing in substantial volume in international trade'. It is certainly not necessary to mill wheat in order to market it in international trade. See ibid at 123, and Jestaedt, supra note 31.

[36] Hudec, supra note 4, at 491.

[37] Ibid.

[38] Ibid, Case No 103.

[39] Ibid at 491.

A panel was formed but could not find any violation of the Subsidies Code. Citing the difficulty of defining 'equitable share' in a complex market situation, the panel was unable to reach any conclusion. They also were unable to find evidence of displacement or price undercutting. In addition, the panel was unable to rule on the nullification and serious injury charges as those concepts were difficult to interpret when third-country trade effects were involved.[40] The report was blocked by the US (after an attempt to have the Subsidies Committee over-rule the panel was rejected by the EC) and not adopted. But the failure of the GATT to resolve this dispute led not to a bilateral deal, as with canned fruit or pasta, but to a trade war, as the US and the EU contested a number of markets for wheat flour, particularly in North Africa and the Middle East.

The use of the GATT to resolve the wheat flour dispute took a different twist a few months later. In April 1983 the EC initiated a GATT complaint against the US.[41] The object of the complaint was the use of subsidies in the Egyptian market, deliberately designed to offset the export subsidies of the EC that were the subject of the US GATT complaint. The subsidy was granted shortly before the panel ruling was known. Sales to Egypt constituted about 50 per cent of EC wheat flour sales, and there was no doubt that the explicit purpose of the subsidy was to challenge the EC in that specific market. The EC complaint was that the US-subsidized sale to Egypt violated Article 10:2 of the Subsidies Code by displacing the traditional supplier (the EC), and Article 10:3 by undercutting the price.[42] A panel was established but never constituted. Apparently, the US withdrew its subsidized exports to the Egyptian market the next year. But the EC had at the least shown that it was prepared to use the GATT mechanism in an attempt to preserve its own markets, rather than merely defend itself against the almost constant attack from other countries.

(b) Pasta (1982–87)

The tensions between the US and the EC in the wheat sector went beyond the sale of wheat flour to the Middle East. US pasta producers had filed a section 301 complaint in October 1981.[43] The US filed a complaint in April 1982 under the GATT Subsidies Code, claiming that the EC was unduly subsidizing pasta exports into the US market.[44] US producers considered that the subsidy that the EC paid to its domestic producers was more than enough to offset the higher cost of durum wheat (the main ingredient for pasta) supported under the CAP.

The case was brought under Article 9 of the Subsidies Code, that prohibited export subsidies on 'non-primary' products. The US argued that the pasta subsidy was illegal as it was paid on a processed product. Only primary products were sheltered from the blanket prohibition on export subsidies. The EC argued

[40] Ibid. [41] Ibid, Case No 123. [42] Ibid at 511.

[43] Hudec reports that the producers chose not to request a countervailing duty investigation as the quantity of imports was not large enough to make a case for material injury to the domestic industry. Ibid, at 493.

[44] Ibid, Case No 105.

that Article 9 was adopted amid widespread use of subsidies that compensated for the additional cost of raw materials and that the subsidy was paid solely on the durum wheat component of the processing cost and thus was covered by the GATT exception for primary products. The panel was convened and delivered a split report in May 1983, with three of the four panellists arguing that pasta was indeed an industrial product, and hence that subsidies on its export were therefore illegal. The dissenting panellist agreed with the EC that the use of an export subsidy on the raw material content of processed food exports was widespread and by implication GATT-legal.[45] The report was never adopted by the Subsidies Code Committee, as the EC chose to block its adoption.[46]

The pasta conflict was not finally settled until 1987. Indeed it became tied up in another trade dispute, over citrus preferences to the Mediterranean countries. The US threatened retaliation against EC pasta exports as a part of its strategy to persuade the EC to remove its preferential access for southern Europe and the North African littoral. In August 1986 the citrus case was settled, and this agreement included a decision to wrap up the pasta case. Some months of acrimonious negotiations followed before the US and the EU signed a Pasta Agreement on 5 August 1987. The EC accepted conditions on the level of export subsidy for pasta that limited it to the extra cost of the durum wheat used. And the EC ensured that its position on the legality of raw-material cost subsidies was enshrined in the WTO. Article 11 of the Agreement on Agriculture explicitly allows subsidies that compensate for the higher cost of raw materials.[47]

(c) Poultry (1982–86)

A third export subsidy conflict arose in 1982 over the EC's use of both domestic and export subsidies in the poultry market.[48] The US and the EU had locked horns on poultry trade before, in the infamous 'Chicken War' of 1963, when the US had taken a complaint to the GATT over the increase in import levies for poultry that were introduced at the time of the establishment of the CAP.[49] By the end of the 1970s the main thrust of the world poultry market had switched away from the sales of whole chicken and turkeys into Europe and toward frozen chicken parts into new markets in other regions of the world. The EC became an exporter of many of these products. The US was also concerned about competition from Brazil, a rapidly emerging player in the poultry trade, and about the impact that

[45] Further details of the pasta decision are found in Hudec, ibid, who describes this case as one that might have been invented by law professors for the purposes of an examination question. The legal intricacies of the case were more evident than its minimal effect on agricultural trade policy.

[46] Featherstone & Ginsberg, supra note 10, at 182, point out that this was the first time that the EC had blocked the adoption of a GATT panel report, and put this down to a growing sense of confidence in the EC in international commercial relations.

[47] The text of Article 11 states that 'in no case may the per-unit subsidy paid on an incorporated agricultural product exceed the per-unit export subsidy that would be payable on exports of the primary product as such'. WTO, *The Results of the Uruguay Round of Trade Negotiations: The Legal Texts* (1994) at 50.

[48] Hudec, supra note 4, Case No 106.

[49] See Josling, Tangermann & Warley, supra note 7, ch 4 for a full discussion of the Chicken War.

low Brazilian prices were having on the EC export prices. The US, as the market leader in the frozen chicken trade, felt obliged to counter the aggressive trade actions of both the EC and Brazil. The US poultry exporters initiated a section 301 complaint that led to the US requesting consultations within the GATT.

The complaint was brought under the Subsidies Code, Article 10:1, charging that the EC had acquired a more-than-equitable share of the poultry market as a result of its export subsidies, and that certain domestic subsidies were inconsistent with Article 8 of the Code which required countries to avoid adverse trade impacts.[50] Conciliation proceeded simultaneously with the parallel complaint against Brazil. No panel was established, though the trilateral discussions continued for some months until suspended in December 1984. In the end, the parties agreed mutually to restrain their export subsidies. The poultry conflict added little to the definition of equitable shares or to the resolution of subsidy cases, but it indicated that in a growing world market consultations can be a useful way of protracting a dispute until the economic and political climate changes.

(d) Sugar (1982)

In contrast to the growing world market for poultry, continued surpluses and high protection in the sugar market have perpetuated trade problems over the past 30 years. The EC world market share had climbed from about 8 per cent in 1971–76 to 18 per cent in 1981.[51] US sugar producers filed a section 301 complaint on the basis that the EC sugar subsidies were depressing world sugar prices and thus hurting their own revenues. The US brought a case against the EC on sugar export policies in April 1982.[52] The case was brought under GATT Article XVI and the Subsidies Code Article 10, claiming that the EU system of export refunds, financed by a levy on domestic sugar, constituted an export subsidy over and above that which would be legal as a price stabilization instrument (as defined in Article XVI:3(2)). In addition, the subsidies had led to the EC gaining more than an equitable market share, in violation of Article 10:1, which constituted price undercutting, as covered by Article 10:3, and caused injury contrary to the obligation contained in Article 8:3.

The US-EC sugar case never went far. Bilateral consultations were adjourned (for reflection) and were never resumed. No panel was ever established. The EC joined the talks about renewing the International Sugar Agreement, though those talks failed to agree on economically meaningful trade restraints. Moreover, the US sugar policy came under increasing scrutiny, and several requests were made for consultations.[53] In 1988, the EC itself chose to challenge the US import regime, specifically the provisions under section 22 of the Agricultural Adjustment Act (as amended) that allowed the US to impose quantitative restrictions on imports.[54]

[50] Hudec, supra note 4, at 495. [51] Ibid at 500. [52] Ibid, Case No 109.

[53] These additional cases are listed as Nos 140, 186 and 187 by Hudec.

[54] As this case was primarily about market access rather than subsidies, it will not be discussed here.

The EC's sugar policy had caused problems to other countries. Australia had challenged the EC in the GATT in 1979, and Brazil followed suit in 1980.[55] Both these countries had become low-cost sugar producers and their search for markets was being hampered by the use of subsidies by the EC. One complication in the interpretation of the GATT in the case of sugar was that an international commodity agreement (the International Sugar Agreement, ISA) had been negotiated to which some but not all producers had become signatories. In particular the EC was not a member of the 1977 ISA and therefore was not obliged to restrict exports under that agreement. Clearly the other exporters resented the 'free ride' that this gave the EC, nominally a champion of commodity agreements and market management. In some respects the GATT cases were designed to put pressure on the EC to join the ISA, and indeed they had limited success in this endeavour.

The sugar disputes did not end with the GATT conflicts over subsidies. Both the US and the EC were conscious of the significance of the sugar conflicts for the ongoing Uruguay Round negotiations, and 'each side accused the other of misusing dispute settlement procedures to jockey for advantage' in the negotiations.[56] But over time the tensions over sugar became more apparent between the EC and low-cost exporters such as Australia and Brazil.

B. WTO Disputes

Since the establishment of the WTO, and the setting up of the Dispute Settlement Body, trade dispute activity has increased. But the share of agricultural cases did not keep up with the general increase. Of the 231 consultations recorded by the WTO Secretariat between 1995 and May 2001, only seven involved agricultural disputes between the US and the EC.[57] In fact, there have been very few cases that have arisen over the agricultural subsidies of any country in the period since the Uruguay Round (not counting AD and CVD cases): only one case has related to domestic subsidies, and three cases have been complaints about export subsidies.

Of these cases only one involved a conflict between the US and the EC. The one case related to export subsidies was initiated in October 1997 by the US against EC export subsidies to processed cheese.[58] The US charged that the EC was providing export subsidies, including under an inward processing arrangement, without regard to the export subsidy reduction commitments of the EC

[55] The US had supported these two cases, but in a rather low-key way. Hudec suggests that the US had already decided, by signing off on a somewhat weak Tokyo Round Subsidies Code, that it would not fight the EC subsidies through the GATT process. A 'secret' letter from the US to the EU authorities undertook to avoid the use of the Subsidies Code to attack the CAP: Hudec, supra note 4, at 131.

[56] Ibid at 567.

[57] About 50 of the consultations involved the US and the EC.

[58] Details are in WTO document WT/DS104/1.

with respect to processed cheese. These export subsidies, it was claimed, distorted markets for dairy products and adversely affected US sales of dairy products. The subsidies were claimed to be inconsistent with the obligations of the EC under the Agreement on Agriculture and the Agreement on Subsidies and Countervailing Measures.[59] No panel was established, and a bilateral settlement was reached relatively quickly.

The reasons for the relative lack of agricultural export and domestic subsidy cases brought under WTO rules are not hard to find. The Agreement on Agriculture includes, in Article 13, an injunction for members to exercise 'due restraint' in bringing certain cases before the WTO. In addition, the binding of subsidy levels in each member's WTO schedule is a major contribution to the transparency of such instruments. Members have to notify the WTO periodically about their subsidy levels, and these can be challenged by cross-notification. And if a country were to appear to exceed its allowed export subsidy levels, specified both in expenditure and quantity of product, or its limit for trade-distorting domestic subsidy, then a discussion in the Committee on Agriculture (set up as a part of the Uruguay Round) would act as a first avenue for multilateral pressure on that country.[60]

But institutional changes are not the only reason why subsidy disputes have proved rare under the WTO. Reform of the agricultural policies of many countries has led to a lesser reliance on export subsidies by countries that have reformed and less need for those that have not undergone such reform to continue such subsidies.[61] The US has reduced considerably its use of export subsidies for cereals, and the EC has also cut subsidy payments, though to a lesser extent. Domestic policies no longer rely on the ability to clear surpluses off the domestic market (at least, not in the grains market). This has also made it easier to live within the constraints of the WTO on domestic support. In particular, a large part of both the EC and US domestic subsidies are sheltered in the 'blue' and 'green' boxes as a result of broadly decoupling the payments from current output and price.

[59] The provisions of these agreements with which these measures were claimed to be inconsistent included the Agreement on Agriculture, Articles 8, 9, 10 and 11; and the Agreement on Subsidies and Countervailing Measures, Article 3.

[60] Whether as a result of the greater transparency or out of respect for the stronger dispute settlement process, countries have been remarkably careful not to exceed their allowable subsidy limits contained in the schedules. Of course, it helps that the domestic support constraints have been less than onerous as a result of aggregation across products, and that export subsidy expenditures in the first two years of the Agreement on Agriculture were sharply down as a result of a period of high world prices. See S. Tangermann, 'Agriculture on the Way to Firm International Trading Rules' in D.L.M. Kennedy & J.D. Southwick (eds), *The Political Economy of International Trade Law. Essays in Honor of Robert E. Hudec* (2002), for a fuller discussion of the implementation of the Agricultural Agreement.

[61] For a full account of the reforms in the 1990s of agricultural policies in the EC and the US see H.W. Moyer & T. Josling, *Agricultural Policy Reform: Politics and Process in the EU and US in the 1990s* (2002).

III. Lessons from past disputes

Whether to take a conflict to the GATT or WTO and make use of the dispute settlement process is ultimately a matter of trade policy. Domestic pressures will often attempt to push governments to that stage, as there is relatively little cost to the industry. (Action through domestic channels, such as anti-dumping requests, by contrast may involve financial and organizational costs.) Clearly, the economic significance of the subsidy being challenged will also be a factor, as will the extent to which the offending policy abroad causes policy problems at home. But the overuse of international panels clearly has a diplomatic cost. Considerations of which cases to take to the GATT/WTO will therefore have to include the likelihood of a favourable ruling from a panel, as well as the prospect of rapid action by the country that is found in violation and the likelihood of counter-challenges by the other party involved. The lesson from past agricultural disputes is that several of these factors have to point in the direction of taking action in the GATT/WTO before the trade irritant warrants the full weight of trade diplomacy. In many other cases the alternatives, including bilateral and other channels, may seem more attractive.

The agricultural disputes described above illustrate these lessons. Only a few cases seemed to meet the criteria for serious attempts at solution within the GATT. Pressure from domestic interests was usually the starting point for each trade conflict, in most cases resulting in a section 301 investigation as a precursor to the GATT consultations. But the US administration clearly uses a filter to ensure that the cases are both economically important and winnable. The importance of the oilseed and wheat flour cases reflect their economic as well as political significance. By contrast, the US is not a sugar exporter and has much less at stake in preventing low prices on world markets.

It is also interesting that all of the US-EC agricultural subsidy cases reviewed above (pasta, flour, wine, poultry, canned fruits, sugar, and oilseeds) had to do with processed foods or the processing sector. There are probably two main reasons for this. One is that the competition among exporters in the area of processed foods is sometimes more intense. Lucrative markets arise and exporters jostle for competitive advantage. Governments help as a way of generating revenue for primary producers and reducing pressures on farm policy. Undifferentiated raw commodities, such as wheat and corn, are sold in bulk through a network of private and public traders. It is not so clear that subsidies in one supplier country have such a negative impact on the profitability of the companies involved. And the farm interests are often cushioned by price support systems from the effect of subsidies abroad. The second reason is that the GATT rules on subsidies are less well defined and more subject to interpretation in the case of processed foods. Indeed much of the legal dispute in these cases has revolved around the scope of the 'primary product' exemption and the extent to which raw material costs can be offset by subsidies.

Under the GATT, it was fair to say that agricultural policies were decided domestically and that trade implications were usually only second-order concerns. Though the subsidy rules in the Subsidies Code did have some impact on the formulation of domestic policy, as was the case with oilseeds in the EC, the export subsidies proved impossible to constrain under the GATT.[62] Countries often did not consider the rules on export subsidies for primary products as binding constraints. In effect, countries took the view that there was not much point in pursuing export subsidies under the GATT once panels had shied away from bold interpretations under Article XVI:3, and thus no firm rulings were made.

The main lesson that many drew from the weakness of Article XVI:3 was that bilateral negotiations offered a more direct and reliable way to prevail upon a subsidizing competitor than a GATT complaint. And when the bilateral process broke down, resort to competitive subsidization was always possible. The 'subsidy wars' of the 1980s arguably had an impact on trade policy in both the US and the EC. Changes in attitudes toward the GATT were noticeable in both the EC and the US over the period. The US changed its policy from passive to aggressive in its use of the dispute settlement mechanism in the period after the Tokyo Round. About the same time the EC also decided that it should be more assertive, and formulated a defensive plan to avoid being forced to change the CAP at the directive of GATT panels.[63] The conflicts during the 1980s should therefore be seen as an aspect of domestic and trade strategy as much as a reflection of the adequacy of the GATT to resolve agricultural subsidy disputes.

IV. Prospects for the future

The impact of the introduction of new trade rules for agriculture under the WTO has very sharply changed the relationship between domestic and trade policy. The significance of the Uruguay Round in changing the legal basis for trade disputes cannot be too strongly emphasized. After the Uruguay Round Agreement on Agriculture, the rules and commitments became much clearer. The EU and the US have broadly honoured their commitments, including exhibiting 'due restraint'. Scope for conflict has indeed been constrained, or perhaps redirected into areas not so clearly covered by the Agreement on Agriculture.[64]

62 The success of the two actions against domestic subsidies should not be underestimated. In both cases the EC changed its domestic policy. The oilseeds case had a particularly important role in the development of the CAP.

63 P.W.B. Phillips, *Wheat, Europe and the GATT: A Political Economy Analysis* (1990).

64 The most intractable transatlantic agricultural disputes since the establishment of the WTO have been the beef hormone and banana disputes. The beef hormone dispute was about whether the EC had used risk analysis as required by the SPS Agreement in banning the use of six hormones in beef production—see T. Josling, D. Roberts & A. Hassan, *The Beef-Hormone Dispute and its Implications for Trade Policy*, European Forum Working Paper, Stanford University, September 1999. The banana

Are we in for more agricultural trade disputes in the future? Will they clog up the dispute settlement system? Traditional conflicts over subsidies may not be so important in the future. The use of export subsidies in agriculture is on the retreat. The US makes little use of export subsidies and the EC would be happy to be able to give up its dependence on a policy instrument that costs money and benefits foreign consumers (who rarely appreciate the largesse). The EC Commission has signalled in the context of the current agricultural negotiations that it is prepared for further reductions in export subsidies. One would therefore be surprised if conflicts over export subsidies ever became as contentious as in the 1980s.

Conflicts over domestic subsidies to agriculture are likely, by contrast, to continue. They may, however, change in nature, with tensions moving from subsidies to processing to environmental and rural amenity payments, compensation for the costs of animal welfare regulations, and structural assistance to rural areas. And it is probable that there will be trade tensions between the EC and the US over the definitions of subsidies falling into the various categories of the Agreement on Agriculture.[65]

Perhaps the most controversial issue at present is the status of 'counter-cyclical' payments. For the past three years the US has supplemented the 'green' box payments authorized under the 1996 Federal Agricultural Improvement Reform Act with large emergency payments ('Market Loss Assistance') to counter the effect of weak commodity prices on farm incomes. Versions of the next Farm Bill that are being discussed in Congress at the time of writing (May 2003) include a continuation of these counter-cyclical payments. The question is how will they be notified to the WTO? As green box payments, even though they are clearly not divorced from price levels? Or as amber box payments, in which case the limit on such payments (currently $19 billion) would be breached?

Underlying all these issues is the significance of the Peace Clause, ie, Article 13 of the Agreement on Agriculture, that expires in 2003. The question is will there be an explosion of subsidy disputes when the Peace Clause is no longer in place to shelter agricultural subsidies? The Peace Clause has a significance in direct

conflict involved violations of GATT Article XIII and the GATS in its allocation of licences for banana imports from Latin America—T. Josling & T. Taylor (eds), *Banana Wars: A Multifaceted Story of Policies in Conflict* (2002). Neither involved any aspect of EC subsidies for agriculture. Similarly, the long-simmering 'non-dispute' about the slow pace of licensing transgenic crops for use on the European market does not relate to agricultural subsidies or farm programmes—I. Sheldon & T. Josling, *Biotech Regulations and the WTO*, paper presented at the IATRC Conference, Tucson, December 2001.

[65] The Agreement on Agriculture specifies three types of domestic support policies: 'amber' box policies that operate directly as price support or are tied to the price of inputs; 'blue' box policies that constitute subsidies conditional on restrictions on output, land use or animal numbers; and 'green' box policies that are not related to current output or prices. Support under 'amber' box policies is calculated (the Aggregate Measure of Support, or AMS) and the allowable expenditures on such policies are agreed in the WTO schedules. Thus disagreements over the definition of a subsidy are most likely to arise when a country is accused by another WTO member of avoiding the bound constraints on amber box policies by labelling (notifying) them as green.

proportion to the likelihood (or the perception of the likelihood) of the success of subsidy challenges under the WTO. The story of the GATT cases discussed in this paper is relevant to this issue. The Peace Clause effectively protects export subsidies (and green box domestic subsidies as well) from the disciplines of Article XVI:3.[66] Experience does not suggest that resort to Article XVI:3 is a sure remedy for aggrieved exporters attempting to restrain export subsidies. 'Open season' on farm subsidies may depend on panels being much more definitive in considering the meaning of 'equitable share of world trade'.

If the WTO dispute settlement mechanism will not necessarily be the locus of the resolution to the trade disputes over subsidies to farm products, between the US and the EC as between other countries, where will the action be? Experience in the Kennedy, Tokyo and Uruguay Rounds suggests that subsidy disputes can be used as a lever in GATT/WTO negotiations. Clearly the current round of trade negotiations will be pivotal in regard to agricultural subsidies. The outcome will determine the future of the special treatment of domestic agricultural subsidies as well as the fate of export subsidies for primary products. One might therefore expect to see some activity aimed at 'clarifying' the interpretation of the WTO agreements as a way of encouraging the negotiation of further reductions in agricultural support and subsidy levels.

With hindsight, the period 1995–2001 may prove to have been the lull before the storm for domestic subsidy disputes between the EU and the US.

[66] In addition, export subsidies are protected from challenge under countervailing duty not supported by evidence of injury or threat of injury and from action under the Subsidies Agreement Articles 3, 5 and 6. See R. Steinberg & T. Josling, 'Vulnerability of EU and US Agricultural Subsidies to WTO Challenge with the Expiry of the Peace Clause', *Journal of International Economic Law*, Spring 2003, for a detailed examination of the significance of relaxing the Peace Clause.

ANNEX: AGRICULTURAL SUBSIDY DISPUTES BETWEEN THE US AND THE EC

Our ref.	*Title / Complainant / Defendant/Case Type*	*Date / Start/ End*	*Panel*	*Outcome*	*301 case / Date Initiated / Initiator*	*301 actions*	*Comments*	*Reinhardt case no*	*Hudec case no*
1	Subsidies of Malt Exports US / EC /				301–5 / 13-Nov-75 / Great Western Malt Company	EC reduced subsidy in 1976; with petitioner's agreement, USTR terminated investigation (19 Jun 1980)			
2	Subsidies on Wheat Flour US / EEC / SCM case	10/8/81 / 1981 / 1983	Panel could not find violation; report not adopted in SCM	Subsidy war	301–6 / 1-Dec-75 / Millers' National Association	Consultations held under GATT in 1977 and 1980; President directed USTR to pursue dispute settlement (1 Aug 1980)	301: US retaliated with subsidy on US wheat flour exports to Egypt (resulted in Hudec case 123) shortly before GATT issues inconclusive panel report	119	103
					301–16 / 2-Nov-78 / Great Plains Wheat, Inc.	After public hearings and consultations, parties agreed to monitor development and consult further, USTR terminated investigation (1 Aug 1980)			

3	Subsidies on Pasta Products US / EEC / SCM case	2/24/82 / 1982 / 1986	Panel split: 3:1, majority found EU subsidy illegal, report non-adopted in SCM	Tariff war; 1986 tentative bilateral settlement of pasta and citrus cases—EU reduced subsidies	301–11 / 12-Nov-76 / Florida Citrus Commission et al	Formal GATT consultations held under Art XXIII (20 Apr 1982), full GATT panel report submitted (14 Dec 1984); after earlier agreement fell through, US and EC reached agreement to concede tariffs and retaliatory duties (10 Aug 1986); further agreements increased EC cheese quota and lowered US tariffs under authority of the Omnibus Trade and Competitiveness Act of 1988 (21 Dec 1988); settlement also led to pasta agreement (see case 301–25)	GATT: US responded with increased tariff on EU pasta, in retaliation for EU citrus tariff preferences for Mediterranean; EU retaliated with higher tariffs on US lemon and walnuts. 301: President determined that EC practices constitute an unfair burden, imposed duties on pasta products (6 Jul 1985); EC imposed retaliatory tariffs on US lemons and walnuts (8 Jul 1985)	121	105

(*Continued*)

ANNEX: (*Continued*)

Our ref.	*Title / Complainant / Defendant/Case Type*	*Date / Start/ End*	*Panel*	*Outcome*	*301 case / Date Initiated / Initiator*	*301 actions*	*Comments*	*Reinhardt case no*	*Hudec case no*
					301–25 / 16-Oct-81 / National Pasta Association	After several US-EC consultations, US requested dispute settlement panel from Subsidies Code Committee (7 Apr 1982); panel report favouring US submitted to the Committee (19 May 1983); US raised tariffs on pasta imports in retaliation against EC discriminatory citrus tariffs in 1985 and 1986, US reached agreement with EC to negotiate pasta dispute in connection with citrus settlement, see case 301–11 (10 Aug 1986); agreement reached to reduce EC pasta export subsidies by 27.5 per cent (15 Sep 1987)			

4	Subsidies on Poultry US / EEC / SCM case	2/24/82 / 1982 / 1984	No panel established	Trilateral consultations; mutual restraint on X-sub agreed	301–23 / 17-Sep-81 / National Broiler Council	US-EC consultations held under Art. 12:3 of the Subsidies Code (16 Feb 1982); President directed expeditious examination of Brazilian subsidies, in response to EC claims that their subsidies were necessary to compete against subsidized Brazilian poultry exports (12 Jul 1982); US conducted several informal and formal consultations with Brazil and the EC (30 Aug 1982–23 Jun 1983); US requested 'conciliation', Subsidies Code Committee held five conciliation meetings with no resolution (16 Oct 1984); no action reported in 1990	GATT: US also involved Brazil	122	106

(Continued)

ANNEX: (*Continued*)

Our ref.	*Title / Complainant / Defendant/Case Type*	*Date / Start/ End*	*Panel*	*Outcome*	*301 case / Date Initiated / Initiator*	*301 actions*	*Comments*	*Reinhardt case no*	*Hudec case no*
5	Production Aids—Canned Fruit US / EEC / GATT case	3/19/82 / 1982 / 1986	Panel found violation for subsidies to processors of peaches and pears, but not for growers, and not for dried grapes; adoption of report blocked by EU	Bilateral settlement with EU reducing subsidies and limiting amount	301–26 / 23-Oct-81 / California Cling Peach Advisory Board et al	US consulted with EC under GATT Art XXIII (25 Feb 1982); final dispute panel report issued (20 Jul 1985); President directed USTR to recommend retaliation unless case resolved by 1 Dec 1985 (7 Sep 1985); after threat of retaliation, US and EC reached settlement to phase out processing subsidies (Dec 1985); following consultations over EC failure to fully implement agreement, new investigation (301–71) initiated, and this investigation terminated (1 Oct 1989)		123	107
					301–71 / 8-May-89 / USTR	EC agreed to reduce its canned fruit subsidies, US and EC clarified interpretation of 1985 Canned Fruit Agreement (see case 301–26) (Jun 1989); USTR terminated investigation (1 Oct 1989)			

6	Export Subsidies on Sugar US / EEC / SCM case	4/7/82 / 1982 / 1983	No panel established; related to failed negotiations on ISA	Bilateral consultations adjourned and never resumed	301–22 / 20-Aug-81 / Great Western Sugar Company	US-EC consultations held under Art. 12:3 of the Subsidies Code (16 Feb 1982); President directed USTR to continue international efforts to eliminate or reduce EC subsidies (28 Jun 1984); USTR denied request of petitioner to reactivate investigation, citing agricultural export subsidies negotiations underway in Uruguay Round (29 Jul 1987); no action reported in 1990	GATT: later, EU (and others) raised complaints about US sugar import restrictions (Hudec 140, 186, 187)	125	109
7	Export Subsidy—Flour to Egypt EEC / US / SCM case	4/7/83/ 1983 / 1983	Panel established but never constituted	According to US sources, US did not offer subsidized low price to Egypt in following year			GATT: explicit purpose of US subs. was to retaliate against EU subsidies (Hudec case 103)	149	123

(*Continued*)

ANNEX: (*Continued*)

Our ref.	*Title / Complainant / Defendant/Case Type*	*Date / Start/ End*	*Panel*	*Outcome*	*301 case / Date Initiated / Initiator*	*301 actions*	*Comments*	*Reinhardt case no*	*Hudec case no*
8	Oilseeds Subsidy US / EEC / GATT case	4/22/88/ 1988 / 1992	Panel finds violation of Art III.4 and nullification or impairment, report adopted; reconvened panel finds Art III.4 violation removed by not nullification or impairment	Bilateral settlement at Blair House I	301–63 / 16-Dec-87 / American Soybean Association	US consulted with EC several times both informally and under GATT Art XXIII, EC acquiesced to forming a dispute panel (27 Jun 1989), after favourable panel decision, USTR concluded that US rights were being denied, decided to conclude the investigation and monitor EC compliance with the panel report (31 Jan 1990)	GATT: after adoption of first report, EU changes regime; after second panel, EU tries unsuccessfully to renegotiate tariff binding; US prepares for retaliation	208	179
9	301 Retaliation Threat-Oilseed EEC / US /	7/18/89/ 1989 / 1989						228	200
10	Measures Affecting the Exportation of Processed Cheese US / EC / WTO complaint	1997					WTO document WT/DS104/1		
11	Definition of Wine Industry for CVD EC / US / SMC case	1984					US grape growers (but not wine producers) complained about EU export subsidies for wine; WTO document: WT/ DS137/1		

CHAPTER 10

Agricultural Trade Disputes in the WTO

Tim Josling

Freeman Spogli Institute, Encina Hall, Stanford University, Stanford, CA 94305, USA
E-mail address: josling@stanford.edu

Abstract
Agricultural trade has generated more than its share of disputes in the past fifty years. Lack of a clear structure of rules to constrain government activity in these markets, coupled with the particularly sensitive nature of trade in basic foodstuffs, has been the main cause of this disproportion. New rules agreed in the Uruguay Round provided an improved framework for government policy in this area, and a temporary exemption was given to certain subsidies from challenge in the WTO (the Peace Clause). However, the expiry of the Peace Clause in 2003 and a growing willingness on the part of exporters to challenge domestic farm programs in other countries through action under the Dispute Settlement Understanding has once again stirred the agricultural pot. Now trade disputes are frequently leading to litigation, encouraged by the slow progress in the Doha Round of trade negotiations. In particular, the scope for domestic subsidies, under the Agreement on Agriculture and the Agreement on Subsidies and Countervailing Measures, has increasingly become the subject of litigation. Countries may have to further modify their domestic policies so as to reduce their vulnerability to challenge in the WTO.

Keywords: WTO trade disputes, agricultural trade conflicts, trade litigation

JEL classifications: F13, F53

1. Introduction

Agricultural trade accounts for a small and declining share of global merchandise trade.[1] But its share of trade disputes is large and shows few signs of declining.[2] For the first fifty years of the General Agreement on

[1] Agricultural exports now make up 8 percent of global exports.
[2] Of the 367 requests for consultations made to the Dispute Settlement Board, 100 have primarily been about agricultural trade, a share of 27 percent.

Frontiers of Economics and Globalization
Volume 6 ISSN: 1574-8715
DOI: 10.1108/S1574-8715(2009)0000006013

Tariffs and Trade (GATT)/WTO multilateral trade system, one could have put this down to imprecise rules and inadequate enforcement mechanisms in that sector (Josling *et al.*, 1996). With the introduction of the Uruguay Round Agreement on Agriculture (URAA) much of the ambiguity was removed, but this did not stem the flow of disputes. Indeed, the strengthened legal provisions of the Dispute Settlement Understanding (DSU) gave encouragement to complainants to attempt to settle long-standing disputes that had eluded the weaker GATT dispute settlement process.

New disputes also emerged, reflecting changing trade concerns. Many of these new disputes related to health and safety issues, took advantage of the more structured rules included in the sanitary and phytosanitary (SPS) Agreement. Others dealt with market access issues, in part over the interpretation of the new obligations. Recently, agricultural disputes have challenged the scope for domestic and export subsidies, under the Agreement on Agriculture and the Agreement on Subsidies and Countervailing Measures (SCM). In the absence of an agreement in the Doha Round one might expect these conflicts to intensify, as countries attempt to use litigation to achieve what might otherwise be gained through negotiation. And if the Agreement on Agriculture does become revised in a successful Doha conclusion, there will be no doubt that several more issues will need to be resolved through the DSU. The prospect of litigative peace in agriculture remains remote.

This chapter reviews the agricultural disputes since the end of the Uruguay Round. After a section that provides an overview of the 100 or so cases that focus on agricultural products, the chapter identifies several disputes that have been taken through all the stages of the dispute settlement process, and have therefore shed significant light on the obligations that countries adopted in the Uruguay Round. Following a discussion of these cases, a concluding section reviews their significance for trade and policy developments in agriculture.

2. *An overview of agricultural trade disputes under the WTO*

There have been about 100 disputes over agricultural trade notified to the Dispute Settlement Body (DSB) over the lifetime of the WTO.[3] Figure 1

[3] The definition of an "agricultural" case is somewhat arbitrary. In this chapter I include all cases that deal largely with agricultural trade even if the dispute is over an aspect of the SPS Agreement. However, in these cases I do not dwell on the implications for the SPS Agreement, but focus on the importance for agricultural trade and policy. I have excluded cases dealing with fish and fish products. Where the disputes have a broad scope (such as the challenges to India's use of quantitative restrictions) I have chosen to exclude them, although many agricultural products may have been affected.

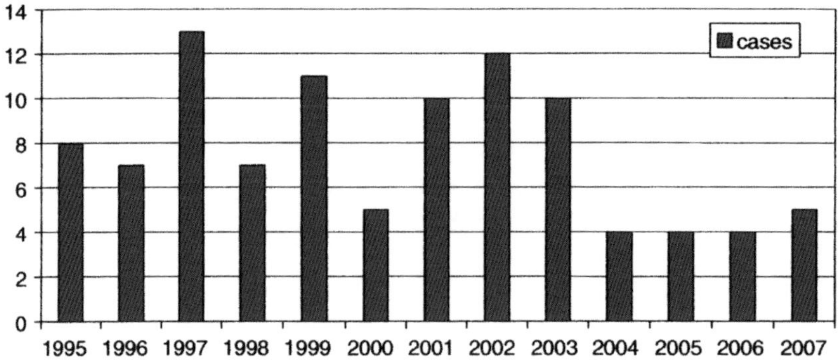

Fig. 1. WTO disputes: agricultural cases. Source: Annex Table.

shows the distribution of these agricultural cases over time.[4] On an average there have been about eight disputes every year that can be classified as agricultural.[5] In the first couple of years of the WTO 15 agricultural disputes were notified to the DSB. Four of these agricultural disputes focused on issues of implementation by the European Community (EC) of the Uruguay Round commitments (DS 9, 13, 17, and 25; see Annex Table).[6] Over this period, the United States initiated three disputes with Korea about the treatment of imported agricultural products, reflecting a long-running concern by US exporters (DS 3, 5, and 41). And two of the most prominent of the agricultural disputes were litigated in 1996, both with their origin in the GATT and each involving the United States and the EC (as was typical of many of the trade disputes at that time). These "legacy" disputes were over the EC's (1992) import regime for bananas (DS 16, 27, and 105) and the (1988) EC regulations over the use of hormones in beef (DS 26 and 48).[7] At least in the United States, the justification for the strengthening of the GATT dispute settlement process through the DSU was in part based on the prospect of finally resolving these conflicts.

As these disputes were being adjudicated, a burst of new litigation occurred in 1997, with 13 disputes that year, perhaps reflecting the lag

[4] For the purposes of this chapter a dispute is initiated by the request for consultations that is notified to the Dispute Settlement Board. It is then given a "DS" number. The WTO website keeps track of these individual disputes, and records any action taken.

[5] The average number of requests for consultation notified to the CSB has been 28 per year since 1995.

[6] The convention followed by the WTO of referring to the European Union as the EC (European Community) is adopted here. Although technically correct, this convention may seem a little anachronistic to the reader.

[7] Another dispute that had been prominent in the GATT era was over the EC subsidies to oilseeds. The final agreement that ended this dispute was negotiated at the same time that the modalities for agriculture in the Uruguay Round were agreed between the United States and the EC, at Blair House in November 1992.

from commercial concern to formal request for consultations. Most of the 1997 cases were concerned with the operation of tariff rate quotas (TRQs) and other import regulations, representing the tensions that accompanied the process of "tariffication" and the removal of non-tariff import barriers. Typical of the disputes at this time were the challenges to the operation of TRQs by the EC and Brazil (DS 69) on poultry and by New Zealand (DS 72) on butter, and to the TRQs of the Philippines on pork and poultry by the United States (DS 74 and 102). One exception was the challenge by the United States and New Zealand to the Canadian dairy policy (DS 103 and 113, discussed in detail in the following).

Disputes in 1998 also focused on market access issues, and the number of cases fell into more "normal" levels. Among these complaints was a challenge by Canada to transport restrictions on cattle, hogs, and grain by the United States (DS 144) that also reflected an attempt to settle an older dispute using the newfound legal structure of the WTO.[8] A renewed burst of activity in 1999 was followed by a less contentious year in 2000, with the focus again on import regulations in both the years.[9] The year 2001 saw a number of safeguard complaints, in part due to the weakening of world prices at the turn of the century.

A significant shift in the type of agricultural disputes is noticeable in 2002, with the challenge by Australia, Brazil, and (later) Thailand to the EC sugar regime. The conflict was over the extent to which that regime in effect provided export subsidies about the scheduled limits. This was followed by a challenge from Brazil to the US policy toward upland cotton, on this occasion questioning the subsidies given to US producers. Thus the emphasis had shifted from disputes over import regulations and contingent protection to the farm policies that were becoming exposed to legal scrutiny. Litigation began to be discussed as a complement to the slow-moving Doha Round in the effort to curb subsidies notably in the United States and EC. The cat was out of the bag.

The year 2003 saw another 10 disputes on agricultural issues reported to the DSB. Two cases reflected the changed nature of food trade: the resurrection of an earlier challenge by the United States to the EC's system of protecting Geographical indications (GIs), and a challenge by three countries to the slow process of authorizing the release of biotech products on the EC market (DS 291, 292, and 293).[10] At the end of 2003 the Peace Clause expired, widening the net of subsidies that could be appealed

[8] For a more detailed history of US–Canadian agricultural trade disputes see Barichello *et al.*, 2005.

[9] An interesting issue was raised by Brazil (DS 154) on the preferential treatment for coffee imported by the EC from competitor countries under regional trade agreements.

[10] The original US GI case (DS 174) had been held in abeyance, and was revived following a new policy initiative by the EC. Australia took out a case in 2003 (DS 290) that then was joined with the earlier case.

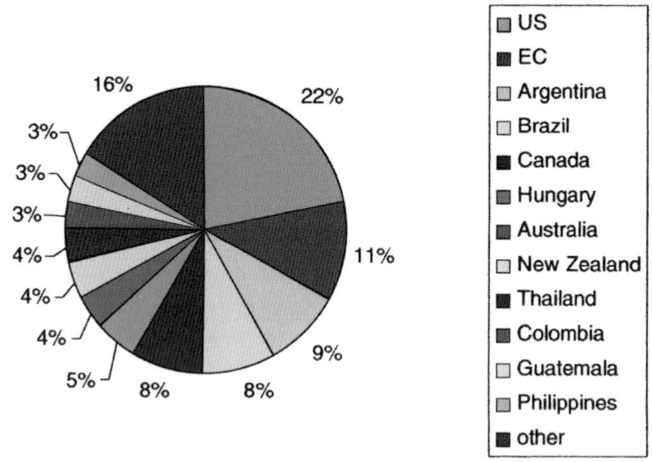

Fig. 2. Shares of requests for consultation on agricultural trade, by complainant. Source: Author's calculations based on WTO website.

under the SCM.[11] There was no immediate rush to litigation, though a number of countries actively explored the possibility for successful challenges. The panel report on the US-cotton dispute (DS 267) emerged in September 2004 and that on EC-sugar (DS 265, 266, and 283) was circulated in October 2004. The reports and their broad confirmation by the Appellate Body gave renewed hope to those who saw the DSU as an effective way of forcing policy change in the EC and the United States. But, in fact the number of new cases initiated since 2004 has been markedly less than before, perhaps reflecting the influence of continued negotiations in the Doha Round. Nevertheless, the most significant cases in the past three years have been those that have challenged US domestic support notification (DS 357 and 365), again reflecting the emphasis since 2002 on using current agreements to rein in farm support policies.

In contrast to the GATT dispute settlement process, which was used primarily by developed countries, the DSU mechanism has been used by a number of developing countries to resolve agricultural disputes.[12] The number (and percentage) of cases brought by individual WTO members is shown in Figure 2. About half of the complaints have been lodged by four countries, namely, the United States, the EC, Argentina,

[11] For more detail on the effect of the Peace Clause on agricultural disputes see Steinberg and Josling, 2003.

[12] For a comprehensive treatment of the difficulties faced by developing countries in using the GATT dispute settlement process see Barton *et al.*, 2006.

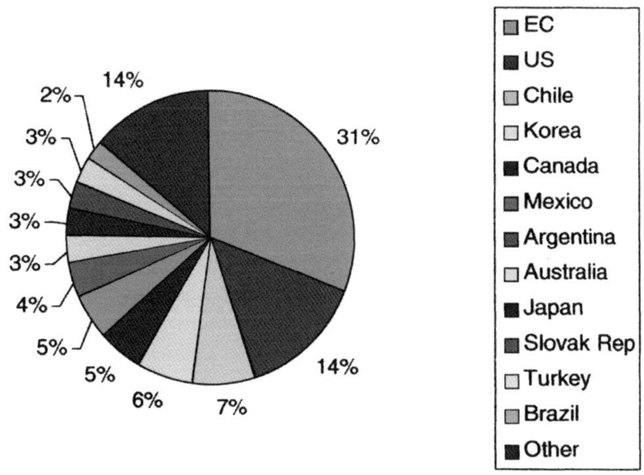

Fig. 3. Shares of requests for consultation on agricultural trade, by respondent. Source: Author's calculations based on WTO website.

and Brazil. It is of course normal for exporters to bring challenges to the policies of importing countries, and for the larger countries to be able to afford the expense of litigation. Small countries may hesitate to use the dispute settlement mechanism knowing that even if successful they have little chance of achieving the desired policy change. But the fact that 23 countries initiated requests for consultation (and many more joined disputes as third parties) shows that there appeared to be a need for such an outlet for commercial tensions in agricultural trade.

If agricultural cases are initiated by frustrated exporters it is natural that their complaints would be focused on the major (and most protected) import markets. Imports of agricultural products tend to be less concentrated than agricultural exports, reflecting the balance between population and land. But the same concentration of disputes among a few countries is evident from the list of respondents. Figure 3 shows the distribution of post-WTO agricultural disputes by respondent.

The distribution of respondents does not appear to reflect the trade pattern. Once again, 23 countries have been named as respondents in requests for consultations, and many of these are exporters. In fact, the EC, the United States, and Chile have had to respond to over one-half of all complaints. And exporters such as Argentina, Australia, Brazil, Canada, Hungary, and Mexico have all been the respondents in agricultural disputes. This emphasizes the often overlooked feature of agricultural trade policy that exporters are sometimes as protectionist as importers when it comes to parts of the agricultural sector that are less than competitive. Therefore, the disputes are often among exporters for

Table 1. Classification of agricultural cases in the WTO, 1995–2007

	Number of cases	Panels established	
		Number	Percent
Market access	40	13	33
Domestic support	3	3	100
Export subsidies	7	5	71
SPS	11	6	55
A/D, CVD	15	4	27
Safeguards	11	7	64
UR Implementation	4	2	50
Other	9	4	44
Total	100	44	44

Source: Author's calculations based on WTO website.

whom domestic politics often complicates commercial diplomacy and leads to ambivalence in trade policy.[13]

It was indicated earlier that many of the cases involving agricultural trade were focused on import regulations and other aspects of market access. This is confirmed in Table 1, where the 100 disputes are grouped on the basis of the grounds for challenge. Forty percent of the requests for consultations were on market access issues: if one includes challenges over health and safety standards imposed by importers and the contingent protection through antidumping duties, countervailing levels and safeguards, the share increases to 77 percent. By contrast, only 10 percent of the disputes were over issues related to domestic support and export competition.[14]

As with other disputes, agricultural challenges are often settled without the aid of a panel and formal litigation. Table 1 also shows the proportion of cases in each category that resulted in the establishment of a panel. The relationship between the grounds for complaint and the likelihood of a panel being established is significant. Forty-four percent of agricultural disputes reached the panel stage. But in the case of market access challenges, only one-third of the cases resulted in a panel: only one-quarter of the disputes over antidumping and countervailing duties reached that stage.

[13] One would expect these intra-exporter conflicts to be less when trade negotiations are in progress, as the tendency will be for exporters to focus on importing countries. But the Doha Round has progressed so haltingly that disputes among exporters have not been noticeably muted.

[14] The Agreement on Agriculture distinguishes between market access, domestic support, and export competition. This distinction is not always useful when considering disputes. Nor is the distinction between complaints under the URAA and other parts of the WTO (GATS, SCM, etc.). Complainants regularly include multiple grounds for challenge. The categories in the table are therefore based on a subjective view of the main issues involved and not a listing of the legal grounds for challenge.

Table 2. Current status of agricultural disputes in the WTO

	Number of cases
Adopted by DSB	32
Report awaited	8
No report issued	2
Withdrawn	2
Replaced	1
Resolved	12
Resolution not notified to DSB	43
	100

Source: Author's calculations based on WTO website.

So these cases are apparently easier to resolve, in part because the trade remedies and often the challenged import regulations are themselves temporary.[15] Disputes over export subsidies and domestic support tend to be more intractable, and involve potentially significant domestic policy changes.

The current (January 2008) status of the agricultural cases considered here is shown in Table 2. Of the 44 panels established to consider agricultural cases, 32 have reported and a further 8 have yet to report.[16] In the other four cases the challenge was withdrawn, or the panel has been in abeyance for several years; a further case was replaced by another one covering the same complaint.[17] Twelve cases were notified to the DSB as having been resolved bilaterally, without the need for as panel, and a further 43 cases were presumably resolved, though the DSB was never notified of the outcome.[18]

The number of disputes that are notified to the DSB overstates the number of policies or procedures that are actually in dispute. It has been common for two or more countries to complain about the same alleged violation of WTO rules. Correcting for this duplication, and for the fact that some countries revise or extend their complaints, the number of separate perceived violations falls to 83. The number of these that actually went to panels also overstates the number of panel decisions. In a number of cases, similar complaints have been grouped and dealt with by the same panel.

[15] Note, however, that the SPS cases more often resulted in the establishment of panels, as many of these trade barriers are less likely to be transitory (Josling *et al.*, 2004).

[16] In the two cases, the DSB has agreed to establish a panel but the panelists are yet to be appointed.

[17] A challenge by Colombia against Chilean safeguards (DS 228) was replaced by a similar challenge with slightly revised complaints (DS 230).

[18] The reluctance of the parties to a dispute to report the successful resolution of that dispute to the DSB is understandable in strategic terms. However, one assumes that all interested parties are aware of the details of the solution, so it would make the assessment of the significance of the DSU simpler if notification were mandated.

Indeed, many of the most contentious cases have been brought by countries acting in concert: the grouping of countries in the banana disputes, the EC-hormones case, the EC-GI case, and the EC-biotech case are examples of coordination among complainants. The number of separate cases that went to panels is therefore 35, generating 31 separate legal opinions.

To see the impact of these opinions, it is necessary to consider the details of several of the most important cases. Six such cases are discussed here: three of them relate to issues of market access and import regulations, the other three to subsidies given to domestic producers under farm support programs. The market access cases include the banana case, with a rich history of market discrimination by the EC in favor of its own former dependencies and colonies; the beef hormone case, considered a landmark in the litigation over health and safety standards; and the EC-GI case that touched upon the provisions of the TRIPS that mandate the protection of regionally named foods. The subsidy cases include the landmark Canada-dairy case that addressed the question of whether export subsidies could result from domestic price setting; the US-cotton case that explored the application of the SCM Agreement to agricultural subsidies; and the EC-sugar case that extended the Canadian dairy ruling.

3. *Market access complaints in agriculture*

3.1. Bananas

Trade in bananas has elicited a series of disputes over the years, pitting the postcolonial regimes of the EC countries against the US-based multinational companies that had a foothold in those parts of Europe that did not have tropical colonies. The banana controversy in the GATT was stimulated initially by the changes in the European import rules implied in the EC's policy of "Completing the Single Market," which were introduced at the start of 1993.[19] Moving from the varied import systems run by individual countries to an EC-wide policy that could be operated without internal trade barriers proved to be a challenge. "Dollar" bananas appeared to lose some of their market access to those coming from the former colonies of France and the United Kingdom. Some countries in Latin America settled on a market sharing deal with the EC but others complained to no avail.

The Uruguay Round, with its strengthening of the Dispute Settlement process, came along at an opportune time for the disaffected group. Two panel reports under the GATT, in 1993 and 1994, had failed to improve

[19] For more detail on the Banana case see Josling (2003), Chapter 9.

the market position for dollar bananas.[20] The third panel, reporting on May 22, 1997, proved to be more effective. "Bananas III," as the report became known as, found the EC in multiple violation of trade rules (WTO, 1997a). The various steps taken to resolve this conflict continue to this day.

As a "pure" market access case, the banana issue would have been interesting. But the case tackled much more than the conflicts over postcolonial discrimination. It was the first panel to consider an argument that a country had contravened the General Agreement on Trade in Services (GATS). By allocating import licenses to domestic firms based on past shipments, the banana import regime gave valuable trading permits to the competitors of the US-based multinationals. The EC had agreed to end discrimination in "wholesale trade services" in the Uruguay Round. This aspect of the case increased its importance and provided a potentially useful clarification of the relationship between rules for goods trade and those for trade in services.

Four different stages in the unfolding dispute can be distinguished. The first stage was that leading up to the request for consultations in September 1995. During this stage, the dispute was essentially one of market access by Central American companies in the EC market as a result of the consolidation of import quotas when the Single Market regime was adopted. The process of accommodation of these bananas was not easy, but the Banana Framework Agreement (BFA) at least in part met these concerns. The second phase began when the impact of the BFA became apparent and the firms that felt that they were losing market opportunities began to pressure their governments for action. This phase continued through the adoption of the panel report as amended by the appeal process and the EC's announcement that it would change its policies to comply. The third stage of the process started with the realization by the complaining parties that the change in regulations had not in fact solved the problem and that further action was needed. This stage continued for another year, and could only be resolved by a change in policy that was safe from WTO challenge. Such a change was finally agreed between the EC and the United States on April 11, 2001, about eight years after the deliberations of the first banana panel. The changes revolved around the substitution of the import license regime for a "tariff only" approach, while keeping the preferential tariff for African, Caribbean and Pacific (ACP) suppliers. The fourth phase of the dispute (still under consideration) centers on the height of the most favored nation (MFN) tariffs faced by the Central American exporters.

Though GATT and WTO complaints often cite more than one Article which the offending country is supposed to have violated, the banana case is unusual for the lengthy list of purported violations. To illustrate this, the list of legal bases for complaints in the banana case is given in

[20] The panel reports had no impact. The EC effectively prevented their adoption by the General Council, following a long GATT tradition of blocking unfavorable reports.

Table 3. Basis for complaints about the EC banana import regime

GATT Article I:1	Non-discrimination
Article II	Schedule of concessions
Article III	National treatment
Article X	Transparency
Article XI	Elimination of quantitative restrictions
Article XIII	Non-discriminatory administration of quantitative restrictions
Import Licensing Agreement Article 1	General provisions
Article 3	Nonautomatic licenses
Agricultural Agreement Article 4.2	No discretionary import licensing
GATS Article II	Most favored nation treatment
Article XVI	Market Access
Article XVII	National treatment
TRIMS Article 2	National treatment and quantitative restrictions

Source: Josling (2003).

Table 3. The essence of the case was the discriminatory allocation of quotas and the license procedures used to affect the quotas. But non-discrimination as a principle recurs throughout the GATT and the GATS, and thus the same policy measures can be in multiple violation. The EC may have thought that the Lomé waiver was satisfactory cover, but this did not survive the scrutiny of the panel.

The failure of the BFA to satisfy the varied interest of the Latin American producers led directly to the request on February 5, 1996 by Ecuador, Guatemala, Honduras, Mexico, and the United States for consultations with the EC. After the necessary consultations had reached no conclusion the complainants requested the formation of a panel.[21] The panel was established by the DSB on May 8, 1996.

The list of complainants is also of interest. Columbia, Costa Rica, Nicaragua, and Venezuela had been the "beneficiaries" of the BFA, and apparently were not willing to risk the wrath of the EC by trying to better their access. But the EC had not managed to satisfy Guatemala, and that country joined with Honduras in an exactly parallel complaint. Ecuador had joined the WTO only on January 26, 1996, and so was anxious to test its newly acquired rights.[22] The United States had originally intended to stay on the sidelines: it would not have been consistent with the attempt to

[21] The EC was to argue before the panel that this period of consultation had been inadequate: given the long gestation period of this conflict it seems unlikely that any further interchange of information or explanations would have improved the situation.

[22] The EC indicated in its submission to the panel that Ecuador had been persuaded with undue haste (only two weeks after its membership) to join the others as a co-complainant. But one imagines that the Ecuadorian government had anticipated such action before its membership was approved.

build up relations with the Caribbean to be seen to challenge the EC's preferences in that region. But 1996 was an election year. Having sold the WTO to the US Congress partly on the basis of the strengthened DSU, it was vulnerable to the argument that holding the EC to the trade rules was an important aspect of US trade policy. Direct pressure from the US-based multinational corporations, in particular the Chiquita corporation, swung the Clinton administration behind the complaint. At a stroke, this raised the stakes and turned a thorny issue of preference systems into a matter of high principle and policy.[23] Along with the beef hormone dispute the banana case focused attention on the willingness of the EC to subjugate its policy preferences to the judgment of a WTO panel. If it proved unwilling, this would not be lost on those whose support for the extension of multilateral trade rules was tenuous at best.

The substantive issues covered by the GATT that were considered by the panel were of three types: tariff questions, quota allocation questions, and the legality of the import-licensing regime. Several of these issues had also to be considered in the light of agreements that came out of the Uruguay Round, including the Licensing Agreement as well as the Agreement on Agriculture and the Trade-Related Investment Measures (TRIMS) Agreement. In addition, the panel considered the compatibility of the licensing regime with the EC's obligations under the GATS.

The tariff issue was perhaps the easiest of the three. The complainants charged that the differential tariff rates that applied between third country bananas and non-traditional ACP imports was a violation of MFN.[24] No objection was lodged against the duty-free imports from the ACP where these were necessary to conform to the requirements of the Lomé Convention. The WTO had granted the EC a waiver from its Article I obligations in December 1994 (extended in October 1996): the EC argued that this was adequate to cover the whole import regime, and not just the traditional ACP imports. The only tariff question of particular interest to the panel, then, was whether this waiver covered non-traditional imports from ACP countries. They decided that as the waiver was not specifically limited to the traditional trade quantities, it must be assumed that "the preferential tariff for the non-traditional ACP bananas is clearly a tariff preference of the sort that the Lomé waiver was designed to cover." (WTO, 1997a, p. 333) As a consequence, the EC "won" the tariff

[23] Mexico followed the lead of the United States in part because of the Mexican ownership at that time of one of the firms (del Monte) and in part as an expression of North American solidarity on a matter of WTO principle.

[24] Guatemala and Honduras, in their joint complaint, added a further tariff issue, arguing that the tariff on third country bananas was above the bound rate of 20 percent. This was in violation of Article II, which refers to the schedules of bindings.

argument and defined in part the relationship between the Lomé Convention and the WTO.

The EC was less fortunate in the case of quota allocation. The argument over the allocation of quotas went to the heart of the complaints over the EC banana regime. At its simplest, the argument revolved around whether the quotas under which banana imports are allowed were allocated in a way consistent with Article XIII of the GATT, which stipulates that they should be allocated in a non-discriminatory way and one that disturbs trade as little as possible. The chapeau of Article XIII:2 states that

> In applying import restrictions to any product, Members shall aim at a distribution of trade in such product approaching as closely as possible the shares which the various Members might be expected to obtain in the absence of such restrictions...
>
> (WTO, 1995)

The complaining parties charged that the EC had allocated the banana import quotas in a way that was inconsistent with this Article. Some countries (the ACP and those that had signed the BFA) had country-specific quotas, while other countries had no such quotas but had to compete for the "other" category of imports. Moreover, they argued that the quotas given to those countries were too large and did not reflect market developments. The allocation method also gave the BFA countries exclusive right to fill any shortfall in supplies under the BFA quotas.

The EC argued that the WTO waiver covered any discrimination under Article XIII as well as Article I. It further argued that it was in effect running two import regimes in parallel, and thus any discrimination between countries covered by different quota schemes was not in violation of the GATT. The traditional ACP bananas were given preference, but this was undoubtedly covered by the waiver and thus could be put on one side: the rest of the banana imports were covered by a tariff quota as entered in the EC schedule, although ACP countries received a (waiver consistent) preference on the tariff to be paid. The panel pointed out that this was the first time a whole quota regime had been called into question, as opposed to the operation of an isolated quota provision. It could also have been said that the spread of tariff quotas that emerged from the Agreement on Agriculture made this an issue of much greater significance. The allocation of quotas (as well as the distribution of licenses, as discussed in the following) is of increasing interest in agricultural trade policy.

The panel found that the EC only had one quota regime for purposes of analyzing its compatibility with Article XIII, regardless of how the EC has chosen to administer the different quotas (WTO, 1997a, para. 7.82). The EC had reached an agreement with the BFA countries, allocated shares in respect of non-traditional ACP bananas, and granted country-specific quotas to ACP countries. This was the regime as laid down in Regulation

404/93. Moreover, it did discriminate against the countries outside the BFA and the ACP. Columbia and Costa Rica had a substantial interest in the EC market and thus could reasonably have been included in the BFA: Nicaragua and Venezuela did not have such a substantial interest and had less of a claim than some of the complaining countries (Guatemala, Honduras, and Mexico).[25] The EC's quota allocation scheme thus violated Article XIII and would have to be modified. However, the panel found that the quota allocation for the ACP bananas, even if in violation of Article XIII, was covered by the WTO waiver for the Lomé Convention.[26]

If the quota allocation system ran afoul of Article XIII, the licensing system that gave expression to the quotas came in for the most severe condemnation by the panel. This system was judged with respect to its transparency and its tendency to discriminate. The system itself was complex, which in itself made for a lack of transparency. But the complaining parties charged that the intention of the license system was to favor firms that had historically imported bananas from the Windward Isles and French overseas territories. This discrimination was contrary to Articles I (non-discrimination) and III (national treatment) of the GATT. It was also claimed that the CMOB violated Article X of the GATT that requires that countries administer trade measures, including licenses, "in a uniform, impartial and reasonable manner." Moreover, it was argued that the EC's licensing system contravened the Agreement on Import Licensing Procedures (Licensing Agreement) that had been incorporated into the basic rules of the WTO at the conclusion of the Uruguay Round.[27] In addition, it was charged that the arrangement violated the TRIMS agreement, which contains a list of trade-related investment measures such as purchasing requirements that are deemed to be inconsistent with national treatment in the GATT. The requirement that firms have to purchase bananas from the ACP to apply for "B" Licenses was therefore a violation of this provision.

Perhaps, the most significant challenge to the import-licensing regime was the suggestion that it was inconsistent with the GATS. The GATS was one of the major innovations of the Uruguay Round, putting service trade on a similar footing to that in goods. Non-discrimination and national

---

[25] Ecuador and Panama were not GATT/WTO members at the time of the BFA. Ecuador was deemed by the panel to have the right to challenge the quota allocation of the BFA upon joining ("all Members have rights") though as the EC pointed out it might have been better to have dealt with this issue in the Protocol of Accession.

[26] The Appellate Body later reversed this finding (WTO, 1997b).

[27] The Licensing Agreement provided more detail on the way in which licensing measures were to be administered, and is included as an Annex 1A agreement in the Marrakesh Agreement which established the WTO.

treatment are fundamental principles of the GATS, as they are in the GATT. But the GATS contains some restrictions on the applicability of these principles. The banana case was the first major test of the scope of these rules and their relation to those in goods trade.

The first task of the panel was to clarify the relationship between the GATT, with its emphasis on the conditions under which goods are traded, with the GATS, which deals with services. Clearly, the trading of goods requires a number of services. If goods markets are distorted by discriminatory trade policies, does it follow that the provision of services that accompany those goods and effectuate the trade is also distorted? Or would that constitute "double jeopardy" for the country implementing such contested regulations? The EC argued before the panel that it should not be made to justify its policy under both the GATT and the GATS, as it was not imposing any measure that discriminated directly on the provision of services. The fact that the "necessary" quota system impacted service providers was not enough to establish a violation of the GATS. The United States argued that, to the contrary, the way the license system worked was to make it much more difficult and expensive for the US corporations to compete with those based in Europe.[28] Thus the licensing system was indeed contrary to GATS.

The panel had little difficulty in deciding that the same measure can violate both GATT and the GATS. Indeed, the specificity with which the import regime for bananas distributed licenses, by operator category and activity, made it difficult to argue that measures had no effect on the competitiveness of particular firms.[29] The panel found that the EC regime did indeed violate the non-discrimination and national treatment provisions of the GATS. The Lomé waiver was of no help here, of course, as it related to the obligations under the GATT, specifically Article I. Once again, though, the issue was not the import of traditional ACP bananas but the BFA quotas and the third-country quotas. The panel ruled that the EC be required to change its import regulations to avoid conflict with the GATS.

---

[28] The US had a particular reason to push the GATS complaint, as it had championed the inclusion of services in the WTO. As with the DSU, the GATS was a major selling point within the US to convince skeptics that the WTO was worthwhile. To have at hand a convenient case to explore the implications of the GATS was fortunate. The EC, in general content to include services in the Uruguay Round, chose to nominate "wholesale trade services" as one of the sectors in its liberalization offer. This meant that it was subject to the general "national treatment" provision of the GATS, along with "non-discrimination".

[29] An important aspect of the GATS is that it takes the WTO a significant step toward considerations of the impact of policies on firms as opposed to goods. Thus, the arguments that the panel had to consider dealt with the competitive position of companies and involved commercially sensitive information.

3.2. Beef hormones

Similar to the banana case that started well before the establishment of the WTO, the beef hormone dispute was also a legacy from the GATT. The events leading up to the EC ban on the domestic use of hormones in cattle raising and hence on imports of hormone-treated beef are important in explaining the political longevity of this US/EC dispute.[30] European livestock producers were searching for ways to stimulate growth in cattle, and took eagerly to the use of hormones, but sometimes with inadequate knowledge of the consequences of misuse of such chemicals.[31] Regulatory control sometimes slipped between the cracks, as coordination and harmonization of national regulations progressed haltingly in the EC.

European authorities first proposed a hormone ban in response to public anxieties that emerged following highly publicized reports of "hormone scandals" in the late 1970s. The first incident was reported in 1977, when some schoolchildren in northern Italy exhibited signs of premature hormonal development that investigators initially suspected was linked to illegal growth hormones in veal or poultry served in school lunches. Although exhaustive examination of possible causes of the abnormalities produced no concrete conclusions, a public furor arose over the use of hormones in livestock production. The second incident occurred three years later, again in Italy, when numerous samples of veal-based baby food were found to contain residues of the illegal hormonal drug diethylstilbestrol (DES), further alarming European consumers.[32] Consumer organizations called for a boycott of veal that had a significant adverse effect on the market and incidentally on the administration of the agricultural market policy which at that time supported veal as well as beef prices.

The United States took the issue of the EC hormone ban to the GATT in March 1987, alleging that there was no legitimate basis for the ban under the Tokyo Round Standards Code. When bilateral consultations between the EC and the United States failed to resolve the matter, the United States requested that a technical expert group be convened

---

[30] The discussion in this section draws heavily from Josling *et al.*, 2006.

[31] Naturally occurring hormones in cattle and humans can be added to feed or applied to increase the rate of animal growth (growth promotion purposes), to synchronize the estrus cycles of dairy cattle to lower production costs (zootechnical purposes), or to correct certain endocrine dysfunctions (therapeutic purposes). "Synthetic" hormones, which mimic the action of natural hormones, are only used for growth promotion.

[32] DES is a synthetic estrogen that had been widely used since the late 1930s for both human and animal health purposes until epidemiological evidence linked the use of DES by pregnant women to the development of cervical cancer in their daughters. Medical and livestock uses of DES were eventually banned in the United States (in 1979) and in Europe (in 1981).

pursuant to Article 14.5 of the Code to examine the issue of scientific support for the EC's measure. Under the GATT rules, the EC blocked formation of the group, arguing that its ban was related to a processing standard (known as PPM, for production and processing method) rather than a product standard (PS) that was not covered. The EC had argued that its sole obligation under the Standards Code was to abstain from the *intentional* circumvention of the disciplines by formulating its measures as PPMs rather than PSs.

As this dispute escalated, both sides publicly considered trade restrictions against the other.[33] When the ban went into effect, the United States retaliated with 100 percent *ad valorem* duties on a range of products imported from Europe. The EC requested a panel to examine the legitimacy of the retaliation, but this request was blocked by the United States. Later in 1989, a joint US–EC Task Force agreed to a limited compromise to allow imports of some US beef products that were certified to be "hormone free" (the ban previously applied to all US beef, as hormones are widely used in the US cattle sector) as well as other beef products destined for pet food. The United States, in response, withdrew some products from its retaliation list.

Further compromise, however, was precluded by the increasing polarization of domestic political forces on both sides of the Atlantic. The US beef industry was convinced that the ban was a protectionist device aimed at restricting trade. The US government worried that in addition to the technical criteria of effectiveness, safety and reliability, a "fourth criterion" of the economic and social impact of the adoption of a particular technology was being endorsed by the EC in its standard for veterinary and other substances, and would become established as an excuse for protecting other agricultural markets. The European producer was determined that US beef should not escape the hormone ban, and the Parliament appeared desirous of hanging onto a popular cause even at the expense of some embarrassment for the Commission. The legal stalemate and ensuing exchange of tit-for-tat measures was widely viewed as one of the more visible failures of the GATT dispute settlement mechanisms. It was the hormones dispute, more than any other case, which motivated negotiation of stronger disciplines on technical regulations in the GATT Uruguay Round. Yet, even knowing that the hormones issue was going to re-emerge under these stronger rules, the EC did not thwart the adoption of the SPS Agreement.

---

[33] For example, in 1988, the US Food Safety and Inspection Service (FSIS) began to request certification from EC authorities that meat produced in EC countries met US safety requirements for hormone residues and conformity assessment procedures were equivalent to US standards. The EC responded with the announcement of a counter-retaliation valued at $360 million (that it never implemented) that targeted products such as California walnuts (Kramer, 1989).

With new Uruguay Round rules for SPS measures and dispute settlement procedures in place, the United States renewed its complaint against the beef import ban. In January 1996, the United States requested formal consultations with the EC, which were joined by Australia, Canada, and New Zealand. The United States charged that the EC ban violated not only the basic GATT provisions, but the technical barriers to trade (TBT) and SPS agreements as well. The central claim was that the ban was not based on science. The EC responded that the ban was the only feasible option for meeting its very high public health goals. The parties met in March, but a mutually satisfactory solution could not be found. The following month, the United States requested that the WTO establish a panel to hear the dispute. The EC countered by requesting a panel to review the legitimacy of the US retaliatory tariffs, whereupon the United States unilaterally rescinded them in July 1996. The first meeting of the panel to hear the complaint by the United States (later joined by Canada) against the EC hormone ban was set for October 1996. As long anticipated, the *Hormones* dispute became the bellwether test of the new disciplines in the SPS Agreement.

The outcome of the Hormones case was favorable to the United States and Canada. In its report issued on August 18, 1997, the WTO dispute settlement panel concurred with the complainants that the EC ban on beef treated with hormones for growth-promotion purposes was inconsistent with its obligations under the SPS Agreement. In support of these findings, the panel noted that the scientific evidence that the EC had reported as informing its regulatory decision fell into two categories. Those studies which had specifically evaluated the potential toxic effects of hormones used to promote growth in cattle concurred that, at present, there was no indication that these substances posed public health risks when properly used. Other research, which the EC argued raised serious questions about the methodology or conclusions of these studies, examined the carcinogenic or genotoxic potential of entire categories of hormones or the hormones at issue in general. As such, the panel stated, these latter studies did not qualify as a risk assessment – in this case, an evaluation of the consequences of consuming beef from cattle treated with growth hormones – as defined in the SPS Agreement.[34]

It was anticipated that, whatever the outcome, the Appellate Body would be asked to review the panel's decision, and indeed, all three parties to the dispute requested a review of both procedural and substantive findings in the panel's report. The Appellate Body released its report in January 1998, ruling on 14 issues. The Appellate Body overruled

[34] Moreover, the panel noted, the scientific experts that it had consulted during its proceedings (under the terms of Article 13 of the DSU) had concurred that this evidence did not invalidate or contradict the scientific conclusions that had been reached by the first group of studies.

the panel on several points, but concurred with the panel that the EC measure was not in conformity with all of the SPS Agreement disciplines.[35] Following the appeal, the EC said that it required four more years to conduct additional risk assessments before policy changes could be considered. The United States and Canada countered that this did not constitute implementation, so the matter went to arbitration in Geneva. The arbitrator concluded that 15 months was a reasonable time to comply.[36] The arbitrator also noted that requests for additional time to conduct new studies or consult experts to demonstrate consistency of a measure was not consistent with the requirement for prompt compliance.

The EC then announced that it would proceed with scientific studies regardless of the arbitrator's decision. In the interim, United States and Canada discussed potential compensation schemes or trade concessions that the EC could offer to compensate the beef producers for loss of the market access due to the hormone ban. Among the options discussed was labeling. The United States agreed that it could label hormone-treated beef as "a product of the USA." It could not agree to a label that would indicate the level of hormones in the beef was higher than a comparable product from the EC, arguing that it is unclear that the level would be higher and such a label would be potentially misleading to consumers.

With no compensation scheme in place, the WTO offered retaliation to the United States and Canada in the form of increased tariffs on EC exports totaling about $128 million. In the meantime, the EC has proceeded with its scientific evaluation of the six hormones through the Scientific Committee on veterinary measures for public health. The Committee opined that it could establish no acceptable daily intake for the hormones. On the basis of this opinion, the EC proposed a permanent ban on estradiol, and a provisional ban on the other five hormones until another committee could review the evidence again to determine if these five hormones might be safely used for therapeutic and technical purposes. The matter was then put before the European Council, but it has not been acted on to date.

[35] The Appellate Body held that the statement in the SPS Agreement that a measure shall be based on an international standard where one exists (except as otherwise provided for in the agreement) does not imply that measures need to conform to international standards. If this were so, contended the judges, the SPS Agreement would vest international standards (that are recommendations under the terms of the Codex) with obligatory force and effect. To sustain such an assumption, the Appellate Body argued, language far more specific and compelling than that found in Article 3 of the SPS Agreement would be necessary.

[36] The arbitrator that established a May 1999 deadline for compliance had noted that "It would not be in keeping with the requirement of prompt compliance to include in the reasonable period of time, time to conduct studies or to consult experts to demonstrate the consistency of a measure already judged to be inconsistent." (WTO, 1998).

The effect that the legal resolution of this landmark dispute would have on the issue of the regulation of hormone use and other food safety cases remains uncertain. But, it has defined the scope of the SPS Agreement and made more public the dilemma that regulations face in balancing consumer safety based on science with consumer sentiment based on perception.[37] The beef hormone case has dramatically demonstrated the limits of the DSU in imposing politically unacceptable solutions on powerful countries. It has also shown that not all legally sanctioned results of SPS dispute settlement cases give desirable trade outcomes. This landmark case has thus (for the moment at least) resulted in less rather than more international trade. Trade sanctions are by far the least preferable of the possible outcomes of the WTO dispute settlement process. But the granting of authorized retaliation under the rule of law may still be superior to undisciplined unilateral tit-for-tat measures, such as those that occurred between the United States and EC in the 1980s, which can be described as the equivalent of "vigilante justice" in trade. Sanctions are tolerated by the EC, as they are small in cost and diffuse in impact. Short of a change of heart by the US beef industry, which might eventually accept compensating market access for additional hormone-free beef into the EC, it is not easy to see a resolution to this conflict.

3.3. EC-GIs

Trade disputes in agriculture in the area of intellectual property have been almost absent. But, as with other sectors of the economy, the establishment of intellectual property rights has become an important aspect of trade and global commerce. The TRIPS agreement addresses agricultural and food products directly, in the provisions (in Articles 22 and 23), which define members' obligation to protect GIs within their

[37] The WTO dispute over EC measures regulating biotech products raised some of the same legal issues as the hormones case. Argentina, Canada, and the United States argued that the EC Commission's failure to complete the process set out in its own directives and regulations for the premarketing review of 27 biotech products between October 1998 and August 2003 constituted a *de facto* ban on these products, which was not based on a risk assessment. The complainants also argued that nine specific prohibitions by EC member states on biotech products that had been formally approved by the EC were likewise not based on a risk assessment. The EC argued that there have been no undue delays in its scientific approval processes, that were "premised on the application of a prudent and precautionary approach." The WTO panel issued its report in this highly visible dispute in September 2006, concurring with the complainants that the EC had maintained a *de facto* ban on biotech products that violated its obligations under the SPS Agreement. Specifically, the panel noted that "it is clear that application of a prudent and precautionary approach is, and must be, subject to reasonable limits, lest the precautionary approach swallow the discipline" imposed by the SPS Agreement. The panel likewise agreed with the complainants that the prohibitions maintained by EC member states were not based on a risk assessment.

markets. The TRIPS provisions on GIs have been the subject of a trade dispute that led to the setting up of a WTO Dispute Settlement Panel. This has given the opportunity to clarify some key issues. The challenge was initiated by the United States in June 1999, when it requested consultations with the EC on the alleged lack of protection for US trademarks and GIs in the EC. Specifically, the United States contended that the EC did not accord as much protection to US GIs or similar trademarks as it did to EC producers. Such a situation would be a violation of the WTO principle of "national treatment," which holds that foreign and domestic products should be subject to the same rules. It would also violate several provisions of the TRIPS Agreement, which reasserts the right of national treatment in the case of intellectual property protection.

Initially, the United States objected to the Regulation 2081/92 governing GIs (except in the wine sector), as amended. This led to inconclusive talks but neither a resolution nor the selection of a panel. But the revision of the legislation in the EC in April 2003 raised more concerns in the United States, and this time the United States was joined by Australia in the complaint. A panel was requested by the United States and Australia in August 2003, and agreed in October of that year. The panel ruled in April 2005 that the EC has indeed failed to give the US trademark holders adequate protection, as required. The main points of the Panel decision, as confirmed by the Appellate Body, are summarized in Table 4.

The outcome of the WTO case managed to give comfort to both sides to the dispute. The EC was able to claim that its GI protection program was not WTO-incompatible as such and the United States could point to the fact that the EC was found to have violated WTO articles in the way in which it implemented that policy. The EC would have to change its policy regarding the registration of foreign products in the EC market considerably.[38] Its own GI regime will in essence have to be opened to all countries selling GI goods into the EC market. This could undermine the strategy of encouraging quality improvements through regional product protection over time. Having other countries protect EC GIs in their markets, as they are requesting in the current WTO negotiations, would restore some measure of balance in this respect.

The regulations at issue in the WTO case did not apply to wines and spirits. But some aspects of the ruling do relate to this area of trade. The panel report clarified one aspect of the complications of having GI and trademark systems intersect, by considering the issue of the rights to the names Bud and Budweiser. This contentious issue, involving one of the world's largest food-and-drink firms, had been simmering for a century, ever since Adolphus Busch emigrated from Germany to the United States and chose a German-sounding name (actually the German translation of a

[38] Subsequently, the EC has simplified its registration requirements for foreign GIs.

Table 4. Summary of WTO panel ruling on GIs

Issue	Ruling
Violation of Article III: discrimination against non-EC firms and producer groups	EC GI regulation discriminates against non-EC persons and products. EC cannot deny protection on the grounds that the foreign government does not grant "equivalent protection" nor can the EC make protection conditional on "reciprocal" protection in another country.
Violation of Article III: interpretation of process of challenge of GIs by foreign firms	Non-EC firms should be able to register and challenge GIs directly without requiring intervention by their governments. Private rights holders should receive protection under domestic law without needing the intervention of their own government.
Violation of Article 16.1 of TRIPS dealing with potential conflicts between trademarks and GIs	EC regulations should allow holders of preexisting trademarks to prevent confusing use of GI. The EC argument that TRIPS allows for coexistence of GIs and pre-existing trademarks but limits trademark holders' rights was rejected by the panel. The EC should take steps to avoid registering GIs where there is a "relatively high" likelihood of confusion with a trademarked product. This protection against confusion was specifically extended to the registration of GIs that used a translation of a trademarked term.

Note: Complain dealt with GIs for products other than wines and spirits, which are covered by different EC regulations.
Source: Author, based on WTO panel report following Josling (2006).

Czech town name Budjovice) to the dismay of the brewers in that town who had several centuries of experience. When the Czech Republic emerged from the blanket of central planning and tried out the competitive marketplace they persuaded four countries to grant GI status to Budweiser as well as its Czech language equivalent. The EC took over this protection when the Czech Republic joined the EC, and hence had to defend its actions when the United States challenged the EC Regulation.[39]

Although the complaint against the EC has been settled, Anheuser-Busch still has outstanding complaints against Budejovicky Budvar, the current Czech brewer of the beer in question. The UK courts have allowed both brewers to use Bud and Budweiser as trademarks in that markets,

[39] Under the TRIPS Agreement, trademarks that overlap with GIs are granted protection. The EC was thus, in the view of the United States, delinquent in not protecting the Bud and Budweiser names. They could register the Czech name as a GI but not its German translation.

and a similar ruling in Japan allows both to use the term Budweiser (O'Connor, 2004, p. 226). Resolution to this issue is still pending in other large markets such as Russia. Coexistence could be a reasonable outcome to this dispute if no consumer confusion is demonstrated.

4. Agricultural subsidy cases

Although the cases that actually involve subsidies (domestic and export) are a minority of the total agricultural conflicts, they have the most significance for rule changes through negotiations. Four such subsidy cases are discussed in this section: the Canada-dairy case, US-cotton and EC-sugar, and the Canadian and Brazilian cases against the United States notification of its trade-distorting support – the Total Aggregate Measure of Support (AMS) (US-TAMS). It is these four disputes that are redefining the concept of a subsidy and the usefulness of the "boxes" of the URAA. A brief account of each of these cases is given in the following sections.

4.1. The Canadian dairy case

In the aftermath of the Uruguay Round, the Government of Canada instituted a new policy designed to assist exporters of dairy products (mainly cheese) made with expensive domestic milk. A separate "export" class of milk was defined which could be sold at a price lower than that for domestic use.[40] The architects of the policy no doubt assumed that, as no government funds were involved, such a scheme would not be seen by trading partners as an export subsidy.

New Zealand, supported by the United States, took issue with the policy and, after the requisite consultations, it became the subject of a WTO dispute.[41] The panel ruled that the program did indeed constitute a subsidy to exports as it resulted from government action even though no funds were involved. The Canadian policy was changed to reduce the role of

[40] Before 1995, the Canadian Dairy Commission, the Federal body charged with the management of the dairy market and the coordination of the Provincial Milk Marketing Boards through the National Milk Marketing Plan, assisted exports through levies paid by dairy farmers. The new regulation at issue established five Special Milk Classes (Classes 5(a) through 5(e)) for milk and dairy products not exclusively for the domestic market. This Class 5 milk is sold at negotiated prices or set by formula based on US industrial milk. The Special Milk Classes 5(d) and (e) were the focus of the dispute, and covered exports of cheese and dried milk mainly to the United States and the United Kingdom, as well as surplus milk from the domestic market.

[41] The dispute also included a complaint about the administration of Canadian dairy import regulations, but that raised different issues and will not be discussed here (WTO, 1999).

the government, leaving it up to the private sector to negotiate sales of the milk for processing and sale to export destinations.[42] New Zealand and the United States were not convinced that this had solved the problem. The panel was asked to rule on the new policy, and again found it to be in violation of Canada's export subsidy commitments on the grounds that the price of domestic milk was controlled by the government and that this in itself could be enough to subsidize exports.[43] Importantly, the Appellate Body in ruling on the second case directed the panel to use the test of whether the cost of the milk to the export processors was less than the cost of production incurred by the farmers. The panel reconvened and decided that as most farmers produced for both the domestic and the foreign market that they in effect sold the milk surplus to their domestic allotment at a "subsidized" price (WTO, 2001).

The case was settled when the Canadian provinces abolished their CEM programs. Changes in the Federal programs are ongoing. New Zealand and the United States have withdrawn their request for sanctions, and argued that the outcome vindicated the working of the dispute settlement machinery. But the significance of the outcome of the challenge by New Zealand and the United States to the Canadian dairy policy was soon obvious to export interests in other countries. If selling farm products for exporting (or processing for export) at a price less than the cost of production was indeed regarded as an export subsidy then any situation where high, administered domestic prices coexisted with exports might be shown to be contrary to the WTO – or at least would need to be counted against the export subsidy commitments. Sugar policies in the EC were an obvious target, but other cases could subsequently emerge.

In the present context this outcome has another implication. The WTO rules and commitments are based on the notional separation of domestic support from market access and export competition. These aspects are clearly linked economically and politically, but it was assumed that they were at least possible to separate in administrative terms. But if an administered price can grant a subsidy on exports, then the link between domestic support and export competition is exposed. In other words, the legal avenue has made obvious what the pillars of the URAA had attempted to conceal: that the root cause of trade problems is high domestic prices set by farm policy and that these have not been effectively reduced by the constraints imposed on the "at the border" instruments or on domestic subsidies.

---

[42] Canada abolished the Special Milk Class 9(e) and restricted sales under Class 5(d) to conform to its export subsidy commitments. A new milk category of Commercial Export Milk (CEM) was established.

[43] The challenge to Canadian dairy policy was not covered by the Peace Clause as it charged that the export subsidy commitments had been violated.

4.2. The US cotton case

The case against US cotton subsidies appears also to question the distinction between amber and green boxes.[44] The rulings of the panel are best summarized by considering the nine elements of the US programs that were the subject of the challenge by Brazil. Five of these elements (direct payments, production flexibility contract payments, market loss assistance payments, counter-cyclical payments and marketing loan payments) relate to the major instruments of farm policy adopted for the "program crops" in the Farm Bills that cover the period 1999–2003.[45] Two more are specific to cotton (Step 2 subsidies and cottonseed payments), and the other two are of more general application (crop insurance and export credit guarantees). The panel ruled basically on two issues: whether these subsidies were allowed or prohibited and whether they caused "serious prejudice" (even if allowed) to Brazil.

The two subsidies that were not price-related (and which had therefore been notified by the United States as being in the green box) were found not to be the cause of "price suppression" in world markets. They were, however, found to contain provisions that made them ineligible for the green box: specifically the restrictions on the alternative crops that farmers could grow on cotton land. These, the panel decided, could keep more acres in that crop than would totally "decoupled" payments have done. The three subsidies that were price-related were found to have caused price suppression through their impact on keeping cotton production high in the United States at a time of low world prices.[46]

The panel ruled that the Step 2 subsidies paid to domestic users were prohibited under the SCM and the Step 2 subsidies available to export users were prohibited because they were not included in the US schedule of subsidies. Moreover, the Step 2 subsidies also caused significant price suppression in world markets. Cottonseed subsidies and crop insurance

---

[44] Brazil requested consultations with the United States on September 27, 2002. After three abortive discussions, a panel was established on May 19, 2003 and issued a report on June 18, 2004 (WTO, 2004b). This ruling was appealed by the United States, and the Appellate Body issued its report on March 3, 2005. The report as amended was adopted on March 21, 2005 (WTO, 2005).

[45] The two Farm Bills in question are the 1996 FAIR Act and 2002 FSRI Act. Production flexibility contract payments were authorized under the FAIR Act, and marketing loss assistance payments were added as emergency measures in 1998–2001. The FSRI Act replaced these with direct payments and counter-cyclical payments. Marketing loans for cotton have been in place since 1986 and Step 2 subsidies since 1990. The cottonseed payments are emergency payments authorized by the ARP Act in 2000. Crop insurance is authorized by separate legislation, the Federal Crop Insurance Act.

[46] The panel rejected the US argument that the low world prices were from other causes and that the high US exports were an exception rather than the rule.

payments were deemed not to have caused price suppression, and were not prohibited subsidies.

The final aspect of the US programs on which the panel ruled was the set of export credit guarantees that are available to US firms when they sell into overseas markets where credit risks are a factor. The finding in this case was that the export credit guarantees given to cotton producers constituted an export subsidy, and since no such subsidy had been included in the US schedule it was in effect prohibited.[47]

The panel ruling required the United States to end the prohibited subsidies within six months of the adoption of the report or by July 1, 2005 at the latest. This ruling applied to the Step 2 payments, to both domestic and export users, and to the export credit guarantees for cotton. The United States decided that it could make these changes in legislation without having to await the next Farm Bill at that time expected in 2007.[48] The Administration urged Congress to scrap the Step 2 payments, and these will cease at the end of the crop year, in August 2006. The USDA has also proposed changes to the export credit arrangements by eliminating the 1 percent cap on the fees that are charged for borrowing through the GSM-102 program, and by terminating the GSM-103 program that provides for longer repayment periods.

More problematic for the United States is how to adjust the programs that the panel found to cause significant price suppression. Withdrawing the marketing loan and counter-cyclical payments would require major changes in the US legislation and could not easily be done outside the context of the next Farm Bill. Taking other steps to remove the adverse impacts on Brazil might seem easier to achieve, but any attempt to restrict US cotton exports could prove difficult. Compensation to Brazil for lost exports would also seem politically implausible, and a deal to boost Brazilian exports of other commodities would be similarly unpopular. So the prospect is for no change in these aspects of US policy at least until the 2007 Farm Bill, at which time the policies may in any case need to be modified as a result of the Doha Round.

An interesting side issue raised by the panel report is the conclusion that the direct payments and production flexibility contract payments are not eligible for the green box. This would seem to indicate that countries might ask the United States to resubmit notifications of domestic support for the years in question. This would almost certainly put the United States in excess of its amber box limits, and raise serious problems with trading partners. If this were to be resolved by litigation (an easier task since no serious prejudice issues would be relevant) then the United States

---

[47] The ruling also declared the export credit guarantees for rice exceeded its allowed export subsidy limit, but did not find fault with other aspects of the program

[48] The Farm Bill was eventually passed in early 2008.

would have to make major changes to its farm policy. But again, the chances are that these issues will be resolved in the context of the Doha Round.

The signal importance of the cotton case for WTO jurisprudence is that it clarifies several aspects of the application of WTO rules to agricultural subsidies. The Peace Clause effectively dissuaded members from challenging agricultural subsidies under the SCM before 2004. Though the panel ruled that the Peace Clause did not provide shelter for the US subsidies in question, the case is best considered as the first "post-Peace Clause" challenge to farm subsidies. The consistency of agricultural subsidies with the provisions of the SCM is a fertile ground for speculation. But the panel indicates that, at least in this case, these restrictions are both onerous and comprehensive. Though the ruling on serious prejudice was based on the impact of US subsidies on world cotton prices, the same provision of the SCM also includes the effect of subsidies in impeding exporters in domestic and third country markets as well as the impact on market shares. Moreover, though it was not found germane to this case, the SCM has provisions for cases where the "threat" of serious prejudice exists.

The case may or may not usher in a flurry of similar litigation; much depends on the success of the Doha Round in reducing subsidies. But the panel report certainly gives encouragement to countries that have refrained from making challenges because they felt that panels would have difficulties in finding evidence of serious prejudice. In markets where there are many factors contributing to the export performance of particular countries, establishing causal relationships is problematic. But the panel seemed to be un-phased by the conflicting opinions of expert witnesses on the magnitude and direction of the impact of US subsidies on world cotton prices. They made their ruling on the basis of a preponderance of evidence from economic studies that production of cotton in the United States has a significant impact on the world market price. Although they avoided linking their decision to any particular study, they certainly paid more attention to such evidence than many previous panels. So the cotton panel continues the trend toward rulings based on economic reasoning and quantification as a way of bringing precision to terms such as "substantial" and "significant" that pepper the rules on the trade impacts of subsidies (Table 5). The cotton case is likely to be cited in many panel reports in future years.

4.3. The EC sugar case

The impact of the Canadian dairy case on the approach taken by exporters toward farm policies in other countries can be seen in the challenge brought by Brazil, Australia, and Thailand against the EC sugar

Table 5. US cotton programs and main elements in the cotton panel ruling

Program	Panel ruling
Direct payments (DP)	Not eligible for green box because of restrictions on use of land Do not cause significant price suppression on world markets
Production flexibility contract payments (PFC)	Not eligible for green box because of restrictions on use of land Do not cause significant price suppression on world markets
Market loss assistance payments (MLA)	Caused significant price suppression on world market
Counter-cyclical payments (CCP)	Caused significant price suppression on world market
Marketing loan payments (ML)	Caused significant price suppression on world market
Step 2 payments	Caused significant price suppression on world market For domestic users, payments were import substitution subsidy For export users, payments were export subsidies not included in US schedule
Cottonseed payments	Do not cause significant price suppression on world markets
Crop insurance	Do not cause significant price suppression on world markets
Export credit guarantees	Credit guarantees for cotton (and several other products) were export subsidies and were not included in US schedule. (Rice export subsidy exceeded its scheduled level)

Source: Author, based on WTO Panel Report following Josling (2005).

subsidies.[49] Complaints about EC sugar policy are not new. Australia had challenged the EC sugar regime in 1979 in the GATT and Brazil followed in 1980, but these were complicated by the fact that there was an International Sugar Agreement (ISA; to which the EC was not a signatory) that restricted exports. Under such circumstances, the panels were unable to determine the extent of injury that the plaintiffs had suffered and the policies continued unchecked (Josling and Tangermann, 2003). The United States also challenged the CAP sugar policy in the GATT in 1982, but no panel was established. The EC indicated its willingness to join the ISA, and proceeded in turn to challenge the US sugar regime.

[49] The Australian and Brazilian challenges were initiated in September 2002 and Thailand joined the complaint in March 2003. The dispute numbers are DS265, DS266, and DS283, respectively. The panel report was presented on October 15, 2004 and was appealed. The Appellate Body gave their opinion on April 28, 2005 and the DSB accepted the report as modified (WTO, 2004a).

One of the contentions of these sugar exporters in the recent WTO case was that the EC grants *de facto* export subsidies by means of the high price paid for sugar used on the domestic market. The domestic market price is maintained for sugar produced under two quotas (the "A" and "B" quotas): production over those quotas (usually called "C" sugar) cannot be sold on the domestic market and receives no direct subsidy. At issue is whether the C sugar benefits indirectly as farmers can cover their fixed costs from returns from the high-price quotas. The analogy with the exported milk products from Canada is close if not exact. The complainants maintain that if such subsides were included, the EC would be in breach of its export subsidy commitments under the URAA.

A second contention was that the EC exports the equivalent of the 1.4 million tons of sugar that is imported under preferential agreements enshrined in the Cotonou Agreement with former colonies. This sugar is sold to the EC at the internal price but re-exported at the world price. This was not notified as a part of the EC's schedule of exports that benefit from subsidies: it was explicitly excluded in a footnote.

The panel found, and the Appellate Body agreed, that the EC was in breech in both respects. The exports of C sugar did benefit from the high price of A and B quotas awarded to the same farms. As the C sugar was solely destined for exports, the effect was to cross-subsidize.[50] By implication, if C sugar were sold on the internal market to any extent, the argument would have required a further stage of showing that the exports were harming other exporters. But as the implicit financial benefits to producers of C sugar were not notified as export subsidies, they were *de facto* prohibited regardless of their market impact. Similarly, the panel found that the re-export of the ACP (and Indian) sugar was prohibited as it did not appear in the EC schedule. Thus, the EC sugar case differs from that of US cotton in that it centers primarily on the notification of export subsidies. The fact that these notifications were not challenged at the time raises questions about how the activities of the Agriculture Committee might be linked more usefully to the issue of the nature of these policies.

The sugar case is complicated by an additional element. If the EC cannot either re-export the ACP imports or sell C sugar on the world market, then the domestic price has to be reduced and/or the quotas have to be reduced. The EC Commission realized this link with reform of the EC sugar regime, and used the argument effectively to persuade member states of the need for policy change. The political decision was made by the

[50] Investigations of subsidies in nonagricultural markets often explore the possibility of cross-subsidization within firms. The economics of cross-subsidization is not as well accepted as the accounting conventions.

EC's Council of Ministers on November 22, 2005, to undertake a reform that cut the sugar price support level by 36 percent and compensated farmers with decoupled payments. Although the support price will stay significantly above the world price level, the incentive to produce for export (over and above the quota volume) will be significantly reduced. If the output falls as expected, the EC will come into compliance with the Panel ruling: cross subsidized production will not find its way into export markets, and the ACP sugar will be absorbed largely in the domestic market.

Suppliers of raw sugar to the EC have also been promised compensation. Under the Cotonou Agreement, these suppliers benefit from guaranteed access at internal prices, and so will lose from the reduction in price levels. Although this preferential access is already under threat from the opening up of tariff and quota-free access to the least developed countries under the "Everything but Arms" agreement of the EC, it remains of economic and political importance to a number of countries. Furthermore, they will also benefit from reductions in the sales of "C" sugar on world markets. Thus the link with the trade negotiations is more complex than just the connection with the reform of the EC sugar regime.

5. *Conclusion*

The proliferation of agricultural cases in the WTO reflects both the ambivalent nature of the multilateral trade rules in the sector and the sensitive nature of the trade itself. In addition, the perceived vulnerability of the major farm programs of industrial countries to challenge under the URAA and the SCM has led to some recent high-profile disputes. The nature of technological changes in food production, particularly the uneven adoption of biotech seeds, has led to other disputes. Countries are still grappling with the trade policy consequences of the search for attributes in production that are desirable to consumers. The dividing line between providing consumers with adequate decisions on which to base decisions and cooperating with domestic producers to restrict imports is often difficult to determine. More of these issues will be tested in the WTO in future years. Indeed, it would be risky to predict any sharp decrease in the numbers of agricultural disputes brought before the DSB in the next decade.[51]

[51] In some areas of trade, complaints can trigger retaliatory filings as an element of trade strategy. This does not seem to be a problem in agriculture at present but it may emerge as more sensitive cases are litigated.

The URAA constituted a negotiated solution to several market access issues in agriculture. The URAA mandated the removal of non-tariff border measures and the binding of most tariffs. It introduced the Special Safeguard for Agriculture (SSG) as new safeguard mechanism and TRQs to maintain access in cases where non-tariff measures were converted to tariffs. In addition, the URAA helped to clarify the issue of subsidies that had proved to be so difficult to discipline under the GATT. The URAA circumscribed the use of export subsidies, obliging countries to notify all such aids and include schedules for their reduction. New export subsidies were banned. For domestic subsidies the URAA introduced a classification of domestic support instruments that attempted to limit the use of the more trade-distorting subsidies. The URAA also implemented notification procedures to track compliance with the provisions and the schedules of commitments.[52] But each of these issues left room for interpretation and were grist for the litigation mill.

Market access issues were the most important in the early days of the WTO, as countries explored through the DSB the practical implementation of the new rules and the agreed schedules. The process of tariffication was fairly smooth, and the introduction of the SSG also was without major problems. However, the establishment of TRQs did lead to several conflicts, as one might imagine in cases where government decisions had immediate commercial impact. The success in limiting trade-distorting subsidies has been somewhat more elusive. Export subsidies that were included in the schedules in general caused few disputes, in part because the limits were well above actual levels. But panels examining country policies unearthed several policies that acted as export aids within the terms of the WTO but had not been notified as such. Thus the major challenges to domestic farm programs in the EU and the United States came from other exporters complaining that the export subsidy restrictions were being circumvented.

Cases brought against particular types of domestic support have been infrequent. With inconclusive debates in the Committee for Agriculture and without the guidance of panel reports, countries were able to decide largely for themselves whether particular policies were consistent with the definitions of the green and blue boxes, and hence not subject to reductions. As long as countries were way below their limits on domestic

[52] Commitments on subsidy levels are treaty provisions, and the commitments in a Member's Schedule are "an integral part" of the URAA and other WTO agreements (WT/DS265/R, paragraph 7.128). Conformity with scheduled commitments is a necessary but not a sufficient condition for escaping challenge. Panels have made clear that compliance with a Domestic Support commitment in a Member's Schedule does not in itself preempt or exclude the operation of other WTO obligations (WT/DS267/R, paras. 7.1066 and 7.1067).

support, it was not a priority to challenge the notifications themselves. But the jump in funding for the 2002 US Farm Bill caused a re-think of this situation, with the possibility that the limits may have been breached if notifications had been erroneous. The statement of the US cotton panel that some of the expenditures that the United States had claimed as "green" may have been mislabeled, turned this possibility into a contestable proposition.

The current case brought by Canada and Brazil, challenging the level of US farm subsidies as notified under the categories used by the URAA, illustrates that ambiguity still exists.[53] On the one hand, it is a remarkable case, which if it ever went to a panel would clarify the somewhat fuzzy nature of the "boxes." On the other hand, it refers to past notifications that were alleged to wrongly classify certain subsidies. So the remedy in the event of a successful challenge is presumably to oblige a re-notification by the United States of its domestic support for several historical years. But the United States could well argue that in the current period of high prices, support levels are already well below the limits set in the schedules even with renotification. So it would not be clear what the United States could do to make amends: changing current policies would not be an appropriate remedy, and compensation for past violations is not contemplated in the DSU.

This does not drain the interest away from the case. The reclassification of direct payments in the United States away from the green box in a revised notification would indeed be a small prize for competing exporters. But added the possibility of a new set of limits in the Doha Round, and the case becomes critical. If the Doha Round succeeds in reducing allowable trade-distorting subsidies (as calculated by the AMS), the allocation of subsidies to these boxes becomes sensitive. The prospect exists that the major driver of change in US farm policy could indeed be the WTO dispute settlement process, and the decisions on the classification of subsidies. That could also set up some controversy over the role of WTO rules when they clash with powerful political interests. Agricultural trade will continue to provide vexing issues for the multilateral trade system and its judicial processes.

[53] The two cases brought by Canada and Brazil (DS 357 and 365 respectively) have been merged. The complaint is that United States exceeded its Total AMS limits in several recent years.

Annex

Table A1. WTO Disputes initiated since January 1995 related to agricultural products

Date	DS#	Complainant	Respondent	Commodity	Issue
1995	3	United States	Korea	Agricultural products	Import testing
1995	5	United States	Korea	Agricultural products	Shelf life
1995	9	Canada	EC	Cereals	UR implementation
1995	13	United States	EC	Grain	UR implementation
1995	16	Guatemala, etc.	EC	Bananas	Import regulations
1995	17	Thailand	EC	Rice	UR implementation
1995	22	Philippines	Brazil	Coconut	CVD
1995	25	Uruguay	EC	Rice	UR implementation
1996	26	United States	EC	Meat	SPS
1996	27	Ecuador, etc.	EC	Bananas	Import regulations
1996	30	Sri Lanka	Brazil	Coconut milk	CVD
1996	35	Argentina, etc.	Hungary	Agricultural products	Export subsidies
1996	41	United States	Korea	Agricultural products	Import testing
1996	48	Canada	EC	Meat	SPS
1996	49	Mexico	United States	Tomatoes	A/D
1997	66	EC	Japan	Pork	Import measures
1997	69	Brazil	EC	Poultry	TRQ
1997	72	New Zealand	EC	Butter	TRQ
1997	74	United States	Philippines	Pork, poultry	TRQ
1997	76	United States	Japan	Agricultural products	Quarantine
1997	98	EC	Korea	Dairy	Safeguards
1997	100	EC	United States	Poultry	SPS

Table A1. (continued)

Date	DS#	Complainant	Respondent	Commodity	Issue
1997	102	United States	Philippines	Pork, poultry	TRQ
1997	103	United States	Canada	Dairy	Export subsidies
1997	104	United States	EC	Processed cheese	Export subsidies
1997	105	Panama	EC	Bananas	Import regulations
1997	111	Argentina	EC	Groundnuts	TRQ
1997	113	New Zealand	Canada	Dairy	Export subsidies
1998	133	Switzerland	Slovakia	Dairy	Import restriction
1998	134	India	EC	Rice	Import restriction
1998	143	Hungary	Slovak Rep	Wheat	Import duties
1998	144	Canada	United States	Cattle, swine, and grain	Transport restrictions
1998	145	EC	Argentina	Wheat gluten	CVD
1998	148	Hungary	Czech Rep	Wheat	Import regulations
1998	149	EC	India	Nonspecific	Import quotas
1999	154	Brazil	EC	Coffee	Differential treatment
1999	158	Guatemala, etc.	EC	Bananas	Import regulations
1999	161	United States	Korea	Beef	Import regulations
1999	166	EC	United States	Wheat gluten	Safeguards
1999	167	Canada	United States	Cattle	CVD
1999	169	Australia	Korea	Beef	Import regulations
1999	174	United States	EC	Agricultural Products	GIs
1999	177	New Zealand	United States	Lamb	Safeguards
1999	178	Australia	United States	Lamb	Safeguards
1999	180	Canada	United States	Sugar	Classification
1999	185	Costa Rica	Trinidad	Pasta	A/D

2000	187	Costa Rica	Trinidad	Pasta	A/D
2000	203	United States	Mexico	Live swine	A/D
2000	205	Thailand	Egypt	Tuna in oil	Import regulations
2000	207	Argentina	Chile	Agricultural products	Price band
2000	210	United States	Belgium	Rice	Import duties
2001	220	Guatemala	Chile	Agricultural products	Price band
2001	223	United States	EC	Corn gluten	TRQ
2001	226	Argentina	Chile	Edible oils	Safeguards
2001	228	Colombia	Chile	Sugar	Safeguards
2001	230	Colombia	Chile	Sugar	Safeguards
2001	235	Poland	Slovakia	Sugar	Safeguards
2001	237	Ecuador	Turkey	Bananas	Import regulations
2001	238	Chile	Argentina	Peaches, preserved	Safeguards
2001	240	Hungary	Romania	Wheat/flour	Import prohibition
2001	241	Brazil	Argentina	Poultry	A/D
2002	245	United States	Japan	Apples	SPS
2002	250	Brazil	United States	Citrus products	Florida excise tax
2002	256	Hungary	Turkey	Pet food	SPS
2002	263	Argentina	EC	Wine	Import regulations
2002	265	Australia	EC	Sugar	Export subsidies
2002	266	Brazil	EC	Sugar	Export subsidies
2002	267	Brazil	United States	Cotton	Domestic support
2002	269	Brazil	EC	Poultry	Classification
2002	270	Philippines	Australia	Fruit and vegetables	Quarantine
2002	271	Philippines	Australia	Pineapple	Quarantine
2002	275	United States	Venezuela	Agricultural Products	Import licensing
2002	276	United States	Canada	Wheat	Import restrictions, STE
2003	283	Thailand	EC	Sugar	Export subsidies

2003	284	Nicaragua	Mexico	Black beans	SPS
2003	286	Thailand	EC	Poultry	Classification
2003	289	Poland	Czech Republic	Pigmeat	Import duties
2003	290	Australia	EC	Agricultural Products	GIs
2003	291	United States	EC	Biotech products	Import regulations
2003	292	Canada	EC	Biotech products	Import regulations
2003	293	Argentina	EC	Biotech products	Import regulations
2003	295	United States	Mexico	Beef, rice	A/D
2003	297	Hungary	Croatia	Meat	SPS
2004	310	Canada	United States	Hard wheat	A/D
2004	314	EC	Mexico	Olive oil	CVD
2004	320	EC	United States	Beef	Continued suspension
2004	321	EC	Canada	Beef	Continued suspension
2005	329	Mexico	Panama	Milk products	Classification
2005	330	EC	Argentina	Olive oil, etc.	CVD
2005	334	United States	Turkey	Rice	TRQ
2005	338	United States	Canada	Corn	CVD, A/D
2006	341	EC	Mexico	Olive oil	CVD
2006	349	Argentina	EC	Garlic	TRQ
2006	351	Argentina	Chile	Milk products	Prov. Safeguards
2006	356	Argentina	Chile	Milk products	Def. Safeguards
2007	357	Canada	United States	Agricultural products	Domestic support
2007	361	Colombia	EC	Bananas	Import duties
2007	364	Panama	EC	Bananas	Differential treatment
2007	365	Brazil	United States	Agricultural products	Domestic support
2007	367	New Zealand	Australia	Apples	Quarantine

Source: WTO website.

References

Barichello, R., Josling, T., Sumner, D. (2005), *Agricultural Trade Disputes Between Canada and the United States: Costly but Diminishing*, Commentary, No. 224, December, CD Howe Institute, Toronto.

Barton, J.H., Goldstein, J., Josling, T., Steinberg, R.H. (2006), *The Evolution of the Trade Regime: Politics, Law and Economics of the GATT and WTO*. Princeton University Press, Princeton, NJ.

Josling, T. (2003), Bananas and the WTO: testing the new dispute settlement process. In: Josling, T.E., Taylor, T.G. (Eds.), *Banana Wars: The Anatomy of a Trade Dispute*. CABI Publishing, Wallingford, pp. 169–194.

Josling, T. (2005), Unraveling the cotton case. *Bridges*. Year 9, No. 4, April–May, pp. 3–5.

Josling, T. (2006), The War on *Terroir:* geographical indications as a transatlantic trade conflict. *Journal of Agricultural Economics* 57 (3), 337–366.

Josling, T., Tangermann, S. (2003), Production and export subsidies in agriculture: lessons from GATT and WTO disputes involving the US and the EC. In: Petersmann, E-U., Pollack, M. (Eds.), *Transatlantic Economic Disputes*. Oxford University Press, Oxford.

Josling, T., Roberts, D., Orden, D. (2004), *Food Regulation and Trade: Toward a Safe and Open Global System*. Institute for International Economics, Washington, DC.

Josling, T., Tangermann, S., Warley, T.K. (1996), *Agriculture in the GATT*. Houndmills, London and New York.

Josling, T., Zhao, L., Carcelen, J., Arha, K. (2006), Implications of WTO litigation for the WTO agricultural negotiations. *IPC Policy Brief*.

Kramer, C.S. (1989), Food safety and International Trade: the US-EC Meat and Hormone Controversies. In: Kramer, C.S. (Ed.), *The Political Economy of US Agriculture*. National Center for Food and Agricultural Policy, Resources for the Future, Washington, DC, pp. 210–211.

O'Connor, B. (2004), *The Law of Geographical Indications*. Cameron May, London.

Steinberg, R.H., Josling, T.E. (2003), When the peace ends: The vulnerability of EC and U.S. agricultural subsidies to WTO legal challenge. *Journal of International Economic Law* 6 (2), 369–417.

World Trade Organization. (1995), The results of the Uruguay Round of multilateral trade negotiations, The Legal Texts, WTO, Geneva.

World Trade Organization. (1997a), European Communities-regime for the importation, sale and distribution of bananas, complaint by the United Sates, Report of the Panel, WT/DS27/R/USA, May 22, 1997.

World Trade Organization. (1997b), European Communities-regime for the importation, sale and distribution of bananas, Report of the Appellate Body, WT/DS27/AB/R, September 9.

World Trade Organization. (1998), EC – measures concerning meat and meat products (hormones), WTO/DS26 & 48/AB/R, February 13.
World Trade Organization. (1999), Canada – measures affecting the importation of milk and the exportation of dairy products, WT/DS103/R and WT/DS113/R.
World Trade Organization. (2001), Canada – measures affecting the importation of milk and the exportation of dairy products, Report of the Appellate Body, WT/DS103&113/AB/RW.
World Trade Organization. (2004a), European Communities – export subsidies on sugar, Reports of the Panels, WT/DS265/R, WT/DS266/R, & WT/DS283/R.
World Trade Organization. (2004b), United States – subsidies on Upland cotton, Report of the Panel, WT/DS267/R.
World Trade Organization. (2005), United States – subsidies on Upland cotton, Reports of the Appellate Body, WT/DS265/AB/R, WT/DS266/AB/R, & WT/DS267/AB/R.

Part V

Monitoring the Compliance of Country Policies with WTO Disciplines

Chapter 12
WTO Compliance and Domestic Farm Policy Change

Tim Josling

Abstract The establishment of the WTO in 1995 posed a challenge for the conduct of domestic farm policies. Both the levels of support and the instruments used were constrained by the Agreement on Agriculture and other parts of the Uruguay Round Agreement. This chapter explores the experience of the period since 1995 to see to what extent the WTO commitments have shaped domestic farm policies, particularly in the United States and the European Union. This influence can come about either through the negotiated constraints on policy outcomes or through the litigation of complaints by other countries. Notifications of domestic support levels show little direct impact on US farm policy but the outcome of litigation has had some influence on policy choices. In the European Union, the reform of the CAP has been much more influenced by WTO subsidy constraints but somewhat less by litigation.

12.1 Introduction

One major objective of the WTO Agreement on Agriculture was to influence domestic agricultural policies, particularly in the developed countries. The idea was to promote less trade-distorting means of support so as to work toward a more open trade system for agricultural products. The United States was a strong supporter of this aim, and maintained the pressure during the Uruguay Round to bring domestic support under the disciplines of trade rules. The disciplines that were developed influenced both instrument choice and the levels of support. Though domestic politicians have had a natural tendency to downplay the significance of these constraints, there is abundant evidence of the growing influence of WTO rules on farm policies. Completion of the Doha Round would make the link between trade rules and domestic policy even more apparent. In the absence of a Doha Round agreement

T. Josling (✉)
Freeman Spogli Institute for International Studies, Stanford University, Stanford, CA, USA
e-mail: josling@stanford.edu

V.E. Ball et al. (eds.), *The Economic Impact of Public Support to Agriculture*, Studies in Productivity and Efficiency 7, DOI 10.1007/978-1-4419-6385-7_12, one might expect to see the more vigorous enforcement of existing restraints on domestic policies through the litigation process of the WTO.

Twenty-four years after the Punta del Este Declaration that launched to Uruguay Round, and which for the first time incorporated the mandate to include domestic policy in the negotiations, it is appropriate to pull together the evidence to see what impact the Agreement on Agriculture (URAA) and other aspects of the Uruguay Round agreement has had on farm policy. For convenience, the focus is on the United States and the European Union as the two trading partners that have the most extensive domestic farm support systems and the strongest interest (both offensive and defensive) in the disciplines of the WTO in this area. But the picture is not complete without some mention of other countries, such as Australia, Canada, and Brazil, that have been major players in the game.

The chapter starts with a brief review of what restraints the URAA was designed to impose on developed country farm policies and continues with a discussion of the significance of these restraints over the period since 1995. The importance of these constraints was enhanced by the expanded use of litigation by other countries in order to challenge perceived violations. Section 12.2 discusses the cases that have had a noticeable impact on the development of domestic policy. Section 12.3 poses the question of what further impact the WTO rules would have if the currently proposed provisions of the Doha Round were to be adopted. By implication, the failure to adopt these provisions would reopen the question of whether existing rules are being applied correctly. A final paragraph attempts to summarize the arguments and conclusions of the chapter.

12.2 The URAA

The Uruguay Round of trade negotiations under the General Agreement on Tariffs and Trade (GATT) marked a transition of the multilateral trade system from a limited intergovernmental agreement on rules of conduct for trade in goods to a more comprehensive treaty covering trade in services and trade-related aspects of intellectual property protection as well as goods trade. It set up a secretariat to assist members in their application of the rules and established a dispute settlement system that could ensure that the broader rules were respected and interpreted in an agreed manner. All members undertook the full set of obligations (the "single undertaking") though the rules themselves allow for limited differentiation by development status ("special and differential treatment" for developing countries).

One key part of the Uruguay Round was the Agreement on Agriculture. The Uruguay Round Agreement on Agriculture (URAA) was a new departure in the treatment of agricultural goods in the multilateral trade system.[1] It devised agriculture-specific rules that obliged the conversion of non-tariff border measures to tariffs as well as placing restrictions on border policies including, for the first time, restraints on export subsidies. And, in particular, it addressed the question of the impact of domestic farm policies on trade flows. The URAA imposed restraints on the level of support provided by domestic programs and introduced incentives to shift to less trade-distorting measures. Moreover, it introduced institutional monitoring of compliance with the rules and schedules, temporarily sheltered some types of agricultural subsidy from challenge under a new subsidy agreement, and committed member governments to further talks on agricultural policy reform.

Though the URAA specifically relates to agricultural programs and trade policies, other aspects of the WTO are of actual or potential importance. One of the most significant aspects is the Agreement on Subsidies and Countervailing Measures (SCM), which governs all subsidies. The clause in the URAA that sheltered agricultural subsidies from challenge under the SCM expired in 2003, and since that time the provisions have applied to a range of agricultural programs. Another aspect is the Sanitary and Phytosanitary (SPS) Agreement, which obliges WTO members to base health and safety standards on scientific risk assessment. For certain sectors of agriculture, particularly livestock and fruits and vegetables, rules that ensure science-based import regulations in other countries are of considerable importance (Josling et al., 2004). These agreements came into effect in 1995 as a part of the Marrakesh Agreement that established the World Trade Organization. As a part of the set of WTO agreements, they are subject to litigation under the Dispute Settlement Understanding that also emerged from the Uruguay Round.[2]

The central elements of the URAA are often referred to as the three "pillars": market access, domestic support, and export competition. In all three areas, new rules were added and reductions in trade distortions were agreed. Together they form a comprehensive framework for the regulation of measures that restrict trade in agricultural products. US and EU farm policy must comply with these rules if they are not to risk challenge by other countries. On the other hand, competing agricultural exporters and those countries that are markets for US and EU farm goods also have to adhere to the rules. The full impact of the URAA includes the benefits that the developed countries might get from the restraint on other country's policies as well as the restraints that are accepted for themselves.

Market access rules include the conversion of all non-tariff import barriers (quotas and restrictive licenses) to tariffs. Moreover, it was agreed that tariff levels were to be bound and that tariff-rate quotas (TRQs – quantities that can be imported at a zero or low tariff) were to be established to maintain market access as "tariffication" took place. These TRQs were to represent "current access" in cases of existing trade or a "minimum access" of 3% of domestic consumption (rising to 5% over the implementation period) in cases where there were no imports in the base period. Tariffs were to be reduced from the base period (1986–1990) by an (unweighted) average of 36%, with a minimum cut of 15% for each tariff line, over a 6-year period (1995–2000).[3] In addition, the agreement established a special safeguard regime (SSG) that countries could use to counter import surges or price drops in markets where they had newly established tariffs.

Domestic support was defined to include payments to farmers in addition to the transfers from consumers through border policies. These included deficiency payments, direct payments, administrative price systems, public research and extension programs subsidies based on compliance with environmental regulations, and other programs that benefited farmers directly.[4] These elements of domestic support were put into three categories, which have become known as the Amber Box (those tied to output or input prices or to current output levels), the Blue Box (those that were tied to supply control programs), and the Green Box (those unrelated to price and output). The Amber Box payments were subject to a reduction of 20% over the transition period as indicated in individual country schedules: neither the Blue Box nor the Green Box payments were subject to reduction.

The rules regarding export competition included a prohibition on new export subsidies and a reduction of existing subsidies by both volume and expenditure. A list of export subsidy practices that are covered is given in Article 9.1. Following the agreed modalities, country schedules were drawn up that provided for reductions relative to the base period of 36% by expenditure and 21% by quantity subsidized. In addition, rules were made more explicit with regard to food aid and countries agreed to negotiate limits on export credit guarantees (government underwriting of sales to purchasers that might lack creditworthiness).

Though the new rules offer the possibility of more open markets, market access for agricultural products did not greatly improve as a result of the tariff reduction schedules. Many of the tariff cuts merely reduced the "water" in the tariff schedules (the superfluous protection given by a tariff that is higher than that which would close off any imports). Ceiling bindings were often set at high levels even though applied tariffs were much lower. The introduction of TRQs, though arguably an improvement on the quantitative restrictions that they replaced, still restricted trade in the more sensitive products. So the task of reducing tariffs to a level more in keeping with non-farm tariffs was left to subsequent rounds of negotiations. The Doha Round shows how difficult it is to take this next step.

12.3 The Impact of the URAA on Policy

The impact of the introduction of the URAA on farm policies has been profound but subtle. Few farm support policies that existed in 1995 had to be abandoned. But the development of policies since that time has been within the framework of the URAA. The URAA was designed to be permissive of the major types of policy in use, but to set up incentives for changes over time. The changes have generally been along the lines that have been favored by "reformers" in domestic policy discussions, but that does not mean that they have been ineffective. The process of domestic and trade policy reform have gone hand in hand. Domestic policy change has allowed the introduction of more discipline in international trade: the trade rules have steered countries in general along the path chosen for domestic policies. The common theme is the use of tariffs as the sole means of border protection and of direct supports as the approved vehicle for farm income supplements. The removal of non-tariff trade barriers changes the nature of domestic policy as it makes supply control difficult to administer at the market level (though resource retirement at the producer level is still possible). Direct payments break in large part the link between farm support and output decisions, and enables a link to be made to the provision of public goods by the farm sector.

How has this played out in practice? The most significant changes that have come along with the implementation of the Uruguay Round in the United States have been in market access. The United States finally abandoned the use of quotas as required by Section 22 of the Agricultural Adjustment Act (as amended) as a result of tariffication of all non-tariff import measures. This also meant that the 1955 waiver that had been renewed annually since that date was no longer needed. The action may not have caused much comment at home, but the implications were not lost on trade partners. The US trade policy for agricultural products was no longer in (waivered) violation of the GATT rules. Also significant was the abolition of "voluntary" export restrictions (VERs) that exporters chose to impose under the implicit threat that there would be mandatory import restrictions if they did not do so. This policy had been used extensively to protect the meat market in the United States from imports of beef and sheep meat from Australia and New Zealand at times when US prices were low. The legal status of VERs in the GATT had never been established, but they were seen as an intrusion into the desirable working of the market.[5] The European Union also saw a major change in its domestic agricultural policy, the CAP, as a result of the application to agricultural goods of the "tariffs only" principle. The "variable levies" that had been used since the inception of the CAP to keep domestic prices stable when world prices fluctuated were always challenged by exporters as not being consistent with the GATT. But, like VERs, they were considered "gray area" measures that fell into no category defined in the GATT. Variable levies were not straightforward tariffs that could be put in a schedule, but they were not quotas as the quantities imported were not constrained. The URAA specifically banned their use, along with other dubious import restrictions. The European Union complied and changed its variable levies into tariffs (tariffication) and bound the resulting tariffs.

A more subtle change came about as a result of the introduction of TRQs in cases where non-tariff import measures were converted into tariffs. Caution by the exporters that the new bound tariffs may still be too high for some significant market access opportunities to open up led to the introduction of TRQs: the importers then used these to favor countries to which they had offered preferential access. So the TRQ emerged as a way of squaring the need to offer some market access to partners in regional and bilateral trade agreement with the imposition of the URAA.

Even the binding of tariffs has implications for domestic policy. The fact that it is difficult to renegotiate a bound tariff, in that one has to satisfy principal suppliers, means that it is not an appropriate tool for managing domestic markets. So in effect the tariff is locked up in a schedule in the WTO and cannot be used by agricultural ministers or congressional committees as they make regular policy decisions.

The limits on export subsidies and the prohibition on new such subsidies have also had a restricting impact on farm policy in the United States and the European Union. In the United States, the use of (overt) export subsidies has virtually been abandoned in the period since 1995: some small programs remain for dairy products. This could of course have happened even without the URAA, but the trade rules reinforce and lock in these changes even if made for domestic reasons. The European Union still uses export subsidies, but has moderated its reliance on such subsidies for clearing domestic markets. Export subsidies are expensive and tend to benefit foreign consumers and to penalize domestic consumers. It may be that no new subsidies would have been introduced in the past 15 years, but it has been important to competing exporters to know that such subsidies would not have been allowed by the URAA.

The new rules for food aid that were incorporated in the URAA had as their intent the avoidance of commercial displacement by concessional sales. Food aid quantities have trended downward in the past decade, and so it is difficult to see the impact of the URAA. And the talks that were suggested in the URAA to negotiate limits on export credits were not successful No advance was made on the contentious issue of the activities of single-desk export agencies, once used extensively by Canada, Australia, New Zealand and a few other exporters to organize and expand export markets: these state trading activities have been somewhat curtailed in the past decade, but not as a result of the introduction of the URAA.

The most difficult question to answer is whether the URAA has made any significant impacts on domestic policies. The discussion between the United States and the European Union at Blair House in November 1992 was a key turning point in the Uruguay Round negotiations. The outcome was to frame the constraints on domestic policy that were to be included in the URAA in such a way that current legislation would not be in gross violation of the agreement and that the option of forcing change through litigation was circumscribed. Thus the Blue Box was introduced to relieve the US direct payments for program crops under the 1990 Farm Bill from reduction (though increases over and above the 1992 level were prohibited), and to ensure that the EU compensatory payments for grains and oilseeds that were introduced in the 1992 reform of the CAP were not going to be challenged by other countries. To ensure the lack of legal challenges, a Peace Clause was agreed for the URAA (Article 13) that sheltered many, but not all, domestic policies from the Subsidies and Countervailing Measures (SCM) Agreement (Steinberg and Josling, 2003).

The first year of US notifications covered the last year of the 1990 Farm Act. The United States still had deficiency payments with acreage idling provisions and this is reflected in the Blue Box component of the notification. Crop prices were relatively high and so the notified total AMS and *de minimis* were both small. With the passage of the 1996 Farm Act, direct income support payments were introduced to replace the deficiency payments: the direct payments were notified in the Green Box. AMS support remained low until crop prices started to deteriorate in 1998 (Fig. 12.1). From that time until the passage of the 2002 Act, production-linked "emergency" payments were authorized that increased AMS support and its share of total support. During the life of the 2002 Act AMS support has generally remained high and variable. More recently, strengthening commodity prices have led to a significant estimated reduction in the total AMS (in 2006, for example) – a condition that has continued into 2008.[6] Weaker prices would increase the expenditure on trade-distorting policies. As discussed below, this could pose some significant

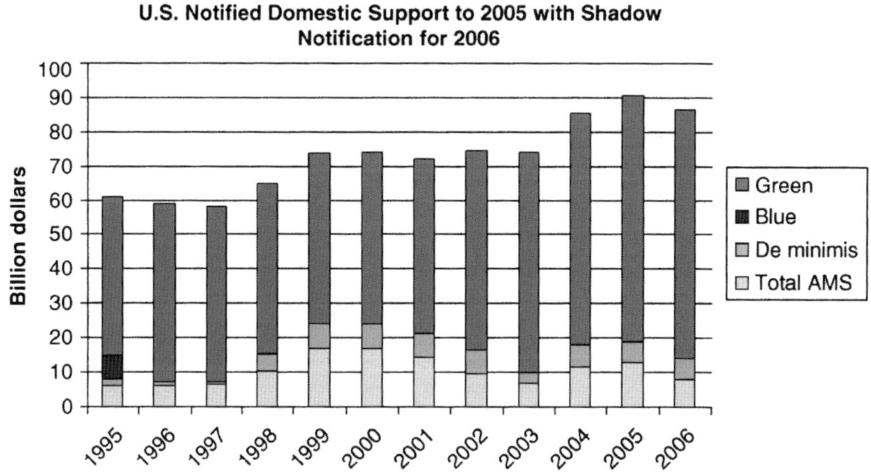

Fig. 12.1 US notifications of domestic support, 1995–2005, with shadow notification for 2006. *Source*: Blandford and Josling, 2008

challenges for the United States in meeting future commitments under a DDA Agreement.

The Uruguay Round Agreement included bindings on the level of the most trade-distorting domestic support, as included in the Total AMS. The Current Total AMS was not to exceed the Final Bound AMS level after the transition period. Figure 12.2 shows the Current Total AMS and the Final Bound AMS for the United States. Support was comfortably within the bindings, although the pronounced variability of notified support by the United States is apparent. As discussed in Blandford and josling (2008) support would probably have exceeded the binding if direct payments

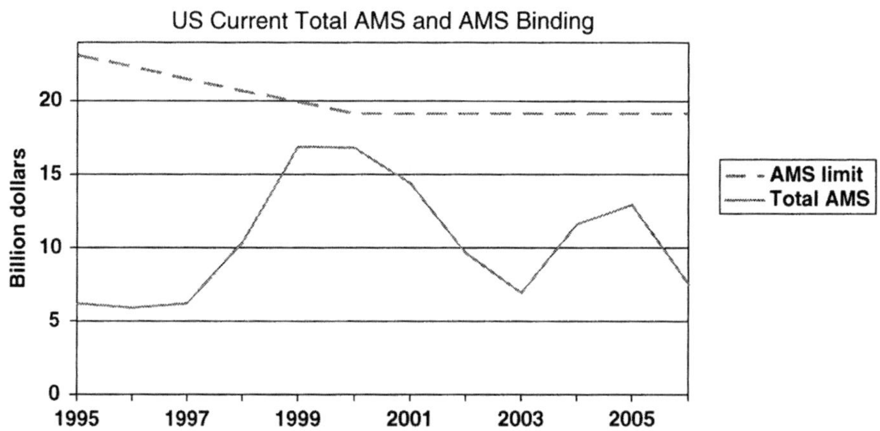

Fig. 12.2 Current total AMS in the United States relative to WTO AMS binding. *Source*: Blandford and Josling, 2008

(notified as Green Box) and counter-cyclical payments (notified as non-product-specific AMS) had been included in the PS AMS. The possibility that this may be required in the future has been raised in an ongoing WTO dispute-settlement case brought by Brazil and others (see below).

The first notification of domestic support by the European Union, in 1995–1996, coincided with the final years of the implementation of the MacSharry reforms.[7] Direct payments (the area payments on cereals and oilseeds, and the headage payments on beef and sheep) were placed in the Blue Box, as they were associated with limits on production. As a result, the original notifications, from the 1995–1996 marketing year, included a large AMS component (48 billion euro) and smaller but sizable Blue Box element (21 billion euro), and a relatively modest amount of Green Box payments (19 billion euro).[8]

The European Union further notified its level of domestic support in December 2006. The period covered support up to the 2003–2004 marketing year. The nature of the CAP reforms since 1995 is reflected in the notifications of domestic support to the WTO. The changes in policy show up as a major shift in the pattern of the notification among the different categories of domestic support. Support prices have been reduced for most of the major products, to close somewhat the gap between EU prices and those in world markets. Export subsidies have also been reduced, in part, as a result of the WTO constraints.

The "new" CAP, starting with the MacSharry reforms, places heavy reliance on direct payments to farmers based on past production patterns and broadly unrelated to current prices and output decisions. Thus the nine notifications from 1995–1996 to 2003–2004 show a marked reduction in price supports compensated by an increase in direct payments. Current Total AMS payments fell from around 50 billion euro in 1995–1996 to 30 billion euro in 2003–2004 – a 40% decline. Blue Box payments rose over the period, from 20 to 25 billion euro, and Green Box payments from 18 to 22 billion euro.[9]

The mix of policies in the European Union changed relatively little from 1995 to 2000, as the reforms in the cereal and oilseed sectors were being assimilated. But budget pressures and the prospect of ten new members from eastern and central Europe led the European Union to consider further reforms. These were incorporated in a decision known as the Agenda 2000 reforms that were agreed in 1999. These reforms had a noticeable impact on the EU domestic support notifications, maintaining the direction of the 1992 reforms but pushing somewhat further. Intervention prices were reduced by 29% for cereals (including a more substantial cut for rice) and, from 2005, they were to be reduced by 15% for butter and skimmed milk powder, reducing the gap between these "administered" prices and the fixed reference prices.[10] The AMS fell from 48 billion euro in 1999–2000 to 29 billion euro in 2002–2003. Changes in the beef regime also modified the notifications somewhat: to the existing subsidies for suckler cows and the special beef premium was added a slaughter premium and some supplementary payments, notified as Blue Box payments as they were limited to base levels of livestock numbers. Blue Box payments increased by 5 billion euros over this period.

Even more significant in their impact on the European Union's domestic support notification have been the reforms enacted since that time, notably the 2003 Fischler Reforms, the changes in the regime for the Mediterranean crops in 2004, the reform of the sugar policy in 2005, and the reform of the fresh and processed fruit and vegetable policies in 2007. The introduction of a Single Farm Payment, the key ingredient of the 2003 Reform, further separates payments from current production. An estimate of the notifications for the years 2004–2005 and 2006–2007 are included in Fig. 12.3.[11] The 2004–2005 notification of domestic support will include some of these decoupled payments under the Fischler reforms, those that were made in 2004, but the main impact will be on the notifications from 2005–2006 and 2006–2007, by which time many of the policy changes will have been implemented.

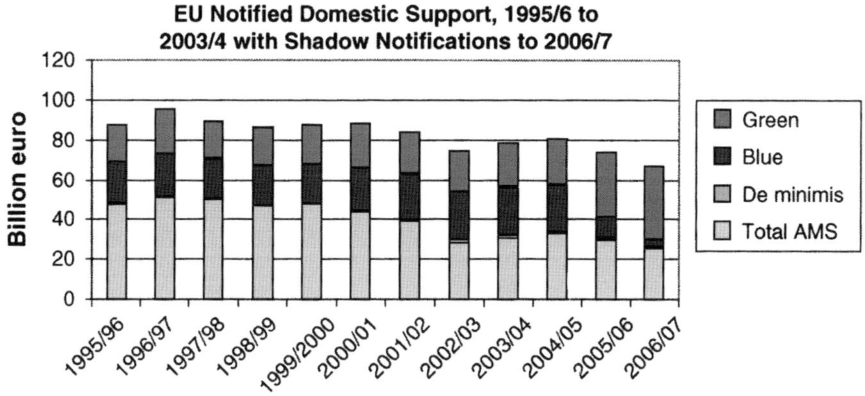

Fig. 12.3 EU notifications of domestic support, 1995–1996 to 2003–2004 with estimates to 2006–2007. *Source*: Blandford and Josling, 2008

The result of these reforms is that a significant shift from Blue Box to Green Box is likely to occur in the next few notifications, as the Blue Box could be reduced to about 4 billion euro in 2006–2007 from about 25 billion euro in the most recent notification, and the Green Box could expand from 22 billion euro to 38 billion over the same period. A significant further reduction could occur in the AMS, from 31 billion to 21 billion euros between 2003 and 2006, reflecting the changes in policy, as many payments that were previously linked to production are shifted to the Green Box. By 2006–2007 the transformation of the CAP into a predominantly Green Box policy will be well underway, with a further increase in decoupled direct payments and a reduction of those in the Blue Box and the Product-Specific AMS (Blandford and Josling, 2008; Josling and Swinbank, 2008).

Under the URAA limits on trade-distorting measures the Current Total AMS as calculated by the European Union (and agreed by other countries) was to be reduced by the year 2000 to 67.2 billion euro.[12] These commitments continue until a revised set of limits is agreed, as would be the case if the Doha Round arrived at a conclusion. The European Union is well within the limits set by the Agreement on

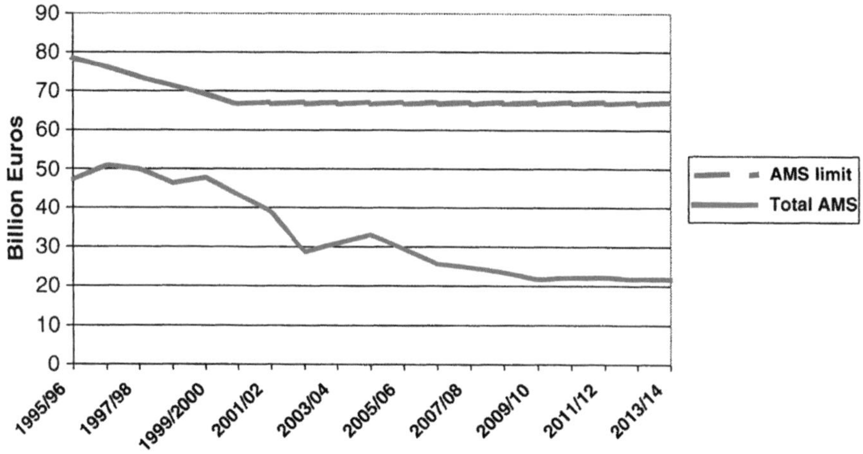

Fig. 12.4 Current total AMS in the European Union relative to WTO AMS binding. *Source*: Blandford and Josling, 2008

Agriculture, in part because of the high AMS recorded in the base period and in part as a result of the steady progress of reform, moving away from price support toward direct payments. Figure 12.4 shows the Current Total AMS in relation to the negotiated AMS limit. In the latest official notification, the AMS stood at 30.9 billion euro, and the estimated notification for the year 2006–2007 shows the level at 21.2 billion euro. Projected notifications for the years beyond 2006–2007 indicate that one can expect the level of AMS payments to drop to about 20 billion euro with the full impact of the CAP reform, and to be stable after 2009 (Josling and Swinbank, 2008). This situation gives the European Union considerable scope for agreeing to reductions in the ceiling for the AMS as a part of a Doha Round agreement.

12.4 WTO Litigation and Agricultural Policies

The Peace Clause did not, of course, stifle all disputes in the area of agriculture. There have been about 100 disputes over agricultural trade notified to the DSB over the lifetime of the WTO.[13] On average there have been about eight disputes every year that can be classified as agricultural.[14] In the first couple of years of the WTO fifteen agricultural disputes were notified to the DSB. Four of these agricultural disputes focused on issues of implementation by the European Union of the Uruguay Round commitments. Over this period, the United States initiated three disputes with Korea about the treatment of imported agricultural products, reflecting a long-running concern by US exporters. And two of the most prominent of the agricultural disputes were litigated in 1996, both with their origin in the GATT and each involving the United States and the European Union (as was typical of many of the trade disputes at that time). These "legacy" disputes were over the European Union's

(1992) import regime for bananas and the (1988) EU regulations over the use of hormones in beef.[15] At least in the United States, the justification for the strengthening of the GATT dispute settlement process through the DSU was, in part, based on the prospect of finally resolving these conflicts.

As these disputes were being adjudicated, a burst of new litigation occurred in 1997, with 13 disputes that year, perhaps reflecting the lag from commercial concern to formal request for consultations. Most of the 1997 cases were concerned with the operation of tariff rate quotas (TRQs) and other import regulations, representing the tensions that accompanied the process of "tariffication" and the removal of non-tariff import barriers. Typical of the disputes at this time were the challenges to the operation of TRQs by the European Union by Brazil on poultry and by New Zealand on butter, and to the operation of TRQs by the Philippines on pork and by the United States on poultry. One exception was the challenge by the United States and New Zealand to the Canadian dairy policy (discussed in more detail below).

Disputes in 1998 also focused on market access issues, and the number of cases fell to more "normal" levels. Among these complaints was a challenge by Canada to transport restrictions on cattle, hogs, and grain by the United States that also reflected an attempt to settle an older dispute using the new-found legal structure of the WTO. A renewed burst of activity in 1999 was followed by a less contentious year in 2000, with the focus again on import regulations in both years.[16] The year 2001 saw a number of safeguard complaints, in part due to the weakening of world prices at the turn of the century.

A significant shift in the type of agricultural disputes is noticeable in 2002, with the challenge by Australia, Brazil, and (later) Thailand to the EU sugar regime. The conflict was over the extent to which that regime in effect provided export subsidies about the scheduled limits. This was followed by a challenge from Brazil to the US policy toward upland cotton, on this occasion questioning the subsidies given to US producers. Thus the emphasis had shifted from disputes over import regulations and contingent protection to the farm policies that were becoming exposed to legal scrutiny. Litigation began to be discussed as a complement to the slow-moving Doha Round in the effort to curb subsidies notably in the United States and the European Union. The cat was out of the bag.

The year 2003 saw another ten disputes on agricultural issues reported to the DSB. Two cases reflected the changed nature of food trade: the resurrection of an earlier challenge by the United States to the European Union's system of protecting geographical indications (GIs), and a challenge by three countries to the slow process of authorizing the release of biotech products on the EU market.[17] At the end of 2003 the Peace Clause expired, widening the net of subsidies that could be appealed under the SCM.[18] There was no immediate rush to litigation, though a number of countries actively explored the possibility for successful challenges. The panel report on the US-cotton dispute emerged in September 2004 and that on EU-sugar was circulated in October 2004. The reports and their broad confirmation by the Appellate Body gave renewed hope to those who saw the DSU as an effective way of forcing policy change in the European Union and the United States. But in fact the number of new cases initiated since 2004 has been markedly less than before, perhaps reflecting the influence of continued negotiations in the Doha Round. Nevertheless the most significant cases in the past 3 years have been those that have challenged US domestic support notification, again reflecting the emphasis since 2002 on using current agreements to rein in farm support policies.

To see the impact of these opinions it is necessary to consider the details of several of the most important cases. Four such cases are discussed here, including the banana case, with a rich history of market discrimination by the European Union in favor of its own former dependencies and colonies; the landmark Canada-dairy case that addressed the question of whether export subsidies could result from domestic price setting; the US-cotton case that explored the application of the SCM Agreement to agricultural subsidies; and the EU-sugar case that extended the Canadian dairy ruling.

12.4.1 The EU Banana Case

The common agricultural policy of the European Union contains a common market organization for bananas. Indeed this commodity achieved some notoriety in the early discussions of the European Economic Community. The French overseas departments were major producers, as were the Cameroons and other African colonies. Germany, with no colonies left opted for "dollar" bananas from Central and South America. Trade in bananas has elicited a series of disputes over the years, pitting the post-colonial regimes of the EU countries against the US-based multinational companies that had a foothold in those parts of Europe that did not have tropical colonies.

The banana controversy in the GATT was stimulated initially by the changes in the European import rules implied in the European Union's policy of "Completing the Single Market" which were introduced at the start of 1993. Moving from the varied import systems run by individual countries to an EU-wide policy that could be operated without internal trade barriers proved to be a challenge. "Dollar" bananas appeared to lose some of their market access to those coming from the former colonies of France and the United Kingdom. Some countries in Latin America settled on a market sharing deal with the European Union but others complained to no avail. The Uruguay Round, with its strengthening of the dispute settlement process, came along at an opportune time for the disaffected group. Two panel reports under the GATT, in 1993 and 1994, had failed to improve the market position for "dollar" bananas.[19] The third panel, reporting on May 22, 1997, proved to be more effective. "Bananas III", as the report became known, found the European Union in multiple violation of trade rules. The various steps taken to resolve this conflict continued for a decade.[20]

The United States had originally intended to stay on the sidelines: it would not have been consistent with the attempt to build up relations with the Caribbean to be seen to challenge the European Union's preferences in that region. But 1996 was an election year. Having sold the WTO to the US Congress partly on the basis of the strengthened DSU, it was vulnerable to the argument that holding the European Union to the trade rules was an important aspect of US trade policy. Direct pressure from the US-based multinational corporations, in particular the Chiquita corporation, swung the Clinton administration behind the complaint. At a stroke this raised the stakes and turned a thorny issue of preference systems into a matter of high principle and policy.[21] Along with the beef-hormone dispute the banana case focused attention on the willingness of the European Union to subjugate its policy preferences to the judgment of a WTO panel. If it proved unwilling, this would not be lost on those whose support for the extension of multilateral trade rules was tenuous at best.

The substantive issues covered by the GATT that were considered by the panel were of three types: tariff questions, quota allocation questions, and the legality of the import licensing regime. Several of these issues had also to be considered in the light of agreements that came out of the Uruguay Round, including the Licensing Agreement as well as the Agreement on Agriculture and the Trade-Related Investment Measures (TRIMS) Agreement. In addition, the panel considered the compatibility of the licensing regime with the European Union's obligations under the GATS.

The tariff issue was perhaps the easiest of the three. The complainants charged that the differential tariff rates that applied between third country bananas and non-traditional ACP imports was a violation of MFN: no objection was lodged against the duty-free imports from the ACP where these were necessary to conform to the requirements of the Lomé Convention. The WTO had been granted the European Union a waiver from its Article I obligations in December 1994 (extended in October 1996): the European Union argued that this was adequate to cover the whole import regime, and not just the traditional ACP imports. The panel decided that as the waiver was not specifically limited to the traditional trade quantities, it must be assumed that "the preferential tariff for the non-traditional ACP bananas is clearly a tariff preference of the sort that the Lomé waiver was designed to cover." (WTO, 1997, p. 333) As a consequence the European Union "won" the tariff argument and defined in part the relationship between the Lomé Convention and the WTO.

The European Union was less fortunate in the case of quota allocation. The argument over the allocation of quotas went to the heart of the complaints over the EU banana regime. At its simplest, the argument revolved around whether the quotas under which banana imports are allowed were allocated in a way consistent with Article XIII of the GATT, which stipulates that they should be allocated in a non-discriminatory way and one that disturbs trade as little as possible. The complaining parties charged that the European Union had allocated the banana import quotas in a way that was inconsistent with this Article. Some countries (the ACP and those that had signed the BFA) had country-specific quotas, while other countries had no such quotas but had to compete for the "other" category of imports. Moreover they argued that the quotas given to those countries were too large and did not reflect market developments. The allocation method also gave the BFA countries exclusive right to fill any shortfall in supplies under the BFA quotas.

If the quota allocation system ran afoul of Article XIII, the licensing system that gave expression to the quotas came in for the most severe condemnation by the panel. This system was judged with respect to its transparency and its tendency to discriminate. The system itself was complex, which in itself made for a lack of transparency. But the complaining parties charged that the intention of the license system was to favor firms that had historically imported bananas from the Windward Isles and French overseas territories. This discrimination was contrary to Articles I (non-discrimination) and III (national treatment) of the GATT. It was also claimed that the CMOB violated Article X of the GATT that requires that countries administer trade measures, including licenses, "in a uniform, impartial and reasonable manner". Moreover, it was argued that the European Union's licensing system contravened the Agreement on Import Licensing Procedures (Licensing Agreement) that had been incorporated into the basic rules of the WTO at the conclusion of the Uruguay Round.[22] In addition it was charged that the arrangement violated the TRIMS agreement, which contains a list of trade-related investment measures such as purchasing requirements that are deemed to be inconsistent with national treatment in the GATT. The requirement that firms have to purchase bananas from the ACP in order to apply for "B" Licenses was therefore a violation of this provision.

In the case of bananas the European Union changed somewhat drastically a commodity market regime in the CAP on the basis of a WTO ruling. Though perhaps not as visible as the cereal and livestock regimes to other temperate zone producers, the banana regime was very sensitive within the European Union. In fact, one could say that the exporters of dollar bananas bet that the German view of the single market regime for bananas would prevail over that favored by the French and the British. When they were proved wrong, they successfully mounted a legal challenge through the US administration. This seems a very clear-cut example of the way in which domestic policy can be influenced by trade rules.

12.4.2 The Canadian Dairy Case

If the banana case was about market access into the European Union, the first major case on export subsidies involved Canadian dairy policy – a somewhat improbable situation given that country's high-cost dairy sector. In the aftermath of the Uruguay Round, the Government of Canada instituted a new policy designed to assist exporters of dairy products (mainly cheese) made with expensive domestic milk. A separate "export" class of milk was defined which could be sold at a price lower than that for domestic use. The architects of the policy no doubt assumed that, as no government funds were involved, such a scheme would not be seen by trading partners as an export subsidy.

New Zealand, supported by the United States, took issue with the policy and, after the requisite consultations, it became the subject of a WTO dispute.[23] The panel ruled that the program did indeed constitute a subsidy to exports as it resulted from government action even though no funds were involved. The Canadian policy was changed to reduce the role of the government, leaving it up to the private sector to negotiate sales of the milk for processing and sale to export destinations.[24] New Zealand and the United States were not convinced that this had solved the problem. The panel was asked to rule on the new policy, and again found it to be in violation of Canada's export subsidy commitments on the grounds that the price of domestic milk was controlled by the government and that this in itself could be enough to subsidize exports (WTO, 1999).[25] Importantly, the Appellate Body in ruling on the second case directed the panel to use the test of whether the cost of the milk to the export processors was less than the cost of production incurred by the farmers. The panel reconvened and decided that as most farmers produced for both the domestic and the foreign market they in effect sold the milk surplus to their domestic allotment at a "subsidized" price (WTO, 2001).

The case was settled when the Canadian provinces abolished their CEM programs. This was a further case of a policy that was popular at home – as the cheese sector in Ontario and Quebec had taken full advantage of the export opportunity – but terminated as a result of an unfavorable WTO ruling. New Zealand and the United States withdrew their request for sanctions, and argued that the outcome vindicated the working of the dispute settlement machinery. But the significance of the outcome of the challenge by New Zealand and the United States to the Canadian dairy policy was soon obvious to export interests in other countries. If selling farm products for exporting (or processing for export) at a price less than the cost of production was indeed regarded as an export subsidy then any situation where high, administered domestic prices coexisted with exports might be shown to be contrary to the WTO – or at least would need to be counted against the export subsidy commitments. Sugar policies in the European Union were an obvious target but other cases could subsequently emerge.

In the present context this outcome has another implication. The WTO rules and commitments are based on the notional separation of domestic support from market access and export competition. These aspects are clearly linked economically and politically, but it was assumed that they were at least possible to separate in administrative terms. But if an administered price can grant a subsidy on exports, the link between domestic support and export competition is exposed. In other words, the legal avenue has made obvious what the pillars of the URAA had attempted to conceal: that the root cause of trade problems is high domestic prices set by farm policy and supported by high tariffs. The levels of support have not been effectively reduced by the constraints imposed on export subsidies or on domestic subsidies.

12.4.3 The US Cotton Case

The case against US Cotton subsidies appears also to question the distinction between different types of subsidies. The issue on this occasion was the inclusion of upland cotton as a commodity eligible for the full range of domestic policies covering grains and oilseeds. The rulings of the panel are best summarized by considering the nine elements of the US programs that were the subject of the challenge by Brazil.[26] Five of these elements (direct payments, production flexibility contract payments, market loss assistance payments, counter-cyclical payments, and marketing loan payments) relate to the major instruments of farm policy adopted for the "program crops" in the Farm Bills that cover the period 1999–2003.[27] Two more are specific to cotton (Step 2 subsidies and cottonseed payments), and the other two are of more general application (crop insurance and export credit guarantees). The panel ruled basically on two issues: whether these subsidies were allowed or prohibited and whether they caused "serious prejudice" (even if allowed) to Brazil (WTO, 2004b; WTO, 2005b).

The two subsidies that were not price related (and which had therefore been notified by the United States as being in the Green Box) were found not to be the cause of "price suppression" in world markets. They were, however, found to contain provisions that made them ineligible for the Green Box: specifically the restrictions on the alternative crops that farmers could grow on cotton land. These, the panel decided, could keep more acres in that crop than would totally "decoupled" payments have done. The three subsidies that were price-related were found to have caused price suppression through their impact on keeping cotton production high in the United States at a time of low world prices.[28]

The panel ruled that the Step 2 subsidies paid to domestic users were prohibited under the Subsidies and Countervailing Measures Agreement (SCM) and the Step 2 subsidies available to export users were prohibited because they were not included in the US schedule of subsidies. Moreover, the Step 2 subsidies also caused significant price suppression in world markets. Cottonseed subsidies and crop insurance payments were deemed not to have caused price suppression, and were not prohibited subsidies.

The final aspect of the US programs on which the panel ruled was the set of export credit guarantees that are available to US firms when they sell into overseas markets where credit risks are a factor. The finding in this case was that the export credit guarantees given to cotton producers constituted an export subsidy, and since no such subsidy had been included in the US schedule it was in effect prohibited.[29]

The panel ruling required the United States to end the prohibited subsidies within six months of the adoption of the report or by July 1, 2005, at the latest. This ruling applied to the Step 2 payments, to both domestic and export users, and to the export credit guarantees for cotton. The United States decided that it could make these changes in legislation without having to await the next Farm Bill expected in 2007. The Administration urged Congress to scrap the Step 2 payments, and these ceased at the end of the crop year, in August 2006. The USDA has also proposed changes to the export credit arrangements by eliminating the 1% cap on the fees that are charged for borrowing through the GSM-102 program, and by terminating the GSM-103 program that provides for longer repayment periods.

More problematic for the United States is how to adjust the programs that the panel found to cause significant price suppression. Withdrawing the marketing loan and counter-cyclical payments would require major changes in the US legislation and could not easily be done outside the context of the next Farm Bill. Taking other steps to remove the adverse impacts on Brazil might seem easier to achieve, but any attempt to restrict US cotton exports could prove difficult. Compensation to Brazil for lost exports would also seem politically implausible, and a deal to boost Brazilian exports of other commodities would be similarly unpopular. So the prospect is for no change in these aspects of US policy at least until the 2012 Farm Bill, at which time the policies may in any case need to be modified as a result of the Doha Round.

An interesting side issue raised by the panel report is the conclusion that the direct payments and production flexibility contract payments are not eligible for the Green Box. This would seem to indicate that countries might eventually ask the United States to resubmit notifications of domestic support for the years in question. This would almost certainly put the United States in excess of its amber box limits, and raise serious problems with trading partners. This issue has been taken up in the TAMS (Total AMS) case (see below) brought by Canada and Brazil.

12.4.4 The EU Sugar Case

The impact of the Canadian dairy case on the approach taken by exporters toward farm policies in other countries can be seen in the challenge brought by Brazil, Australia, and Thailand against the EU sugar subsidies.[30] Complaints about EU sugar policy are not new. Australia had challenged the EU sugar regime in 1979 in the GATT and Brazil followed in 1980, but these were complicated by the fact that there was an international sugar agreement (ISA) (to which the European Union was not a signatory) that restricted exports. Under such circumstances the panels were unable to determine the extent of injury that the plaintiffs had suffered and the policies continued unchecked (Tangermann and Josling, 2003). The United States also challenged the CAP sugar policy in the GATT in 1982, but no panel was established. The European Union indicated its willingness to join the ISA, and proceeded in turn to challenge the US sugar regime.

One of the contentions of these sugar exporters in the recent WTO case was that the EU grants *de facto* export subsidies by means of the high price paid for sugar used on the domestic market. The domestic market price is maintained for sugar produced under two quotas (the "A" and "B" quotas): production over those quotas (usually called "C" sugar) cannot be sold on the domestic market and receives no direct subsidy. At issue is whether the "C" sugar benefits indirectly as farmers can cover their fixed costs from returns from the high-price quotas. The analogy with the exported milk products from Canada is close, if not exact. The complainants maintain that if such subsidies were included, the European Union would be in breach of its export subsidy commitments under the URAA.

A second contention was that the European Union exports the equivalent of the 1.4 million tons of sugar that are imported under preferential agreements enshrined in the Cotonou Agreement with former colonies. This sugar is sold to the European Union at the internal price but re-exported at the world price. This was not notified as a part of the European Union's schedule of exports that benefit from subsidies: it was explicitly excluded in a footnote.

The panel found, and the Appellate Body agreed, that the European Union was in breech in both respects (WTO, 2004a; WTO, 2005a). The exports of C sugar did benefit from the high price of A and B quotas awarded to the same farms. As the C sugar was solely destined for exports, the effect was to cross-subsidize.[31] By implication, if C sugar were sold on the internal market to any extent, the argument would have required a further stage of showing that the exports were harming other exporters. But as the implicit financial benefits to producers of C sugar were not notified as export subsidies they were *de facto* prohibited regardless of their market impact. Similarly, the panel found that the re-export of the ACP (and Indian) sugar was prohibited as it did not appear in the EU schedule. Thus the EU-sugar case differs from that of US cotton in that it centers primarily on the notification of export subsidies. The fact that these notifications were not challenged at the time raises questions about how the activities of the Agriculture Committee might be linked more usefully to the issue of the nature of these policies.

The sugar case is complicated by an additional element. If the European Union cannot either re-export the ACP imports or sell C sugar on the world market, the domestic price has to be reduced and/or the quotas have to be reduced. The EU Commission realized this link with reform of the EU sugar regime, and used the argument effectively to persuade member states of the need for policy change. The political decision was made by the European Union's Council of Ministers on November 22, 2005, to undertake a reform that cut the sugar price support level by 36% and compensated farmers with "decoupled" payments. Though the support price will stay significantly above the world price level, the incentive to produce for export (over and above the quota volume) will be significantly reduced. As the output falls, the European Union will come into compliance with the panel ruling: cross-subsidized production will not find its way into export markets, and the ACP sugar will be absorbed largely in the domestic market.

12.4.5 The TAMS Case

Cases brought against countries for the way they have notified policies that come under domestic support have been infrequent. With inconclusive debates in the Committee for Agriculture and without the guidance of panel reports, countries were able, largely, to decide for themselves whether particular policies were consistent with the definitions of the Green and Blue Boxes, and hence not subject to reductions. So long as countries were way below their limits on domestic support it was not a priority to challenge the notifications themselves. But the jump in funding for the 2002 US Farm Bill caused a re-think of this situation, with the possibility that the limits may have been breached if notifications had been erroneous. The statement of the US-Cotton panel that some of the expenditures that the United States had claimed as "green" may have been mis-labeled turned this possibility into a contestable proposition.

The recent cases by Canada and Brazil raise the broader question of whether the United States has violated its total AMS commitment under the URAA during certain years.[32] A primary issue is again whether direct payments to farmers have been correctly notified as meeting the criteria of the Green Box or should be included in the AMS. A second issue concerns whether US counter-cyclical payments under the 2002 Farm Bill (and the similar prior emergency payments) are non-product-specific (NPS) AMS as notified by the United States or should be considered product specific (PS), because they are inherently linked to specific commodity prices and like direct payments are paid without regard to the type of farm production but with exception for certain restrictions on base acreage land use. Canada also has questioned whether certain disaster relief programs reported in the Green Box meet its criteria. Brazil has raised questions on whether certain other policies provide subsidies that have not been counted in notified support. The outcomes of these dispute settlement cases, in conjunction with any negotiated outcome of the Doha Round, will have implications both for the United States and other countries in terms of the manner in which certain policies are notified, whether domestic support is judged consistent with WTO obligations, and policy reforms that might be undertaken in the future.[33]

The TAMS case illustrates that ambiguity still exists. On the one hand, it is a remarkable case, which when decided by a panel would clarify the somewhat fuzzy nature of the "boxes". On the other hand, it refers to past notifications that were alleged to wrongly classify certain subsidies. So the remedy in the event of a successful challenge is presumably to oblige a re-notification by the United States of its domestic support for several historical years. But the United States could well argue that in the current period of high prices, support levels are already well below the limits set in the schedules even with re-notification. So it would not be clear what the United States could do to make amends: changing current policies would not be an appropriate remedy, and compensation for past violations is not contemplated in the DSU.

This does not drain the interest away from the case. The reclassification of direct payments in the United States away from the Green Box in a revised notification would indeed be a small prize for competing exporters. But add the possibility of a new set of limits in the Doha Round, and the case becomes critical. If the Doha Round succeeds in reducing allowable AMS expenditure, the allocation of subsidies to these boxes becomes much more sensitive. The prospect exists that the major driver of change in US farm policy could indeed be the WTO dispute settlement process, and the decisions on the classification of subsidies. That could also set up some controversy over the role of WTO rules when they clash with powerful political interests. Agricultural trade will continue to provide vexing issues for the multilateral trade system and its judicial processes.

12.5 The Significance of the Doha Round

The agreement to include agriculture as a key part of the Doha Development Agenda in 2001 has led to further changes in the nature of the relationship between domestic farm policy and trade rules. The United States pushed for the elevation of agriculture from the "built in agenda" that was mandated by the Uruguay Round to a pivotal aspect of the Doha Round. But the game has changed considerably since that decision was taken. The United States is now under pressure in the Round to make "real" cuts in its farm programs.

The European Union has been playing a more active role in setting the agenda for the agricultural component of the Doha Round than it did in the Uruguay Round and in earlier GATT rounds.[34] The Commission, negotiating on behalf of member states, has tried to avoid the defensive position that gave it little room to suggest changes in the rules that it would favor. In particular it wanted to avoid being isolated as the main defender of protectionist agricultural programs, and risk being blamed for resisting further progress in bringing agricultural trade rules closer to those in the non-agricultural sector.

This new position has indeed had a major impact on the conduct of the negotiations. Although transatlantic tensions still exist, often over issues such as regulations regarding biotech food and the use of place names for trademarks, the past 5 years have seen a noticeable convergence of EU and US positions on agricultural trade rules. The conflicts that are prolonging the Doha Round agricultural talks are more often between the United States and the European Union on the one hand and developing countries on the other. Both the United States and the European Union have agreed that there will be significant cuts in tariffs, subject to partial exclusions for sensitive products, and major reductions in the allowable level of trade-distorting domestic support. The elimination of export subsidies is no longer a significant point of contention, although there are still differences in the area of food aid.

The main reason why the European Union can be so much less defensive in its approach to trade talks is in the progress it has made with domestic reform of agricultural policy. The MacSharry reforms of 1992 allowed the European Union to agree to disciplines on domestic and export subsidies in the Uruguay Round Agreement on Agriculture (URAA), as well as resolving the oilseed controversy. Cereal prices were cut to bring them closer to world prices and oilseed hectarage was restrained. Payments that were made in compensation for price cuts were placed in the Blue Box, and thus avoided mandated reductions. Support given through administered prices also declined, in part as a result of the use of the difference between these prices and fixed reference prices for the calculation of the subsidy element. So the partially-reformed CAP had no difficulty staying within the bounds of the European Union's schedule of subsidy reductions in the first few years.

Further reforms have had a similar impact, lowering the level of trade-distorting subsidies and making it easier for the European Union to contemplate and accept further restrictions on agricultural policies in the WTO. In this connection, the changes in 1999 (the Agenda 2000 reforms) and the subsequent significant changes in 2003 and 2004, under the leadership of Commissioner Fischler, have continued and developed the approach taken by MacSharry. Price support has been removed or weakened for many commodities, and payments are now made to farmers on the basis of historical production of a wide range of products with no obligation to produce any particular product to claim payment. This "Single Farm Payment" has made the CAP significantly more consistent with the "tariffs and decoupled payments" model that underlies the URAA.

To what extent would a successful conclusion of the Doha Development Agenda (DDA), along the lines of the modalities in the Revised Draft Modalities paper of July 10, 2008, require further changes in the Farm Bill and the common agricultural policy? Will those changes be made easier by corresponding disciplines on the domestic programs of other countries? How much increased market access is likely to be generated as a result of cuts in tariffs that would be required of the European Union and the United States? Will the termination of the European Union's use of export subsidies to balance its internal market have any significant impact on price levels and on world market conditions? What other issues will the European Union insist on as it moves toward a package that is acceptable to member states?

12.6 The Revised Draft Modalities for Domestic Support

WTO members are at present considering a number of changes to the URAA that would have an impact on the constraints on EU policy from WTO obligations. In July 2008, Ambassador Crawford Falconer, the chair of the special session of the WTO Committee on Agriculture, released a revised set of draft modalities for agriculture that included detailed proposals for future disciplines on domestic support (TN/AG/W/4/Rev.3). The Falconer revised draft modalities paper was an attempt to frame the parameters of such increased restraint so as to enable countries to converge on a single document, and formed the basis for the July Mini-Ministerial.

There has recently been an attempt to project the levels of AMS, OTDS, and other components of domestic support under assumptions about the outcome of the negotiation on modalities. The discussion in this section is based on the report of that study (Blandford and Josling, 2008). The United States is projected to stay comfortably within its total bindings for the duration of the projection period (see Fig. 12.5).

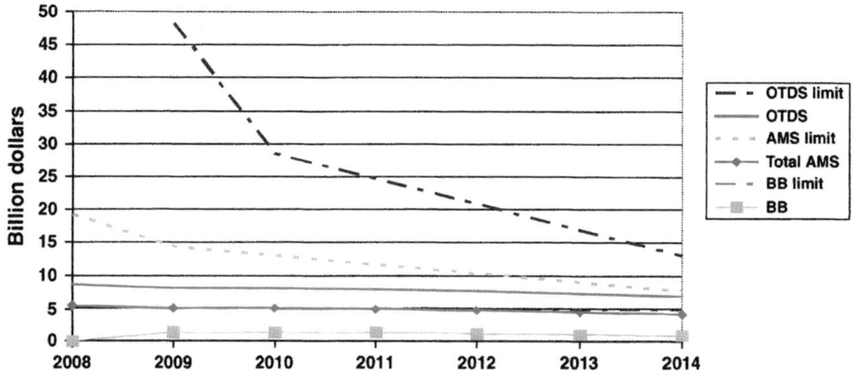

Fig. 12.5 Projected notifications of domestic support, the United States, 2008–2014, and proposed limits to OTDS, AMS and Blue Box. *Source*: Blandford and Josling, 2008

In addition to the relatively high crop prices projected by USDA an important contributing factor to this result is a change in dairy policy included in the 2008 Farm Act. Prior to this Act, the US dairy support program was defined with respect to a support price for milk. That structure was reflected in US notifications in that the per unit market price support calculation was applied total milk production. The 2008 Act redefines the support program with respect to support for three dairy products – butter, cheddar cheese, and non-fat dry milk.[35] Those support prices are defined to be consistent with the previous support price for milk ($9.90 per hundred weight). The effect of this change is to allow the United States to notify market price support for dairy on the basis of the volume of the three dairy products concerned, rather than the total volume of milk production. We build this change in notifications into the projections beginning in 2008. There remain some technical questions associated with how the calculation would be made, but the estimate is that the change in methodology would reduce notified market price support for dairy by roughly 65%. The application of the revised approach results in a projected notification of $1.9 billion in 2014, compared to $5.5 billion under the previous method. If it were not for this change, we project that the United States would exceed its Total AMS binding in 2014 by roughly $0.2 billion, rather than being $3.4 billion below the binding.

Although the overall bindings relative to aggregate support would seem to suggest few problems for the United States, there are issues with some commodities. The projections suggest that the draft modalities would result in product-specific AMS and Blue Box bindings being exceeded for cotton throughout the implementation period of an agreement, with an excess for peanut Blue Box payments (CCPs) and for AMS support for sugar. As noted above the change in the dairy program removes a potential problem of exceeding the PS AMS binding for dairy. These results indicate that there are likely to be significant issues to be faced for a limited number of commodities, two of which (cotton and sugar) have proved to be highly politically sensitive in the United States.

In terms of other possibilities for box-shifting the projections for US notified support suggest that the greatest potential for the United States lies in an expansion of the non-product-specific support category. With a projected payments equal to $6.9 billion of the "available" $13 billion OTDS, the United States would still have $6.1 billion in non-product-specific support that could be used, while still staying within WTO commitments. The exact amount could change depending on what happens to PS AMS and Blue Box payments under the ACRE program in the 2008 Farm Bill, but some shifting of support into the non-product-specific category would appear to be a possibility for the United States. Given the considerable pressure that was exerted for a reduction in direct payments (Green Box), in the debate on the 2008 Farm Bill, the popularity of such payments among farmers might well decline in the future with less support for box-shifting in that direction.

The Falconer proposals, as they would apply to the European Union, would place a limit on overall trade-distorting support (OTDS). This OTDS limit would be subject to reductions over the implementation period of the agreement. There would also be reductions in the limits for the total AMS from the final values applying under the Uruguay Round Agreement as well as in the *de minimis* percentages. The Blue Box would have limits imposed based on the percentage of the value of production. Limits would also be imposed on the product-specific AMS and on product-specific Blue Box support, as described in the table.

The implications for the European Union of these proposals are striking. The Base OTDS, from which reductions would be measured, would be 110.3 billion euro. Thus the range for the Final Bound OTDS would be from 16.5 to 27.6 billion euro. This corresponds to an estimate of 24 billion euro for the Current Total OTDS in the year 2013–2014.[36] Thus the more restrictive limit would appear to bind and impose further policy changes of a nature consistent with developments since 2003. The overall picture is shown in Fig. 12.6, which shows the projected notifications relative to the more ambitious limits in the range indicated in the Draft Modalities paper. The AMS limit would be reduced from the current level of 67.2 billion to 20.1 billion euro (augmented minimally by allowance for the enlargement of the European Union).[37] The estimated Current Total AMS for the year 2013–2014 is 24.0 billion euro, indicating a significant restraint on EU policies in the final year of the transition period if they continue on their current course. The year 2013–2014 is the year when a new budgetary cycle starts in the European Union at which time the funding for the CAP could well be trimmed for internal reasons.

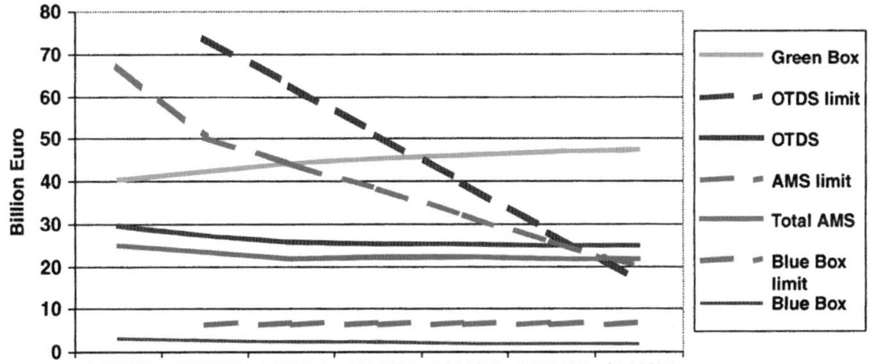

Fig. 12.6 Projected notifications of domestic support, European Union, 2007–2008 and 2013–2014, and proposed limits to OTDS, AMS, and Blue Box. *Source*: Blandford and Josling, 2008

In addition to the constraints on total AMS and Blue Box support, the Revised Modalities draft also proposes restrictions on product-specific AMS and Blue Box amounts. These constraints might well be binding in specific instances. The Revised Draft suggests caps on product-specific AMS payments at the 1995–2000 levels. Increases in administered prices are effectively restricted by this constraint. Changes in fixed reference prices are not envisaged in the URAA, and would presumably have to be negotiated. But variations in the level of "eligible production" for both the products where the market price support is calculated and for those where an equivalent measure of support is used could well lead to AMS limits being violated.

Blue Box limits at a product-specific level are also likely to have some impact. Though the total Blue Box spending may be decreasing, as payments move to the Green Box, those for individual products cannot increase to make use of that "slack". Although these payments are currently tied to fixed yield, areas and head of livestock, the restriction implies no possibility of any re-basing of such payments that would violate the limits.

Although it would appear that the European Union can continue to run the CAP for some years in the face of cuts of 70% for the AMS limit and the introduction of a cut of 85% in overall trade-distorting support, these results should not be interpreted as an indication that the WTO constraints introduced by the Doha Round will not ultimately affect EU policy. In order to stay within the new limits, changes would have to be made to ensure that direct payments can continue to be notified as Green Box without being challenged by other countries. And further transfers of subsidies from the blue to the Green Box will be necessary.

The extent to which the Single Farm Payments are truly compatible with the Green Box has been raised by some commentators (McMahon, 2007; Swinbank, 2007; Swinbank and Tranter, 2005). Were they to be notified in the AMS or Blue Box, under current WTO constraints, the impact would not be great. The limit of 67.2 billion euro for the AMS would not be approached, and the Blue Box is not limited.[38] However, the situation would be drastically changed if the Doha Round were to be completed along the lines of the Revised Modalities. In all cases except where the direct payments are notified in the Green Box (where no limit exists) the new WTO constraints would be violated by the year 2013–2014. If direct payments were to be notified in the Blue Box, the total would far exceed the limit of 5.6 billion euro suggested in the Revised Draft. Up to 28 billion euro would have to be notified in the AMS and this would well exceed the limit of 20.1 billion euro suggested in the same draft. *A fortiori*, if all the direct payments were to be notified in the AMS, the limit of 20.1 billion euro would again be violated. Perhaps more relevant is the effect on the OTDS of any decision to place direct payments outside the Green Box. The OTDS limit of 16.5 billion euro suggested by the Draft would be less than the level of direct payments alone, leaving all other support to be cut or changed to Green Box compatible payments.[39]

12.7 Conclusions

In the United States, domestic farm policy has largely been separated from trade policy. Domestic policy is under the watch of the agricultural committees of Congress and the USDA: other Congressional committees have oversight of trade issues and the USTR is the agency within the administration that negotiates and watches trade matters. Coordination is through interagency contact and through the interests of individual senators and representatives. Thus it is common to assert that the WTO has little impact on domestic policy on the basis of the fact that the debates about domestic policy appear remarkably unconstrained by and unaware of trade rules and obligations. But this does not mean that trade issues are not important to domestic policy in the United States: it has much more to do with the division of labor in the Congress and in the administration. This chapter has attempted to trace some of these linkages and show that it is quite possible to have a domestic policy process that is apparently unaware of trade issues but in practice passes legislation that is linked with the trade policy of the country.

The division of labor is different in the European Union. The Commission is an executive body but also with the sole power of initiation of (EU) legislation. Moreover it has competence by virtue of the EU Treaty over trade negotiations, subject to a mandate from the ministers of trade. So the European Union can coordinate the domestic and trade policy functions somewhat easier by virtue of the function of the Commission. The mandate and the interpretation of that mandate are the effective controls that the member states have over trade policy. The Commission can, and has, premised its domestic policy initiatives on the constraints, objectives, and opportunities in the realm of trade policy. The contention of this chapter is that the conflicts between trade and domestic policy are likely to be internalized within the decision process so that a more cohesive policy set emerges. Therefore it should not come as a surprise that the impacts of the WTO constraints on the CAP are less than in the case of the United States.

In the United States it has taken litigation to bring home the implications of the WTO URAA. The major challenge to the US farm programs was Brazil's complaint about the upland cotton subsidies: though the focus was on the cotton program, it raised issues that went beyond that commodity to include soybeans and corn and other "program crops". The fact that the panel found broadly in favor of Brazil was a clear indication that the attempt to enforce existing rules could succeed and that litigation could in certain circumstances lead to policy change. First, Canada and then, the European Union also have had to change policies as the result of unfavorable rulings of WTO panels. On the other hand, the judgments that have led to policy change have been those that dealt with export subsidies, direct or indirect. The Canadian responses to the panel reports on its dairy policy have not weakened the main distortive instruments of high domestic milk prices held up by supply control and steep tariffs. But from the viewpoint of dairy exporters the most egregious aspects of the policy, the promotion of cheese exports by means of allowing manufacturers to buy milk at a much lower price has been curbed. The European Union changed its banana policy to bring it in line with the instruments suggested by the WTO panel, those of a simple tariff and duty-free access for the ACP exporters. The European Union also reformed its sugar policy to avoid the subsidy granted on the re-export of ACP sugar and the cross-subsidy implied by the high price for quota sugar relative to the sugar above quotas that had to be exported outside the European Union.

Quantitative constraints on the level of domestic support have not so obviously been influential in policy change. But that is in part because of the somewhat lax process of examining the conformity of domestic support policies with the URAA. So when the panel examining the US-cotton case ruled that the direct payments were not eligible for the Green Box if they restricted the choice of crops that could be grown on base acres, the door was left open for challenges that would focus on whether the maximum levels of support agreed in the URAA had in fact been violated. The ongoing TAMS case brought by Brazil and Canada will clarify the issue, but could indeed lead to the conclusion that the URAA did in fact impose a limit on domestic support (in the United States) even though it was not recognized at the time. The European Union, by contrast, has not been challenged on its Green Box notifications, though this could conceivably change.

The importance of the Doha Round is thus magnified by the legal challenges. The removal of most of the "slack" between AMS limits and actual AMS spending will make it much more likely that countries get close to their maximum allowable trade-distorting subsidy levels. This increases the possibility of challenges against such countries that feel their export interests have been harmed. By contrast, if the Doha Round is not completed then the challenges on domestic support are likely to be more restrained.

Notes

1. The scope of the URAA covers products in HS Chapters 1–24, excluding fish and fish products but including cotton, wool, hides, flax, hemp, and a few other products.
2. Other aspects of the WTO, not discussed in this chapter, include the Agreement on Trade-Related Intellectual Property (TRIPS), which covers patents for agricultural biotech and geographical indications for foods and wines, and the Technical Barriers to Trade Agreement (TBT), which attempts to prevent the use of standards and labels from being used as a disguised trade barrier. In addition, the WTO Anti-Dumping Agreement is sometimes invoked in agricultural disputes.
3. The levels of tariff reduction and the requirements for market opening were included in the "Modalities" document that formed the basis for offers (draft schedules). This document ceased to be relevant after the schedules themselves had been agreed.
4. Deficiency payments are subsidies that make up the difference between the market returns and a predefined target price. Direct payments are paid in ways that do not depend on current output: the usual basis is acreage and yield in some base year. Administrative prices can also give a subsidy if the price level is kept above that which obtains in the market.
5. Of course, from the point of view of the exporting country the collection of a tax on exports is better than the imposition of a tax on imports by the importer. But export sectors will argue for the removal of either tax.
6. Note also the significant increase in Green Box support in the United States, due primarily to a major expansion in expenditures on domestic food assistance programs.
7. The compensation payments were introduced progressively in the marketing years 1993–1994 and 1995–1996.
8. No estimate exists of what would have been the AMS notifications before 1995, had they been required. But it is likely that, in the 8 years between the 1986–1988 base and the first year of the URAA, trade-distorting support (as measured by the AMS) fell from about 80 billion to 50 billion euro. This was due, in large part, to the introduction of the MacSharry reforms and the placing of these payments in the Blue Box. Green Box eligible policies probably rose modestly over the same period.
9. Though this might appear to suggest that about 10 billion euro in less trade-distorting support has replaced 20 billion euro of more trade-disruptive payments, it should be remembered that the much of the AMS is a calculation based on the difference between an administered price

and a fixed reference price. So a drop in this support can be unrelated to either government payments or farm income.

10. The Agenda 2000 package also agreed a new dairy premium from 2005, to compensate dairy farmers for the scheduled reductions in butter and skim milk powder intervention prices. In G/AG/N/EEC/17 the European Union said it intended declaring these payments in the Blue Box.
11. For the details behind these forecasts see Josling and Swinbank (2008).
12. The European Union (at that time the EU12) declared a base period AMS of 73.53 billion euro, which with a 20% reduction would have given an AMS commitment in 2000 equal to 58.82 billion euro. However, a "credit" of 2.38 billion euro was negotiated, and this led to a Final Bound Total AMS of 61.20 billion euro being agreed (see Supporting table 9a in the EU notification). Enlargement to the EU15 necessitated some changes. The initial AMS figure of 78.7 billion euro mentioned in the text was the EU15 limit in the first year of implementation. The revised Final Bound Total AMS was fixed at 67.2 billion euro for the EU15. No limit has been agreed for the EU of 25 or of 27: for the purposes of this chapter we will assume that the EU15 limit is continued.
13. Not all disputes that are notified to the DSB result in the establishment of a panel.
14. The average number of requests for consultation notified to the DSB has been 28 per year since 1995.
15. Another dispute that had been prominent in the GATT era was over the EU subsidies to oilseeds. The final agreement that ended this dispute was negotiated at the same time that the modalities for agriculture in the Uruguay Round were agreed between the United States and the European Union, at Blair House in November 1992.
16. An interesting issue was raised by Brazil on the preferential treatment for coffee imported by the European Union from competitor countries under regional trade agreements.
17. The original US GI case had been held in abeyance, and was revived following a new policy initiative by the European Union. Australia took out a case in 2003 that then was joined with the earlier case.
18. For more detail on the effect of the Peace Clause on agricultural disputes see Steinberg and Josling, 2003.
19. The panel reports had no impact. The EU effectively prevented their adoption by the General Council, following a long GATT tradition of blocking unfavorable reports.
20. As an agricultural policy case the banana issue would have been interesting enough. But the case tackled much more than the conflicts over post-colonial discrimination. It was the first panel to consider an argument that a country had contravened the General Agreement on Trade in Services (GATS). By allocating import licenses to domestic firms based on past shipments the banana import regime gave valuable trading permits to the competitors of the US-based multinationals. The European Union had agreed to end discrimination in "wholesale trade services" in the Uruguay Round. This aspect of the case increased its importance and provided a potentially useful clarification of the relationship between rules for goods trade and those for trade in services.
21. Mexico followed the lead of the United States in part because of the Mexican ownership at that time of one of the firms (del Monte) and in part as an expression of North American solidarity on a matter of WTO principle.
22. The Licensing Agreement provided more detail on the way in which licensing measures were to be administered, and is included as an Annex 1A agreement in the Marrakesh Agreement which established the WTO.
23. The dispute also included a complaint about the administration of Canadian dairy import regulations, but that raised different issues and will not be discussed here.
24. Canada abolished the Special Milk Class 9(e) and restricted sales under Class 5(d) to conform to its export subsidy commitments. A new milk category of Commercial Export Milk (CEM) was established.
25. The challenge to Canadian dairy policy was not covered by the Peace Clause as it charged that the export subsidy commitments had been violated.

26. Brazil requested consultations with the United States on September 27, 2002. After three abortive discussions, a panel was established on May 19, 2003, and issued a report on June 18, 2004. This ruling was appealed by the United States, and the Appellate Body issued its report on March 3, 2005. The report as amended was adopted on March 21, 2005.
27. The two Farm Bills in question are the 1996 FAIR Act and 2002 FSRI Act. Production flexibility contract payments were authorized under the FAIR Act, and marketing loss assistance payments were added as emergency measures in 1998–2001. The FSRI Act replaced these with direct payments and counter-cyclical payments. Marketing loans for cotton have been in place since 1986 and Step 2 subsidies since 1990. The cottonseed payments are emergency payments authorized by the ARP Act in 2000. Crop insurance is authorized by separate legislation, the Federal Crop Insurance Act.
28. The panel rejected the US argument that the low world prices were from other causes and that the high US exports were an exception rather than the rule.
29. The ruling also declared the export credit guarantees for rice exceeded its allowed export subsidy limit, but did not find fault with other aspects of the program
30. The Australian and Brazilian challenges were initiated in September 2002 and Thailand joined the complaint in March 2003. The dispute numbers are DS265, DS266, and DS283, respectively. The panel report was presented on October 15, 2004, and was appealed. The Appellate Body gave their opinion on April 28, 2005, and the DSB accepted the report as modified.
31. Investigations of subsidies in non-agricultural markets often explore the possibility of cross-subsidization within firms. The economics of cross-subsidization is not as well accepted as the accounting conventions.
32. The two cases brought by Canada and Brazil (DS 357, 365, respectively) have been merged. The complaint is that United States exceeded its Total AMS limits in several recent years.
33. Were direct and countercyclical payments and their antecedents to be ruled product-specific support that should have been included in the US Current Total AMS, then the United States would indeed have exceeded its AMS commitment in 1999, 2000, 2002, 2004, and 2005, as suggested in the Brazil and Canada cases (see Blandford and Josling, 2008).
34. The use of the term European Union for the collective position and interest of the European Union rather than the technically correct term EC (European Community), preferred in WTO documents.
35. Economists would argue that a price support program for a subset of dairy products is likely to affect the prices of all dairy products; that is, that the original formulation of the notifications is still appropriate in an economic, if not a legal sense.
36. In order to examine the impact of these changes on future notifications we assume that new WTO support commitments are implemented over the period from 2010–2014, so that all new reductions and bindings apply fully in 2014. Our assumptions about the evolution of agricultural policy in the European Union are that progressively more of the direct payments can be notified as Green Box, as the "health check" consolidates the changes in the 2003 Reforms.
37. The limit for the OTDS at the end of the transition period appears to be less than the AMS limit (a function of the higher percentage cut), implying that the AMS will have to be reduced by even more than indicated here to avoid violation of the OTDS limit. There will in effect be no room for Blue Box and *de minimis* payments by the end of the transition.
38. Inclusion in the Blue Box of new or modified subsidies however could be challenged, but these subsidies could be transferred to the AMS without violating the AMS limit. The AMS limit itself will be somewhat higher that 67.2 billion euro, to take into account the allowable limits of new members.
39. However, another source of uncertainty is less of a problem in the European Union. Unlike the situation in the United States, relatively little of the support provided to farmers in the European Union is subject to increases if market prices fall.

References

Blandford, D., Josling, T. (2008), The WTO July 10th Agricultural Modalities Proposals and their Impact on Domestic Support in the EU and the US, Paper Available from Authors), July 11.

Josling, T., Swinbank, A. (2008), *EU Domestic Support Notifications, Presented at the conference on Improving WTO Transparency: Shadow Domestic Support Notifications*, International Food Policy Research Institute, Washington DC, March 12.

McMahon, J.A. (2007), Trade Policy Reform through Litigation, EuroChoices, Volume 6(2), pp. 42–47.

Steinberg, R.H., Josling, T.E. (2003), When the peace ends: The vulnerability of EU and U.S. agricultural subsidies to WTO legal challenge, *Journal of International Economic Law* 6(2): 369–417.

Swinbank, A. (2007), WTO Challenges to Mr. Fischler's CAP, Paper Presented at a Conference on Agricultural Policy Changes: Canada, EU and the World Trade Organization, University of Victoria, Canada, September.

Swinbank, A., Tranter, R. (2005), Decoupling EU farm support: Does the new single payment scheme fit within the green box? *The Estey Centre Journal of International Law and Trade Policy* 6(1): 47–61.

World Trade Organization. (1995), *The Results of the Uruguay Round of Multilateral Trade Negotiations: The Legal Texts*, WTO, Geneva.

World Trade Organization. (1997), *European Communities – Regime for the Importation, Sale and Distribution of Bananas*, Reports of the Panels, WT/DS27/R/USA, WT/DS27/R/ECU, WT/DS27/R/GTM, WT/DS27/R/MEX.

World Trade Organization. (1999), *Canada – Measures Affecting the Importation of Milk and the Exportation of Dairy Products*, WT/DS103/R and WT/DS113/R, WTO, Geneva.

World Trade Organization. (2001), *Canada – Measures Affecting the Importation of Milk and the Exportation of Dairy Products, Report of the Appellate Body*, WT/DS103&113/AB/RW, WTO, Geneva.

World Trade Organization. (2004a), *European Communities – Export Subsidies on Sugar, Reports of the Panels*, WT/DS265/R, WT/DS266/R, & WT/DS283/R, WTO, Geneva.

World Trade Organization. (2004b), *United States – Subsidies on Upland Cotton, Report of the Panel*, WT/DS267/R, WTO, Geneva.

World Trade Organization. (2005a), *European Communities – Export Subsidies on Sugar, Report of the Appellate Body*, WT/DS265/AB/R, WT/DS266/AD/R, & WT/DS283/AB/R, WTO, Geneva.

World Trade Organization. (2005b), *United States – Subsidies on Upland Cotton, Reports of the Appellate Body*, WT/DS265/AB/R, WT/DS266/AB/R, & WT/DS267/AB/R, WTO, Geneva.

World Trade Organization. (2008), *Revised Draft Modalities for Agriculture*, TN/AG/W/4/Rev.3, WTO, Geneva, 10 July.

11

The difficult task of disciplining domestic support

DAVID ORDEN, DAVID BLANDFORD AND TIM JOSLING

When the WTO was launched at the conclusion of the Uruguay Round negotiations its members committed to a new set of disciplines for agricultural domestic support, market access and export competition. It was recognized at the time that the domestic support disciplines were rather porous. Their architecture was consistent with the modest objectives that WTO members had collectively agreed to reduce distortions in world markets. What was uncertain at that point was just how the agreed-upon disciplines would interact with subsequent domestic agricultural policy decisions. In particular, it was not known to what extent the new rules and commitments would motivate countries to shift their policies in the less trade-distorting direction envisioned by the Agreement on Agriculture.

For domestic support the only fixed numerical commitment under the Agreement was to a nominal ceiling (or zero binding) on the sum of certain trade-distorting amounts of support calculated annually in the Current Total AMS. Countries making ceiling commitments set the ceilings at relatively high levels as a result of using a 1986–88 base period with low world prices and high support. By the time the Agreement was signed prices had increased and support moderated, so it was recognized that these commitments provided substantial flexibility. Green box measures in all countries, and certain types of support through development programs in developing countries, were exempt from any ceiling. The blue box emerged as a late compromise in the negotiations that left exempt from caps or reductions substantial payments linked to supply control programs in the EU and US. Within a product's AMS, market price support was to be measured in a somewhat artificial manner based on the gap between an administered price and a fixed external reference price applied to an (ambiguously-defined) eligible quantity. *De minimis* allowances for product-specific and non-product-specific AMS support were adopted apparently with little consideration of how important these exemptions might turn out to be. Requirements to notify domestic support measures to facilitate verification of compliance with the Agreement also lacked rigorous criteria. Not only were submission deadlines advisory rather than binding, but how various measures should be classified in relation to the agreed rules, and how levels of support should be measured, were subject only to general guidelines.

Under these loose terms, a body of notifications of domestic support began to accumulate. Notifications came fairly steadily in the first few years of the WTO for the eight countries examined in the previous chapters. Yet, for three of these countries, Brazil, the EU and the US that are key players in the often acrimonious international debate over farm policies, the notification delays increased as the Doha negotiations sought to define new disciplines. The timing of the EU and US notifications improved later, but only after it became apparent that the Doha Round was unlikely to be concluded rapidly. This in itself is a perverse pattern. Just at the time that transparency afforded by formal notifications might have been most useful, leading countries chose not to live up to this responsibility. The lack of transparency may be indicative as much of the divisive character of the negotiations as an obstacle to their progress. What is clear from the agreed guidelines is that the notifications should have been provided in a more timely manner. Other key countries, particularly China and India, have lagged even further behind in submitting notifications. The length of some of the delays clearly reflects political decisions not to provide the information, rather than a lack of technical capacity. In deciding whether or not to obscure how they will report their levels of subsidies or shifts in policies, countries reveal their attitude toward the effectiveness of the international rules designed to discipline domestic support.

This chapter builds upon the detailed country experiences evaluated in the book to bring together in the context of the above concerns some conclusions on the usefulness of the disciplines on domestic support provided by the Agreement. The first section summarizes levels of domestic support from 1995 to 2008 from both the notifications submitted by governments to the WTO and the shadow notifications based on official statistics that will in most cases be used in future notifications. Compliance of levels of support with the Agreement and scheduled reductions of commitments is assessed. We are also interested in how well the notifications have tracked changes in farm policies and have contributed to the goal of reducing distortions in world agricultural markets. The interpretation of notified levels of domestic support requires a careful examination of shifts in policy within countries and their economic implications. In some cases variations in notified support reflect real changes in policies, while in others they largely reflect how countries have chosen to categorize and report their policy measures.

We also use the notifications and shadow notifications to examine the evolution of support policies across the countries. Key questions are whether the structure or levels of support have tended to converge toward less trade-distorting forms and whether the Agreement has played a role driving such convergence. Comparisons across countries focus on whether the underlying economic goal of the Agreement has been met, rather than the legal issue of whether individual countries have complied with its terms.

Looking forward, we evaluate the extent to which the proposed 2008 Doha draft modalities would contribute towards stricter limits on agricultural domestic support, drawing on projections of future support notifications made in the preceding chapters. The importance of careful examination of the basis for changes in notified levels of support is reiterated in the context of assessing the consequences of a Doha Round outcome. We then turn to a brief discussion of some issues that remain unresolved in attempting to align the legal framework on domestic support with the goal of reducing distortions in world markets. Meaningful directions for clarification and enhancement of the rules for the long term are outlined, including the strengthening of the notification and monitoring process.

Compliance with WTO commitments

The accumulated database of domestic support notifications has become substantial since the WTO was founded, despite the lack of timeliness in submissions. The addition of shadow notifications where necessary, as described in the previous chapters, makes it possible to evaluate whether the eight countries examined appear to have complied with rules and commitments under the Agreement over a fourteen-year period. The assembling of a consistent time series of information improves policy transparency; countries for which we have supplied missing data could, and eventually will, confirm our unofficial estimates or contribute to an improved database by updating their notifications.

Tables 11.1 and 11.2 present an aggregate picture of domestic support provided by the countries since 1995, its classification into WTO categories, and the extent of compliance with ceiling commitments. The information is consolidated into summary form by deriving averages for the entire period and for its first and second halves, along with showing

Table 11.1 *Summary of domestic support notifications and shadow notifications for four developed countries, 1995–2008*

	EU[a] (billion euros)				US (billion dollars)			
	Averages				Averages			
	All years	First half	Second half	2008/09	All years	First half	Second half	2008
Green box	30.0	20.4	39.6	56.6	61.7	49.9	73.4	99.6
Less food aid and public stockholding	29.6	20.1	39.1	56.1	18.4	15.0	21.8	23.7
Decoupled income support	8.6	0.3	16.8	33.7	5.2	4.5	5.9	6.1
OTDS	56.6	69.1	44.3	28.5	15.2	16.3	14.2	11.2
Blue box	18.1	21.3	14.9	4.7	0.5	1.0	—	—
Current Total AMS	37.4	47.2	27.6	22.1	9.9	11.0	8.9	7.1
of which, MPS	34.5	43.7	25.3	21.4	5.9	5.9	6.0	6.1
Total *de minimis*	1.1	0.6	1.8	1.7	4.8	4.3	5.3	4.2
Product-specific	0.3	0.1	0.6	0.3	0.3	0.1	0.5	0.1
Non-product-specific	0.8	0.5	1.2	1.3	4.5	4.2	4.8	4.1
Total support	86.6	89.5	83.9	85.1	76.9	66.2	87.6	110.8
Less food aid and public stockholding	86.2	89.2	83.4	84.6	33.6	31.3	36.0	34.9
	Assessment of the commitments							
Bound Total AMS	70.7	72.1	69.3	72.2	19.7	20.2	19.1	19.1
CTAMS/Bound Total AMS (%)	52.9	65.4	39.8	31.1	50.4	54.3	46.5	36.9
Total value of production[b]	252.2	226.0	278.4	296.0	226.5	195.4	262.8	335.3
Bound Total AMS/Total value of production (%)	28.0	31.9	24.9	24.4	8.7	10.4	7.3	5.7

	Japan (billion yen)				Norway (billion NOK)			
	Averages				Averages			
	All years	First half	Second half	2008	All years	First half	Second half	2008
Green box	2,380.7	2,781.2	1,980.2	1,887.3	4.8	4.2	5.4	6.9
Less food aid and public stockholding	2,331.0	2,710.2	1,951.8	1,864.5	4.3	3.5	5.1	6.9
Decoupled income support	14.5	–	29.1	102.3	—	—	—	—
OTDS	1,316.0	1,929.5	702.5	632.0	17.1	18.0	16.2	15.0
Blue box	54.2	46.7	61.8	32.4	6.4	7.5	5.3	3.7
Current Total AMS	1,218.7	1,842.6	594.8	510.7	10.6	10.5	10.7	11.1
of which, MPS	1,020.0	1,645.7	394.4	385.3	11.2	10.9	11.5	11.9
Total *de minimis*	43.1	40.3	45.8	88.9	0.1	—	0.1	0.2
Product-specific	18.5	17.4	19.5	15.4	0.0	—	0.1	0.1
Non-product-specific	24.6	22.9	26.3	73.5	0.0	—	0.1	0.1
Total support	3,696.7	4,710.7	2,682.7	2,519.3	21.9	22.2	21.6	21.9
Less food aid and public stockholding	3,647.0	4,639.7	2,654.3	2,496.5	21.4	21.5	21.3	21.9
	Assessment of the commitments							
Bound Total AMS	4,100.2	4,209.4	3,972.9	3,972.9	11.8	12.1	11.4	11.4
CTAMS/Bound Total AMS (%)	29.7	43.8	15.0	12.9	90.1	86.7	94.1	97.6
Total value of production[b]	9,045.5	9,482.3	8,535.9	8,650.9	22.9	22.5	23.3	24.8
Bound Total AMS/Total value of production (%)	45.3	44.4	46.5	45.9	51.5	53.9	48.9	46.0

Notes: — indicates zero.

[a] Reference to the EU15, EU25 and EU27 as presented in Chapter 3. Row "*of which*, MPS" includeds EMS price support.

[b] Determines, in combination with the *de minimis* percentage, the non-product-specific *de minimis* threshold. Product-specific *de minimis* thresholds also apply.

Sources: WTO notifications and authors' calculations.

Table 11.2 *Summary of domestic support notifications and shadow notifications for four developing countries, 1995–2008*

	Brazil (billion US dollars)				India (billion US dollars)			
	Averages				Averages			
	All years	First half	Second half	2007/08	All years	First half	Second half	2008/09
Green box	2.1	2.6	1.6	2.2	6.1	3.4	8.4	12.5
Less food aid and public stockholding	1.4	1.8	1.1	1.5	1.6	0.9	2.2	3.0
Decoupled income support	—	—	—	—	—	—	—	—
Development programs	0.4	0.3	0.6	1.0	7.2	5.1	8.9	11.7
OTDS	1.2	0.7	1.6	2.7	–1.9	–2.5	–1.4	1.4
Blue box	—	—	—	—	—	—	—	—
Current Total AMS	0.1	—	0.1	0.5	—	—	—	—
Total *de minimis*[a]	1.1	0.7	1.5	2.1	–1.9	–2.5	–1.4	1.4
Product-specific	0.3	0.3	0.2	0.1	–2.9	–3.4	–2.5	0.2
Non-product-specific	0.8	0.4	1.3	2.1	1.0	0.9	1.1	1.2
Total support	3.7	3.6	3.8	5.9	11.4	6.0	16.0	25.7
Less food aid and public stockholding	3.0	2.8	3.3	5.2	6.9	3.5	9.7	16.2
	Assessment of the commitments							
Bound Total AMS	1.0	1.0	0.9	0.9	zb	zb	zb	zb
CTAMS/Bound Total AMS (%)	7.9	1.2	14.6	54.8	zb	zb	zb	zb

Total value of production[a]	55.3	50.1	60.5	99.4	106.7	91.4	119.8	141.2
Bound Total AMS/Total value of production (%)	1.7	2.0	1.5	0.9	zb	zb	zb	zb

	China (billion RMB)				Philippines (billion pesos)			
	Averages				Averages			
	All years	First half	Second half	2008	All years	First half	Second half	2008
Green box	260.1	181.5	327.4	397.1	12.4	9.8	15.1	22.6
Less food aid and public stockholding	208.0	133.5	271.8	334.0	11.4	8.5	14.3	21.5
Decoupled income support	5.3	—	9.9	15.1	—	—	—	—
Development programs	na	na	na	na	3.1	2.6	3.7	5.6
OTDS	-20.8	-41.9	-2.7	9.8	2.1	2.0	2.2	8.2
Blue box	—	—	—	—	—	—	—	—
Current Total AMS	—	—	—	—	—	—	—	—
Total *de minimis*[a]	-20.8	-41.9	-2.7	—	2.1	2.0	2.2	8.2
Product-specific	-31.1	-57.0	-8.8	—	2.1	2.0	2.2	8.2
Non-product-specific	10.2	15.1	6.1	9.8	—	—	—	—
Total support	239.2	139.6	324.6	406.9	17.7	14.3	21.0	36.4
Less food aid and public stockholding	187.1	91.6	269.0	343.8	16.7	13.1	20.2	35.2

Table 11.2 (*cont.*)

	China (billion RMB)				Philippines (billion pesos)			
	Averages				Averages			
	All years	First half	Second half	2008	All years	First half	Second half	2008
	Assessment of the commitments							
Bound Total AMS	zb	zb	zb	zb	zb	zb	zb	zb
CTAMS/Bound Total AMS (%)	zb	zb	zb	zb	zb	zb	zb	zb
Total value of production[b]	2,741.9	2,150.4	3,248.8	4,241.5	558.4	428.9	687.8	946.9
Bound Total AMS/Total value of production (%)	zb	zb	zb	zb	zb	zb	zb	zb

Notes: — indicates zero; na indicates that China is not eligible to exempt the development program category of support from AMS; zb indicates a zero Bound Total AMS.

[a] For India and China this is the sum of AMS support including negative values of MPS (see Tables 8.3 and 9.1).

[b] Determines, in combination with the *de minimis* percentage, the projected non-product-specific *de minimis* threshold. Product-specific *de minimis* thresholds also apply.

Sources: WTO notifications and authors' calculations.

estimated 2008 values. The break points are somewhat arbitrary, but the latter three columns provide an indication of trends in domestic support when compared to the overall averages. Notified levels of support are presented in the currency in which the notifications are made.

From the data it is evident that neither developed nor developing countries have had difficulty meeting the domestic support obligations specified in the Agreement. Among the developed countries, Norway stands out as having regularly notified annual CTAMS close to its Bound Total AMS commitment. As described by Gaasland, Garcia and Vårdal in Chapter 6, notifying support close to the commitment arises for two reasons: administered prices for main crop and livestock products serve as an anchor for Norway's border measures and consequently its domestic market prices; and the MPS calculations use total domestic production as the eligible production. Norway's MPS has exceeded its CTAMS, since the latter includes a negative component due to estimated costs imposed on livestock farmers through high prices for feed. With a strong relationship between administered and market prices, the MPS notified by Norway comes closer to reflecting the economic protection provided to farmers than in other countries. With its CTAMS deriving almost entirely from MPS, Norway occasionally employs slight changes in the notified administered prices to keep MPS low enough to avoid any violations of its commitment.

The notified MPS shows differing relationships to the CTAMS and commitment levels among the remaining countries. The United States, like Norway, has notified a stable MPS, but this accounts for a much smaller share of the US support commitment and in the early years a smaller share of its CTAMS. For the EU and Japan, the MPS in the 1986–88 base period (and related EMS price support used primarily by the EU for fruits and vegetables) was the predominant component determining their commitment levels. Since the Agreement was implemented, EU notifications reflect a systematic direction of policy reform that has shifted support from MPS to exempt direct payments, and consequently the notified CTAMS has fallen steadily over time. The EU payments initially were notified as exempt on blue box grounds. As the reforms unfolded, EU payments were further decoupled from production bases or levels of production and have been notified almost entirely in the green box as decoupled income support.

The change in the domestic support regime in the EU has been associated with a decline in economic market price support to farmers, although to a lesser extent in 1995–2008 than the reduction in the notified MPS, as discussed by Josling and Swinbank in Chapter 3. The situation in Japan is even more stark, as described by Godo and Takahashi in Chapter 5. Elimination of the administered price for rice in 1998 resulted in a reduction in the notified MPS from 70 percent of Japan's commitment to just 20 percent, with essentially no change in economic market price support for rice in that year and only a modest decline in subsequent years. While the EU has implemented relatively few measures providing non-exempt AMS support payments, Japan's AMS non-exempt direct payments have accounted for about one-third of the notified CTAMS since its rice MPS was eliminated. Non-exempt payments have been the cornerstone of domestic support for the US. Linked to market prices, these payments have made the CTAMS of the US uniquely variable on an annual basis compared to other countries. The period averages in Table 11.1 include several years when the notified CTAMS exceeded 85 percent of the US ceiling commitment. In contrast, as the EU shifted from a notified MPS unaffected by world price fluctuations to fixed direct payments it avoided introducing variability into its notified support.

Brazil is the only developing country included in our analysis that has a non-zero (though small) Bound Total AMS. It is also the only developing country among the four analyzed that regularly notifies support other than MPS within the AMS category (in Brazil's case, primarily credit subsidies and debt rescheduling, as discussed by Nassar in Chapter 7). The AMS for one or more products (cotton or wheat) has exceeded the *de minimis* threshold in a few years in Brazil, but the resulting CTAMS has always been well below Brazil's commitment.

Among the other developing countries, the MPS for China and India has been negative because administered prices have been below fixed external reference prices for key food staples (rice and wheat). The MPS does not accurately reflect the economic market price support provided in either country because of the way that the price gap is defined in the Agreement and the choice made by these countries to report eligible quantities on the basis of government grain procurements or other limiting criteria, rather than total or marketed production. Farmers growing rice or wheat in China or India have been disprotected (implicitly taxed) in certain years since 1995, but mostly they have received positive economic price support, as described by Gopinath and Cheng in Chapters 8 and 9, respectively.

An exaggerated positive difference between the rate of price support implied by the notified MPS and economic market price support is apparent for the Philippines. In this case, rice is protected by border measures, with domestic prices up to twice world price levels, as Cororaton describes in Chapter 10. The applied administered price in the MPS calculations was three times the fixed external reference price by 2008. Yet, the Philippines notified a rice MPS below the *de minimis* AMS threshold because it counted only small procured amounts as the eligible quantity of production. The policy debate in the Philippines shows that administered prices are an anchor for border policies that determine market prices, similar to the situation in Norway. Calculating the MPS based on procured quantities understates the policy importance of the administered price of rice in the Philippines, while the use of the nominal administered prices relative to a fixed nominal reference price overstates the actual rate of economic protection.

Under the Agreement, a product-specific AMS need only be included in CTAMS if it exceeds the applicable *de minimis* threshold. Countries can make use of this provision to report relatively modest levels of support for identified products. The four developed countries have made relatively little use of product-specific *de minimis* exemptions. A negative MPS has been reported by the EU when administered prices have fallen below its external reference prices (notably for durum wheat, oats, and occasionally beef). In those cases, when the calculated AMS support has been negative the product-specific AMS has been notified as zero.

The non-product-specific AMS can be excluded from CTAMS as *de minimis* if it falls below the threshold percentage of the total value of agricultural production. Some countries choose to include support that is concentrated on a limited number of products in the non-product-specific AMS. Among the eight countries, the US stands out as having made substantial use of the non-product-specific *de minimis* AMS exemption. This has allowed price-dependent payments made in years of relatively low world prices for certain crops (primarily corn, soybeans, wheat, rice, and cotton) to be excluded from the CTAMS. This non-product-specific AMS support actually reflects an element of reform in US policy, with payments less tied to the production of specific products or to supply control requirements than for the blue box measures they replaced. Yet, the classification of these price-linked payments as non-product-specific AMS has been controversial, as discussed by Brink in Chapter 2 and Blandford and Orden in Chapter 4.

The *de minimis* thresholds on AMS support are constraints for China, India and the Philippines under the Agreement because they do not have a Bound Total AMS identified in their schedules of commitments. These countries have notified various types of non-product-specific AMS support below *de minimis* thresholds. India and the Philippines, and also Brazil, have notified similar or identical measures under exemptions for development programs. Such notifications, particularly by Brazil and India, have been subject to both domestic and international scrutiny because they include input subsidies, which are key forms of support in these countries.

The exemption for development programs allows developing countries to address rural poverty by assisting farmers in ways that affect production and trade. In principle, this reduces the effectiveness of WTO rules to direct countries away from trade-distorting forms of support. In practice, the effect of the exemption has not been consequential, at least through 2008. Even if support under development programs were to be included in the AMS, such support has been low enough that the *de minimis* thresholds of Brazil, India and the Philippines would not have been binding. The *de minimis* threshold level of support has only been approached by the sum of the non-product-specific support notified in the two categories (*de minimis* and development programs) for India, in part because in its few notifications India reported subsidies for electricity and irrigation that other countries are less conscientious about including in their notifications. As incomes continue to increase in large developing countries such as China or India, domestic support seems to be growing and MPS may turn positive. For those countries eligible for the development program exemption (China is not eligible, under the terms of its accession to the WTO), this exemption could prove important for future compliance with support limitations in the Agreement. Questions of whether MPS should be computed using government procurements or total production, or whether direct payment programs qualify for the green box or blue box or belong in AMS, could also prove important in determining the scope these countries have for providing support while remaining within WTO commitments.

To summarize, each country has found room within the exemptions and *de minimis* exclusions provided by the Agreement to allocate domestic support among the allowed categories in order to claim it has remained in compliance with the rules and well under its commitment. Alternative assessments of the categorization of measures or measurement of support levels alter the compliance picture in some cases, as earlier chapters have shown. Challenges to notifications can be raised in the WTO Committee on Agriculture and a few have reached the level of the formal dispute settlement process. But overall there has been only limited capacity to demonstrate noncompliance given the porous disciplines that the Agreement enshrines.

Trends in support among countries

The WTO notifications are designed first and foremost to provide transparency in monitoring compliance with legal obligations under the Agreement. But these legal obligations draw their purpose from an underlying economic motivation. Interest in compliance with the Agreement therefore is tied to the objective of correcting and preventing distortions in world agricultural markets. So the broader question is how well the notifications reflect policy reform decisions over time and what they convey about trends in forms and levels of support among countries. Some of these insights can be deduced from notified nominal support levels and from assessments of compliance by individual countries with the Agreement. But the nominal data and unilateral compliance assessments fail to bring out some of the comparative information conveyed by the notifications.

Two key questions in this regard concern the motivation for policy reform under the Agreement and whether it has played a role in promoting policy convergence among countries. Insight into these questions can be obtained from assessment of the composition of domestic support and its level as a percentage of the total value of agricultural production (Table 11.3 and Table 11.4). Within each country, this normalization facilitates comparisons of types and levels of support across years relative to the size of its agricultural sector. Japan stands out (see Table 11.1) in this regard as the only country for which the notified nominal total value of agricultural production against which support levels are evaluated has declined over time.

In terms of the convergence question, the notifications of domestic support expressed as a percentage of the total value of agricultural production provide useful information for drawing comparisons. For these comparisons a caveat is in order because of the manner in which the notifications are prepared and reviewed. Each country exercises substantial discretion in the measures it notifies to the WTO and in the measurement of levels of support. The WTO notifications are not specifically designed to provide a systematic comparison across members, unlike the support estimates provided by the OECD's PSEs for a smaller group of countries. Although some scrutiny of the notifications occurs through the WTO Committee on Agriculture and through dispute settlement, no systematic

Table 11.3 *Summary of domestic support as percent of total value of agricultural production for four developed countries, 1995–2008*

	EU[a]				US			
	Averages(%)				Averages (%)			
	All years	First half	Second half	2008/09	All years	First half	Second half	2008
Green box	11.9	9.0	14.2	19.1	27.2	25.5	27.9	29.7
Less food aid and public stockholding	11.7	8.9	14.0	19.0	8.1	7.7	8.3	7.1
Decoupled income support	3.4	0.2	6.1	11.4	2.3	2.3	2.3	1.8
OTDS	22.4	30.6	15.9	9.5	6.7	8.3	5.4	3.3
Blue box	7.2	9.4	5.4	1.6	0.2	0.5	—	—
Current Total AMS	14.8	20.9	9.9	7.5	4.4	5.6	3.4	2.1
of which, MPS	13.7	19.3	9.1	7.2	2.6	3.0	2.3	1.8
Total *de minimis*	0.4	0.3	0.6	0.5	2.1	2.2	2.0	1.2
Product-specific	0.1	0.1	0.2	0.1	0.1	0.1	0.2	—
Non-product-specific	0.3	0.2	0.4	0.4	2.0	2.1	1.8	1.2
Total support	34.3	39.6	30.1	28.7	33.9	33.9	33.3	33.0
Less food aid and public stockholding	34.2	39.5	29.9	28.6	14.9	16.0	13.7	10.4

	Japan				Norway			
	Averages (%)				Averages (%)			
	All years	First half	Second half	2008	All years	First half	Second half	2008
Green box	26.3	29.3	23.2	21.8	21.0	18.7	23.2	27.8
Less food aid and public stockholding	25.8	28.6	22.9	21.6	19.6	15.5	21.9	27.8
Decoupled income support	0.2	—	0.3	1.2	—	—	—	—
OTDS	14.5	20.3	8.2	7.3	74.7	80.0	69.5	60.4
Blue box	0.6	0.5	0.7	0.4	28.0	33.2	22.9	14.9
Current Total AMS	13.5	19.4	7.0	5.9	46.4	46.7	46.0	44.9
of which, MPS	11.3	17.4	4.6	4.5	48.8	48.4	49.1	48.0
Total *de minimis*	0.5	0.4	0.5	1.0	0.3	—	0.6	0.6
Product-specific	0.2	0.2	0.2	0.2	0.1	—	0.3	0.2
Non-product-specific	0.3	0.2	0.3	0.8	0.2	—	0.3	0.4
Total support	40.9	49.7	31.4	29.1	95.7	98.7	92.7	88.3
Less food aid and public stockholding	40.3	48.9	31.1	28.9	93.4	95.5	91.4	88.3

Note: — indicates zero.

[a] Refers to the EU15, EU25 and EU27 as presented in Chapter 3. Row "*of which*, MPS" includes EMS price support.

Sources: WTO notifications and authors' calculations.

Table 11.4 *Summary of domestic support as percent of total value of agricultural production for four developing countries, 1995–2008*

	Brazil				India			
	Averages (%)				Averages (%)			
	All years	First half	Second half	2007/08	All years	First half	Second half	2008/09
Green box	3.8	5.1	2.7	2.2	5.7	3.7	7.1	8.9
Less food aid and public stockholding	2.6	3.6	1.8	1.6	1.5	1.0	1.8	2.1
Decoupled income support	—	—	—	—	—	—	—	—
Development programs	0.8	0.6	1.0	1.0	6.7	5.6	7.5	8.3
OTDS	2.1	1.4	2.7	2.7	–1.8	–2.8	–1.2	1.0
Blue box	—	—	—	—	—	—	—	—
Current Total AMS	0.1	—	0.2	0.5	zb	zb	zb	zb
Total *de minimis*[a]	2.0	1.4	2.5	2.2	–1.8	–2.8	–1.2	1.0
Product-specific	0.5	0.6	0.4	0.1	–2.7	–3.7	–2.1	0.1
Non-product-specific	1.5	0.8	2.1	2.1	0.9	1.0	0.9	0.8
Total support	6.7	7.1	6.4	5.9	10.6	6.5	13.3	18.2
Less food aid and public stockholding	5.5	5.6	5.4	5.3	6.4	3.9	8.1	11.4

	China				Philippines			
	Averages (%)				Averages (%)			
	All years	First half	Second half	2008	All years	First half	Second half	2008
Green box	9.5	8.4	10.1	9.4	2.2	2.3	2.2	2.3
Less food aid and public stockholding	7.6	6.2	8.4	7.9	2.0	2.0	2.1	2.2
Decoupled income support	0.2	—	0.3	0.4	—	—	—	—
Development programs	na	na	na	na	0.6	0.6	0.5	0.6
OTDS	-0.8	-1.9	-0.1	0.2	0.4	0.5	0.3	0.8
Blue box	—	—	-	—	—	—	—	—
Current Total AMS	zb	zb	zb	zb	zb	zb	zb	zb
Total *de minimis*[a]	-0.8	-1.9	-0.1	—	0.4	0.5	0.3	0.8
Product-specific	-1.1	-2.6	-0.3	—	0.4	0.5	0.3	0.8
Non-product-specific	0.4	0.7	0.2	0.2	—	—	—	—
Total support	8.7	6.5	10.0	9.6	3.2	3.3	3.1	3.7
Less food aid and public stockholding	6.8	4.3	8.3	8.1	3.0	3.1	2.9	3.6

Notes: — indicates zero; na indicates that China is not eligible to exempt the development program category of support from AMS; zb indicates a zero Bound Total AMS.

[a] For India and China, this is the sum of AMS support including negative values of MPS (see Tables 8.3 and 9.1).

Sources: WTO notifications and authors' calculations.

corroboration is undertaken to ensure comparability of the notified support. Thus some caution is appropriate in making cross-country comparisons of levels of support in the notifications, especially at an aggregate level involving summations across multiple measures in various categories, as opposed to comparing support from a specific measure reported by more than one country.

Green box support has increased in nominal value and as a percentage of the total value of production in six of the countries, with the exceptions being Brazil and Japan. The composition of the green box, its level as a percentage of total production value, and the explanation for growth in support differ markedly among countries. Green box support was near or exceeded 20 percent of production value in the EU, Japan, Norway and the US by 2008, but was less than 10 percent in Brazil, China, India, and the Philippines. Green box support is high but declining in Japan particularly because of the inclusion of substantial infrastructure investments. These also make up a large component of China's green box notifications, but such investments are not included to the same extent in the notifications of other countries. Norway's high green box support relative to the total value of production includes a unique program of farm-operator vacation payments that Gaasland, Garcia and Vårdal argue is a labor input subsidy and should not qualify for inclusion.

The green box in India and in the US includes large expenditures directed toward food consumers. Without domestic food aid programs, whose subsidies can be applied to purchases of domestic or foreign produced groceries, US green box support averages about 8 percent of the total value of agricultural production, compared to 27 percent if domestic food aid is included. Without public stockholding for food security, India's green box support is about 1.5 percent of the total value of production, compared to 6 percent with stockholding. For the EU, almost the entire growth of green box support comes from the policy shift to payments notified as decoupled income support to agricultural producers. These payments rose to more than 11 percent of the total value of agricultural production in 2008. The US shifted to direct payments notified as decoupled income support a decade earlier than the EU but annual US payments have remained less than 3 percent of the total value of production. China's payments to grain producers notified as decoupled income support since 2004 are less than 1 percent of total agricultural production value.

The extent to which both the EU and US have abandoned blue box payments is noticeable; notified blue box subsidies have almost disappeared. The blue box was created in the final stages of the Uruguay Round negotiations mainly to provide a haven for some of the support provided by the EU and US that was argued to be less trade-distorting than non-exempt direct payments in the AMS. While levels of blue box support remain unconstrained by the Agreement, the use of this category was subsequently overtaken in both cases by policy decisions that involved movement away from supply control measures. Norway has continued its use of blue box measures and notifies significant blue box payments, but even in Norway's case the value and relative importance of these payments has declined. Japan continues to enact policies to divert land from rice production into other crops but has notified only limited blue box payments associated with these measures.

India has reported a relatively high level of support under the development program exemption. In its notifications for 1996/97 and 1997/98, 80 percent of the reported subsidies for fertilizer, electricity, and irrigation were included in the development program category based on the share of small farms in the total number of farms, as described by Gopinath. Brazil and the Philippines have notified smaller amounts of support under the development program exemption. The level of China's non-product-specific AMS notified as *de minimis* is much lower as a percentage of the value of production than the sum of India's non-product-specific support under development programs plus *de minimis* AMS, as already noted. China has not notified subsidies for irrigation or electricity, a potentially important omission that Cheng examines.

A broad measurement of support is provided by the concept of the OTDS (overall trade-distorting support: the sum of CTAMS, *de minimis* AMS support and blue box payments) as discussed in the Doha Round. This measurement has declined slightly in nominal value in Norway and the US, and more dramatically in the EU and Japan, over the period 1995–2008. The decline in the EU reflects changes in policy, with the significant qualification that the MPS notified to the WTO is not an accurate measure of the economic value of market price support. For Japan, there is little correspondence between its low notified MPS, and hence the OTDS, and its continued border protection of rice. This results in a major disconnect between the illusion of policy reform through a reduction in notified MPS and the reality that domestic rice prices in Japan have remained substantially above world levels because of high tariffs and Japan's diversion of land from rice production. Even with a reduced MPS, both the OTDS and the total of all support (including also that in the green box) is higher in the EU and Japan than in the US as a percentage of the total value of agricultural production when domestic food aid is excluded. The OTDS and the total of all support are particularly high as percentages of the value of production for Norway.

The developing countries have notified less support than the developed countries but the level has been increasing in all four cases, except for the total of all support for Brazil as a percent of value of production because of its declining green box support. When domestic food aid and public stockholding for food security programs are excluded from the green box notifications, the estimated total of all support for China and India relative to the total value of agricultural production in 2008 is of a similar order of magnitude to that for the US. Of course, there are many more farms in China and India producing that agricultural output and receiving low levels of support per farm, though per farm support is not disciplined in the WTO.

When all notified support is combined, the nominal level among developed countries has risen in the US, been stable in Norway, declined slightly in the EU, and declined sharply in Japan between 1995 and 2008. Total support has declined in the four developed countries as a percentage of the total value of agricultural production, whereas it has increased in China, India and the Philippines. With a porous international Agreement on Agriculture, domestic support policies remain heterogeneous across the countries in our analysis.

Doha's enhanced disciplines on domestic support

In the Doha Round countries have been negotiating over new rules and commitments to achieve further reductions in agricultural support and protection. The potential disciplines for domestic support incorporated in the draft modalities of December 2008 reflect progress toward that objective. They could have the effect of reducing the disparity among countries in the level of domestic support provided, though the rules will still reflect the continued accommodation of differences in the measures and levels of support that have been discussed in this book. Though some disagreement persists on how much additional discipline should be introduced and how quickly, detailed and intense negotiations lie behind the proposed rules, initial commitments and phased-in commitment reductions reflected in the draft modalities.

The potential Doha commitments are shown side-by-side for the eight countries in Table 11.5. The top portion of the table shows commitments in the currency used by each country for its notifications, while the lower portion provides a basis for comparison by expressing commitments in

Table 11.5 *Doha limits on OTDS, CTAMS, and overall blue box in currency of notification and Doha* de minimis *percentages*

	EU27	US	Japan	Norway	Brazil	India	China	Philippines
	Billion euro	*Billion US$*	*Billion Yen*	*Billion NOK*	*Billion US$*	*Billion US$*	*Billion RMB*	*Billion pesos*
Basis for calculations								
Pre-Doha Final Bound Total AMS (FBTAMS) (%)	72.2	19.1	3,972.9	11.4	0.9	—	—	—
Value of production (1995–2000)	259.3	195.9	9,849.6	22.6				
Value of production (1995–2004)					48.7	102.5	2,337.6	468.8
10 percent of value of production (1995–2000)	25.9	19.6	985.0	2.3				
20 percent of value of production (1995–2004)					9.7	20.5	467.5	93.8
5 percent of value of production (1995–2000 or 1995–2004)	12.9	9.8	492.5	1.1	2.4	5.1	116.9	23.4
Notified blue box (if greater than 5 percent of value of production)[a]	20.8			7.5				
Base OTDS (sum of selected components above)	118.9	48.5	5,450.3	21.2	13.1	25.6	584.4	117.2

Table 11.5 (*cont.*)

	EU27	US	Japan	Norway	Brazil	India	China	Philippines
Full reduction percentage from Base OTDS (%)	80	70	75	55	37	—	—	—
Final Bound OTDS after any reduction	23.8	14.5	1,362.6	9.5	8.3	25.6	584.4	117.2
Full reduction percentage from pre-Doha FBTAMS (%)	70	60	70	53	30			
Final Bound Total AMS after reduction	21.7	7.6	1,191.9	5.4	0.6	—	—	—
Overall blue box limit (2.5 percent or 5 percent of value of production)[b]	6.5	4.9	246.2	3.6	2.4	5.1	116.9	23.4
De minimis percentage after any reduction (%)	2.5	2.5	2.5	2.5	6.7	10.0	8.5	10.0
	Commitments in US dollars[c]							
Final Bound OTDS	33.1	14.5	14.6	1.5	8.3	25.6	85.5	2.5
Final Bound Total AMS	30.1	7.6	12.7	0.9	0.6	—	—	—
Overall blue box	9.0	4.9	2.6	0.6	2.4	5.1	17.1	0.5

	Commitment as a share of base-period value of production (%)							
Final Bound OTDS	9.2	7.4	13.8	42.1	17.0	25.0	25.0	25.0
Final Bound Total AMS	8.4	3.9	12.1	24.0	1.3	—	—	—
Overall blue box	2.5	2.5	2.5	15.7	5.0	5.0	5.0	5.0

Notes: — indicates zero. Value of production in base periods is average of those reported in WTO (2010), which includes certain qualifications attaching to the data.

[a] Tests for paragraph 1(c) condition, picks up blue box payments when above 5 percent of value of production (See Table 2.2 and Appendix B).

[b] Norway is treated as a special case under paragraph 39.

[c] Country data were converted from currency of notifications to US dollars using IMF average yearly exchange rates for 2009.

Source: Based on WTO (2008) and prepared for this chapter by Lars Brink with country chapter authors.

US dollars (using 2009 average exchange rates) and as percentages of the base-period total agricultural production value for each country.

Among the developed countries, Final Bound Total AMS levels are brought down by 70 percent in the EU and Japan and by somewhat smaller percentages for the US (60 percent) and Norway (53 percent). These significant reductions would not only cut allowable nominal levels of CTAMS but also would rebalance the relative magnitude of commitments among countries, measured on a dollar basis or as a percentage of the value of production. The ratio of FBTAMS of the EU compared to that of the US measured in US dollars at 2009 exchange rates falls from 5.2 under the Agreement to 4.0 under the Doha proposals as the EU27 limit drops from 72.2 billion euro to 21.7 billion euro and that of the US from $19.1 billion to $7.6 billion. Japan and Norway retain higher FBTAMS commitments than the EU or US as a percentage of the 1995–2000 base-period value of production; the support limit is brought closer to the EU or US levels than in the past using this criterion for Japan but less so for Norway.[1] The *de minimis* thresholds are reduced uniformly for the developed countries from 5 percent of the future annual nominal value of production to 2.5 percent. The overall blue box would be limited to 2.5 percent of the 1995–2000 value of production, instead of being unconstrained (Norway's constraint would be calculated differently). Product-specific caps would apply to AMS support and to blue box payments – these additional commitments are discussed in the previous chapters but are not shown in Table 11.5.

The Doha commitments would create a Base OTDS for developed countries that includes the FBTAMS under the Agreement plus 10 percent of the total value of production for the period 1995–2000. The Base OTDS also includes either an additional 5 percent of the 1995–2000 production value or the average of notified blue box payments in that period if it is higher (as is the case for the EU and Norway). The Doha OTDS commitments would cap the sum of CTAMS, *de minimis* AMS support and blue box payments for the first time. Substantial reductions from the base would be phased in as Bound OTDS commitments for the developed countries over five years. The percentage reductions are largest for the EU, followed by Japan, the US and Norway.

[1] The projected total value of production is subject to uncertainty, but using the projections of the preceding chapters leads to similar findings about relative levels of support that would be allowed under the proposed Doha commitments.

For the EU and Japan, the Final Bound OTDS exceeds the Final Bound Total AMS by only small amounts (2.1 billion euro and 170 billion yen, respectively) under the proposed Doha modalities. As a result, *de minimis* and blue box support would be tightly constrained unless the CTAMS were held well below its commitment level. Conversely, for Norway and the US the formulas negotiated into the 2008 Doha draft modalities leave a substantial gap between the two commitments. This gives the Norway and the US more room to provide blue box or *de minimis* AMS support even with CTAMS near its limit. The OTDS limit for the US is closer to the OTDS limit for the EU than the FBTAMS of the US is to that of the EU. The same is true for the US relative to Japan. Norway retains higher commitments as a percentage of its value of production.

The commitments for Brazil have a similar pattern as those of the developed countries under the Doha draft modalities but the reductions reflect the more lenient treatment for developing countries. Brazil's Base OTDS is calculated using a more recent period (through 2004) and higher percentages of the base-period value of production (totaling 25 percent). Its small FBTAMS is reduced by 30 percent (to $0.6 billion), its *de minimis* thresholds by one-third (to 6.7 percent of value of production), its OTDS by 37 percent, and its overall blue box limit is set at 5 percent of the 1995–2004 total value of agricultural production.

The Doha implications for the commitments of the other three developing countries differ. China, India and the Philippines remain constrained by their obligation under the Agreement to provide no more than *de minimis* levels of AMS support. Their Base OTDS is calculated using the longer 1995–2004 period and the higher percentage of total value of production. Overall blue box support also would be capped at 5 percent of base-period production value for these developing countries.

For China, India and the Philippines no reductions from Base OTDS or in *de minimis* thresholds are required by the Doha draft modalities and product-specific AMS caps are determined quite loosely. As a consequence, their allowable OTDS will be double or more those of the EU, US or Japan as a percentage of base-period value of production. On a dollar basis, the OTDS support that could be provided by China and India would be $85.5 billion and $25.6 billion, respectively. These are much higher nominal values than for Japan or the US and, in the case of China, more than double the limit for the EU. The design of the Doha modalities thus shifts the balance of future support commitments compared to the historical support patterns among these six countries. These results re-illustrate the point made more broadly by Brink for developed and developing countries in Chapter 2.

Within their overall scope for allowable support, the three developing countries face the additional constraint of maintaining a zero CTAMS. This imposes significant limits on how their OTDS can be provided: in particular, it constrains product-specific AMS support to be less than future *de minimis* thresholds. These limits on product-specific support are much less than the support developed countries have provided in the past to certain products. However, as the value of production grows in nominal value, the *de minimis* thresholds also grow while the relatively tighter product-specific AMS limits the Doha draft modalities would impose on developed countries stay constant. Past *de minimis* thresholds are therefore not reliable guides for the future patterns of allowable product-specific AMS support across countries. Brazil retains two-thirds of its modest FBTAMS, amounting to 1.3 percent of the 1995–2004 total value of production. Because it has a non-zero FBTAMS Brazil takes reduction commitments from its Base OTDS, in contrast to the other developing countries. Consequently Brazil's latitude for OTDS is 17 percent of base period total value of production, compared to the 25 percent for other developing countries.

How binding are the potential Doha constraints?

One perspective on the degree to which the draft Doha disciplines would exert a tighter constraint on domestic support comes from analyzing how the support notified in the past would have related to the new rules and commitments. As summarized in our introduction and discussed in more depth in the country chapters, this question was particularly relevant during the early years of the negotiations (2001–05) when the broad outlines of possible commitments were being hammered out and world market prices were generally expected to remain relatively low. Japan has been well positioned to accept tighter domestic support disciplines after it stopped notifying rice MPS in 1998. The EU has positioned itself since the MacSharry reforms of 1992 and the Fischler reforms of 2003 to accommodate tighter domestic support commitments, through its shift from MPS to blue box and subsequently to green box payments. It would have had to move in this direction much faster if the Doha commitments had been in effect in the past. For Norway and the US, the proposed Doha commitments would also have compelled changes in policies pursued through 2005 in order to achieve compliance. Higher market prices during 2006–2008 subsequently brought US support to nominal levels within the limits set in the Doha proposals, but Norway's policies would still have required modifications to comply with the proposed commitments. For the developing countries we have examined in this analysis, the levels of support provided in the past have been in compliance with the proposed commitments under a Doha agreement.

More germane to the future are projected levels of support compared to the proposed commitments. Estimates from the previous chapters are summarized in Table 11.6. For the developing countries, anticipated support remains well below the relatively loose commitments of the Doha draft modalities. China and India might face some nominal constraints on MPS provided to staple crops – a somewhat artificial constraint as we have argued and one that may be alleviated by the Doha provision to allow price support associated with public stockholding in developing countries to be exempted in the green box, as discussed by both Brink and Gopinath. It is anticipated that India will continue to provide substantial exempt support under development programs. Brazil and the Philippines remain far below allowed support levels in all dimensions. Thus, these developing countries have substantial flexibility with respect to trade-distorting domestic support under the Doha proposals.

For the developed countries that have provided most of the domestic support historically, the Doha commitments would be a somewhat more substantive constraint on future policies. The EU's projected decoupled income support in the green box remains high but this is not subject to WTO nominal constraint. The EU's CTAMS and OTDS would have been projected to be near or above its Doha commitments by the year 2015/16, without a decline of EMS first notified for 2007/08. Past reforms would be locked in were the Doha agreement in place. Likewise, the support for the US is projected to be 30–35 percent below the Doha FBTAMS and Final Bound OTDS commitments. This is the result of some additional flexibility the US achieved in 2008 by reducing its dairy MPS through modest re-definitional policy changes with little economic effect. Even so, given the price-dependent character of past US support, the Doha constraints could require future policy modifications in periods of declining prices. In particular, new countercyclical support such as that provided through the ACRE revenue-guarantee program introduced in 2008 could be constrained.

For Japan, the Doha ceilings would preclude levels of AMS and blue box support that Godo and Takahashi argue were planned by the government

Table 11.6 *Projected levels of support (mid 2010s) and Doha constraints (2008 draft modalities fully implemented) for eight countries*

	EU27		US		Japan		Norway	
	Projection[a]	Ceiling	Projection[a]	Ceiling	Projection[a]	Ceiling	Projection[a]	Ceiling
	Billion euros		*Billion dollars*		*Billion yen*		*Billion NOK*	
Green box	56.7		117.5		1,526		6.9	
OTDS	17.2	23.8	10.2	14.5	1,558	1,362	15.3	9.5
Blue box	4.7	6.5	—	4.9	560	246	3.7	3.6
Current Total AMS[b]	10.9	21.7	5.0	7.6	909	1,192	11.4	5.4
of which, MPS	10.3		5.0		334		11.9	
Total *de minimis*	1.6		4.9		89		0.2	
Product-specific[c]	0.3	7.5	0.1	7.3	15	209	0.1	0.6
Non-product-specific	1.3	7.5	4.8	7.3	73	209	0.1	0.6
Total support	73.9		127.7		3,084		22.2	
Total value of production[d]	299.7 [e]		265.2		8,378 [e]		24.1 [e]	
	Brazil		India		China		Philippines	
	Projection	Ceiling	Projection	Ceiling	Projection	Ceiling	Projection	Ceiling
	Billion US dollars		*Billion US dollars*		*Billion RMB*		*Billion pesos*	
Green box	2.3 [e]		22.1		522.0		25.1	
Development programs	0.7 [e]		13.5		—	—	6.2	
OTDS	2.0	8.3	8.4	25.6	183.4	584.4	8.5	117.2
Blue box	—	2.4	—	5.1	—	116.9	—	23.4
Current Total AMS[b]	—	0.6	—	—	—	—	—	—

Total *de minimis*	2.0		8.4		183.4		8.5	
Product-specific[c]	0.3	5.3	6.8	17.7	92.3[f]	444.1	8.5	191.0
Non-product-specific	1.7[e]	5.3	1.7	17.7	91.1	444.1	—	191.0
Total support	5.0[e]		44.0		705.4		39.8	
Total value of production[d]	78.7[e]		177.2		5,224.9		1,910.0	

Notes: — indicates zero and a blank means that no entry is applicable.

[a] Projected support levels assuming no adjustment to accommodate possible Doha ceilings (see Chapters 3–6).

[b] Cannot exceed ceiling on CTAMS (i.e., Doha Final Bound Total AMS) or, if no FBTAMS exists in the country's Schedule, cannot exceed zero.

[c] The AMS for any product (sum of MPS and EMS, non-exempt direct payments and other non-exempt support) is subject to the product's *de minimis* threshold (for the countries with a FBTAMS commitment) or limit (for those with a zero ceiling on CTAMS). These thresholds or limits are not shown individually: see chapters for details.

[d] Determines, in combination with the Doha *de minimis* percentage, the projected non-product-specific *de minimis* threshold and the sum of all product-specific *de minimis* thresholds as entered in the ceiling column (the sum of the values of production for all products is the total value of production).

[e] Average value during 2006–08 as no projection is made in the country chapters.

[f] Projected AMSs for wheat, corn and soybeans exceed *de minimis* thresholds under certain assumptions as the result of a large market price support component (see Chapter 9).

Source: Authors' calculations.

holding power in 2009 – the levels of support involved are not precluded under the Agreement, but would exceed Japan's overall blue box and OTDS Doha commitments. Likewise, a Doha agreement would require significant policy changes for Norway, as assessed by Gaasland, Garcia and Vårdal. Although domestic support measures could be introduced that would maintain most of Norway's production under the Doha disciplines, this would require a shift from MPS to direct payments and changes in Norway's policies that have been subject to little reform since 1995.

Taking these projections into account, we conclude that a Doha agreement built on the December 2008 draft modalities would achieve real progress on the path toward substantial progressive reductions in agricultural support envisioned in the preamble of the 1994 Agreement on Agriculture. A Doha agreement with tightened and extended commitments would impose some meaningful constraints, especially for developed countries that have provided high levels of support in the past. The Doha disciplines would clearly alter the tone of policy discussions about compliance by countries as the tighter limits loomed larger in national deliberations. The EU reform path would be locked in by its commitments, although room would remain for some increases compared to recently notified trade-distorting support. The disciplines would be particularly germane for the US if nominal agricultural prices move sharply downward or resume a downward trend. Japan would be constrained in pursuing measures that have entered its domestic policy debate and Norway would have to undertake a reconfiguration of its support programs. These would all be steps in the direction of a progressive reduction in trade-distorting support.

Strengthening international disciplines beyond Doha

The disciplines on domestic policies embedded in the Agreement and monitored through the notifications are designed to limit the support that countries provide under certain measures to their agricultural sectors. A new agreement in line with the Doha Round proposals would do so to a greater extent. The main rationale for the disciplines has always been that they are necessary to reduce production and trade distortions resulting from domestic support.

While the constraints rarely have proved binding, the policies of developed countries have shown a degree of convergence in the past twenty years, anchored by the Agreement but also related to national developments and changes in the nature of their agricultural industries. Developing countries have, in general, taken a somewhat different path in their agricultural policies; again not heavily constrained by WTO rules but consistent both with the limits the Agreement imposes and the flexibility it affords.

In the nine years of unsuccessful Doha negotiations through 2010, one persistent question has been whether and how to take further steps to tighten the disciplines on domestic support so as to draw a stronger link between WTO agreements and national policy decisions. The Doha draft modalities would establish rules and support ceilings that are more complicated than those of the Agreement and more heterogeneous across countries. These characteristics were necessary to satisfy competing aims and to achieve even a tentative blueprint for a new agricultural agreement. There are risks inherent in locking such diversity into the architecture of the international disciplines, yet even this compromise has not yet been enough to forge a consensus and bring the negotiations to closure.

The purpose of strengthening the Agreement through the Doha Round and beyond is to achieve the long-term objective of limiting protection and the distortions national policies create in world agricultural markets. It implies further movement towards policy convergence that would include five main dimensions: moderate tariffs and related impediments to imports; elimination of explicit and implicit export subsidies; limited scope for trade-distorting domestic support; the provision of support for public goods and other agreed purposes under well-defined green box criteria; and the transparent monitoring of international commitments.

If this is to happen, greater attention will need to be directed to the appropriate end point of policy convergence, the path for achieving this, and how consensus on the need for convergence can be secured. One can no longer view domestic support for agriculture as merely a developed country aberration that needs to be eliminated. Multilateral and comprehensive disciplines on domestic support are in a real sense the embodiment of an agricultural policy for the global economy. The parameters of such a policy still need to be determined.

The analysis of what has already been achieved under the Agreement and what might be achieved under proposed Doha disciplines on domestic support lays some of the groundwork for a strategic exploration of the longer term policy issues. We close with some observations that have emerged from our analysis that are germane to the ultimate aim of achieving greater policy cohesion around domestic support, recognizing that this will involve a very long period of deliberations and policy evolution. Some of the ideas we propose and the related recommendations have been aired in the Doha negotiations. However, countries have not yet been prepared collectively to adopt the expanded disciplines and obligations that are implied.

Greater international transparency

The role of the notifications as a device for monitoring policies and verifying compliance has been hampered by delays in submissions to the WTO. Shadow notifications and projections of likely future notifications along the lines we have presented add transparency to the monitoring process, but cannot substitute for formal submissions.

The Doha draft modalities would strengthen the notification obligations of countries and subject implementation of commitments to enhanced monitoring and review. For domestic support, an annual notification would be required. A complementary approach that could further improve the timeliness and content of reporting for certain members would be to link the WTO domestic support notifications to the mechanism of the annual policy review process of OECD. The OECD's regular publication of PSEs was initiated in 1987 during the Uruguay Round negotiations with the aim of improving transparency about agricultural policy measures, including domestic support and border measures, and the support they provide. An enormous investment has been made in the OECD's reporting and evaluation system. It makes sense to benefit from this investment in strengthening transparency in the WTO.

Linking the preparation of WTO notifications for some countries to OECD's annual monitoring process would not require the OECD and governments notifying the WTO to use exactly the same categories or even measurements of support, nor a completely common process for generating their reports. But instituting this linkage could ensure annual submissions on a regular basis by a large group of countries. The adoption of such linked reporting could also result in adherence to more uniform guidelines for notifications across countries. Transparency would not be improved for all WTO members under this mechanism (unless the country coverage under the OECD's system were expanded), but it would include most of the main importers and exporters engaged in agricultural trade, including emerging-market, non-OECD members such as Brazil and China that participate in OECD agricultural policy reviews. A mechanism of this type would demonstrate an increased level of commitment by leading countries to the integrity of WTO monitoring through timely notifications, which could only have beneficial effects on the credibility of commitments and the process of verifying compliance. The notifications would be subject to more prompt review through the Committee on Agriculture, to possible challenges by other WTO members, and to public scrutiny.

A more dramatic step for addressing late notifications would be to introduce disincentives for delayed submissions. Putting teeth into the agreement's notification requirement would have to recognize normal lags inherent in their preparation. Some delay is inevitable due to the nature of the information required – it takes time to collect and organize the detailed data underlying calculations in the notifications some of which may not be available until well after the particular period for which support was provided. The responsibility that governments bear under WTO processes, including those through dispute settlement, means that care is taken in the preparation of notifications.

Countries also want to take advantage of rules for exempting support under certain measures from their commitments. This could be automatically disallowed for a given year if notification was not made within a specified period of time, such as a year or eighteen months after the end of the period to be notified. If applied uniformly, both developed and developing countries would have a strong incentive to provide timely notifications under this stipulation in order to take advantage of the substantive distinctions that WTO rules make among different categories of support. Even *de minimis* allowances could be disallowed after the grace period. This would make almost mandatory the timely notification of domestic support by developed and developing countries and signal greater seriousness about the commitments. The processes for finding a country to be in violation of its obligations through WTO dispute settlement (see Chapter 1) would not change by adding a provision that late notification precludes exempting from commitment certain support that otherwise would be eligible for exemption, but the range of circumstances that could give rise to a violation would expand.

Accurate and meaningful measurements of support

We have emphasized the importance of accurate and meaningful notifications of domestic support not only as a legal requirement but also to achieve the economic objectives that underlie the Agreement. A troubling characteristic, as we have shown, is that countries often calculate key measurements of domestic support in different ways. Countries exercise substantial discretion in the types of policies they report, their placement in categories, and methods for calculating support levels. In part this arises from different agricultural circumstances across countries and consequent differences in policies. But it also results from the use of approaches that best appear to show that a country is complying with its WTO commitments.

A more coordinated process for the preparation of notifications, such as the proposal to link this to the OECD's annual monitoring and evaluation exercise, could reduce the heterogeneity apparent in the notifications for many countries. A more widespread understanding of what types of policies fit the criteria of the green box could lead to less divergence among countries in the measures that have been included or excluded from this category. Input subsidies could also be reported more uniformly among countries.

A critical issue in disparity that we have highlighted concerns the discretion that countries have in measuring market price support, in addition to inherent technical limitations of the WTO measurement. As we have shown, reductions in notified MPS often run ahead of real changes in the economic value of price support that countries provide. This precludes the notified MPS from being an accurate and meaningful measurement of support – and hence of the extent of trade distortion. In turn, this undermines the meaningful measurement of AMS and thus the usefulness of the ceiling commitments as indicators of restraint on levels of certain trade-distorting support.

Ambiguity in measurement of the MPS is going to be difficult to resolve. The initial decision to combine measures providing MPS and certain non-exempt direct payments and other non-exempt support into the AMS category has a rationale based on the potential economic effects of these measures. MPS is potentially the most distorting policy, since effective price support influences both production and consumption decisions, while the principal effect of direct payments is on production incentives. Thus, implicit in the Agreement is that it is desirable in terms of reducing and preventing distortions in world agricultural markets to substitute AMS (i.e., non-exempt) direct payments for MPS or to introduce new exempt payments that would qualify for the blue or green boxes in lieu of MPS. However, our analysis has shown that countries often reduce notified MPS without corresponding effects on price-linked market distortions.

Some progress can be made by adopting clearer rules for what constitutes an applied administered price and the eligible quantity of production. One might argue further along this line that the domestic support disciplines should be applied to the economic measurement of price support, as calculated by the OECD and as used in economic studies. But a difficulty arises from the separation of domestic support measures from market access and export competition measures for purposes of imposing disciplines under three distinct pillars in the WTO.

As we have emphasized, MPS through administered prices, market access as determined by tariffs and other import policies, and export competition as affected by taxes and subsidies have intertwined effects on domestic markets. Outcomes of policies considered under any one pillar are affected by the conditions defined by the other pillars. Adopting an economic measurement of market price support for commitments under the domestic support disciplines would introduce variation in the notified support that agricultural policymakers cannot control, due to fluctuations in world prices and exchange rates. Moreover, it would subsume under the domestic support discipline the effects of tariffs and other border policies, including levels of TRQs, export subsidies, and the effects of non-tariff measures, that are the domain of other WTO commitments and agreements. Such a breadth of commitment was rejected early in the Uruguay Round negotiations and is unlikely ever to be ceded to the domestic support disciplines alone.

Given the severe limitations of the MPS it could be dropped from inclusion in AMS support in the future and commitments adjusted downward accordingly. We reject this alternative because of the important policy role of administered prices in some cases and the desirability of disciplining their use.

A better alternative would be to take steps within the domestic support disciplines to ensure that the latitude allowed by the MPS provisions does not undermine commitments to limit other forms of AMS and OTDS support. A distinction could be drawn between MPS and non-exempt direct payments and other support within the AMS. With this distinction, countries with Final Bound Total AMS or Final Bound OTDS commitments attributed to MPS in the relevant base period would retain the option of using MPS to a corresponding level as long as they are in compliance with other domestic support rules and commitments. The non-exempt direct payments and other budgeted outlays reported in AMS would also be bound by these other commitments, less the support attributable to MPS. Without this distinction, eliminating MPS opens up an equivalent amount within CTAMS for substitute non-exempt measures. Those countries we have examined that have reduced MPS the most (the EU and Japan) have not substituted non-exempt payments for the MPS. But our analysis suggests that other countries, such as the US, if they were to face a tight FBTAMS constraint, might use reductions in MPS that do not reduce economic price support to make room for expanded non-exempt direct payments. Making a distinction between MPS and other non-exempt support within AMS could avoid such substitutions.

Green box disciplines

The legal provisions of the Agreement and its proposed Doha Round extension divide domestic support measures at a fundamental level into two types: those that have at most minimal trade-distorting effects in the green box category and all others that are included in OTDS categories (unless exempted in development programs as an aspect of special and differential treatment for developing countries). Many of the green box measures have desirable social objectives and many have less of an effect than other support on a country's competitors, while most of the trade-distorting measures stimulate production and drive down world prices to the detriment of non-subsidized producers. The WTO rules are designed to maintain the separation between these types of policies, and to guard against the possibility that trade-distorting measures slip into the green box for which expenditures are not capped.

Strengthened WTO rules and OTDS commitments would encourage shifts to green box measures. This will require greater scrutiny to assure consistency of notified measures and their implementation with specific green box criteria, in order to achieve the public benefits that green box programs are designed to encourage while discouraging new forms of subsidies that distort production and trade. The need for enhanced scrutiny of green box measures receives considerable attention in a collection of policy and analytical papers edited by Meléndez-Ortiz, Bellmann, and Hepburn (2009). Their overall policy orientation, as we would also argue, is that green box policies appropriately disciplined and administered provide the foundation for permanent agricultural support policy.

Meléndez-Ortiz, Bellmann, and Hepburn trace the Uruguay Round negotiations that determined the green box rules and examine how to make them most effective. They focus on those measures that legitimately meet the agreed non-distorting criteria and the enforcement needed to preclude the inclusion of distortionary measures. The green box policies notified since the Agreement came into effect are described for numerous countries and their social implications, such as effects on the distribution of income among large and small farms, are evaluated. The environmental impacts of green box policies are examined, as well as the use of green box policies to enhance rural income and promote poverty reduction in developing countries.

Our analysis has highlighted a number of cases where further disciplines on green box measures are warranted in order to exclude measures that have more than minimal effects on production or trade. We focus here on one of these issues: the subcategory in the green box of decoupled income support payments to farmers. We believe that greater discipline on these payments will be necessary if a consensus on long-term policy for agricultural support is to be achieved.

The reasoning underlying the inclusion of measures that meet the decoupled income support criteria in the green box is that in principle these payments neither depend on nor affect current prices or production. There has been an economic presumption to this effect, in part based on a longstanding literature suggesting that quota rents from supply control programs are captured in the price of quotas or land (Orden, Paarlberg, and Roe 1999). The decision on the level of decoupled income transfers to agricultural producers is therefore left as a sovereign issue. There has been some convergent policy movement towards payments notified in this category among China, the EU, and the US. But large differences remain among these three countries in the levels of the payments, and there is a clear division between the few countries that make such payments and all others that do not. In the EU and US, decoupled income support has been subject to substantial internal public debate, indicative of sovereign policy choices being made and contested and consistent with their discretion under the Agreement.

The problem that arises given these differences in levels of decoupled income support is whether payments, especially at high levels, have more than a minimal trade-distorting or production effect, and thus should be constrained. A number of mechanisms through which decoupled income support might stimulate production have been identified (Elbehri and Sarris 2009; Abler and Blandford 2005). Among these mechanisms are a wealth effect, making producers less risk averse; easing of credit constraints, so additional purchased inputs are utilized; impacts on labor allocation decisions, such that more labor is devoted to farm production; coverage of fixed costs, so that the number of farms or levels of profit-maximizing output are increased; and anticipation of future rebasing of payment eligibility criteria, that rewards the expansion of current production.

With the increased adoption of payments notified as decoupled income support, greater attention has been directed towards assessing their effects. Various analytical techniques have been utilized, but the time series of data on these payments are short. Analysis has focused not only on those payments notified as decoupled income support in the green box but also on measures such as the US countercyclical and similar payments provided since 1998 that are price-linked but not dependent on current production levels.

Some of the analysis shows the quite limited effects of these measures on output (Goodwin and Mishra 2005, 2006). However, several recent studies have questioned this conclusion. De Gorter, Just, and Kropp (2008) present theoretical arguments that fixed and countercyclical payments can have a substantial impact by deterring exit and affecting choice of output levels. They show substantial effects on dairy output due to US Milk Income Loss Contract payments. Kirwan (2009) concludes that less of the value of US fixed direct and countercyclical payments is passed through to landowners than earlier studies have implied. He finds that 75 percent of the value of payments is retained by operators of rented land, with only 25 percent reflected in rental rates. Kirwan does not address the effects of the payments on production, but their retention by farm operators could enhance production along several of the lines mentioned above. Femenia, Gohin, and Carpentier (2010) demonstrate that earlier studies underestimated the wealth effects of income support. Gardner, Hardie, and Parks (2010) use advanced statistical techniques to evaluate the effects of US support programs since 1987 – a point in time at which those programs became increasingly separated from production decisions and include (since 1996) the US direct payments notified as decoupled income support. Gardner, Hardie, and Parks find that US support has induced 45 to 90 million more acres into agricultural production than would otherwise have been the case.

In light of this newly emerging evidence and the remaining uncertainty about the extent to which decoupled income support affects production, we conclude that some nominal limits will be required on this type of support. As long as a reasonable case can be made that alleged decoupled income support has production effects, a consensus will not form around policy convergence where a few countries that can afford to make unlimited payments of this type.

Ensuring fair markets for food consumers

The final issue we raise places domestic support disciplines in the context of the broader forces that will influence agriculture in the coming decade.

The existing rules of the Agreement for domestic support and those being negotiated in the Doha Round are targeted primarily toward disciplining policy measures and support that stimulate production and depress world prices to the detriment of agricultural producers in other countries. This has been a concern of non-subsidizing exporters, who see their competitive position in world markets eroded, and of food-importing countries, who blame low world prices for undermining farmers' incomes and long-term investments in their agricultural sectors.

The emergence during the late 2000s of a period of relatively high agricultural prices does not eliminate the need for traditional disciplines on price-depressing domestic support. We have shown evidence to this effect in evaluating such measures as continued price support interventions by Norway, the new ACRE revenue-guarantee program enacted by the US in 2008, and the increased subsidies middle-income countries provide to agriculture as their economies grow. But production-stimulating policies are the not the only ones that create economic distortions in world markets. Measures that restrict supply or augment demand beyond market-driven levels are also potentially trade distorting. Such measures have become more prevalent, have contributed to the relatively high agricultural prices since 2007, and could come to dominate policy interventions affecting agriculture in the future.

Supply-restricting and demand-augmenting policies come under scrutiny when higher world food prices create difficulties for low-income food importers and poverty rises in these countries. Karapinar and Häberli (2010) examine these concerns about the dramatic price increases in 2008 in an historical perspective and offer assessments of the extent to which these can be addressed in the WTO.

In the framework of WTO domestic support notifications, one set of supply-control measures are those notified in the blue box, for which subsidy payments but not the level of supply restraint is reported. Use of these measures is waning, as we have described.

Some other supply-restricting policies are notified in the green box, particularly conservation programs that have the effect of reducing planted crop acreage. Green box rules limit payments for environmental measures to revenue forgone or additional costs entailed in their adoption. This has not been a sufficient constraint to preclude subsidy payments large enough to draw land out of production. More discipline on these payments may be necessary if a convergence consensus is to emerge on future agricultural policies, especially if prices remain relatively high for staple grains and oilseeds.

Moreover, the green box environmental support rules are inadequate to address two of the most policy-laden challenges facing agriculture: the rising demand for farm-based biofuels and the other, still undetermined, mitigation opportunities and adaptation strategies that may arise from global climate change. These challenges will place significant new demands on agricultural markets – for example, as rising fossil fuel prices create incentives to produce biofuels or as increased trade is needed to moderate greater climatically induced variability in agricultural production. The demands on agriculture as a source of biofuels and for other responses to climate change will also be driven to a large extent by policy decisions that involve mandates or incentives for certain uses of land and other agricultural resources.

We have noted that the demand-augmenting effects of biofuel subsidies and mandates in Brazil, the EU and the US already have had significant impacts on production and prices. Yet, such policy measures remain largely outside existing or proposed WTO disciplines. Certainly, the most important of these measures have not been notified under the Agreement as agricultural domestic support.

The domestic support rules could be strengthened to address the problems that arise from policies that reduce production, limit exports or increase demand for non-food uses of agricultural products to the detriment of consumers. Doing so is complicated, as we have discussed in chapters on Brazil and the US, and it seems unlikely that countries will attempt to negotiate disciplines on measures that increase the demand for agricultural products, even though such measures have an impact on world prices and hence on poor consumers. A case can be made for a cohesive approach to a multilateral food security initiative that would include disciplines on certain measures of this kind of domestic support.

The need for greater transparency in the area of biofuel subsidies has been emphasized in a study by Josling, Blandford, and Earley (2010). Such transparency has not been forthcoming from the system of notification to the WTO under either the Agreement on Agriculture or the Agreement on Subsidies and Countervailing Measures. In both cases, basic notification information is scant and the information needed to estimate the trade impact of the subsidies has been lacking. Under the Agreement on Agriculture, governments in their notifications to the WTO seem content to ignore support to ethanol through biofuel mandates or tax concessions, even though an argument can be made that at least part of this should be reported as domestic support in favor of agricultural producers. Nor have governments been persuaded to report biofuel subsidies in enough detail to allow analysis of their effects under the ASCM. These measures will require more discipline for convergent domestic support policies to evolve.

The challenge ahead

This book has spelled out in depth the international rules and commitments, subsequent policy decisions, and notification and monitoring of those policies that have led to the current juncture in disciplining agricultural domestic support. Domestic support disciplines are a key part of the Agreement on Agriculture and new disciplines on domestic support will have to be part of any successful further negotiations on a new agricultural agreement. It may or may not prove possible for a consensus to emerge in the near-term on an architecture of strengthened multilateral rules and commitments. Meanwhile, countries continue to utilize many unilateral domestic support measures with adverse effects. Notification of those domestic support measures has been slow and inconsistent. The result has been to devalue the process of reporting and the integrity of the international disciplines, even if explicit violations have been rare. Should there be a Doha Round agreement, its credibility will hinge on more timely and consistent monitoring as many more countries will find themselves closer to agreed limits.

Longer term, the challenges we have identified are indicative of both the importance of disciplining agricultural domestic support and the difficulty of doing so. Many complex issues in terms of goals, rules, commitments, implementation, and monitoring will have to be tackled in any attempt to bring greater cohesion to a global regime for agricultural policies. The experiences of countries under the Agreement provide a tangible starting point for such an attempt, illuminate potential pitfalls to be avoided, and offer lessons to guide the negotiations and future policy developments. There is a need to make agricultural domestic support policies more consistent and beneficial in a world economy in which future production technologies and the food supply are uncertain and in which the efficient functioning of agricultural markets and trade is increasingly needed to contribute to an effective, robust and sustainable global food system.

References

Abler, D., and D. Blandford. 2005. A review of empirical studies on the acreage and/or production response to US production flexibility contract payments under the FAIR Act and related payments under supplementary legislation. OECD report AGR/CA/APM(2004)21/Final.

de Gorter, H., D. R. Just, and J. D. Kropp. 2008. Cross-subsidization due to infra-marginal support in agriculture: A general theory and empirical evidence. *American Journal of Agricultural Economics* 90(1): 42–54.

Elbehri, A., and A. Sarris. 2009. *Non-distorting Farm Support to Enhance Global Food Production*. Rome: FAO.

Femenia, F., A. Gohin, and A. Carpentier. 2010. The decoupling of farm programs: Revisiting the wealth effect. *American Journal of Agricultural Economics* 92(3): 836–848.

Gardner, B., I. Hardie, and P. J. Parks. 2010. United States farm commodity programs and land use. *American Journal of Agricultural Economics* 92(3): 803–820.

Goodwin, B. K., and A. K. Mishra. 2005. Another look at decoupling: Additional evidence of the production effects of direct payments. *American Journal of Agricultural Economics* 87(5): 1200–1210.

2006. Are "decoupled" farm program payments really decoupled? *American Journal of Agricultural Economics* 88(1): 73–89.

Josling, T., D. Blandford, and J. Earley. 2010. Biofuel and biomass subsidies in the US, EU and Brazil: Towards a transparent system of notification. IPC Position Paper. International Food and Agricultural Trade Policy Council.

Karapinar, B., and C. Häberli (ed.) 2010. *The End of Cheap Food and the WTO*. Cambridge University Press.

Kirwan, B. E. 2009. The incidence of US agricultural subsidies on farmland rental rates. *Journal of Political Economy* 117(1): 138–164.

Meléndez-Ortiz, R., C. Bellmann, and J. Hepburn (ed.) 2009. *Agricultural Subsidies in the WTO Green Box: Ensuring Coherence with Sustainable Development Goals*. Cambridge University Press.

Orden, D., R. Paarlberg, and T. Roe. 1999. *Policy Reform in American Agriculture: Analysis and Prognosis*. University of Chicago Press.

WTO. 2008. Revised draft modalities for agriculture. TN/AG/W/4/Rev.4, 6 December.

2010. Total value of agricultural production: Note by the Secretariat. TN/AG/S/21/Rev.4, 23 February.

World Trade Review (2013), 12: 3, 533–547
 doi:10.1017/S1474745612000535 First published online 28 February 2013

Transparency and timeliness: the monitoring of agricultural policies in the WTO using OECD data

TIM JOSLING*
FSI, Stanford University
KLAUS MITTENZWEI
NILF, Oslo

Abstract: Transparency in the multilateral trade system is fundamental. Monitoring the compliance of WTO members with their obligations is an important part of that transparency, and timeliness in the notification of compliance is crucial. In the case of domestic support to agriculture, the notifications of compliance with obligations has been slow and opaque. But another database exists that could both illuminate the extent to which policy instruments are correctly notified and provide a convenient way to ensure timely 'pre-notifications' in the event that delays occur in the future. This note shows how the OECD database can be used, for example, to shed light on the extent to which payments to producers that require production as a matter of eligibility are presently notified to the WTO as having no effect on production. We also demonstrate the feasibility of using OECD data to construct 'pre-notifications' by calculating the (as yet un-notified) domestic support notifications for the EU for the years 2009/10 and 2010/11.

Introduction

Transparency is a fundamental aspect of an effective and efficient trade system and a major part of the task of the World Trade Organization (WTO) (Kerr, 2008). A recent article in this journal has provided a framework for systematically evaluating the efficiency of the many aspects of WTO transparency (Collins-Williams and Wolfe, 2010). This framework identifies a progression of transparency functions from addressing the 'right to know' through 'targeted' transparency that structures information to address particular policy issues to 'external' transparency that

* Email: josling@stanford.edu
The authors are grateful for comments on an earlier draft by Lars Brink and for constructive suggestions from two reviewers. Responsibility for remaining errors of commission or omission is however ours alone. We would like to recognize the support of NILF in enabling Mittenzwei to spend time at The Europe Center, Stanford University, during the preparation of the paper.

makes possible the use of this information to improve public understanding of the nature of the trade system and the performance of trade policies. The provision of basic information about trade flows and tariff levels has been enhanced by improvements in data collection and analysis, though non-tariff trade measures (NTMs) still pose a significant challenge.[1] However, monitoring and surveillance, a key aspect of targeted transparency, is highly variable in its effectiveness, ranging from the relatively data-rich notifications of information on health and safety regulations to the Sanitary and Phytosanitary (SPS) Committee to the essentially vacuous notifications to the Subsidies and Countervailing Measures (SCM) Committee. Collins-Williams and Wolfe point out that notifications to the Agriculture Committee mandated by the Agreement on Agriculture by WTO members are often delayed and incomplete, and the monitoring and surveillance of these notifications is 'spotty' (2010: 569).[2]

The monitoring of agricultural support has indeed been useful in tracing the developments in domestic farm policies in the light of the constraints introduced by the Agreement on Agriculture (AoA) and embedded in country schedules (Orden *et al.*, 2011). But the notifications have been of limited use in improving the 'external' transparency of the link between farm policies and world trade.[3] This limited usefulness is reduced even more by the slow reporting: transparency would be considerably enhanced by more timely notification of support levels. But this should not be an insuperable problem.

Data exist in the public domain for the construction of provisional WTO notifications within months of the end of the reporting period. These data are collected by the Organization for Economic Cooperation and Development (OECD) in connection with its own agricultural policy monitoring. In 1982, the OECD ministers mandated a report from the Agriculture and Trade Committees on the farm policies of the member states and the trade implications of these policies (OECD, 1982). The Secretariat adopted (and adapted) the PSE (producer support estimate) that had been developed by the FAO in the context of a program of International Agricultural Adjustment (FAO, 1975). The PSE measure proved useful in the 'monitoring and evaluation' of adherence to a set of guidelines, required of the Secretariat on an annual basis (OECD, 1988). This process has continued until the present, though the link with the policy guidelines has essentially gone. The purpose of the data collection by the OECD is notably different from that of

1 Recognition of this lack of organized data on NTMs has recently spawned intensive efforts by several institutions, including the WTO which devoted its 2012 World Trade Report to the topic (WTO, 2012).

2 Though the emphasis in this paper is on the notification of domestic support, members also have to notify their use of export subsidies and of tariff-rate quotas. These too can be delayed and incomplete, but the OECD database is less relevant in these cases.

3 Economic modelling of the trade system has generally avoided the use of WTO notifications for data on farm policies and has preferred the more economically intuitive and consistent data collected by the OECD for major countries.

the WTO monitoring, and the classification system used reflects these differences. But the two datasets are based on essentially the same data, so the calculation of provisional notifications (or counter-notifications) from OECD data is a relatively straightforward if somewhat detailed technical task.

The existence of these two overlapping datasets on farm policies has posed its own problems for transparency. The interpretation of the information (by politicians, government officials, and academic scholars) contained in both the WTO notifications and the OECD support estimates has been hindered by the differences in the classification systems used. In particular, the AoA makes a somewhat artificial distinction between market access (tariffs and border measures), export competition (subsidies and export credit), and domestic support (price support, direct payments, and other subsidies). The OECD implicitly incorporates border measures into its measurement of support by using domestic producer prices. Thus, the WTO notifications treat support through border measures as being additional to that from domestic 'administered prices' even though the one is a necessary component of the other.

In addition, there is a clear difference in the use of the data accumulated by the two institutions. The WTO notifications address compliance rather than illuminating policy change. In the Collins-Williams and Wolfe framework, the transparency is 'targeted'. The OECD database is organized in such a way as to focus on policy changes, but is not monitoring compliance with any specific agreement.[4] In this sense, it is addressing an issue of 'external' transparency.

Our argument is that the two systems should be viewed as complementary rather than competitive: as each contributing to the understanding of farm support policies rather than being a source of confusion. By treating the two classification systems as revealing different facets of the same set of policies, we would claim that these two contributions taken together significantly enhance the overall transparency of indicators for agricultural policy analysis. The two systems nicely complement each other precisely because they are structured differently, and that using one to throw light on the other can yield new insights into policy developments, and to the task of disciplining farm policies in the interests of a more responsive trade system.[5]

A major benefit of looking at both datasets as being complementary is to suggest the use of the OECD classification as a way of contributing to the improvement of WTO monitoring practices. Such an examination could, for instance, show the

4 The full 'monitoring and evaluation' report on agricultural policies in OECD Countries is published in alternate years with a shorter version 'agricultural policies at a glance' appearing in the intervening years (e.g. OECD, 2010b; OECD 2011). The updated country-specific databases can be downloaded from Hhttp://www.oecd.org/document/59/0,3746,en_2649_37401_39551355_1_1_1_37401,00.html.

5 Collins-Williams and Wolfe (2010) mention the OECD database but declare themselves 'not persuaded' of its relevance to the WTO notifications (page 573, fn. 14). Their caution is based on the different purposes for which the data are collected.

extent to which key policy attributes (such as the requirement to produce) identified in the OECD dataset match up with definitions embedded in the AoA.[6] One major issue that will have to be tackled eventually (regardless of the outcome of the Doha Round) is the extent to which payments notified in the green box are actually being administered in a way that conforms to the criteria.[7] Though legal considerations dominate the present notification procedure when allocating payments to the green box, the underlying policy question is the usefulness of the notifications themselves to monitor the movement to less trade-distorting support. Although the issue of green box payments is perhaps the most prominent one, the merits of looking at both datasets are not limited to the green box. This includes looking at measures notified within the blue box, which covers payments under production-limiting programs, and matching these payments to the OECD labels regarding production limits. Indeed, the comprehensive nature of the OECD support estimates, which include the impact of border measures, may itself be of value in understanding the significance of the disciplines imposed through the WTO on policies that impact trade in agricultural products.

A second benefit of exploiting the complementarity between the two databases is the ability to calculate provisional WTO notifications from recent OECD data, thus reducing the time-lag common with official notifications.[8] This contributes to the attribute of timeliness, an essential aspect of transparency. This benefit primarily rests on the OECD's ability to quickly update the dataset. The almost continuous process of keeping up-to-date with policy developments in the OECD Secretariat gives that institution an advantage in timeliness over the WTO. It also makes use of the accumulated knowledge of the Secretariat and the OECD Committee for Agriculture that has been an important part of the credibility of the PSE database. The concept of provisional notifications has already been introduced in the Doha Round negotiations, and so the opportunity could present itself in the future to make up-to-date information on the implementation of WTO commitments available on a regular basis. Annex M of the latest draft of the modalities (Rev 4) addresses the issue of Monitoring and Surveillance (WTO, 2008). The Annex states that 'as a matter of urgency' the basic documents defining procedures and formats for notification be revised, and the Agriculture Committee play an 'enhanced role' in reviewing and monitoring implementation of commitments. In addition, the

6 Such an examination of policy attributes would in no way alter the legal requirements of countries to notify support levels in order to monitor compliance with the AoA. While members' questions in the WTO Committee on Agriculture sometimes draw on the policy detail provided in OECD monitoring, this is not done systematically.

7 The problem of monitoring the accuracy and validity of member notifications extends beyond the green box, but the complexity of the WTO criteria in this case suggests that this is an area where transparency is particularly lacking.

8 One could also construct 'proto-notifications' for the period before the entry into force of the WTO AoA in 1995. This could illuminate the extent to which the changes that occurred were guided by the Agreement or whether the Agreement was possible because of changes in farm policy already under way.

Annex provides a suggested replacement for AoA Article 18 (Review of the Implementation of the Commitments) that includes, *inter alia*, a provision for provisional notifications 'in the event that a member is unable to submit the final notification by the appropriate deadline' (Annex M, para. 4).[9]

The remainder of this note illustrates these benefits with two examples: the potential light that the OECD classification of some payments under the heading 'production required' can shed on the placement of these payments under the various headings of the WTO green box; and the feasibility of 'pre-notification' of domestic support levels using OECD data so as to add timeliness to transparency.[10]

Appropriate notifications: production requirements and the green box

Domestic support for the producers of agricultural goods is categorized in the Agreement on Agriculture to reflect presumed degrees of trade distortion. Payments that are deemed to be the most trade distorting (price supports and direct payments linked to output or price) are constrained in country 'schedules' as are those that are tied to production limits. No such constraints are placed on spending that meets the green box criteria. The basic notion of the green box is to shelter from support reductions such programs that have little or no effect on production. The payment for the provision of public goods by the farm sector would often come within this category.[11] The aggregate effect could still be to increase production from the sector even when the size of any individual producer's payment did not depend on his production. But the legal manifestation of this notion is by no means clear-cut. The conditions under which a policy is exempted from reduction are given in AoA Article 6, para. 1 (WTO, 1994). This article, *inter alia*, refers to Annex 2 of the Agreement (the green box) that specifies that domestic support measures 'shall meet the fundamental requirement that they have no, or at most minimal, trade-distorting effects or effects on production' (para. 1). This would appear to exclude from the green box any payment that has any impact (in either direction?) on

9 Given the absence of any progress in completing the Doha Round, the Agriculture Committee has already been discussing improvements in monitoring. Indeed the suggestions for transparency and timeliness made in this paper may be even more pertinent in a situation where the Doha Round draft suggestions are not implemented.

10 We use the term 'pre-notifications' in a general way to indicate any estimate made before the official notification to the WTO. The changes envisaged in the Doha Round for improving transparency include the possibility of 'provisional notifications' by WTO member governments as mentioned above. This would be one way to institutionalize the pre-notifications. The term 'shadow notifications' was used by Orden *et al.* (2011), implying an unofficial monitoring, and this may be the better term when governments are not directly involved.

11 To the extent that agricultural producers contribute to the cost of these public goods, by levies or restrictions, should be counted as a tax to be set against the payments. In general, general services such as marketing information and research and development are provided with little cost to the producer: environmental payments are allowed in the green box to the extent that they cover the extra costs of compliance with the relevant regulations.

production. However, the paragraph continues 'accordingly, all [green box] measures shall conform to the following basic criteria': (a) support is provided by a publicly funded government program, and (b) it does not have the effect of providing price support to producers. In addition, specific criteria and conditions apply for each of twelve sub-categories of the green box.

Two of these specific criteria are of special interest with regard to production requirements and production-based payments. The first of these criteria requires that the amount of the payment must not be related to or to be based on the type or volume of production, prices, or factors of production. This criterion applies to payments under the headings related to decoupled income support, natural disaster relief, resource retirement, investment aid, and regional assistance, and to other direct payments. The second criterion states that no production shall be required in order to receive the payment. This applies only to decoupled income support and 'other direct payments' not covered by the specific categories. The criteria for the other categories of payments do not include the requirement that the payment, in order to qualify for the green box, must not require production: a payment can be unrelated to production volume or type and still be paid only if some production occurs. In fact, many programs necessarily imply that there is some 'requirement' for production: governments are unlikely to pay a subsidy for meeting some environmental production standard and then make payments even in those cases where there is no production. Some production is *de facto* required to receive that payment. In these cases, the eligibility for receiving a payment (and the size of the payment) is defined with reference to, for example, the extent of income loss due to natural disasters, structural or regional disadvantages, or environmental program compliance.[12] And, for another group of green box categories (such as general services and food aid) there are no payments to producers, and hence no opportunity to place a restriction on payments on the basis of production.

The relationship between the green box criteria and the production requirements is summarized in Table 1, which also identifies the categories in the notification format used by WTO members. There has not yet been a panel ruling on the interpretation that countries have put on these criteria.[13]

The OECD database identifies programs that have specific production requirements. The focus is on the distinction between policy instruments for which production is required (PSE categories A1, A2, B1, B2, B3, C, and D) and those for

12 It is, however, difficult to reconcile the 'fundamental requirement' that there be no (or only minimal) effect on production with the specific criteria that allow compensation for losses or for regional cost disadvantages.

13 The *US–Cotton* case did touch on green box requirements with respect to production, in part to address the US claim that the cotton subsidies were sheltered by the Peace Clause (WTO, 2004). The panel considered the question of restrictions on the eligibility for payments that precluded some types of production (vegetables and wild rice). Their opinion was that these restrictions meant that the payments were in fact tied to production. This did not address the issue of whether, if any production is required, the Green Box conditions are violated.

Table 1. Categorization of domestic support measures in the WTO green box

Categories	Appearance in AoA Annex 2	Appearance in WTO notification requirement and format	Policy-specific criteria	
			Amount of payment: '*Not be related to, or based on, the type or volume of production*'	Eligibility for payment: '*No production shall be required in order to receive such payments*'
General services	Para. 2	(a)		
Public stockholding	Para. 3	(b)		
Domestic food aid	Para. 4	(c)		
Decoupled income support	Para. 6	(d)	X	X
Income insurance and income safety-net programmes	Para. 7	(e)	X	
Natural disaster relief	Para. 8	(f)		X(1)
Structural adjustment assistance through producer retirement	Para. 9	(g)		
Structural adjustment assistance through resource retirement	Para. 10	(h)	X	
Structural adjustment through investment aid	Para. 11	(i)	X	X(1)
Environmental programmes	Para. 12	(j)		
Regional assistance programmes	Para. 13	(k)	X	
Other direct payments	Para. 5(2)	(l)	X	X

Notes: (1) Regards future production.
(2) 'Other direct payments' are defined in para. 5 as payments 'other than those specified in paras. 6 through 13', and all except one of the criteria of para. 6 apply to those payments.
Source: WTO (1994), WTO (1995).

which production is not required (PSE categories E to N, all GSSE categories). This feature was presumably introduced as an indication as to the extent to which the policy instrument in question might distort production and hence trade: this is an important part of the process of quantitative evaluation of policy change in OECD members. The modeling of the quantitative effect of farm policies relies crucially on the extent to which direct payment policies give an incentive to producers.[14] However, the link with the WTO green box criteria discussed above is somewhat obscure. Some payments can fall under the OECD heading of 'no production required' and still be ineligible for the WTO green box. A prominent example is the counter-cyclical payments in the US: no current production is required to receive such payments, as they are paid on base acreage. But the counter-cyclical payments do not qualify for the green box as they are triggered by and related to price movements. Thus the most interesting link with the OECD categories is in the criteria for 'decoupled income support'. The OECD category of 'no production required' seems to cover cases where production is not required for eligibility and the payments are not related to production. Both these conditions must be met in order place these payments under AoA Annex 2, paras. 5 or 6.[15]

Using the OECD database and matching individual policy instruments with payments notified in the WTO green box reveals the extent of this grey area between production requirements, production-based payments, and green box eligibility (Table 2). Payments for which a match was found, and which were classified by the OECD as 'production required', were notified in the seven (of the 12) sub-categories of green box payments that prohibit payment on the basis of production.[16]

As mentioned above, it is not inconsistent to require production but base the payments on other criteria. But in the case of 'other direct payments' (para. 5) and 'decoupled income support' (para. 6), there is no such ambiguity. Norway and Switzerland each notified significant payments that appear *a priori* to be ineligible for the green box. For example, NOK 1.232 billion or 100 of Norway's payments in the category 'other direct payments' were regarded as requiring production by the OECD. This includes the Vacation and Replacement Scheme that reimburses farmers for the costs of hired labor during vacation and illness.[17] The Swiss

14 There is an extensive literature that explores the production impact of decoupled payments (reviewed in Abler and Blandford, 2007). The broad conclusion of these studies is that there are a number of mechanisms by which direct payments unrelated to output could in fact act as incentives to producers. These include a wealth effect, an income effect, and an effect on the rate of exodus from the sector.

15 The term 'decoupled' income support is used in the heading of Annex 2, para. 6, but not defined. The OECD uses the term 'decoupled' in a 'weak' form to indicate that production would be the same with or without the support and in a 'strong' form implying that changes in the level of income support will not affect production. Both are presumably subsumed by the WTO 'fundamental requirement' for green box eligibility that payments have no, or at the most minimal, effects on production (Annex 2, para.1).

16 Values above 100% indicate differences in reported values in the two classification systems or possible inconsistencies in the matching process.

17 Similar anomalies show up in the matching of instruments from the OECD categories to the notifications in the blue box. Norway, for instance, notifies regional deficiency payments to meat producers in this category. In order to be eligible for the blue box, payments have to be 'under production-limiting programs' (along with other criteria). Although there exists an upper limit on the amount of meat that is eligible for the payments it is not binding. The regional deficiency payments to meat differ in this respect from regional deficiency payments to milk as the latter are made under a (binding) milk quota scheme.

Table 2. Support classified as requiring production by the OECD and notified as green box payments to the WTO in 2008 by green box sub-category:
(I) amount of payment requiring production in sub-category (million units of national currency),
(II) total amount of payment in sub-category (million units of national currency),
(III) share of support requiring production in sub-category (per cent)

	Norway			Switzerland			EU			US		
Category (AoA Annex 2 paragraphs)	I mill. NOK	II mill. NOK	III %	I mill. CHF	II mill. CHF	III %	I mill. €	II mill. €	III %	I mill. $	II mill. $	III %
Decoupled income support (para. 6)				406	1,618	25	349	35,646	1			
Other dir. paym. to prod. (para. 5)	1,232	1,232	100									
Income insurance (para. 7)								17	0			
Natural disaster relief paym. (para. 8)	14	95	15				1,041	1,165	89	660	98	673
Str. ad. – resource retirem. (para. 10)		111						303	0			
Str. ad. – investment aids (para. 11)	354	444	80	113	88	127	3,218	7,772	41			
Reg. assist. pro-grammes (para. 13)				664	674	99	4,669	3,720	126			
Total green box paras. 5 – 8, 10 – 11, and 13	1,600	1,882	85	1,591	3,558	45	9,277	48,623	19	660	98	673

Source: Own calculation based on OECD (2011) and WTO (var.).

Payment for the Holding of Roughage Eating Farm Animals (PHREFA) accounts for roughly one fourth of decoupled income support notified by Switzerland. The OECD has put PHREFA in PSE category C that covers payments made on current animal numbers for which production is required. This would seem to be inconsistent with the criteria for the green box. In the case of the EU, the amount of such ambiguous payments is small relative to the total payments notified under paras. 5 and 6. For the US, there appeared to be no such conflicting notifications.

Though the case of decoupled income support and other direct payments to producers (AoA Annex 2, paras. 5 and 6) is the most clear-cut example of where the OECD data can help to focus on the consistency of WTO notifications, other categories of the green box also raise issues that need to be explored – including the compatibility with the 'fundamental requirement' of Annex 2 para. 1 that payments have no, or at most minimal, effects on production.[18] Table 2 shows the total green box notifications for categories that bar the use of production as a basis for payments (paras. 8,11,12,and 13) and the payments in those categories that are reported by the OECD as requiring production. For European countries, typical examples of green box measures that require production are environmental protection programs, regional assistance programs, and investment aid. Two other Swiss programs, the Milk Price Supplement for Cheese Production (MPSCP) and the Payments for Non-Silage Feeding of Cows (PNSFC), have been notified as green box payments in the category 'Regional assistance'. But these are classified by the OECD as output payments and hence depend on 'the type and volume of production'. Examples of EU programs notified in the green box include (regional) support to Less Favoured Areas (LFA), investment aids, and agri-environmental support. These are considered as requiring production by the OECD, thus at least raising the question of compatibility with the 'fundamental requirement' in para. 1 of Annex 2.

Timely notifications: the case for pre-notifications of WTO domestic support

The second example of where the complementarity between the WTO notifications and the OECD database can be exploited relates to timeliness. The notification rules require notifications to be submitted 'no later than 60 days following the year in question' (WTO, 1995). This rule has been broken frequently by almost all major WTO members in the past. Serious concerns about these lags have arisen

Consequently, the OECD considers the milk deficiency payments as being subject to a production limit, while it does not consider such a production limit being in place for the meat deficiency payments.

18 Discussion of the compatibility with the fundamental requirement raises issues beyond the scope of this paper, such as the import of the word 'accordingly' that links the fundamental requirement with the 'basic criteria' in the rest of the paragraph.

among members as the notifications are intended to facilitate the review of members' implementation of commitments, and this has led to discussions on how to improve notification procedures (Brink, 2009, 2011). This raises the question as to why countries have taken, in some cases, several years to submit the required notifications. Data availability may account for a minimal delay, but this is not credible as the major cause. Indeed, several members have revised their notifications in subsequent years, in response to improved data. WTO members may have tactical reasons for delaying their notifications, particularly during trade negotiations, but this seriously undermines the effectiveness of the WTO system. To remove these lags could even ease the path of trade talks, though the main benefit would still be on monitoring the implementation of existing commitments.

In this section we provide WTO pre-notifications, by which we mean synthetic notifications for years for which official WTO-notifications are not yet available. The pre-notifications are achieved by adding up support under individual support measures as identified in the PSE database by the WTO categories of market price support, non-exempt direct payments, blue box, and green box.

Some additions to the OECD database have been made to improve the fit, so as to accommodate the definitional differences between WTO notifications and OECD classifications. We include market price support only for those commodities that are listed as receiving MPS in the WTO-notifications and for which data are also available in the PSE database. Moreover, we use administered prices (instead of producer prices) and WTO (fixed) reference prices instead of OECD (current) reference prices to conform to WTO definitions. We do however apply the price difference to the total quantity of production reported in the OECD database rather than to 'eligible' production as used in the WTO MPS calculations. This departure from the WTO notification procedures is intended to avoid the (somewhat subjective) choice of an 'eligible' production quantity. The designation of eligible production is one of the ways in which WTO members have controlled their notified MPS (Orden *et al.*, 2011). Using the total production may therefore give MPS levels that would be higher than those eventually reported by the country.[19] We also disregarded *de minimis* exemption of product-specific and non-product-specific support from current total AMS (aggregate measurement of support) so as to focus on the issue of comparability.[20]

As an example of such a pre-notification process, Figure 1 compares official notifications and our constructed pre-notifications for the EU. The period from 1995 to 2008 acts as a check on the ability to reconstruct the notifications based on

19 One could correct for this by linking the notified eligible production in previous years with the corresponding production levels, but this has not been attempted in this paper.

20 We do so mainly to keep the comparison as straightforward as possible. One could of course use the value of production contained in the PSE database to check whether the *de minimis* exemption applies to a specific commodity (or to all commodities).

Figure 1. Official WTO notifications (left column for each year) for the EU for 1995–2008 and pre-notifications (right column for each year) for 1995–2010 (million Euro)

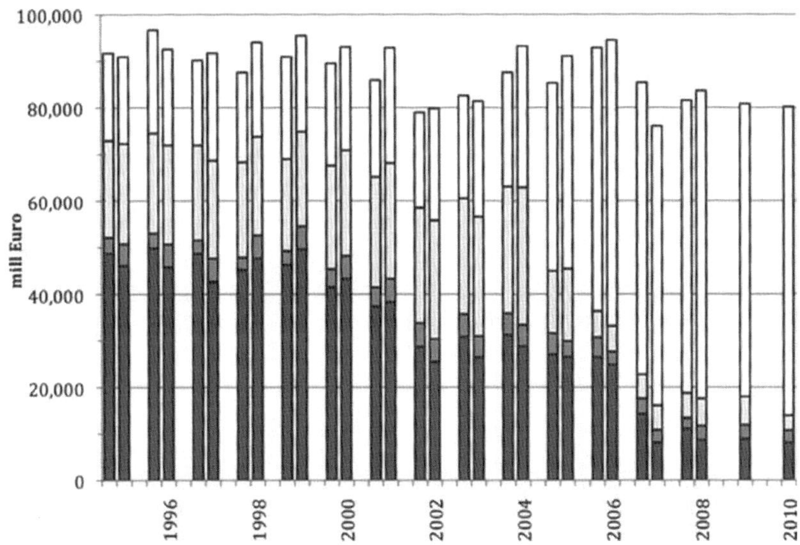

Note: Shading, from the top: green box, blue box, non-exempt direct payments, and market price support.

data available from the OECD database at the time when the notification was 'due'. The figure shows reasonable correspondence between the actual notifications and the reconstructions. The policy changes that moved support among the boxes is captured adequately. This suggests that such pre-notification is feasible.

As the latest EU notification of domestic support is for the marketing year 2008/09 (i.e., 2008 in the OECD convention), pre-notifications can be calculated for the two years from 2009 to 2010. The pre-notifications for the years 2009 to 2010 show no increase of total support compared to 2008. The differences mostly reflect higher green box payments. Market price support and non-exempt direct payments have apparently remained at their 2008 level. The continued phasing-in of the Single Payment Scheme (SPS) is illustrated in the shift from blue box support to green box support from 2008 to 2010. SPS payments (green box) are increased at the expense of per hectare payments to crops (blue box), roughly maintaining the total of blue box and green box payments.[21] So WTO members could have this

21 It should be emphasized that the pre-notifications are not in any sense projections of notifications based on the past. They are constructed from current OECD data, most of which will form the basis for the official notifications when submitted.

information well in advance of the formal notification without any need for additional data beyond that collected by the OECD.

Conclusion

The two datasets that monitor the development of agricultural policies in OECD countries and several non-OECD countries need to be seen as complementary resources in the search for transparency. The OECD PSE dataset includes more policies but fewer commodities. The WTO notifications of domestic support are more inclusive on a product basis (covering all domestic support in favor of agricultural producers) but employ classification conventions that are less transparent as a result of the drafting of the AoA. By comparing the two, through the tracing of the treatment of individual policy instruments, the WTO dataset can be enhanced with the better policy detail of the OECD estimates. The intention is not to interfere with the notification of compliance *per se*, as this is a legal rather than an economic matter, but to make the discussion of the possible improvements of the AoA monitoring less obscure. Knowledge of the extent to which policies placed in the Green Box policies require production is one example of the benefits from making use of both datasets together.

Our argument for the possibility of pre-notifications rests on the technical feasibility of the use of OECD data for constructing plausible WTO notifications in advance of the formal notification by the government to the WTO. For this to happen would require major countries to embrace the idea as being strategically desirable. The conclusion of the Doha Round would tighten the constraints on farm policy and enhance the monitoring provisions. Under such conditions, the improved transparency of more-timely notifications could be even more valuable, as one would anticipate several cases of potential violations of new domestic support limits. Without a Doha Round outcome, the focus will remain on the trade impact of the set of policies currently in use. Though less politically charged, the improved transparency of more timely notifications would still be of value.

Two major hurdles stand in the way of exploiting the complementarity of the two farm policy monitoring efforts. First, if countries really wish to hide their policies from scrutiny in the WTO, they might withdraw their cooperation within the OECD so as to prevent the construction of pre-notifications. The OECD itself is premised on transparency and the open discussion of policy issues among its members. It seems unlikely that OECD members would compromise such useful cooperation merely to hide data most of which is readily available within the countries concerned. And, in any case, the cooperation of countries with the OECD Secretariat is more in the nature of confirming interpretation and refining judgments rather than providing confidential data.

The second problem is that the OECD membership comprises mainly countries that are considered developed countries in the WTO context. But the OECD follows and monitors policy developments in a group of non-OECD members and collects the same information on their farm policies.[22] The links between the two monitoring exercises would not immediately resolve issues such as the slow WTO notifications in the case of India, but it could provide some urgency to the situation. Other studies are underway for similar policy monitoring in Latin America and Africa. It is possible that the provisional notifications could be expanded from the countries monitored by the OECD to include most of the WTO members when these databases are completed.

Inevitably the question would arise as to who would undertake to implement the improvements in transparency and timeliness suggested in this paper? The WTO is naturally concerned with the accuracy of notifications as well as with their timeliness. But it is unlikely that the WTO Secretariat could be asked to undertake the additional task of mapping the notifications with the data available at the OECD. Similarly, the OECD Secretariat would probably not be asked to monitor WTO notifications. But WTO members that are impacted by the imperfect system of notification currently in place could well institute a monitoring process that made use of both databases. And the Agriculture Committee provides a venue for discussion of the outcome of such monitoring.

To date, the issue of the trade distortion caused by farm policies has primarily been framed in terms of developed countries. But this is changing as the programs that have caused most trade problems in the past recede and new policies are put in place to meet a growing demand for food (Brink, 2009). In the future, the main interest in monitoring domestic support may shift from the impact of the farm policies of the developed world to those of developing and emerging countries. At that stage transparency and timeliness could become a major issue.

References

Abler, D. and D. Blandford (2007), 'Getting out of the Box: Transitioning Out of Direct Payments', available at http://cnas.tamu.edu/SessIIBPaperAblerBlandford.pdf.

Brink, L. (2009), 'WTO Constraints on Domestic Support in Agriculture: Past and Future', *Canadian Journal of Agricultural Economics*, 57(1): 1–22.

—— (2011), 'The WTO Disciplines on Domestic Support', in D. Orden, D. Blandford, and T. Josling (eds.), *WTO Disciplines on Agricultural Support: Seeking a Fair Basis for Trade*, Cambridge: Cambridge University Press.

Collins-Williams, T. and R. Wolfe (2010), 'Transparency as a Trade Policy Tool: The WTO's Cloudy Windows', *World Trade Review*, 9(4): 551–581.

FAO (1973), *Agricultural Protection: Domestic Policy and International Trade*, C 73/LIM/9, Rome: Food and Agriculture Organization.

22 By expanding the coverage of the OECD database to include new OECD members and those non-OECD members that are deemed to be potential members, the coverage of domestic farm policies has improved. The use of data relating to non-OECD members in the context of WTO monitoring could raise some sensitive issues: the government of India has reportedly objected to the calculation and publication by the OECD of agricultural support estimates for that country.

—— (1975), *Agricultural Protection and Stabilization Policies: A Framework for Measuring in the Context of Agricultural Adjustment*, C 75/LIM/2, Rome: Food and Agriculture Organization.

Kerr, W. A. (2008), 'Trade Agreements: The Important Role of Transparency', *Estey Centre Journal of International Law and Trade Policy*, 9(1): 1–11.

OECD (1982), 'Minutes of the Council at Ministerial Level as adopted on 10–11 May 1982, C(82)58 (Final), Organization for Economic Cooperation and Development, Paris.

—— (1988), *Monitoring and Outlook of Agricultural Policies, Markets and Trade*, Paris: Organization for Economic Cooperation and Development.

—— (2010), *OECD's Producer Support Estimate and Related Indicators of Agricultural Support: Concepts, Calculations, Interpretation and Use (The PSE Manual)*, Paris: Organization for Economic Cooperation and Development.

—— (2010), *Agricultural Policies in OECD Countries: At a Glance*, Paris: Organization for Economic Cooperation and Development.

—— (2011), *Agricultural Policy Monitoring and Evaluation 2011: OECD Countries and Emerging Economies*, Paris: Organization for Economic Cooperation and Development.

Orden, D., D. Blandford, and T. Josling (2011), 'The Difficult Task of Disciplining Domestic Support', in D. Orden, D. Blandford, and T. Josling (ed.), *WTO Disciplines on Agricultural Support: Seeking a Fair Basis for Trade*, Cambridge: Cambridge University Press.

—— (eds.) (2011), *WTO Disciplines on Agricultural Support: Seeking a Fair Basis for Trade*, Cambridge: Cambridge University Press.

World Trade Organization (WTO) (1994), 'Agreement on Agriculture', Part of Annex 1A 'Multilateral Agreements on Trade in Goods' of the Agreement Establishing the World Trade Organization, Marrakesh Declaration of 15 April, Marrakesh.

—— (1995), 'Notification Requirements and Formats', G/AG/2, World Trade Organization, Geneva, 30 June.

—— (2004), *United States – Subsidies on Upload Cotton*, Report of the Panel, WT/DS267/R.

—— (2008), 'Revised Draft Modalities for Agriculture', TN/AG/W/4/Rev. 4, World Trade Organization, Geneva, December.

—— (2012), 'Trade and Public Policies: A Closer look at Non-tariff Measures in the 21st Century', World Trade Report, Geneva.